RAMSEY CAMPBELL, PROBABLY WAS originally published by PS back in 2002 since which time the author has expanded some of the essays, added others and generally tinkered around with the running order... as is his wont. Thus the original 140,000-or-so words compiled from Ramsey's non-fiction of three decades have been considerably (and entertainingly) expanded to represent getting on for half-a-century of Campbelliana now well in excess of 150,000 words.

The subjects range from the perils of authorship to the delights of amateur fiction and film, from drugs to nightmares, from the Highgate Vampire to the Dracula Society's marching song. Friends are remembered and so is Mary Whitehouse. A seminal study of schoolgirl spanking is brought up to date. Many thoughts on the history of horror fiction are included. And, at last, it is revealed why Harlan Ellison is responsible.

May the reader variously laugh, weep, ponder, disagree and turn uneasily in bed.

Ramsey Campbell, Probably

Ramsey Campbell, Probably

RAMSEY CAMPBELL

EDITED BY S. T. JOSHI

Ramsey Campbell, Probably
Copyright © Ramsey Campbell 2015

Cover Art
Copyright © J. K Potter 2015

Title page photograph by Kathleen Probert

Published in September 2015 by Drugstore Indian Press, a division of PS Publishing Ltd., by arrangement with the author. RAMSEY CAMPBELL, PROBABLY was originally published by PS Publishing in September 2002. It has been extensively revised by the author. All rights reserved by the author. The right of Ramsey Campbell to be identified as Author of this Work has been asserted by him in accordance with the Copyright, Designs and Patents Act 1988.

First DIP Edition

ISBN
978-1-848639-11-9

This book is a work of fiction. Names, characters, places and incidents either are products of the author's imagination or are used fictitiously. Any resemblance to actual events or locales or persons, living or dead, is entirely coincidental.

Design & Layout by Michael Smith
Printed and bound in England by T. J. International

PS Publishing Ltd
Grosvenor House
1 New Road—Hornsea
HU18 1PG—England

editor@pspublishing.co.uk
www.pspublishing.co.uk

Contents

1. On Horror Fiction

2. On Horror and Fantasy Film

3. On Horror in Society

4. *On Some Writers*

5. *On Ramsey Campbell*

ACKNOWLEDGMENTS

Essays collected herein first appeared as follows:

"Fiedler on the Roof", *Fantasy Review*, volume 7, number 8, whole # 71, September 1984 (revised for this Drugstore Indian edition)

"The Crime of Horror" (as "Contemporary Horror: A Mixed Bag"), *Fantasy Review*, volume 8 (shown as "9"), number 6, whole # 80, June 1985 (revised for this Drugstore Indian edition)

"Dig Us No Grave", *Fantasy Review*, volume 9, number 3, whole # 89, March 1986

"A Horror Writer's Lexicon", *Necrofile* 5, Summer 1992

"Horror Fiction and the Mainstream", *Necrofile* 12, Spring 1994

"Unconvincing Horror", *Necrofile* 25, Summer 1997

"To the Next Generation", *Writers of the Future* volume IV, edited by Algis Budrys (New Era, 1988)

"Beyond the Pale", *Fantasy Review*, volume 8, number 8, whole # 82, August 1985

"Horror Films and Society", *Necrofile* 11, Winter 1994; *Necrofile* 19, Winter 1996

"The Quality of Terror", *Cut! Horror Writers on Horror Film*, edited by Christopher Golden (Berkley Books, April 1992)

"Alone in the Pacific with Projector, Screen and Ten Best Films" (as "Alone in the Pacific with My 10 Best Films"), *Shock Xpress* 4, May-June 1986

"Pulsating Posteriors and Submissive Misses or, Strapped for Cash" (as "Pulsating Posteriors and Masochistic Misses or Strapped for Cash"), *Shock*, edited by Stefan Jaworzyn (Titan Books, September 1996: severely revised for the present volume)

"Floundering on the Bottom", *Shock Xpress 2*, edited by Stefan Jaworzyn (Titan Books, March 1994) (revised for this Drugstore Indian edition; the review of *The Legend of Harrow Woods* originally appeared as *Ramsey's Rambles* in *Video Watchdog* 168, May/June 2012)

"Turn Off" (as "The Whitehouse Way"), *Shock Xpress* volume 2. Issue 1, Summer 1987

"The Nearest to a Ghost", *Dancing with the Dark*, edited by Stephen Jones (Vista, 1997) (expanded for this Drugstore Indian edition)

"The Strange Case of Sean Manchester", *Shock Xpress 1*, edited by Stefan Jaworzyn (Titan Books, August 1991) (revised for this Drugstore Indian edition)

"Tim Powers" (as "Introduction"), *The Anubis Gates* by Tim Powers (Mark V. Ziesing, 1989)

"Terry Lamsley" combines "Introduction" to *Conference for the Dead* by Terry Lamsley (Ash-Tree Press, 1996) and "LAMSLEY, Terry" in *St. James Guide to Horror, Ghost & Gothic Writers*, edited by David Pringle (St. James Press, 1998)

"*American Psycho*" (as "In My Opinion: Psycho by Design"), *Fear* 31, July 1991

"S. Hudson", *Necrofile* 3, Winter 1992

"Shaun Hutson", *Necrofile* 6, Fall 1992 (revised for this Drugstore Indian edition)

"Pete Atkins" (as "Introduction"), *Wishmaster and Other Stories* by Peter Atkins (Pumpkin Books, October 1999) (revised for this Drugstore Indian edition)

"Bob Shaw", *Necrofile* 32, Spring 1999

"John Brunner", www.thespook.com, June 2002 (revised for this Drugstore Indian edition)

"K. W. Jeter", *In the Land of the Dead* by K. W. Jeter (Morrigan Publications, 1989)

"Alan Price" (as "Introduction") *The Other Side of the Mirror* by Alan David Price (Citron Press, 1999) (revised for this Drugstore Indian edition)

"Richard Christian Matheson" (as "Ramsey Campbell: Matheson"), *Dystopia: Collected Stories* by Richard Christian Matheson (Gauntlet Publications, 2000)

"Poppy Z. Brite", www.thespook.com, June 2001(revised for this Drugstore Indian edition)

"Lovecraft: an Introduction", *The H. P. Lovecraft Centennial Guidebook*, edited by John B. Cooke (Montilla Publications, 1990)

"Robert E. Howard" (as "Introduction"), *Solomon Kane* by Robert E. Howard (Baen Books, 1995)

"R. R. Ryan", *Necrofile* 27, Winter 1998

"Robert Aickman", *Necrofile* 30, Fall 1998 (revised for this Drugstore Indian edition)

"Stephen King" (as "Welcome to Room 217"), *Kingdom of Fear: the World of Stephen King*, edited by Tim Underwood and Chuck Miller (Underwood-Miller, 1986); "Introduction to *Pet Sematary*" (PS Publishing, 2013)

"Clive Barker" (as "Introduction"), *Clive Barker's Books of Blood* (Sphere Books, 1984); "Weaver of Wonders", *Sunday Times* Magazine, 18 October 1987

"Peter Straub" (as "Foreword"), *Shadowland* by Peter Straub (Gauntlet Publications, 1995)

"Dennis Etchison" combines "Introduction" to *Darkside* by Dennis Etchison (American Fantasy / Airgedlámh Publications, 1996) and "Introduction" to *The Dark Country* by Dennis Etchison (Scream/Press, October 1982)

"James Herbert" (as "James Herbert: Notes Towards a Reappraisal"), *Fantasy Review*, volume 8, number 2, whole # 76, February 1984; introduction to *The Fog*, Centipede Press, 2010

"Thomas Ligotti" (as "Introduction"), *Songs of a Dead Dreamer* by Thomas Ligotti (Silver Scarab Press, 1985)

"Donald R. Burleson" (as "Introduction"), *Beyond the Lamplight: Stories from the Dark* by Donald R. Burleson (Jack O' Lantern Press, 1996)

"How I Got Here", *Contemporary Authors* volume 228 (Thomson Gale, Farmington Hills, 2005) (expanded for this Drugstore Indian edition)

"A Small Dose of Reality", *Fantasy Review*, volume 8, number 11, whole # 85, November 1985

"Why I Write Horror Fiction", *Necrofile* 2, Fall 1991; "The H Word", *Nightmare* no. 17, February 2014

"On Reading My Stories", *Necrofile* 7, Winter 1993 (revised for this Drugstore Indian edition)

"Nightmares", *Necrofile* 8, Spring 1993 (subsequently revised)

"Taking Drugs", *Necrofile* 9, Summer 1993 (expanded for this Drugstore Indian edition)

"Fame!", *Necrofile* 14, Fall 1994

"A School Visit", *Necrofile* 17, Summer 1995

"Writing and Depression", *Necrofile* 15, Winter 1995 (expanded for this Drugstore Indian edition)

"Editing Horror Anthologies", *Necrofile* 20, Spring 1996

"A Transient Engagement", *Necrofile* 31, Winter 1999 (revised for this Drugstore Indian edition)

Afterword to *The Inhabitant of the Lake and Other Unwelcome Tenants* (PS Publishing, 2011)

"Foreword to *Demons by Daylight*" (as "Foreword"), *Demons by Daylight* (Carroll & Graf, 1990)

"Introduction to *The Height of the Scream*" (as "*introduction and allergies*"), *The Height of the Scream* (Arkham House, 1976); *Still Shrill After All These Years* from the Babbage Press reprint (2004)

"Afterword to *The Doll Who Ate His Mother*" (as "Afterword"), *The Doll Who Ate His Mother* (Headline, 1993)

"Afterword to *The Parasite*" (as "Author's Afterword"), *The Parasite* (Headline, 1993)

"Afterword to *The Nameless*" (as "Afterword"), *The Nameless* (Little, Brown, 1992)

"Introduction to *Dark Companions*" (as "Introduction"), *Dark Companions* (Macmillan, 1982; afterword (as "Afterword"), Samhain, 2011

"Afterword to *Night of the Claw*" (as "Afterword"), *The Claw* (Little, Brown, 1992)

"Afterword to *Incarnate*" (as "Afterword"), *Incarnate* (Futura, 1990)

"Afterword to *Obsession*" (as "Afterword"), *Obsession* (Samhain, 2011)

"Afterword to *The Hungry Moon*" (as "Afterword"), *The Hungry Moon* (Samhain, 2011)

"Afterword to *Scared Stiff*" (as "Afterword"), *Scared Stiff* (Tor, September 2002)

"Introduction to *Dark Feasts*" (as "Introduction"), *Dark Feasts* (Robinson Publishing, 1987)

"Afterword to *The Influence*", *The Influence* (Centipede Press, 2011)

"Introduction to *Alone with the Horrors*" (as "So Far"), *Alone with the Horrors* (Arkham House, 1993)

"Introduction to *Far Away and Never*" (as "Introduction"), *Far Away and Never* (Necronomicon Press, 1996)

"All The Ghosts That Made Me", *The Guide / Der Reiseführer* (Edition Phantasia, 1994)

All essays first published in *Necrofile* or on www.thespook.com appeared under the title "Ramsey Campbell, Probably".

THANKS!

. . . to Scott David Aniolowski, Barbara Boote, Algis Budrys, Robert A. Collins, Jeff Conner, John B. Cooke, Stefan Dziemianowicz, Les Escott, Christa Faust (not least for my guest appearance in *Control Freak*), Carl Ford, Robert and Nancy Garcia, John Gilbert, Christopher Golden, Barry Hoffmann, Anthony Hogg, John Jarrold, Stefan Jaworzyn, Steve Jones, Joachim Körber, Peter Lavery, Glenn Lord, David Marshall, Chuck Miller, Harry O. Morris, Michael A. Morrison, Kevin Owen, Terry Parkinson, David Pringle, Nick Robinson, Barbara and Christopher Roden, Anthony Sapienza, Milton Subotsky, Jack Sullivan, James Turner, Tim Underwood, Douglas E. Winter, Mark Ziesing, and of course S. T. Joshi, Mike Smith, Pete and Nicky Crowther, not to mention my wife Jenny. I abase myself to anyone I've missed.

INTRODUCTION

FOR THOSE WHO WRITE HORROR FICTION, THE QUESTION comes spinning around as inevitably as the sun: What scares you? What's the scariest thing you've ever read?

My answer, for years now, has been offered in two honest words: My mortgage. Then I try to explain why scares rank low in my reading priorities and my assessment of great horror fiction. The horror-as-rollercoaster metaphor is as timeworn as it is trite, and discerning readers begin to understand that as soon as I mention two more honest words: Ramsey Campbell.

Not that Ramsey himself scares me (although there was that curious business about the talking manikin hand beneath the staircase of his home in Wallasey). He is kind, thoughtful, welcoming—the most gentle of men. He is also, to my mind, the essential living example of an artist for whom horror is not a kind of fiction but literature's core value. Scares? You'll find them throughout the Campbell canon, but his narratives take readers past the visceral and into the realm of the genuinely disturbing.

Two nights ago, I sat in a local movie theatre watching Steven Spielberg's latest multi million-dollar mall magnet, *Minority Report*. Dulled to distraction by its relentless blur of faux science fiction,

CGI, and backlighting, I jumped, startled, at a well-crafted "pop up." That was a scare, pure and simple: Spielberg went for a visceral response, and in my case, he got it. Yet sitting here now, only two days later, I remember my reaction, but I cannot, for the life of me, remember the scene.

On the other hand, I read *Demons by Daylight* almost thirty years ago, and its stories still haunt me, summoning me back, time and again, to consider them with reverence. Even in the earliest of his mature fiction, Ramsey Campbell wrote horror with respect and with a singular ambition: To touch those dire places inside us all where we question the frailty of our flesh or our resolve, where we question reality and our place in it, where we question our sanity—and the sanity of our gods. His is a fiction of horror, not about horror.

The distinction explains Campbell's critical success, as well as his commercial difficulties. In a marketplace that treats storytelling as commodity entertainment, and exalts appearance and expectation—where book covers and film trailers tell all—safety is paramount. A horror fiction that is about escape, about scares—that good old rollercoaster ride—is Pat Boone doing rock-and-roll, George Lucas doing science fiction, George W. Bush doing politics: The threatening and uncomfortable elements that might demand thinking or incite transgression are supplanted, and reality is whitewashed into a didactic of good versus evil, whether an empire or an axis.

Here, then, is Campbell's enduring bond with his youthful inspiration H. P. Lovecraft, whose fiction, however baroque or bathetic or brilliant, concerned itself with the interstices of reality and the imagined, posing the question of what lurks beyond and summoning the courage—or the temerity—to interrogate the forbidden in search of answers. That the young Campbell also embraced the more elegant, if equally eccentric, Vladimir Nabokov should come as no surprise. Despite HPL's mechanistic protestations, his essential stories ache with the hope, however bleak, that life might fulfill Nabokov's vision: "not flimsy nonsense, but a web of sense."

Ramsey Campbell writes horror fiction. He does so without

apology, and without inventing more palatable catch phrases for his work. Let me bear witness.

In 1998, while I was whirlwinding through England to promote the anthology *Millenium* (aka *Revelations*), an eager someone at HarperCollins arranged for me to appear with Ramsey on Liverpool cable television—a thin cut above American "cable access" programming. After finishing a radio interview (and more than a few glasses of wine), we crawled dutifully into the bowels of an unkempt studio, where the diminutive presenter urged us into seats that were fixed a foot below his own, in order to compensate for his (lack of) height.

Lights, robot camera, action.

Introductions and hollow praise for *Millenium* complete, our host read his first question from a teleprompter—which I guarantee was more than he read of the book:

"Mr. Campbell, you don't like being called a writer of horror fiction, do you ?"

Fortunately for the presenter, I was seated in the middle of what suddenly seemed like horror's only episode of *The Jerry Springer Show*. I've wondered ever since whether the tape was aired. What I remember most about the mad minutes that followed is the passionate and profound defense of horror that Ramsey offered—and my disappointment that his words would be heard by so few.

I had similar feelings when asked to write this introduction. Exhilaration at Campbell's insight and integrity. Disappointment that this volume is offered only in a limited edition whose several hundred copies will be read eagerly by enthusiasts but not by the far broader audience it deserves.

That is, of course, the nature of the beast known as genre, which these essays examine in all its grime and occasional glory. Few writers with true devotion to the fiction and film of horror have found a bully pulpit from which to offer their critical opinions (as opposed to self-promotion). Fewer still have found favor in anything approaching the mainstream.

For several years David J. Schow tilted against the windmills of Hollywood (and, occasionally, publishing) in his "Raving and Drooling" column for *Fangoria*. Kim Newman appears with some frequency in the pages of well-regarded film journals, while Tim

Lucas pursues his perfectionist vision through Video Watchdog. S. T. Joshi, Gahan Wilson, and I have managed to review horror fiction (and urge its legitimacy) with some consistency in a patchwork of magazines and newspapers, but only Ramsey Campbell has rattled the cage of this genre with the regular dispatches that give this book its name.

The eponymous essays of Ramsey Campbell, Probably have served as horror's "Op-Ed" journalism for more than a decade, livening the pages of *Necrofile* and, more recently, **thespook.com**. Expanded here with the best of Campbell's critical contributions to other venues and a selection of his introductions and afterwords to his own fiction and the books of others, this volume offers some of the better critical autobiography of this generation.

Read in the cumulative, Campbell the critic is as idiosyncratic and compelling as Campbell the storyteller. These essays are infectious reading—sometimes humorous, sometimes heart breaking, and consistently candid.

Doctors tell us that often the most difficult, and unfortunate, of psychiatric patients are those who are the most aware of their illness. The same is no doubt true of writers.

Campbell is remarkably self-conscious of his art and his industry. More than that, he is a writer with an admirable yet brutal honesty about himself, as underscored by "Near Madness," a revision of his wrenching introduction to the unexpurgated edition of *The Face That Must Die*. Whether examining his childhood, his creative choices, or certain intriguing distractions (such as his adventures in Soho's Spankarama), Campbell refuses to indulge the filters that blur and soften so much autobiography. His candor is not merely refreshing, but also revelatory: A life this rich, expressed so genuinely, shames the authorial myth-making of the tedious self-promoters .

Little is sacred in these pages save the ideal of artistic conscience. The critique aims high, low, and in between, tackling everyone from academic icon Leslie Fiedler to vampire-hunter Sean Manchester; but more often than not, Campbell's true target is horror—and through horror, himself.

You don't have to read far to realize that Ramsey Campbell holds tough, challenging opinions, but that he remains open-minded, willing to reassess, willing to change, even willing to apologize.

Consider his ruminations on James Herbert, Britain's most popular—and, for a time, most vilified—horror novelist. A re-reading of Herbert in the context of this overheated criticism gave Campbell new respect for his novels, and insight into the class bias of the British horror tradition.

An essential theme of Ramsey Campbell, Probably is horror's time-honored animus, repression. From reflections on the James Bulger tragedy and a visit with Mary Whitehouse to the less obvious (and thus more insidious) censors of genre, commerce, and apathy, Campbell reminds us of the curious symbiosis between horror and inhibition—and that repression, like horror, begins within.

The title of this collection is taken from an essay by Harlan Ellison published (with regret, one would hope) in the January 1991 issue of *The Magazine of Fantasy & Science Fiction*. With a remarkable lack of prescience, Harlan chose to name names, awkwardly and incorrectly, in penning yet another death knell of "horror." It's Ramsey Campbell's story and I won't pre-empt it here. I'll simply state the obvious:

Ramsey Campbell, absolutely.

Douglas E. Winter
Oakton, Virginia August 2002

Ramsey Campbell, Probably

for Jenny and David—
much to discuss

1: On Horror Fiction

Fiedler on the Roof

HORROR FICTION IS BESET WITH IGNORANCE masquerading as informed criticism. I'm sharply reminded of this by reading the text of a speech by Leslie Fiedler, printed in the June 1984 issue of *Fantasy Review* (formerly *Fantasy Newsletter*). Fiedler is the author of *Love and Death in the American Novel*, a tome sometimes cited as providing insights into horror fiction. He gave the speech to the Fifth International Conference on the Fantastic in the Arts, where he was Academic Guest of Honour. It rather disproves my impression that the wider the audience the less informed the criti-cism will be, for Fiedler's is one of the shoddiest and most inaccurate examples of horror criticism I have read. To demon-strate the kind of thing the genre has to suffer, and because some readers might be misled by Fiedler's reputation into swallowing his claims, I want to look at the speech in some detail.

"By the late Victorian era," Fiedler says, "macabre fiction had come to be considered disreputable schlock . . . Gothic horror was left to modest hacks." These two statements are taken from consecutive paragraphs, and I can see no evidence that Fiedler distinguishes "Gothic Horror" (his capitals) from macabre fiction; this kind of blurring of distinctions proves to be characteristic of his argument. Which hacks (a term my dictionary defines as "a literary drudge") is he thinking of? Ambrose Bierce, John Buchan, Conan Doyle, Rudyard Kipling, Vernon Lee, Arthur Machen, Guy de Maupassant, Sir Arthur Quiller-Couch? I can't tell if he hadn't time to think of them or hoped his audience wouldn't have, for in his next sentence he leaps ahead thirty years: "In the 1930s . . . such works of horror which had somehow survived the critics' scorn . . . were translated into images on the American screen." He thus, while implying (or perhaps wishing) that works which are disliked by critics ought not to survive, ignores all the intervening fiction—the work of, for example, E. F. Benson and his brothers, Algernon Blackwood, Lafcadio Hearn, William Hope Hodgson, M. R. James, Edith Nesbit, Oliver Onions, Saki, H. G. Wells (who wrote a good deal of horror as distinct from science fiction), Edith Wharton, Mary E. Wilkins-Freeman. . . . Perhaps he simply didn't know their work—I can find no evidence in his speech of his having read anything but best-sellers—or perhaps he's testing his audience to make sure they're awake. If not, his claim that EC comics were "the most horrific examples of the [comic book] genre" (the truth being that most imitators of the EC comics devoted whatever talent they had to piling on the gruesomeness, since that was the only way they could compete) may have jarred them back into awareness in time to savour his next, extraordinary, paragraph.

The "kids" of the fifties, he tells us, surreptitiously indulged in "the literature of horror even as they listened to rock music and took psychedelic drugs. . . . Nor did their tastes change when they came of age in the sixties." What happened then, according to Fiedler, was that these "college-bound or college-educated offspring of the most privileged classes" embraced comics and the monster films of the thirties. I've tried my best to banish from my mind a vision of millions of twelve- or thirteen-year-olds (little older if they were "college-bound" in the mid-sixties) out of their heads (on substances I should have thought had scarcely emerged from the laboratory in the McCarthy era) while listening to Bill Haley as they read Poe. Or is Fiedler still talking about horror comics when he refers to "the literature of horror"? Perhaps he feels he doesn't need to make himself clear, or to reflect on whether college students of the sixties really preferred thirties horror movies to the numerous horror films that were being newly released (many of them, especially the American movies, aimed straight at that youthful audience). Still, perhaps it's a more economical way of making his point than the truth would have been, much like his claim that *Night of the Living Dead* was patterned after thirties monster films (I can think of few horror films up to that date which owed less to the thirties). Or perhaps it's simply that his excitement is getting the better of him as he sidles closer to the subject of the guilty pleasures of horror.

"The formerly despised pop forms of horror had for them [the generation that had "come of age"] the added appeal of the taboo, providing not only the traditional *frisson* of fear but the added titillation of guilt." Remember that, as far as one can tell, Fiedler is still talking about thirties horror films. Is it likely that any generation except possibly his own felt that way about those films? Can he be transferring his own feelings of guilt onto a generation which is most unlikely to have felt anything of the kind? "Nor has horror ceased to function for us as pornography. . . " he claims (the academic "we" differing from the royal "we" in that it means "everyone must feel as I do"), and to prove it he launches into a lip-smacking description of the opening scene of *Carrie.* "Somehow," he continues, "the combination of blood, running water and sanitary plumbing has a special appeal for contemporary movie fans." Presumably he means that there have been dozens of imitations of the shower scene in *Psycho.* One might object that the appeal is rather for, on the one hand, filmmakers (such as de Palma) who admire Hitchcock and, on the other, for slavish imitators of past successes, but perhaps Fiedler doesn't think it worth distinguishing between artists and their audience. Perhaps it's true that "de Palma served his apprenticeship making low budget skin-flicks," though I thought that was Coppola, but perhaps it's enough for Fiedler that they're of the same generation; at any rate, it enables him to prop up his argument about guilty pleasure. So does the claim that the most successful horror films of recent years have been those which "combine the horrific and the lubricious" (such as, according to Fiedler, *The Exorcist* and *Rosemary's Baby*). Admittedly *The Exorcist* had box-office figures second only to *Jaws* in the horror field, but *Rosemary's Baby* must give way to *The Amityville Horror* and *The Omen.* Perhaps the latter pair don't matter, or would complicate his argument that the two films he names "demonstrated during the seventies the fail-safe box office appeal" of sex & horror. In fact, *Rosemary's Baby* was made in 1968, but what's a few years to Fiedler?

Now his argument lurches to pop music and *Thriller*, Michael Jackson's video. Fiedler reflects on "how conventional our responses to horror have become, and how cannily Jackson's record [*sic*] exploited these responses." Surely it's rather that one's responses to *Thriller* are conventional because the video itself is; its progenitors are the Universal monster reunions (*House of Frankenstein/Dracula*) and the Abbot & Costello monster films. What distinguishes *Thriller* is Michael Jackson's prefatory disclaimer, which both turns the video into a soft sell for Christianity and announces (like the opening of *Indiana Jones*, which, I'm afraid, put me just as much on my guard) that we aren't to take seriously what follows. Alas, the effect on poor Fiedler of even such an emptily knowing film as *Thriller* is to revive his unease about enjoying horror.

"We find something absurd about the fact that we do so . . . our sense that there is something shamefully regressive about our enjoyment of this genre, a stubborn refusal to grow up." It's hardly surprising Fiedler feels this way if, as the gaps in his account of the field suggest, he's restricted himself to material to which he can feel superior. His explanation of why he feels uneasy illuminates his preconceptions, not the field: "Precisely because modern science threatens to divest the Cosmos of all mystery and dread, we are driven desperately to manufacture fantasies of the weird and the uncanny." Is he now using the academic "we" in order to pass himself off as a creator of fantasy, or to acknowledge that there's a good deal of it in his argument? I have to say that I don't write my fiction for the reason he gives at all, and I can't accept that it applies to the genre either, since horror fiction surely predated modern science (though obviously that depends on when Fiedler believes modern science to date from). Fiedler wishes (or, according to him, "we" wish) for a genre that would imagine "supernatural or unnatural beings" explicable in terms of science, and his "ingenious solution" to what seems to be a non-existent problem is, of course, science fiction. "It is true," he says, "that science fiction has typically been set in the future"—which I suppose is true—whereas "horror fiction early and late" has been set in the past, which is simply untrue except presumably of such examples of the field as he has read. He quotes two science fiction titles to prove that science fiction is the solution, and gets one of them wrong. I can't tell if his gibe at Stephen King (at whom he sneers as "the master of horror schlock") shows that he doesn't realise King is precisely what he's wishing for, or that Fiedler resents him for being so, or simply resents having to appear on the same programme as a writer of the fiction he can't cope with.

I do think the editor of *Fantasy Review* has done the field a service by printing Fiedler's text where it can be exposed to informed criticism. Sadly, it is by no means the only example of its kind the genre has had to deal with recently. I suspect I may have to return to the subject in my next column.

THE CRIME OF HORROR

POE, LE FANU, STEVENSON, BIERCE, MARION Crawford, Machen, the Victorian and Edwardian anthologies of Hugh Lamb, *The Supernatural Omnibus, Dracula*, M. R. James, Blackwood, Hodgson, Onions, de la Mare, Lovecraft, Bloch, Wellman, both the Bowens, Metcalfe, Leiber, Bradbury, *Great Tales of Terror and the Supernatural*, Jackson, Matheson, David Case, *The Surly Sullen Bell*, Aickman, *Lost Souls* . . . I assume my readers have read a substantial amount of all this, but if not, there's a reading list to help you become acquainted with the distinguished tradition of horror fiction, while Douglas Winter's *Shadowings* will enable you to sort out what's worthwhile from the debris that the explosion of contemporary horror fiction has produced. Now, if all this is old news to you, there still may be an area you've overlooked, as for a long time I did: where crime and the tale of terror overlap.

I've heard it said that the pseudonymous hackwork that infested the carcass of van Thal's Pan Horror series was (besides being a crime in itself) crime fiction, and I suppose it was, of a degraded and degrading kind. No doubt it had an audience, but I wouldn't want to live next door to them. I'm concerned rather with Woolrich, Dickson/Carr, Thompson, and the author of the most frightening psychological horror novels I have ever read.

Woolrich does enjoy some reputation among students of the

macabre, but until recently only collectors could decide how merited it was. Access was easier to the films (particularly *The Leopard Man, Phantom Lady* and *Rear Window*) based on Woolrich's work. Now Ballantine are reprinting a series of his novels, and the reappraisal can begin. For myself, I find that the intensity of Woolrich's vision, the constant sense of a recurring urban nightmare, is capable of making me forgive the shortcomings of his style. *Phantom Lady*, for example, takes the standard theme of the race against time to find the witness who can save an innocent man so deep into paranoia that it qualifies as a true tale of terror, and it's worth remembering that Woolrich was responsible for probably the greatest scene of terror in all Val Lewton's films, the young girl's fatal shopping expedition in *The Leopard Man,* reproduced virtually image by image from the novel *Black Alibi.* But where the film shows us only the trickle of blood under the door, Woolrich opens the door like the notorious dramatiser of "The Monkey's Paw" and shows us the chewed remains. Perhaps Woolrich was less at his ease with overt horror, as some of the contents of *The Fantastic Stories of Cornell Woolrich* (Southern Illinois University Press, 1981) suggest. The book benefits from an introduction by Francis M. Nevins Jr., who defines the underlying terror of Woolrich's fiction by pointing out that if the pattern of coincidence in the tales is too complex for mere coincidence, it bespeaks a god "whose existence . . . we would be much happier without".

Elsewhere Nevins claims that noir fiction is "always redeemed by a breathtakingly vivid poetry of word." At the risk of seeming partisan, I would suggest that crime fiction is less dependent than horror fiction on literary style. (Woolrich regarded himself, rather like Lovecraft, as "a guy who could write a little publishing in magazines surrounded by people who couldn't write at all.") God knows that horror suffers from a great deal of gratingly bad writing—look in any bookstore that has a horror section. But while some very considerable crime fiction has been written awkwardly, with little if any stylistic distinction(I take Hammett to be a prime example*), I'm not

* That's what I said, and I was wrong. Hammett's style is pared to the minimum and conveys very precisely what the author wants to communicate, morally as well as narratively. Whereas Raymond Chandler often reads as though he's presuming to improve the genre, Hammett based much of his work on his own experience as a Pinkerton detective and doesn't try to interpose his style between himself and the material. An admirable contemporary crime writer whose work shares Hammett's moral rigour and is at least as challenging is Dennis Lehane.

at all sure that this is or can be true of horror fiction. Perhaps this is why Woolrich's fantastic tales often seem less nightmarish than thoughtless, and sometimes read ("She grabs for the gun and her eyes light up. 'I am going, but you are coming with me!' she pants") like a parody whose point one is missing.

By contrast, Jim Thompson's workmanlike style generally quickens in the scenes of horror. Thompson clearly believed that horror is best conveyed obliquely. This isn't invariably true—neither reticence nor gross explicitness can ever be a substitute for imagination, and I for one find "In Amundsen's Tent" no more rewarding than the excesses of Shaun Hutson—but one sentence of implication is very often worth a paragraph of gore. (Sometimes reticence of language is inadvertently more horrible: "terminate with extreme prejudice," "defensive weapon," "star wars"...)

In Thompson's work horror is almost always the outcome. *The Getaway* begins as a heist thriller, but traces consequences with a grimness that passes beyond logic into a non-supernatural vision of hell on earth (a Poesque outcome suppressed by, of all people, Sam Peckinpah). Thompson excels at trapping the reader in a psychotic consciousness, in the horrible made circumstantial: having fatally injured one of his victims, the homicidal sheriff of *Killer Inside Me* "sat down and tried to read the paper." (That book and Thompson's extraordinary *Savage Night* employ a technique closely associated with horror fiction, the impossible first-person narrative.) Like Woolrich, Thompson tried his hand at the overtly fantastic, but his only such tale that I've read ("Forever After")—reminiscent of an EC comic or a black Bloch joke—is lightweight compared to the novels.

After all this, John Dickson Carr and his alter ego Carter Dickson may seem like light relief, but only to an extent. Perhaps I should own up to a special interest in Carr: I wrote two unfinished drafts of a novel-length pastiche of his work (*Murder by Moonlight*) before falling under Lovecraft's spell, and more recently my novel *To Wake the Dead* had to be retitled because Carr's book of that name was already on my American publisher's list. Now that publisher's paperback division, Collier Books, is reissuing Carr, and I'm delighted to find that their appeal for me hasn't faded. (Too often it does: my bitterest disappointment for years has been rereading

Weird Tales in search of unreprinted gems and realising how abysmally bad most of the unreprinted stories are.) Sometimes Carr employs the cosy conventions of the detective story, but his sense of the absurd is far more fully and variously developed than, say, Agatha Christie's, so that in some of his work events and characters have the qualities of a sliding panel or a paradox incarnate (shades of Chesterton, of course, an obvious influence): one could almost believe him capable of writing Sebastian Knight's detective parody as summarised in Nabokov's novel. Carr also has a particular feeling for the macabre, not only in his out-and-out ghost stories ("Blind Man's Hood," "New Murders for Old") or even in the ghost stories he sometimes tells, and leaves unrationalised, in his detective novels (*The Red Widow Murders, The Plague Court Murders*), but in the extraordinary eeriness and sense of evil that pervade novels such as *The Crooked Hinge* (perhaps the best of the Collier reprints to sample if you don't know Carr's work—not for nothing does the book quote mottoes from Bierce and Huysmans). Detective stories they may be, but sometimes the cosiness grows chill, the setting slips to let something out of M. R. James peer through.

Generic conventions prove far less comforting in the first three novels of John Franklin Bardin, published as an omnibus by Penguin. No crime novels I have read (indeed, perhaps no novel except Paul Ableman's astonishing *I Hear Voices*) have come so close to conveying the terror of insanity. *The Deadly Percheron* reads like a paranoid fantasy based on the private-eye genre. George Matthews, the narrator, is a psychiatrist forced to play detective, but he is also a narrator who comes to seem as unreliable as any of Poe's. (Phillip Marlowe is unreliable in a different way, in his adolescent view of the world.) Matthews tries to help a patient who claims to be directed by midgets, only for Matthews to meet one of the midgets himself. A page in which the midget insists on being called a leprechaun wouldn't look out of place in *Unknown* magazine, but the only *Unknown* story to resemble Bardin's is L. Ron Hubbard's *Fear.* Hardly has Matthews become embroiled in a plot involving murder and impersonation than he himself ends up in a mental ward, his identity denied by everyone he knew. Marlowe would have talked his way out, but Matthews' knowledge of schizophrenia only makes him aware of how delusory his claims sound. Even his own reflection is unrecognisably monstrous, and in a scene that (for me at any rate) finally tips the book into sheer horror, his photograph turns into his new monstrous face. He escapes by inventing an identity the doctors will believe in, an identity that then begins to take him over. Eventually he sets about regaining Matthews by sorting out the plot and tracking down the culprit, and it looks as if the conventions of the private-eye genre may finally come to the rescue—but the plot he pieces together is indistinguishable from a schizophrenic fantasy. The last line of the novel is "Then I just let go and swung off into space."

The Last of Phillip Banter is in theory more conventional; it's the old tale of a plot to drive an already unbalanced victim (Banter, a businessman and alcoholic) into madness or suicide, later a staple of innumerable British film and television would-be thrillers. Bardin, however, conveys Banter's growing insanity with dismaying vividness, and makes it the focus of the book. While the reader knows early on that the central device—a manuscript Banter keeps finding, apparently written by himself and describing his next day's events—is being written by someone else, this is by no means as reassuring as one might expect. Ominously, Banter seeks help from George Matthews, whose attempts at detection are as tragic in their effects as they were in *Percheron.* I can think of no novel in which the final marshalling of suspects by the detective, and the outcome of this, bring so little relief.

There's a moment in *Banter* where a potential murder victim seems to hear her dead father stumbling upstairs to rape her. This appalling glimpse proves to be the basis for *Devil Take the Blue-Tail Fly,* a study of a musician's descent into insanity. Now there are no generic conventions to hang on to, and nothing but an inexorable progression toward the utter horror of the final pages. If it was the failure of these novels in America that caused Bardin to turn to more conventional crime writing, it's difficult to see where else he could have headed after *Blue-Tail Fly.* Alas, his later novel *Purloining Tiny* is perverse but reads like someone imitating Bardin.

I believe the contents of the Penguin omnibus to be essential to any library of horror fiction. It's a neglected example of horror fiction as the opposite of escapism (an opposition that defines what's worthwhile in the genre)—fiction that shows its audience what they might otherwise be unable to bear. Interested readers (all who have read this, I hope) should visit the website at:

www.johnfranklinbardin.com

The body of this piece was written in 1985. One relevant author who has appeared since then is Steve Mosby, who deserves an essay to himself. Until I write it, let me take the opportunity to recommend his novels to anyone seriously interested in horror and its intersection with crime writing. I began with his *Black Flowers*, which manages to be both metafictional and compellingly suspenseful while it analyses the relationship between fiction and reality with considerable intelligence. It's impressively disturbing, as are (among others) Mosby's *50/50 Killer* and *Still Bleeding*. An equally extraordinary talent is José Carlos Somoza, who is too seldom translated into English. *The Art of Murder* is a bleak near-future vision worthy of (but by no means derivative from) Ballard, while *The Athenian Murders* is a detective novel Nabokov could have been proud to have written. Somoza's only other book to appear in English to date, *The Key of Doom*, uses science fiction to come up with a genuinely new kind of ghost—a memorably frightening one.

Dig Us No Grave

The tale of supernatural terror often deals with the cyclical nature of things: the ghost that always returns, the events that are repeated from generation to generation, the personalities that are reborn. As well as dealing with the cyclical, the genre suffers from the process too. Perhaps it should: we shall see.

"I believe ghost story writing to be a dying art. It's just possible that another Montague Rhodes James may appear one day, but I profoundly doubt it." So wrote H. Russell Wakefield in 1961, and I wonder why. Perhaps he might have overlooked Russell Kirk, whose tales had not then been collected, or even the publication ten years earlier of *We Are for the Dark*, but could he really have been unaware of Cynthia Asquith's ghost books of the fifties, the third of which displayed Aickman's mastery in "Ringing the Changes"? His ignorance is harder to understand than that of Colin Wilson and Nigel Kneale, claiming ten years or so later on television that no good ghost stories were being written any more; there seems to be no reason why either of them should be expected to know (though Kneale's achievements in terms of terror are considerable). They can't really be blamed for having been treated as experts by the media, and the same may be said of Roald Dahl, whose single attempt at a ghost story was, he says, a failure; perhaps a lack of sympathy with the genre explains why his anthology, which remained unpublished for decades, is so derivative.

Even when the recurring claim that the field is moribund is more closely argued, ignorance tends to show through. Take Julia Briggs' *Night Visitors* (Faber, 1977), subtitled "The Rise and Fall of the English Ghost Story." In many ways this is a useful book, far more sensitive to the qualities of the genre than the patronizing blurb suggests. ("Contributions were also made [to the genre] by writers whose reputations rest exclusively on their ghost stories, among them J. S. Le Fanu, Arthur Machen, Algernon Blackwood, and M.R. James"—as well, that's to say, as Dickens, Stevenson, Kipling and that other James.) Briggs is especially perceptive about Walter de la Mare. But like many histories of the genre, her book loses insight as it comes closer to the present day. For her to show that Elizabeth Bowen's ghost stories express "an increasing sense of spiritual dislocation" and "the strange juxtaposition of the everyday and the bizarre, visible wherever one looked" in wartime London, yet then to argue that "the modern urban environment" and contemporary "attitudes to the inner life" have put paid to the ghost story "except as a mode of nostalgia," strikes me as inconsistent, and suggests that she finds the present more solid and readily explicable than I do. Her observation that with L. P. Hartley the use of irony in the genre became self-defeatingly explicit is interesting as a comment on Hartley, but she uses it to make a point against Elizabeth Jane Howard, the only contemporary writer she bothers to note. Since she misquotes the title of Howard's 1951 story in order to make her point, I have to assume that her reading in the field of the last few decades has been sketchy at best. She might otherwise have realised that it's no longer true that "Freud's theories . . . had set the self-aware on their guard lest their fantasy . . . reveal more than they intended." Not only is the supernatural tale still capable of letting the subconscious speak freely—one of its great merits—but there are writers in the field who have found Freudian insights beneficial; I'm one, and Aickman said he was. In fairness to Julia Briggs I should add that she later praised Aickman in the *Times Literary Supplement,* after he had brought his work to her attention.

In *The Literature of Terror* (Longman, 1980), David Punter lays the ghost story to rest even earlier in its career, and convicts M. R. James of the dirty deed. His argument for this doesn't lack insight (nor does the book as a whole): he points to the way James often refers to his own and his readers' shared knowledge of the genre, a self-consciousness that for Punter makes James's stories "extended footnotes . . . a final decay of the Gothic into formalism." But at his best James used that shared knowledge with considerable and disconcerting wit, as in the image of the sheeted spectre which turns out to be "only" a sheet. Play with the conventions of a genre scarcely renders further development impossible; James's notion of the hoax-like ghost which proves not to be a hoax may lead straight to Perceval London's terrifying "Thurnley Abbey"; Fritz Leiber's tales of urban supernatural terror are influenced by James, but not by his self-consciousness, probably because Leiber's work was also a powerful response to cities where he lived; Aickman developed beyond James (about whose work, "A School Story" excepted, he had reservations, because of what he saw as James's lack of sincerity) simply by ignoring his influence. Alas, Punter's book provides no evidence of his having read Leiber or Aickman or any other contemporary writer normally identified with the genre. Instead, the book lurches into a discussion of horror films before defining "contemporary Gothic" in terms of more critically acceptable names (Ballard, Angela Carter, Pynchon, Oates, John Hawkes and others). While I welcome the linking of John Hawkes with the genre (an association Jack Sullivan had already noted), I deplore the way this is achieved by ignoring so many writers working in the tradition Punter set out to discuss*.

By now I've implicitly raised the question of what I mean by "the genre", and here, I think, the recurring arguments become more stimulating than a simple tolling of the knell. I have in mind those arguments that distinguish the ghostly from—well, we shall see. Thus in his introduction to *The Supernatural Omnibus* (1931), Montague Summers laments the *Not at Night* anthologies and suggests that "if there is a note of spiritual horror . . . the story is raised to another plane far higher than the rather nauseous sensa-

* Punter subsequently revised the book and even noticed my work; he spent a paragraph in dismissing *The Long Lost*, which he found of no interest other than to horror fans (although it isn't clear whether, having devoted a book to the genre, he numbers himself among them) and of very little even to them.

tionalism of fiendish serums, foul experiments of lunatic surgeons, half-human plants, monstrous insects and the like." In a similar vein, Algernon Blackwood found Lovecraft's work lacking in spirituality. More recently, I dismissed the fiction that infested the later van Thal horror anthologies as "pornography without sex," but William Schoell objected that "gore is gore, whether presented artistically or in a piece of hackneyed crap." So much for *King Lear*, presumably. I reiterate that to me, context and style matter a great deal.

Summers' argument was recently revived by Susan Hill. Her introduction to her anthology of ghost stories (1983) defines that genre with a niceness even Summers and Blackwood might have questioned. Finding no spiritual sustenance in the sorts of book she sees being marketed as supernatural fiction, she seems to have determined to return to the first principles of the genre, as she perceives them. Now I can sympathise if (to contrive an unlikely example) she bought Shaun Hutson's *Shadows* in mistake for Charlie Grant's, but the trouble with her approach is that it excludes so much. I'm for broadening the genre, not narrowing it, and I should say that a genre is defined by the work its practitioners regard as part of it. If M. R. James thought of, say, "The Ash Tree" as a ghost story, and Aickman "The Trains," then that is what they are. Hill's novel *The Woman in Black* further epitomises her view of the field; it's a fine pastiche and an effective tale, but it seems to me to lack the individuality of *The Green Man*, where Kingsley Amis develops the ghostly novel in his own highly recognisable way and helps to bring it up to date.

As an anthologist as well as a writer, Aickman was for broadening. His Fontana series reprinted such tales as "The Travelling Grave," "The Voice in the Night," "The Dancing Partner," and "Levitation." The breadth of his definition of the ghostly was one of the strengths of the series, but it proved insufficiently marketable for the publishers, who tried to make the books appear more conventional (one cover blurb introduces D. H. Lawrence's "Rocking-Horse Winner" in terms of "eerie sounds, strangled cries"!) and later instructed R. Chetwynd-Hayes, who took over the editorship, to confine himself to ghosts in the narrowest sense, other manifestations of the supernatural to be extradited to a companion series of horror anthologies. This seems not to have proved helpful even in marketing terms, since both series are now defunct. Aickman has a successor, however, in Jack Sullivan (see his anthology *Lost Souls*).

Perhaps the problem of an anthology like Susan Hill's is that it harks back to a supposed Golden Age where definitions were clearer, where ghost stories could be trusted not to be too disturbing or too horrific. Speaking of *The Woman in Black*, she maintained that the ghost story must be set in the past or somewhere that resembles the past, but I must say that I see that not so much as a creative principle as an admission of defeat. For me at least, nostalgia muffles the effect of any good ghost story; I don't want to feel comfortably distanced from the supernatural experience it seeks to communicate, I want that experience to be communicated as intensely as possible. (I do enjoy Basil Copper's work for its nostalgia, I admit, in much the same way as I enjoy Basil Rathbone's Sherlock Holmes.) The same is true for the horror story, a genre recurrently overtaken by nostalgia. Horror fiction is in the business of going too far, of showing the audience things they've avoided seeing or thinking. Very much like humour, it's in the business of breaking taboos, and it follows that once those taboos are broken the fiction tends to lose power, to become "safe." For instance, Hammer Films were the subject of strident condemnation just ten years before the studios received a Queen's Award for Industry.

I'm sidling toward a definition of these genres, I see. Horror fiction speaks the unspeakable, ghost stories try to glimpse the eternal: will that do? Most other definitions that I've seen tend to blur the boundary: Susan Hill accepts stories in which the manifestations are projections from a character's psyche, but that's equally true of a good deal of horror fiction; Peter Nicholls (in a BBC radio programme where he suggested that "the ghost story has seldom been successfully transplanted to America") quoted "Lukundoo" as "an old-fashioned ghost story," while Robert Robinson, bewailing the passing of the Golden Age, expressed nostalgia for E. F. Benson's cancer-on-the-rampage vignette "Caterpillars," so that I begin to wonder if one received definition of "ghost story" is "a horror story over a certain age." Now, as I hope I've made clear, I don't regard the blurring of the generic division as a bad thing; indeed, I think that a great many of the best ghost and horror stories can be claimed by both genres. And yet I'm beginning to wonder if that is still the case.

Susan Hill suggests that the ghost story went into decline in the 1930s because, with the rise of "terror and horror fiction," it was deemed to be no longer frightening enough (whether by editors or by the public she doesn't say). This is far too sweeping a claim, but nevertheless she raises a point that's discussed at greater length in a challenging essay by David Aylward serialised in the first two issues of Raymond Alexander's and R. S. Hadji's excellent journal *Borderland.* While Aylward makes some statements I'd quarrel with (for instance, that "The Beckoning Fair One" and "How Love Came to Professor Guildea" don't inspire fear), he argues toward a point I find hard to dismiss, even if I wanted to: ". . . the writers, who used to strive for awe and achieve fear, now strive for fear and achieve only disgust." But writers such as T. E. D. Klein and Thomas Ligotti don't, nor Reggie Oliver and Terry Lamsley, not to mention Glen Hirshberg and Mark Samuels . . . There are others—a heartening number. Let me put it more simply. As long as the likes of Ash-Tree Press are keeping the best principles alive, in their reprints and in new work they publish, the genre needs no epitaph.

A Horror Writer's Lexicon

agent: 100% of a writer

anthologist: an editor with an idea, e.g.:

Love Your Growth
Dry Bones: Great Horror Fiction About Skulls
The One Thousand Greatest Vampire Stories
Writhe! Great Horror Tales About Worms
Wiggies: Great Horror Stories about Hair
Squish! Squelchy Horror Tales
Sentenced to Death: The World's Horror Writers Each Contributed One Sentence to This Novel
Bugs in the Rugs: Great Horror Fiction About House Pests
Dead Teeth Bite: Great Horror Tales About Dentures

anthology: a book of which contributors seldom receive copies

autograph: an imposition similar to lines, set by readers rather than teachers

author: a social incompetent

author's copies: copies that an author may receive after a book appears in shops

binding: something publishers think contracts should be on authors; something publishers think books hardly need

book: what collectors bet on

blurb: a way of reducing a book to the attention span of the audience; a synopsis of the book the editor would have liked the author to write; an aid to reviewers who lack the time to read

category: a way of hiding quality from readers

character: a device to persuade readers that books are about them

classic: boring

collectible: fashionable

compliment: a conversational approach to an author, e.g.:

"Do you write under your own name?"
"Have you had anything published?"
"How many books do you write a year?"
"Should I have heard of you?"
"What formula do you write to?"
"Do you know Stephen King?"
"Are your readers like normal people?"
"Can you make a living out of that sort of stuff?"
"It's just the same as science fiction, isn't it?"
"Do you get a lot of letters from mad people?"
"I prefer fiction to be about real life."
"What's Stephen King like?"

contract: a way of rendering an author smaller

cover art: a skull

dealer: someone who supplies the addictions of fans

display: a method of comparing cover art (q. v.)

draft: something that creeps through the door from an unpublished author

editor: someone who admires an author's work; the opposite of copy-editor

fan: a reader who thinks he buys the author with the book

fan mail: a way of cheering up an author, e.g.:

"When are you going to write another book like your first one?"
"My friends have never heard of you."
"I can't find your books in any of the shops."
"The shops have never heard of you."
"Do you mind not being famous?"

galleys: somewhere writers are enslaved

genre: a fan's exclusive reading; a term for whichever genre the fan reads

ghost: something people at parties have seen; something they expect writers to be on their behalf *horror fiction:* pornography; unintentional humour; therapy for authors; literature's cloaca

idea: a present from a reader to an author, e.g.:

"And then he wakes up."

"And then he turns into a skeleton."

"And then at the very end you realise that Flowerew spelled backwards is . . . "

"But *she's* a *vampire.*"

"But at the end the monster isn't really dead."

"And then at the very end you realise that Uhluhtc spelled backwards . . . "

"And then you find out the bank he's been going to every night is the blood bank."

"And then at the very end you realise that Nietsneknarf . . . "

interview: statements you can't recall having made

interviewer: a writer who uses people as first drafts

limited edition: an edition of which the author receives fewer copies than usual

literate: boring

page-turner: a book for readers with no time for language

postage: something seldom enclosed with a draft (q. v.)

proof: evidence of incompetence

promotion: an aid that publishers promise an author will have once he's better known

quote: an author's opinion of another or of their work, e.g.:

"Never has ——'s talent been more apparent."

"A unique book—unlike anything else I've ever read."

"Displays all ——'s inimitable use of language."

"A brave and ambitious attempt to write something new in fiction."

"Written with all the wit, intelligence and skill we have come to expect from this author."

"A book that has its place on any bookshelf."

"I couldn't wait to read to the end."

"Everyone who cares about the field should know about this author."

"Perhaps the leading exponent of the loghorreal style."

"Seldom has a writer so skilfully concealed his technique."

review: an inaccurate plot summary, sometimes including comments, e.g.:
"Liverpool's answer to Clive Barker."
"Too disturbing."
"Too much like real writing."
"Fans of gory violence will certainly be disappointed."

royalty: a minus amount

signing, postal: a favour that fans allow writers to do them

signing, public: a way of keeping fans away from bookshops

snobbery, literary: Ursula Le Guin on Lovecraft; Gore Vidal on Le Guin

some: the horror writer's indefinite article

study: a product of its opposite

style: a quality lent to authors by publishers

subtle: boring

title: a publisher's label, e.g.:
Alien Turds
The Itching
Itching 2: The Eggs
Spill Your Guts
Spill Your Guts 2: The Stitching
They Who Suck
Vampire Evil
Evil Vampire
Evil: The Vampire
Vampire: The Evil
Vampire: Evil?

traditional: boring

unpublished: superior to published; misunderstood; conspired against

writers' group: a place where people who can't write are persuaded that they can

Horror Fiction and the Mainstream

Only twenty seven years to go! Arkham House helped me celebrate my first thirty as a horror writer, and already I'm three years into the next. Perhaps by the time I come to the end of that chunk of my life I won't have to explain quite so often what I do. "You're nothing like your stories" continues to be a popular comment from audiences, particularly writers' groups, but I haven't yet been tempted to confound one by entering a lecture crabwise with my face in a hideous rictus, or approaching the podium by squirming under the furniture, or being audible only as a scrabbling and muttering from beneath the floor. The truth, of course, is that I'm exactly like my stories, more like them than anything else. One place writers can't hide is in their fiction, though it can be fascinating to watch their struggles to smooth their tales over themselves, producing only the lumpy outline of what they thought they hid or weren't even aware of trying to conceal. I persist in committing myself to the principle that the purpose of writing is to tell the truth.

An unlikely principle, you might object, to be flourished by a skeptic who mostly writes about the supernatural—at least, that's the substance of another comment I often encounter. Isn't that objection based on a misunderstanding of the nature of fiction?

Must (to draw a parallel) every science fiction writer be required to believe in the literal truth of their imaginings, or at least in the likelihood of them, in order not to be declared artistically fake? Surely truth must be sought in the fiction itself, not in how glued to reality it is. In my case, one truth is that I find the supernatural imaginatively appealing, especially in its more macabre aspects, and that's why I devote so much of my time to writing about it. Yet I'm bound to own that such a career is unusual. You might even call it weird.

I suspect Don Herron might, though he hasn't to my face yet. I have to assume he would include me among "the newer crop of writers who apparently wake up every morning, drink coffee and eat breakfast, then sit down at the typewriter and attempt to get weird", whom he distinguishes from authors such as Lovecraft and M. R. James, who wrote "for the love of the art" (*Kingdom of Fear,* edited by Underwood and Miller, p. 146). I'm happy to say it's precisely for the love of the art that I write, and in the hope of becoming better at it, and it's my moderate commercial success which enables me to carry on doing so. Far from trying to get weird, I want to convey the imaginative glimpses which are urging me to make them vivid. But isn't devoting my life to such a task odd in itself?

Don does touch on an important point, after all. Hardly any of the great work in our field is the product of a career in nothing but horror. The ghost stories of M. R. James span about twenty years, after which he wrote a few lesser attempts that read like the work of an imitator, the possibly autobiographical "A Vignette" excepted, and the whole of his ghostly output is only a fraction of his published prose. If we discount Lovecraft's letters, not that I see why we should, his four books' worth of prose was also the fruit of twenty years in the field. Indeed, twenty years or less seems to be as long as most writers can contribute to it. Some, such as Frank Belknap Long, seem to falter after that and never recover. Some—H. Russell Wakefield was one, and I imagine my readers can list others, me included—stay in it for life only by producing a good deal of work that is mediocre or worse as well as some good stuff.

Of course there have been exceptions. Fritz Leiber looks like one, since he was still writing macabre tales forty years after the seminal

"Smoke Ghost". Ray Bradbury pops up unexpectedly in Robert Bloch's latest anthology with a new tale that wouldn't have been out of place in *Dark Carnival.* But both writers trained much of their imaginations on science fiction or the otherwise fantastic, and here, I believe, is the crux. Even those writers who are most closely identified with the field have been elsewhere much of the time.

Off already goes Clive Barker—indeed, I understand he's toying with the notion that the *Books of Blood* and *The Damnation Game* were never horror so much as "fantastique". Off, ignoring our waves, goes Shaun Hutson, whose new novel purports to be a straight thriller about terrorism, which means that at least three characters have their eyes shot out. (Hutson also writes pseudonymous war novels, and rumour—who knows how malicious—has it he's the author of westerns and romances too.) But am I not ignoring important exceptions—Blackwood, for instance?

I say that not in order to provoke those in the know but to cite Blackwood as an example of a particular trend. Although some of his late fiction is macabre, the essential progression of his career was from achieving terror to achieving awe. A similar development may be seen in Lovecraft—from the loathsome monstrosities of, say, "The Lurking Fear" to the intellectual respect for the Old Ones in *At the Mountains of Madness.* These instances suggest to me that the best—perhaps the only—reason to stay in the field is that one believes it capable of development, and I'm reminded that when Robert Aickman had completed "Growing Boys" he wrote to me that he believed he'd found a new direction for his work to take.

A favourite question from audiences is whether I ever write anything but horror. I reply politely, though if anyone looked close they might see my toes writhe. One answer is much of the time over the last few years. I wasn't aware of writing horror during the production of *The Count of Eleven,* nor during most of *The Long Lost,* and it was only when I stood back from these novels I decided that was still what I'd written. I feel absolutely no need to write outside my field to prove I can, but nor will I force anything I write to be more generic than the theme appears to call for. So a recent story, "Where They Lived", may not seem like a horror tale to many readers. It simply struck me as redundant to introduce a macabre element, because the English couple abroad in it were sufficiently horrendous. When I read the first draft in Florida last year and asked how many of the audience thought it was a horror story, two timid hands arose, neither of them belonging to Pete Atkins, Dennis Etchison or Steve Jones, all present.

That story, and the aforementioned novels of mine, feel to me like natural developments of my previous stuff, and a sufficient answer to the question posed above. Underlying that question in at least some cases, I think, is the assumption that it's somehow preferable not to specialise. Why on earth should this be truer of horror than of science fiction, say, or crime fiction? I'm not arguing the reverse of the assumption; many of the classics of our field were written by writers who mostly wrote outside it, and in quite a few instances, as Robert Aickman pointed out, the writers are remembered solely for those tales. Kingsley Amis—not that he's likely to be so little remembered, or deserves to be—describes the process which led to his writing, among other things, ghost stories: essentially, becoming interested in a genre to the extent of feeling able to contribute. In his case this produced several fine shorter pieces—I continue to regret not including "To See the Sun" in *Uncanny Banquet*, with nothing to blame but my own laziness—and most considerably The *Green Man*, which Brian Aldiss notes in Horror: *100 Best Books* "works as a novel, rather than just as a horror tale". Let's not be too quick to object to that "just" before calling to mind the innumerable book-length horrors which have burdened the last couple of decades. But it's my contention that real novels can be, and have been, written from within the field too. All it takes is literary scope.

I wouldn't want it to appear that I'm sidling towards the mainstream so as to distance myself from such horrors of the wrong kind as have been infesting the field of late. I'd rather be seen as trying to return to the literary roots of the genre, and—not quite the same—to my own roots as a writer. Once I started to see a direction I wanted to take away from imitating Lovecraft, Nabokov and Graham Greene became influences as important for me as M. R. James and Lovecraft were. I must also acknowledge having learned from Thomas Hinde's studies of paranoia, *The Day the Call Came* and *The Investigator*, especially since Hinde is one of the very few omissions from Fiona Webster's useful listing in the first issue of *Horror* of mainstream writers who have contributed to our field.

And while I've occasionally pillaged films—here a face at the window of a moving vehicle from *Carnival of Souls,* there an object that shouldn't be hanging from a hook on a door, courtesy of Danny Kaye—the filmmaker whose influence most shaped my prose was Alain Resnais, with *Hiroshima Mon Amour* and especially *Last Year in Marienbad.* (His third feature, *Muriel,* has haunted me for thirty years, during which time I've been unable to see it again.*) I found the instant flashbacks and other narrative dislocations of these films profoundly disturbing and exciting, and I'm happy to say that recent viewings of the first two proved they'd lost none of their power for me. I've been trying to achieve similar effects in prose for as long as I've sounded like myself. I should also acknowledge my debt to Buñuel, above all *Los Olvidados*, which I first saw when I was fifteen. I'd gone to see the main feature, Bert I. Gordon's *The Cyclops*, but it was the Buñuel that stayed with me—its realism so unflinching that at times it seems surreal, the dream sequence that illuminates the themes with a special light. I believe it influenced my attempts to use the supernatural as a way of talking about contemporary experience.

Where next? What next? I've just completed the first draft of *The One Safe Place,* which grew out of two items in my local newspaper. It isn't supernatural—it may not seem to everyone, or even anyone, to be a horror story. I think it becomes one. The idea clamoured to be written in the way it has turned out, at any rate. Next, though, will be a tale of supernatural terror. I've littered the field with enough failed attempts—*The Parasite, The Hungry Moon, Midnight Sun* come immediately to mind—and I think it's time I had another go. Perhaps I'll never learn.

* I subsequently located it on NTSC videocassette and was delighted to find it had lost none of its power for me. It can now be had on DVD, and should be.

UNCONVINCING HORROR

> "Nobody loves me,
> Everybody hates me,
> Going down the garden to eat worms."

Here's a quiz. Is the above

> a: a children's rhyme?
> b: the start of a bad joke?
> c: the opening of an adaptation of "The Monkey's Paw"?

I IMAGINE SOME OF MY READERS MAY SUSPECT that all three answers are right, and so they are. Picture the scene. A woman in a straitjacket huddles against the wall of her cell, chanting the rhyme, while the psychiatrist to whom she will tell her tale, long stretches of it consisting of direct quotations from W. W. Jacobs' prose, loiters near a primitive ECT machine that will be used for the payoff of the play. Be aware that as a member of the audience you will have noted from the programme that there are only two actors in this adaptation. On the way to the theatre you might have thought "The Monkey's Paw" was well-nigh foolproof as theatrical material—but the first half of that evening's experience might have helped to change your mind.

The venue was the Chester Gateway Theatre. The event was *Nightmares.* To quote the programme, "two chilling tales by Robert Louis Stephenson and W. W. Jacobs—the Stephen Kings of their day—are brought to spine-tingling life on the stage." I shall leave that sentence to my readers to react to as they will, and pass on to the claim that "the stories which terrified Victorian England are the same ones which captivate audiences today"—not a proposal against which an old traditionalist like me is likely to react, but in the context a curious one, suggesting as it does that Jacobs was able to affect Victoria's subjects with a story first published in the year after her death. When I put this point gently in the interval to Jeremy Raison, the artistic director, he apparently felt I was being too precise. He was the adaptor—I'm not using this term in its sense of an appliance with no energy of its own, you understand—of "The Body Snatcher", the first play of the evening.

Like the travesty of Jacobs, this is a two hander. It's set in a pub. Fettes, the body-snatcher, rants his way through a series of speeches that turn most of Stevenson's tale into monologues. Even the final revelation is recounted, not shown. At one point he throws over a chair; at another he climbs on the bar and twines himself around a decorative lamp. Thunder and lightning egg him on, as does the howling of wolves; only the hooting of owls is absent, perhaps having struck the director as too much of a cliché. The pub landlady serves Fettes drinks and several helpings of conscience. Admirers of Val Lewton's film based on the Stevenson story will recall how effectively Lewton developed the material as a moral tale without losing any of its macabre power, and may wonder if the addition of a kind of female Jiminy Cricket can compare. Not favourably, I fear. The landlady is the subject of a twist in the tail that looks uncomfortably like an admission that the play would otherwise not be macabre enough.

Let us return to "The Monkey's Paw" before considering the assumptions made by those responsible for the double bill. The woman in the straitjacket proves to be the mother from Jacobs' tale. Like Fettes in the first half, she too is beset by sound effects. The revenant's "knock, so quiet and stealthy as to be scarcely audible"—

described thus in her speech—is thunderous, and presumably intended to startle the audience rather than to excite the titter it received. I believe it was Basil Davenport who cited a production of "The Monkey's Paw" that showed the mangled revenant; while the Chester play didn't go that far, the actress delivered herself of a prolonged graphic description of the injuries, entirely at odds with the reticence to which the story owes its power. As with the Stevenson, the adaptor—in this case, Adam Fresco—finds the original ending insufficient, and so the mother gets to make an extra wish, psychologically valid but a betrayal of the internal consistency of the tale.

I'm not about to savage the careers of Messrs Fresco and Raison. My point is simply that they ought to have stayed out of a genre which, on all the above evidence, they neither know nor like. I'm confident readers of this magazine could assemble a list of horror stories that could be adapted as two-handers without jettisoning characters and distorting the tale—"August Heat" comes at once to my mind. Both "The Monkey's Paw" and "The Body Snatcher" would have been altogether more potent read aloud by the lead actor and without the heckling of sound effects. In his programme note justifying what he did to Jacobs, Adam Fresco writes ". . . developments in science and medicine have inspired modern tales of terror from Mary Shelley's *Frankenstein* to Stephen King's *Lawnmower Man*"—a very odd context in which to place King's tale of a householder's discovery that the fellow mowing his lawn is a satyr who requires a sacrifice to Pan. Fresco seems to see the field largely in terms of films, and his note suggests that he had *The X-Files* too much in mind when adapting Jacobs. Still, his note is nowhere near as ignorant as the overview of horror fiction which, in four pages of the programme, one Robin Seavill presumes to offer.

The essay is called "Horror of Horrors!" Indeed. The illustrations include a picture of a man tied to a railway track and a detail from Fuseli's "The Nightmare", puzzlingly captioned "The Gothic novel—inspiration of a thousand nightmares." Like far too many accounts of horror fiction, the text swerves away as soon as it can from the prose of the field to concentrate on other media. I shall restrain myself as best I can in the face of its most extraordinary statements.

"The two plays that make up tonight's programme come from the heyday of the Victorian shocker, a time when audiences liked their ghost stories gruesome, grisly and ghoulish." Even leaving aside the considerable number of ghost stories of the period that were none of these flippantly alliterative things, I have to point out that Stevenson and Jacobs told their stories with exemplary restraint; it was the adaptors who pumped up the Stevenson with melodrama and injected the Jacobs with gruesomeness. However, Seavill's opening sentence is unproblematical compared to its successor.

"These days we have become so desensitised by the in-your-face tactics of TV and cinema that it is perhaps hard to appreciate why the Victorians liked them so much." As I read this my growl of "Speak for yourself, pal" must have been heard by quite a number of my neighbours in the audience, before it became apparent to me that Seavill was apparently saying that the evening's entertainment was unlikely to work. The culprits weren't the adaptors or the production, however, but the cinema, "which was able to put more money into lavish and increasingly outlandish special effects, and year on year the emphasis gradually shifted from implicit suggestion to out and out gore." This notion that horror, and the censorship of it, has consistently progressed towards greater explicitness is so erroneous yet so widespread that I may return to it in a future column. Let me confine myself for now to Seavill's next, and most astounding, sentence. "The pendulum has only just begun to swing back again after the over the top excesses of the video nasties, though it still has a long way to go before we get back to the good old days of plastic fangs and raspberry essence so beloved of Hammer Studios."

I take a breath. I count to ten—no, twenty. I suppress all the expletives provoked by the above, several breaths' worth. I skim over the thoughtless—I use the adjective in its most literal sense—reference to "video nasties", and reflect briefly that, as any number of contemporary reviews and attacks in the media demonstrate, Hammer Films were the nasties of their day. Those points are minor compared with the fundamental attitude Seavill sums up in this sentence. What he wants—and what we may suspect Fresco and Raison of wanting too, given that Seavill's statement is meant to introduce their plays—is horror that isn't convincing. I find this staggering. As well insist on having comedy that doesn't make you laugh or tragedy that you may be assured won't move you. I've rarely seen such inadvertent honesty in a programme note. It tells us that the double bill was intended not to shock, not to disturb, not to frighten, not to do anything that horror fiction might reasonably be expected to do—perhaps only to allow the audience to feel simultaneously superior to the material and nostalgic for an era when they might have found it affecting. I don't know when I've seen a more blatant example in any medium of horror fiction created for people who don't like horror. I only hope that those members of the audience who do, and who were disappointed by the evening, won't be put off the original stories if they don't know them. The plays were regrettable, but that would be unforgivable.

[Messrs Fresco, Raison and Seavill were each sent a copy of this piece. One of them, I'm told, threw it in the nearest bin. I've no sense of how it affected his accomplices.]

To the Next Generation

Why do we write horror stories?

If you write in this field you're bound to be asked that question, and in any case it does no harm to know your reasons. It must be the question I've been asked most often in my career, and I've amassed quite a few answers. However, I don't think it's possible to answer the question until we have defined what we mean by "horror stories", and so here goes my neck on the block.

Horror fiction is the branch of literature most often concerned with going too far. It is the least escapist form of fantasy. It shows us sights we would ordinarily look away from or reminds us of insights we might prefer not to admit we have. It makes us intimate with people we would cross the street to avoid. It shows us the monstrous and perhaps reveals that we are looking in a mirror. It tells us we are right to be afraid, or that we aren't afraid enough. It also frequently embraces, or at least is conterminous with, the ghost story. It flourishes here and there in the fields of science fiction and crime fiction, and not infrequently it bobs up in the mainstream, whatever that is. Despite its name, it is often most concerned to produce awe and terror in its audience, but it is not unusual for a horror story to encompass a wider emotional range.

All these reasons (and maybe more that you can think of) justify one answer I give anyone who wants to know why I write what I write: that horror fiction seems to me to be an extremely broad field—quite broad enough to allow me to deal fully with any theme I want to deal with. Another answer, perhaps the one most likely to strike an echo in any aspiring writer, is that I want to pay back some of the pleasure that horror fiction has been giving me almost since I learned to read. (Indeed, my very first memory of anything I read is of being terrified by a story, presumably intended to be charming, in a British children's comic annual, where a Christmas tree dissatisfied with its lot uprooted itself from the tub and creaked back to the forest, scattering earth on the carpet as it went.) Even simpler, and as true, is the answer that I write horror fiction because I'm proud of my field. If you aren't proud of the field you write in, I can see no point in doing it at all.

Pride in a field involves knowing its history. I've no room here for a reading list, but let me recommend two fine fat anthologies as representative: *Great Tales of Terror and the Supernatural*, edited by Phyllis Wise and Herbert A. Fraser in the late forties and still triumphantly in print, and David Hartwell's more recent *Dark Descent*. One reason to become familiar with the traditions of your field is to discover what has already been done; another is to learn from the masters. The notion that you should learn only from your contemporaries, on the basis that if you look to earlier models then your work is likely to be unsaleably out of date, seems to me to be nonsense, and inimical to the vitality of any field. A field whose writers relate only to their own peers is in danger of disappearing up itself.

I've seen it claimed that Lovecraft and earlier masters are irrelevant to today's writers in the field, on the basis that if they were working today they would bring themselves unrecognisably up to date. In Lovecraft's case the claim is demonstrably rubbish, and I have my doubts about Machen and M. R. James, but that's not the point. The techniques these writers have been imitated, but they have never been bettered as far as I'm aware. If you want to learn the technique of the glancing phrase of terror, the image that goes by almost before you notice and shows enough to suggest far more (and it's worth knowing), study M. R. James. If you want to examine the model of the tale of supernatural terror, where carefully graduated hints and glimpses build to an awesome pitch, Lovecraft is where to look.

Lovecraft is a classic instance of the writer who constructs strengths out of his weaknesses. He had little interest in, or talent for, characterisation, and so he wrote stories in which the insignificance of humanity is the theme and the source of his power. No wonder that his novels were essentially extended short stories. Here I should admit that I first saw print by imitating Lovecraft slavishly. With the benefit of hindsight I feel there's nothing necessarily wrong in beginning by imitation, since if you have any originality of your own to be brought out you will soon become aware of the limits of your model. It seems to me that it can be useful to develop the rudiments of technique by imitation, in order to have gained some fluency before you begin to write more personally. The aim of any literary apprenticeship is to allow you to tell the stories only you can tell.

I hope that doesn't sound more daunting than it is. I'm simply asking you to be true to your own imagination and experience. By all means read voraciously, and don't limit yourself by confining your reading to your own field, but read as a means to finding your own voice. There's only one Stephen King, for instance, but there are far too many writers trying to sound like him. Show us what only you have seen, tell us your secret thoughts and wildest imaginings. Above all, be honest. I believe that good fiction, and good criticism, show us what we hadn't seen before or what we had overlooked. Sometimes they make us look again at what we had taken for granted.

It seems to me that, despite all the claims I made on its behalf at the beginning of this piece, horror fiction too often takes for granted conventions which the field needs to examine in order to develop. Who better than the next generation, yourselves, to do so? Let me suggest a few for you to attack.

Take the theme of evil, as the horror story often does. Writing about evil is a moral act, and it won't do to recycle definitions of evil, to take them on trust. Horror fiction frequently uses the idea of evil in such a shorthand form as to be essentially meaningless: something vague out there that causes folk to commit terrible acts, something other than ourselves, nothing to do with us. That sounds to me more like an excuse than a definition, and I hope it's had its day. If we're going to write about evil then let's define it and how it relates to ourselves. In my view fiction should disturb, and especially disturb the reader's prejudices rather than seek to reassure by indulging and confirming them.

All good fiction consists of looking at things afresh, but some horror fiction seems to have an inbuilt tendency to do the opposite. Ten years or so ago many books had nothing more to say than "the devil made me do it"; now, thanks to the influence of films like *Friday the 13th,* it seems enough for some writers to say that a character is psychotic, no further explanation necessary. But it's the job of writers to imagine how it would feel to be all their characters, however painful that may sometimes be. Perhaps it's a lack of that compassion which has led some writers to create children who are evil simply because they're children, surely the most deplorable cliché of the field.

Some clichés are simply products of lazy writing. Tradition shouldn't be used as an excuse to repeat what earlier writers have done; if you feel the need to write about the stock figures of the horror story, that's all the more reason to imagine them anew. For instance, we might have believed there was nothing new to be written about vampirism until Karl Wagner wrote "Beyond Any Measure," whose stunningly original idea was always implicit in the vampire tradition and waiting for Karl to notice. Again, generations might have thought that the definitive haunted house tale had been written, but it hadn't been until Shirley Jackson wrote *The Haunting of Hill House* (a statement guaranteed to make some of you try to improve on that novel, perhaps). Put it another way: one reason some folk recoil from my own novel *The Face That Must Die* seems to be that it confronts you with how I imagine it might be like to be a psychotic killer, rather than keeping a Halloween face or ski mask between him and the audience, the better to turn him into a bogey-man we can dismiss as being nothing like ourselves. It's only fair to warn you that many readers and publishers would rather see imitations of whatever they liked last year than give new ideas a chance. But I've always tried to write what rings true to me, whether or not it makes the till ring. If you don't feel involved with what you're writing, it's unlikely that anyone else will.

There's another side to the field which is overdue for attack by a new generation: its reactionary quality. A horror writer I otherwise admire argued recently that "it has been a time-honoured tradition in literature and film that you have a weak or helpless heroine"—implying, I assume, that we should go on doing so. Well, tradition is a pretty poor excuse for perpetrating stereotypes (not that the author in question necessarily does); time-honoured it may be, but that doesn't make it honourable. In fact, these days so many horror stories (and, especially, films) gloat over the suffering of women that it seems clear the authors are getting their own back, consciously or not, on aspects of real life that they can't cope with. Of course that isn't new in horror fiction, nor is using horror fiction to define as evil or diabolical whatever threatens the writer or the writer's life-style, but at the very least one should be aware as soon as possible that this is what one is doing, so as to be able to move on. I have my suspicions too about the argument that horror fiction defines what is normal by showing us what isn't. I think it's time for more of the field to acknowledge that when we come face to face with the monsters, we may find ourselves looking not at a mask but at a mirror.

Now all this may sound as if it requires some discipline and dedication, and my experience is that it does. After all, the best way for a writer to compete is with oneself, to do better than one did last time. I'm not the first to say that the most important thing for a writer to do is to write, but I'll add that you should work on whatever you're writing every day until it's finished; to do otherwise is to court writer's block, every blank day adding to the hurdle that prevents you from getting back into the story and making the task seem more impossible. An example of this is my story "Litter", where six months elapsed between my first day's work and my return to the story, which I took up by writing the line "That's how he enters the story, or this is." I should have rewritten the story to improve its shape, of course. Now I rewrite more and more severely, and take great pleasure in cutting thousands of words out of first drafts; I think that's a pleasure worth learning as early as possible in one's career, not least because realising one can do it helps one relax into writing the first draft, where it's better to have too much material for later shaping than not enough. Learning to relax enough with the technique of writing novels comes easier to some than others; you may feel you need to plot a novel in advance (maybe all the way to breaking it down into chapter synopses) before you begin the first chapter, but it's worth trying to regard the synopsis merely as a safety net once you begin writing, trying to let the novel develop itself as it takes on more life. I did that first in *Incarnate,* and since then I've avoided plotting or constructing too far ahead, trying to know only as much as I need to know to start writing and head in the right direction. It can be fearsome to find yourself losing your way halfway through a novel, all by yourself in the unknown, but I find that the solutions are usually somewhere in what you've already written, and I can tell you that the bad days are worth the days when you feel the novel come to life.

I'm still stressing the arduousness, but let me see if I can pass on some tricks I've learned. We all have an optimum period of creativity each day, and it's worth beginning work then if you possibly can. Mine is from about six in the morning until noon or so. It's easy to get distracted away from your work, but music may help; my desk is between the speakers of the hi-fi on which I play compact discs (which last longer than records and keep me there longer) of all sorts of music from Monteverdi onwards. (Steve King uses rock, Peter Straub jazz.) Don't be too eager to feel you've exhausted your creative energy for the day, but if you sense you're close to doing so, then don't squeeze yourself dry: better to know what the next paragraph is going to be and start with that next time. Scribble down a rough version of it rather than risk forgetting it. Always have a rough idea of your first paragraph before you sit down to write, and then you won't be trapped into fearing the blank page. If you must take a day or more out from a story, break off before the end of a scene or a chapter, to give yourself some impetus when you return. Always carry a notebook for ideas, glimpses, overheard dialogue, details of what you're about to write, developments of work in progress. If an idea or something larger refuses to be developed, try altering the viewpoint or even the form: if it won't grow as a short story, it may be a poem. Sometimes two apparently unproductive ideas may be cross-fertilised to give you a story. Then again, you may not be ready technically or emotionally to deal with an idea, and it can improve with waiting.

What else can I tell you? Only to write. Surprise us, astonish us. Enjoy your work. Above all, don't despair. The frustration you will inevitably experience sometimes, the feeling that you don't know how to write, may be the birth pangs of something genuinely new. I know I still suffer that experience every time I write a story. Believe me, it's preferable to playing it safe with a formula. Good luck! I look forward to reading you!

2: On Horror and Fantasy Film

Beyond the Pale

To be quoted back at oneself after almost twenty years can be a disconcerting experience. Certainly I found it so, in the first issue of the British magazine *Gothique* to have been published since 1965. A theme runs through the issue, my own new contribution included: a plea for a more critical attitude toward horror fiction, movies in particular, in response to "certain disturbing tendencies in the modern horror film," as Ernie Harris puts it in his contribution. He means "exploitation of the nastiest and most degrading kind," and quotes my thoughts from 1968: ". . . an increase in cinematic violence could be symptomatic of, and responsible for, the increasing reluctance to be shocked by or sympathetic to forms of human suffering—which is to say a decline in humanism."

Well, I don't want to get into an argument with myself, but I'm less inclined these days to blame fiction for the reality it reflects, more inclined to suggest that fiction, even at its most extreme, expresses the emotions of its chosen audience rather than corrupting them. I hope, all the same, that I've been making clear in *Fantasy Review* that I'm very much in favour of bringing critical standards to bear on the horror genre. Yet I'll sound a note of warning. While I've no sympathy at all with those who would like to keep the genre disreputable, for whatever reason, I should be wary of seeking to regain respectability for the genre by excluding its less respectable examples without regard for their merits.

In the new *Gothique* Stan Nicholls writes: "We could be a little less willing to defend every cheap piece of fiction and film catering to the most basic instincts of cruelty and sexual exploitation which happens to bear a tenuous fantasy label." Fair enough, perhaps even Somtow would agree, but it's a case that can only be tested against specific films and defences of them, as Ernie Harris notes: "Trying to make a case for films like *Driller Killer* or *Nightmares (In a Damaged Brain)* does nothing for credibility." But at whatever risk to my reputation, I've come to agree with Kim Newman's defence of *Driller Killer* as a disturbingly vivid treatment of the everyday life of a psychotic, and one that must have been uncomfortably familiar to its Times Square-42nd Street audience. Given that the director went on to make the equally bleak and unpredictable *Ms .45* I should say he deserves encouragement, even if it may be premature to include him in an encyclopaedia of the genre.

Which brings me, with at least oblique relevance, to the forthcoming Penguin encyclopaedia of horror, for which I wrote a couple of dozen entries about films. Several of these were reappraisals of films I thought to be neglected (*The Beast from Haunted Cave*) or unjustly maligned (*The Shining*). It was probably inevitable that the encyclopaedia would end up overlong and have to be cut, but I was sorry that two of my reappraisals were excised. If only to give the films another chance, I'd like to include them here.

Death Line, made in Britain in 1973, was released in America as *Raw Meat*, cut to obtain a PG rating. It's now available uncut on DVD. I wrote about it for the encyclopaedia as follows:

An unusually bleak and harrowing horror film. The disappearance of a civil servant from a London underground railway station leads to the discovery that workers trapped by the cave-in of a Victorian underground railway and abandoned there have survived for several generations by cannibalism. The civil servant has been carried off by the last cannibal in a vain attempt to revive his dying, and pregnant, mate. Significantly, the cannibal (Hugh

Armstrong) is described as "The Man" on the credits. He is at once the most appalling and the most human of all screen monsters. Some of the scenes of life at the end of its tether are as distressing as any in the genre: the Man's inarticulate howls of anguish as he realises he is now totally alone; his attempts to revive his mate and later, his attempts to communicate with and, however savagely, to protect the young woman (Sharon Gurney) he abducts, with much greater psychological justification than monstrous kidnapping in films generally bears, from the upper world. A welcome touch of grotesque humour—his only words are "Mind the doors," which he has overheard from the station above his lair—was seized upon by most British film reviewers as sufficient reason to treat the film as beneath contempt. Apart from this touch and a blackly comic performance by Donald Pleasance as the policeman in charge of the case, *Death Line* is relentlessly oppressive—indeed, while the most claustrophobic scenes (a prolonged tour of the cannibal's lair, an episode in a lift) are filmed in single takes, there are perhaps half a dozen exterior shots in the film, no daytime exteriors at all, and not a glimpse of the sky; very little in the film offers the audience any relief from the plight of the Man.

The theme of the revenge of the exploited worker predates that of *The Texas Chainsaw Massacre* by several years, and is expressed with more stylistic coherence than in Hooper's film. The compassion of all the upperworld characters is severely limited, where it exists at all: if the abducted young woman is at the opposite pole from Christopher Lee's MI5 man (who simply wishes to see things hushed up, as the industrialists who failed to rescue the workers from the collapsed tunnel presumably did), her compassion breaks down in the face of the Man's grotesque but genuine attempts to calm and communicate with her. The violence would be intolerable if it were not for the tragic dimension of the film, but Hugh Armstrong's performance is one of the greatest and most moving in horror films.

My other deleted entry was for Wes Craven's *Last House on the Left*. This 1972 film was denied British release until the early eighties, when it was briefly available on videocassette before being prosecuted wherever it appeared. (In February 2000 it was submitted to the British Board of Film Classification, who refused it a certificate, but after more adventures with the censor the uncut version was given an 18 rating in 2008.) On the basis of two viewings, I wrote:

Wes Craven's first film is about the inescapability of violence. It borrows its structure from Bergman's *Virgin Spring:* two young women are raped and murdered by criminals, who then take refuge in the house of one of their victims and are killed by her parents. Where Bergman's film is austere and almost ritualistic, Craven's is relentlessly horrific (though, significantly, this doesn't involve lingering on the details of violence). Like David Morrell's novel *First Blood,* with which it is contemporary and which attracted comparable hostility, Craven's film is concerned with the awareness of the universal potential for violence that Vietnam made inescapable. Craven's response to the objection that Vietnam is "over" is that "it's not over—it's going to come in through another door."

A central concern of *Last House on the Left* is the acting out of repressed violence. "What's new in the outside world?" Mari's mother asks the father, who replies "Same old stuff—murder, mayhem." The repression of violence by describing it as "other" is often a stratagem of the horror genre. Mari's parents criticise her for going to see Bloodlust, a violent rock group ("All that blood and violence—I thought you were supposed to be the love generation") but accept it as inevitable. As in *The Virgin Spring,* the daughter is led to her death by another young woman, but where in Bergman's film the other is seeking her downfall, in Craven's she too becomes a victim. The violence is squalid, harrowingly painful, banal and authentic—"authentic," that is, both in its lack of any real motivation beyond casual sadism and in the observation of how the criminals behave. Sometimes embarrassed by their own excesses ("Oh Christ" one mutters as Brenda, the female member of the gang, mutilates Mari's friend, while another giggles uncomfortably), they never have any sympathy elicited on their behalf by the film, but at the same time the audience is never allowed to dismiss them simply as monsters. Nor is the audience given the luxury of detachment (Brenda's first scene, where she is overheard singing "Singing in the Rain," might be an ironic echo of Kubrick's *A*

Clockwork Orange, possibly the most aestheticised of all films about violence). Even the visual style of the scenes of violence is random, "carelessly" framed, precluding any pleasure in the representation, and there is no display of violent special effects for the audience to enjoy as pure technique. In Mari's last scene, she prays "I pray the Lord my soul to take" while a song on the soundtrack declares "You're all alone," but ironically, the criminals seem to kill her out of depression, almost remorse, at their behaviour.

Krug and company dress up as middle-class executives when their car breaks down and seek help at the nearest house, Mari's. The anticipated scenes of vengeance offer none of the mindless satisfaction of, say, Charles Bronson's revenge spree in *Death Wish*. (The film has already made the audience anticipation disturbingly explicit: as the young women are driven to their doom, a jaunty song is heard on the soundtrack—"Let's have some fun with these two lovely children and off them as soon as we're done.") The mother seduces one of the gang before castrating him, the father sets traps for the others. The mother seems disconcertingly adept as a seducer (while in the opening scene she feels sexually overshadowed by Mari); the father's traps are too ingenious and lovingly thought out for comfort—the parents are as convincing, and ultimately as savage, as criminals as the gang were convincing as middle-class travellers. At the end of the carnage the theme song is repeated: "The road leads to nowhere, the castle stays the same." The medieval reference is all that remains of Bergman's original, brought home in contemporary terms.

Two sorry Italian imitations followed Craven's film, *Late Night Trains* (*Night Train Murders*) and *The House on the Edge of the Park*. Both indulge the visual aspects of the violence while playing down the pain and injury, the opposite of Craven's method. Besides being one of the first and most important of the horror films about the contemporary family, *Last House on the Left* anticipates and criticises the anti-feminist trend in horror films ("You been reading those creep women's lib magazines?" Brenda is asked) and serves as a riposte to the urban revenge movies of the later seventies. It was among the last of the so-called video nasties to be banned in Britain, but was finally passed uncut (having previously been allowed with cuts) in March 2008.

Beyond the equally uncompromising *Hills Have Eyes,* Craven's work became increasingly bland, and I can only wonder if he was doing his best to avoid the sort of hostility his early work provoked. (Dennis Etchison and others have given me to understand that *Nightmare on Elm Street* is something of a return to form.*) As for Gary Sherman, director of *Death Line,* he seemed to disappear from the cinema for ten years, resurfacing with *Dead and Buried,* a stylish but excessively violent horror comic, quite possibly the sort of film the reviewers had led him to believe was expected of him. Which brings me to a statement of principle which is as near as this essay is likely to come to a unifying theme: I should rather risk overpraising work in my field than see distinguished work go unremarked. In that I'm one with Lovecraft, I believe.

* It was, but I believe his finest achievement so far to be its final sequel. *Wes Craven's New Nightmare.*

Horror Films and Society

I

As I began to write this column, at the end of November, the best-known horror film in Britain was *Child's Play 3*. It had been cited as an influence in two British cases of sadism, in one of which two ten-year-old boys abducted a two-year-old, James Bulger, whom they then tortured and murdered. In this case there appeared to be no definite proof that the owner of the copy of the film (released direct to video in Britain) allowed his son to watch it, and the police declared themselves unconvinced that films were to blame for the crime, but horror is back in the dock again. Even before the case came to trial the *Guardian* printed a letter insisting that the culprits must have watched horror films, and now the press and politicians are in full cry. A Liberal—readers must decide for themselves what the word means in this context—calls for an extra censorship rating, to signify "Not suitable for home viewing". A *Sunday Times* columnist claims that one boy "must have known his father liked video nasties with plots remarkably evocative of the crime committed", though she seems unable or unwilling to be more specific, and goes on to suggest that the boy imagined his sadism was heroic because his parents (note the switch from "father") liked to watch that kind of thing. Also in the *Sunday Times*

Michael Medved (previously employed by the paper to sneer at Demi Moore and discuss Tom Cruise's salary) appears to sound reasonable: "... even if is only a few thousand—or a few hundred—vulnerable individuals who are encouraged to commit murderous cruelty..." Long before the end of his article the "if" has been forgotten, and I believe there is an important counter-argument—that since the effects of extreme imagery are still a matter of considerable disagreement, it may be more dangerous to censor these expressions of the collective unconscious than to let them regulate themselves, however tardily. Suppressing them will not make them go away, only fester—that's my argument, at any rate.

Two separate BBC researchers—one local, one for a nationwide broadcast—approached me to go on the air about the James Bulger case. "If Bulger happens," one said while the jury at the trial was out, "can we quote you?" Here "quote" means "use", since I hadn't ventured an opinion, and it wasn't only the hardboiled professional language which caused me to refuse. In one sense I was flattered on behalf of our field to be regarded as potentially able to offer insights into the psychology of the situation, which was what I was being asked to talk about, but the notion of anyone involved in the case having to listen to the speculations of a horror writer made me uncomfortable. Besides, imagine the headlines. I might have said that the innocence of childhood must involve the potential to commit acts of terrible irrationality—any other concept of childhood innocence is a dangerous sham perpetrated by people who have forgotten their own childhood state—but that mightn't have gone down too well either. So, coward that perhaps I am, I set myself a lesser task which I'd begun to suspect none of the commentators in the media had bothered with: watching the offending film, a third showing of which Sky Television cancelled after the film was named in the court case.

Child's Play 3 is an undistinguished second sequel to an intermittently imaginative original, on the old theme of the possessed doll. None of the films in the series can hold its own with Blackwood or Wakefield or the Ealing *Dead of Night* or *Magic* (the Goldman novel, not the film), but they do have some satirical fun with the possession of Chucky the Good Guy Doll, a children's mass-produced companion, by the spirit of a killer determined to magic his way into a new human body. In this third film his chosen victim has been enrolled in a military school, a kind of junior version of the first section of *Full Metal Jacket,* to which it has more than a few similarities. Chucky is reintegrated once again and pursues him, killing a handful of mostly unsympathetic secondary characters, as is the way of the standard horror film, while motivations are abandoned amid the mayhem. After substituting real ammunition in a war game, Chucky pursues a new victim to a carnival and is eventually sundered a third time. But where is the scene in which the doll is battered and has paint flung at it, allegedly the source of the behaviour of the two ten-year-old killers? It is not in this film at all, but in its predecessor. So anxious were the media, and the executives at Sky Television, to find something to blame that they got the wrong film.

If rushing to judgement has been better exemplified elsewhere, let me know. And yet . . . In the other, quite unrelated British case, the teenagers who tortured and set fire to their teenage victim, who died after naming them, reportedly used Chucky's catch-phrase to terrorise her. Isn't this a reason to ban the films, even if the criminals were under the influence of drugs? Not, I would suggest, unless we feel that the Beatles' white album must also be banned on the basis that Charles Manson played it to his drugged followers to put them in the mood for killing. If films must be banned if they can be shown to have been imitated, mustn't this policy be consistently applied? There are documented cases of children injuring others in imitation of Tom and Jerry and the Three Stooges, and I must say that if any films parallel the dreadful treatment of James Bulger, who had paint thrown in his eyes and bricks flung at him, they are the *Home Alone* duo, which present exactly that behaviour on the part of a boy about ten years old as amusing and admirable. All of which may sound as if I'm absolving modern horror and telling it that all is well, but not so. Precisely because the tendency of many, perhaps most, of us in the field is to regard ourselves as blameless—precisely because I caught myself doing so—I think it's time to take a closer look.

Let me start with the *Child's Play* series. It exemplifies a tendency to which the studio, Universal, have been prone for at least sixty years—that of bringing their successful monsters back to life and, on the whole, making their viewpoint progressively more central. But there's surely a difference between the way they defrosted Frankenstein's maltreated creature and the modern tendency, which perhaps reaches its nadir in another company's decision to give ingratiating quips and a ridiculous origin to Freddy Kreuger, who began life as nothing more than a killer of children. In *Child's Play 3* Chucky gets a quite a few lines, and even if they're witless, they still have the effect of reducing the audience's critical distance from him, to no very good end. Not that I'm opposed to giving the monstrous a voice—I've been trying to do it in my tales for years—but these scenes tell us nothing about the monster, they simply try and make us feel closer to him without examining that state. Of course he is still made of plastic, and can therefore be spectacularly mutilated in each film without our feeling unduly disturbed by the spectacle; indeed, he's so resilient that he comes back for more of the same. If his blood looks realistic, that's supposed to add to the gory fun we've paid to have. But what are we to make of realism which the audience is meant to recognise as unreal?

Undoubtedly audiences know more about effects in the movies than they used to. Long past are the days when people fled the image of a train entering a station or even screamed at King Kong. Jean-Luc Godard, and others too, might argue that this enables the cinema to address the audience as an equal rather than as a consumer of illusions, but both approaches have produced great films. More to the present point, few things can turn a horror movie inadvertently comic quicker than dud effects, and so it isn't surprising if film-makers seek to convince. In general the increasing realism of makeup effects keeps pace with the audience's ability to perceive them as effects, if sometimes only just. Yet surely these effects also suggest that however convincing violence may look, it need not be real.

The notion of desensitisation inevitably comes to mind. Films become more violent as audiences grow used to a level of violence. I have to say that doesn't wholly relate to my own experience—I'm still perfectly capable of being affected by violence in old movies, because of the context in which it appears. (There is some surprisingly gruesome violence in several Val Lewton films, for instance, which is all the more shocking because of their overall reticence.) Becoming used to violence in fiction doesn't necessarily entail becoming indifferent to it in real life. But that is no excuse for bad art. Nothing is.

Which brings us, I'm afraid, to the state of too much modern horror fiction. I co-edit *Best New Horror* with Steve Jones, which means I have to read a great deal of it, though not as much as the resilient and dedicated Steve, and I've reached a conclusion similar to that forced upon Karl Wagner last year by his reading the multitude of candidates for *Year's Best Horror:* "Most of those short stories are hopelessly awful . . . more of a task each year. . . the same bad stories over and over and over." Perhaps nobody who writes such fiction is likely to read a critical magazine such as ours, but in case they or their friends do, let me ask how they justify what they write. Would they regard that as an unreasonable question? Do they feel that striving to outdo or even equal their fellow competitors in revoltingness is the highest goal they can set themselves? I'd call that an irresponsible waste of any talent they have, and I'm being kind to the horde whose offensiveness is nothing more than a substitute for talent. Angela Carter once, while writing about Lovecraft, described horror fiction as a holiday from morality, but I grow increasingly convinced that it needn't be and that to think otherwise is an inexcusable excuse. Shaun Hutson once, or maybe oftener, said that if anyone was caused to commit crimes by reading his fiction it (the criminal behaviour, not the reading) just proved they were already sick in the head, but to write with such an attitude is simply to refuse to take responsibility for one's work. Dare I propose to our colleagues in the field the possibility of self-censorship? Provided that the writer is aware of exerting it, this can be a useful discipline, productive of wit.

Let me close with two quotes. From the still excellent *New Maps of Hell:* "The impression lingers that a good look through the mailing lists of the fantasy magazines would amply repay anybody setting up in business as an analyst." Lord knows how Kingsley Amis might reword that comment if he had to read much of the current crop (a word in which I'm tempted to substitute a different vowel); as it stands, it is all too appropriate. It may be unfair to the field as a whole, but it, and worse, is true of far too much of the field. I come back yet again to David Aylward: "Writers . . . now strive for fear and produce only disgust." I think it is high time some of them considered that they may be producing something more deplorable and more pernicious. The best I can hope is that their work, with the tedium of its excesses, destroys nothing but itself.

II

> "In *Necrofile* 11 Mr Campbell voiced his hope that the work of certain writers who merely produce disgust destroy nothing but itself, but it is to be feared that horror videos have already done more than that, as witness the James Bulger tragedy. I'm sure most of us can hold our horror, but surely ten-year-olds cannot do so."
>
> Hubert Van Calenbergh (*Necrofile* 12, p. 20)

The James Bulger tragedy witnesses nothing of the kind, as I thought I'd made clear in my piece to which Mr Van Calenbergh refers. To repeat myself, "the police declared themselves unconvinced that films were to blame for the crime, but horror is back in the dock again." I might have added that the old arguments were being rehashed yet again, with both sides going away convinced they were in the right, and—again as usual—the proponents of censorship relying on rhetoric when they ran out of arguments. This kind of thing:

"It may fearlessly be asserted that there never lived an animal of prey of uglier type than this two-legged creature, who poisons the minds of little children to make his bread . . . Beware of him, O careful parents of little lads! He is as cunning as the fabled vampire. Already he may have bitten your little rosy-cheeked son Jack. He may be lurking at this very moment in that young gentleman's private chamber, little as you suspect it, polluting his mind and smoothing the way to swift destruction."

Except for its literacy, that could be a passage from any of the dozens of diatribes against horror films on video which appeared, and continue to appear, in British newspapers. In fact it was published in 1874. It comes from James Greenwood's "Penny Packets of Poison", an attack on the Penny Dreadfuls, included in his collection of essays *The Wilds of London*. You see what I mean by saying that arguments, if any of that can be dignified by such a term, recur. Of course I'm not accusing Mr Van Calenbergh of such overstatement—he would hardly be contributing to our august pages if that were his style—but I do think he may be feeding ammunition to those groups who would use children as a supposed justification for censorship for adults. Since writing my earlier piece I've spoken to Sheila Fogarty, a BBC reporter who was in court throughout the James Bulger trial, and she tells me that videos were never even mentioned except by the judge in his summing-up. That said, I want to thank Mr Van Calenbergh, because it was his comment which troubled me until I worked out why. Can ten-year-olds really not hold their horror? Surely the answer to that can be found within and about the field itself, and most importantly, within our own experience.

I'll come to mine. Meanwhile, I'll ask my readers to cast their own minds back to their first encounter with adult horror fiction in whatever form, written or filmed. It's my observation that a great many people in the field were at least as young as the boys Mr Van Calenbergh cites when they began to consume fiction regarded as unsuitable for children. Let me refer to just a few examples I find in the library of my house. Joan Aiken writes "I first came to E. F. Benson's stories when I was around six years old . . . I had already read *Ghost-Stories of an Antiquary* by M. R. James, and nearly died of delicious terror at 'Oh, Whistle, and I'll Come to You, My Lad . . . children of that age seem to be infinitely tough and infinitely masochistic." Lovecraft was eight when he fell in love with the tales of Poe, despite his already being plagued by bad dreams of night-gaunts. Thana Niveau was nine, but had seen *Friday the 13th* and *Alien* a year earlier. Frank Belknap Long was apparently familiar with Poe's work well before the age of thirteen, though he was that age when Poe's worth became apparent to him. John Llewellyn Probert bought *The Ninth Pan Book of Horror Stories* when he was nine, and found it too much for him, but only for a fortnight before he returned to it. Robert Bloch was ten years old when he began to read *Weird Tales*, with the issue that contained "Pickman's Model". Fritz Leiber might have been younger when he sampled the magazine, only to find it too disturbing, though he was to return to it soon enough. Admittedly Stephen King may have been as old as fourteen when he chanced upon a copy of the Avon *Lurking Fear,* but he notes it "wasn't my first encounter with horror, of course". Brian Aldiss (whose middle initial comes and goes in obedience to principles even more arcane than those governing the M. of Iain Banks) was seven when he bought Dashiell Hammett's *Modern Tales of Horror,* the slightly slimmer British version of *Creeps by Night,* missing the stories by S. Fowler Wright and Harold Dearden. ("For many years," he writes, "it was my favourite book—favourite because it scared the life out of me.") The palm for precociousness, however, must surely be awarded to Pete Rawlik of the South Florida Science Fiction Society. "For me, the first corrupting exposure to the realm of horror came at the tender age of four. I remember sitting on my father's lap . . . slowly, carefully reading the fine text of H. P. Lovecraft's 'The Rats in the Walls'."

More power to Pete Rawlik's father! May there be many more like him! Thank heaven he didn't fall foul of any censor, official or self-appointed, who felt they knew better than he did what was unsuitable for his son. Of course the anecdote might also be taken to demonstrate how sustaining a stable family relationship can be, and I note that Brian W. Aldiss read the Hammett anthology aloud to his mother. Does this mean that to survive a dose of horror fiction early in one's life one needs an at least reasonably unfraught childhood? Well, no: not in my experience.

I imagine some of our readers have read this or that account of my childhood, but for those who don't know, let me summarise it. My mother was clinically schizophrenic, my father lived in our house but didn't let himself be seen by me—a decent basis for a troubled young mind, you might assume, and indeed when I was seven my mother took me to a child psychiatrist in, so my memory suggests, the hope that he would cure my nightmares and night panics. They had various causes, and not only my family life—for a start, I'd suffered a year at a Catholic school run by an Irish madman, whose violent treatment of some of my schoolmates deeply disturbed me. (The atmosphere of fear at that school, and at its teenagers' equivalent, is only hinted in my tale "The Interloper".) But the specific sources of my night terrors were in fiction I'd read and films I'd seen, which may appear to suggest that the stuff ought to have been censored—except that on that basis we would end up censoring some pretty unlikely material, since much of it was considered suitable for children.

For instance, *More Adventures of Rupert*, the 1947 volume of an annual devoted to the adventures of a well-dressed little bear. This was published by the *Daily Express*, and includes a spectacular example of the political incorrectness of the time, in which Rupert meets "Koko the little coon", a black boy kept as a mascot by an airman. "How funny his black face looks on the white pillow," Rupert's mother remarks after tucking up Rupert and his friend together in bed. None of this bothered me, however, but "Rupert's Christmas Tree" certainly did. Rupert chooses a pine sapling in "a secret wood" to which a mysterious little man has led him, and in the night the tree appears in a tub left for it outside the bears' cottage. After the festivities Rupert hears "a small high-pitched laugh behind him" from the direction of the tree. That night in bed he hears "a little scratchy noise in the dark shadows" outside the window, and finds the tub in the downstairs room empty, a trail of soil leading from it into the night. By now the four-year-old Campbell was terrified to see where that led, but the pictures were worse than my imagination—the skeletal silhouette of the tree prancing across a field and then clinging with its roots to a rock-face while it leaned the fairy doll that served it for a head towards Rupert. Perhaps the book's effects on me were visible, because when I searched for it, it had disappeared. Forty years later I tracked down another copy, and the imagery seems as nightmarish as ever, not least because of the livid twilight against which the tree is limned. I may mention that it was the first book I can remember reading, although Disney's *Snow White and the Seven Dwarfs* may have been my first experience of terror in fiction.

Another children's book I read when I was not much older did indeed fall foul of censorship. This was *The Princess and the Goblin* by George MacDonald. Two episodes refused to leave me at night—chapter 13, "The Cobs' Creatures", in which horribly mutated animals swarm out of the goblin mines and are shown doing so in an Arthur Hughes illustration that would not have looked out of place in *Weird Tales*, and an encounter in the next chapter ("That Night Week") with something "with legs as long as a horse's . . . but its body no bigger and its legs no thicker than those of a cat." Its victim considers fleeing up an unknown staircase in the palace, but is afraid that the dark passage may lead to no tower, quite enough of a fear to remain with me for some considerable time. This book also vanished, and I forgot about it until decades later, where I found it in a library where I was working. But the illustrations had gone, and so had most of the cobs' creatures, apparently now considered too much for little minds to cope with. I almost thought I'd imagined the content until I tracked down a facsimile edition published in 1979 by Octopus, illustrations and all.

In retrospect I think MacDonald's book served as my introduction to adult horror fiction. The leggy intruder, and the detached ironic style in which all the monstrosities are described, are so suggestive of M. R. James that I wonder if he could have read the book. And isn't the horde of mutated creatures—"the various parts of their bodies assuming, in an apparently arbitrary and self-willed manner, the most abnormal developments"—uncannily similar to the livestock on the farm in "The Colour Out of Space"? I was, at the most, eight years old when I read that very tale in a Groff Conklin science fiction anthology and was deeply terrified by it, and by then I'd read at least one adult collection of ghost stories—*Fifty Years of Ghost Stories*, half of *A Century* of them. This lodged in my mind two images that wouldn't go away—a pile of linen in a drawer from which a small pink hand came groping, and a dim room in which the unlucky protagonist felt gigantic insect feelers exploring his face. Only later did I identify these scenes as elements in my first reading of M. R. James, and the tale as "The Residence at Whitminster".

It may sound as though there wasn't much pleasure in these premature encounters for me, and yet I sought more. The simple truth appears to be that I valued the emotion of terror—perhaps I could do nothing else with it. By the time I was ten I resented reading supposed tales of terror which lacked that quality, and I wasn't much older when I grasped that it needed good prose to convey it—better prose, certainly, than could be found in the bulk of the first *Not at Night* anthology to appear in British paperback. I was starting to be critical, a necessary stage in the process of becoming a writer. However, I don't think becoming a writer was any kind of a mechanism that was required to deal with what I'd read.

It may be objected that I'm not talking about the kind of horror now available to ten-year-olds. By a coincidence it would be tasteless to invent, I can. The video repeatedly associated with the James Bulger trial was one or other of the *Child's Play* films. At ten years old I read Villy Sørensen's story "Child's Play", and was appalled by it. Interested readers can find it in my anthology *Fine Frights*, but be warned that it concerns two small boys playing at surgery on another child. Can a ten-year-old cope with that level of horror? This one did. I honestly believe that children are in the main far more resilient than they are given credit for—as resilient, perhaps, as we can easily forget we were ourselves. I'm beginning to think that squeamishness comes with advancing years—it has in my case—and sometimes, if it isn't seen for what it is, brings with it censoriousness.

The Quality of Terror

As a child I suffered from sleepless nights after having seen Disney's *Snow White.* That's hardly unusual. I should think most children who saw the film in the first decades of its existence, and quite a few who encountered it later, found scenes from it invading their dreams: the old woman with the apple which is too red, the mirror from which a face peers that doesn't belong to the person in front of it. (Indeed, when the film was originally released there was a good deal of controversy over the British censor's certificate, and later copies of the film were missing some images: the wicked queen kicking a skeleton to pieces in the dungeon, and her being struck by lightning.) However, none of these scenes was the source of my nightmare. That came in the charming interlude in which the dwarfs perform a song and dance for Snow White. The problem was simply that in the background of the scene was an open window that showed pitch darkness, and at five or six years old I knew something worse than I could imagine was about to appear in that window.

This was my introduction to terror in films, and more of the same was to follow. I couldn't have been much older when I saw John Ford's *Mogambo,* a romantic jungle melodrama in whose favour even Lindsay Anderson, one of Ford's earliest and staunchest defenders, could find little to say except "The shots of the gorillas must have been difficult to obtain." Towards the end of the film a boy in the row behind me told his friend that the woman in the film was about to shoot the man—"and," he said enthusiastically, "you see all blood." From that moment, approximately the whole of the last reel was transformed for me into an agony of waiting for the act of violence. It was my earliest encounter with the technique of suspense as expounded by Hitchcock.

Soon I saw *Knock on Wood*, a comedy in which Danny Kaye played a ventriloquist whose doll is used without his knowledge as a hiding place for, as I remember it, a canister of microfilm. Two groups of secret agents want the microfilm. In one scene, a member of each group enters Kaye's flat in his absence, and one spy kills the other—pinning him to the door with a knife—just as Kaye returns. Of course Kaye's obliviousness to the presence of something more than a coat and a hat on the door is a protracted gag, but I found the suspense almost unbearable, and the fact that everyone around me was laughing made the situation all the more nightmarish.

Well, comedy's a funny thing, and so is terror. These early experiences suggest to me that terror can be found in many sorts of fiction, and I value it wherever it occurs. Finding it worthwhile in itself often gets horror buffs looked at askance, but I don't know why this should be the case, any more than I see anything odd about admiring a comedy for provoking mirth or a tragedy for moving its audience to tears (so much, by the way, for the specious argument which links pornography and horror fiction on the basis that both, and only both, seek to achieve a physical response). On the other hand, I'm all in favour of examining what the terror and its context mean, which is why (for instance) I'm wary of *The Exorcist*, book and film both. While the film certainly contains images one would previously never have expected to see on the screen, there's a sense in which the breaking of taboos can be deeply reactionary, and I think that's the case here. Just as mediaeval Norman church carvings often depicted obscene caricatures of sex in order to turn the faithful against their own sexuality, so *The Exorcist* presents an obscene caricature of adolescent rebellion in order to blame the devil for it, a view of rebellion which Dennis Wheatley would have applauded, God bless him.

It occurs to me to wonder when the ambition to frighten, as

distinct from communicating fear as a by-product of telling the story, first declared itself in the cinema. My vote would be for Murnau's *Nosferatu*, in which the use of actual settings challenges the viewer to reject the evidence of his own eyes, the least human Dracula in all cinema*. The same decade gave us a version of *Doctor Jekyll and Mr Hyde* in which John Barrymore revels in a grisly inventiveness far beyond the demands of the narrative. The years immediately preceding the Hays Code are a trove of disturbing images: the torture by bell in *The Face of Fu Manchu*, Kong's revenge on the natives in the complete *King Kong*, the extreme sadism of the developments involving Miriam Hopkins in the Mamoulian *Jekyll and Hyde*, the sewn-up mouth and general grim humour of *Murder at the Zoo* (whose finale, along with the monster's invasion of the bride's room in Whale's *Frankenstein*, is among the earliest examples of scenes prolonged so as to make the audience sweat). Despite or perhaps because of their age, these images retain their power to shock any audience that is sensitive to their context, even if they are restrained by today's standards or lack of standards. In horror films as in many other places, less can often be more, and the greatest justification of this appeared in the forties: the films of Val Lewton.

In *The Leopard Man* (1942) a young girl is sent shopping after dark and is savaged to death. Almost every aspect of the scene is drawn from the book on which the film is based, Cornell Woolrich's *Black Alibi*. Whereas the film shows us only a trickle of blood beneath a door, however, Woolrich flings the door open. ("It was as though clots of red mud had been pelted at the outside of the door, until, adhering, they formed a sort of spattered mound up against it. There were rags mixed in with it, and snarls of hair. . . ") Reading the book after seeing the film is rather like reading "The Monkey's Paw" rewritten by a splatterpunk. All the same, one crucial similarity between the scenes in the book and the film is the willingness to be as frightening as possible.

If the Lewton films directed by Jacques Tourneur contain the finest scenes in the series, this is as much a tribute to Tourneur's delicacy as his skill. But as well as the night-walks in *Leopard Man*

* *Nosferatu* was my choice when this essay was written in the early 1990s, but I hadn't then seen *The Cabinet of Dr Caligari* projected at the correct speed. Since I have, the awakening of Cesare is my nomination for the cinema's earliest image of pure terror (surely an influence on that other great scene of uncanny revival, Karloff's as *The Mummy*.)

and *I Walked with a Zombie* and the scene in the swimming pool in *Cat People*, the finale of *The Body Snatcher* (directed by Robert Wise) and several episodes of *The Seventh Victim* (by Mark Robson) are landmarks of screen terror. Especially in the Tourneur films, the subtlety and suggestiveness of the handling raises terror to aesthetic heights which involve beauty and awe.

Other contemporary evidence of the will to frighten is less impressive, but not to be ignored. By showing victims from the killer's viewpoint in *The Lodger* and *Hangover Square*, John Brahm screws terror one notch tighter. The mummy saga of the forties (*Hand*, *Tomb*, *Ghost* and *Curse*) contains, amidst all the chuntering about tana leaves, scenes of unexpected menace. As I recall the films of the fifties I discover that my memories of true terror are mostly of isolated scenes or images: the first glimpse (not the close-up) of a scuttling Martian in *The War of the Worlds;* the nightmarish episode in *Tarantula* where the heroine is trapped in a collapsing house with a disfigured Leo G. Carroll while the spider crouches over the roof; the Lovecraftian apparition of *The Beast from Haunted Cave* and especially its shadow as it makes for its victims, waving its tentacles, from deep in the earth; the unusually gruesome severed head in *The House on Haunted Hill* (a film enlivened, like the director's *Macabre* and *Mr Sardonicus*, by unexpectedly disturbing images, most of them removed at the time by the British censor). Finest of all was the opening scene of Bergman's *Wild Strawberries*, rendered not at all reassuring by being acknowledged at the outset as a dream, and the finale of the same director's *Magician* (*The Face* in Britain) wasn't far behind. For me the most thoroughly frightening film of the decade was the last great Jacques Tourneur, *Night* (*Curse* in America) *of the Demon*, a rare serious film about the supernatural, in my opinion compromised hardly at all by the decision to show the demon. Showing it at the beginning, however, was as much of a mistake as the voice-over in Siegel's *Invasion of the Body Snatchers* (another masterpiece of the period) which keeps informing the audience how deceptive the film's appearance of normality is.

I think it's fair to say that the ambition to frighten is more widespread in the sixties. Hitchcock gave his colleagues in the business a considerable amount to live up to in *Psycho.* Meanwhile in *Black Sunday* Mario Bava virtually reinvented the Italian horror film and gave the genre at least one of its most unforgettable images, the insects scuttling out of the dead face of the witch as the spiked mask is pulled off. Nor am I likely to forget the disinterment of Vincent Price's wife in *The Pit and the Pendulum,* the dancing dead in *Carnival of Souls,* the bulging door and the cry of "Whose hand was I holding?" in *The Haunting,* the hideous and hideously lively corpse in the first story of Bava's *Black Sabbath,* the grinning mask that conceals worse in *Onibaba* (the last film to give me nightmares), or any number of scenes from *Repulsion*. The sixties were also luridly illuminated by *Night of the Living Dead,* George Romero's most frightening film, though not his best. When the film opened in Britain the critic Tom Milne rightly praised its relentlessness and refusal to compromise. None of us could have realised how quickly Romero's genuine pessimism was to be parroted by almost every minor (or worse) horror film that followed, any more than John Carpenter could have foreseen how his admirable commitment to being nothing but frightening in *Halloween* was to be imitated to excess by a horde of hacks. Between the Romero and the Carpenter came the great delirium of *Suspiria* (a quality Argento brought to several other breathtaking films), *Don't Look Now* (a film whose every aspect the late Robert Aickman loathed, but whose last reel I still find terrifying), *The Texas Chainsaw Massacre,* and *Eraserhead.*

I always find the first half of Hooper's film almost unbearably menacing and the second something of a letdown. Some of my disappointment may have to do with a sense that the timing of shocks is slightly off, but I think the real problem is that in *Chainsaw Massacre* the urge to be terrifying gets out of control, leaving the film with nowhere to go long before the end. (Lord knows my own novel *The Parasite* suffers from the same kind of uncontrollable escalation.) It's a pattern which I fear has been repeated *ad nauseam* since.

I first saw *Eraserhead* at a midnight showing at the London Film Festival, and perhaps that added to the sense that it was something I was trying not to dream. While we're on the subject of dream narratives, I may as well mention that I found J. S. Cardone's *The Slayer* more persuasive and more gripping than most of the *Elm Street* nightmares. The death of the baby in *Eraserhead* is appalling—legitimately so, I think. Soon, however, the screen offered masses of images at least as atrocious, and much of this was mindless escalation. I've nothing against explicitness; I find the monstrous transformations in John Carpenter's *Thing* awesome rather than repulsive; I thought *The Evil Dead* was great scary fun; *Hellraiser* is wholly compelling, and David Cronenberg seems to display excessive images so as to challenge the audience to confront its own reactions. His version of *The Fly* proves that extreme physical explicitness and terror needn't be mutually exclusive, while most of his films—*Videodrome* in particular—demonstrate that these qualities can coexist with intellectual substance. On the other hand, I find Lucio Fulci's zombies (especially those who visit the blind woman in *The Beyond, The Seven Doors of Death,* or whatever title it may next acquire) more unnerving before they set about their gory rending of victims, though I certainly didn't want the British censor to remove these images on my behalf. (As of February 2001 he has ceased to do so.) In general I think that horror films have recently been at least as guilty of the coarsening which David Aylward (writing in the sadly defunct Canadian journal *Borderland*) found in too much of today's horror fiction; whether or not they "used to strive for awe and achieve fear", certainly now they "strive for fear and achieve only disgust", if they can even be bothered to strive.

Let me not end on a pessimistic note. Terror is still capable of higher things. Despite the context of theme-park extravagance in which they occur, Julian Beck's scenes as the preacher in *Poltergeist II*—when he seems about to reveal himself as a cadaver without, as far as I can see, any makeup effects to aid him—convey a real sense of supernatural terror which is worth the whole of the rest of the series. And the most powerfully frightening scenes of the nineties for me so far are Joe Pesci's in *Goodfellas,* where he plays a psychotic who is all the more disturbing because he is so much fun to watch. It's a creation worthy to stand beside Travis Bickle in another Scorsese film, *Taxi Driver.* Horror fans who look for their horror only in films and books which are labelled as such are cheating themselves, and I hope that some of what I've said here makes my readers look again. After all, that's what writers are for.

ALONE IN THE PACIFIC WITH PROJECTOR, SCREEN AND TEN BEST FILMS

EXCUSES, EXCUSES. I'M ABOUT TO START A NEW novel, *The Influence*, and feel the need to relax. I've just bought a word processor and feel as above (though, to be truthful, I find working with the new technology enormous fun). *Shock Xpress* made me do it—that is, asked me to write about my ten favourite horror films. I'm hoping that my comments are stimulating enough to justify reprinting them here.

If I had to choose a single favourite, one candidate would be Carl Dreyer's *Vampyr* (1931). It is certainly one of the unique experiences offered by the cinema. It's only fair to warn anyone approaching the film for the first time that some of its odder elements look awfully like flaws: the hesitant performances of the almost entirely non-professional cast, in particular the glassy-eyed Baron Nicolas de Gunzburg, who backed the film and, under a pseudonym, acted the role of the hero; the inordinate amount of time spent by various characters (much as in Murnau's *Nosferatu*) in poring over a tome about vampirism; the extraordinary subtitles, where a character can't ask "Who are you?" without its being transformed into "How are you?" But on repeated viewings I find that even these elements blend into a unity, together with the film's attitude to the narrative, originally Sheridan Le Fanu's but now ungraspable as a dream. However, let me not fall into the trap of calling the film simply dreamlike, for I regard it as the cinema's greatest evocation of the supernatural in my experience, of a landscape where the extra-ordinary is almost commonplace. Shadows dance independent of their objects, a lake reflects a figure that isn't visible on the bank, the earth of a grave flies back onto a gravedigger's shovel, a face fills a window, the doctor who treats a vampire's victims is the vampire's vanguard, the mediaeval figure of Death who summons a ferry in the opening sequence (a ferry which is used only by the hero and heroine, and only at the end of the film) may be the disfigured old man who has a room above the hero's at the inn . . . All this takes place in the midst of dazzlingly bright natural locations, where the nominally normal characters seem entranced. Perhaps that explains, or is explained by, their fascination with the book, but as I've said, in *Vampyr* language shifts as alarmingly as the narrative: "Dou you hear?" people ask, and the visual continuum is broken by explanatory titles such as "An atmosphere loaden with mystery keeps him avake." Tom Milne describes a press conference Dreyer gave after the premiere of *Gertrud,* his last film, where the director shifted from language to language in his answers until "his way was lost in a jumble of languages and the translators retired, baffled." So, I know, do many viewers of *Vampyr,* but I give you my word that it is a film worth getting to know intimately[1].

It is the only vampire film on my list. I have to reserve judgment on Murnau's, since the only reasonably coherent print of *Nosferatu* that I've seen has to be projected at sound speed, making the dead travel even faster[2]. (The use of natural locations, and Max Schreck's inimitably unlovely vampire, survive this treatment, though.) Tod Browning's vampire films are vitiated either by stiff theatricality or strained last-minute rationalizations. Christopher Lee's Dracula is the most authentic—aristocratic, brooding and seductive—but the direction of his various Dracula films lacks his intensity. A special mention to Klaus Kinski, both as an unexpectedly poignant (as well

[1]Recent restorations—for instance, the Eureka Masters of Cinema DVD and Blu-ray—offer more rational subtitles and the most complete available version of the film.

[2]Again, the Eureka version (among others) plays at the correct speed and restores footage missing from other cuts, demonstrating that it's a remarkable film.

as expectedly frightening) Nosferatu and, in Jesus Franco's dull *Dracula*, a distressingly convincing Renfield. I also admire *Martin*, George Romero's film about the tedium of vampire life in Pittsburgh. The most beautiful vampire films since Dreyer's, though, are Mario Bava's *Black Sunday* and Harry Kumel's *Daughters of Darkness*.

Chronologically, the next film to make my list is Mamoulian's *Doctor Jekyll and Mr Hyde* (1932). A recent BBC television showing of the complete version demonstrated its superiority over all other cinema versions of the story (though I must note John Barrymore's remarkable, cumulatively terrifying, performance in the 1920 version). I was especially pleased to find how disturbing Mamoulian's film remains (so much for the alleged blunting of our sensibilities by the excesses of recent graphic horror movies): Fredric March's gradual slide from delight in his release from staidness to dependence on his sadistic relationship with Miriam Hopkins is both compelling and, I'd venture to suggest, as shocking now as it must have been in its day. Hyde's monstrousness is always presented as an aspect of humanity rather than a rejection of it, and so it's appropriate that when we look in the mirror in this film, we may see Hyde's face. Elaborate as the film's technique sometimes is, it is never meaninglessly so.

I find the film more rewarding than the werewolf movies to which it can be related. *The Wolf Man* is written and directed with intelligence (all of which I tried to respect when I wrote the novel of the film ten years ago), but Lon Chaney's transformation is both too literal for the context and insufficiently lupine (Curt Siodmak wanted the wolfman to be seen only in reflection, as he sees himself; Siodmak later took his subtlety to Val Lewton.) *The Curse of the Werewolf* is broken-backed, but I did like the elaborate Hollywood werewolf films of the early eighties, particularly *Wolfen*, despite its uncertainties. I also value *Company of Wolves*, not least for its willingness to leave some of its images unexplained.

King Kong (1933) is the next of my ten. I have no doubt that it is the greatest of all monster films. When I was nineteen years old I had, and said so stridently in an issue of the British fanzine *Alien*, antagonising many of the readers, Ray Harryhausen for one. That was in the days when I often mistook controversy for criticism, but at least the film will be remembered long after my carping has crumbled to dust. The characterisation of the giant ape is incomparable (and, as the 1976 remake demonstrated, inimitable), and the film is one of the very few monster movies that convey a sense of genuine terror. It's a pity that most copies tone down Kong's violence, rather as Sylvester Stallone originally did to Rambo (or they used to; the restorations now available are as uncensored as can be). At least no version gives Kong a final monologue to justify himself.

My list leapfrogs over the forties, to my surprise. I should certainly have expected to include a Val Lewton film: perhaps *The Body Snatcher* (for moral clarity) or *Cat People* (for psychological subtlety and the delicacy of its scenes of terror)—*The Curse of the Cat People* and *I Walked with a Zombie* take the Lewton virtue of restraint so far that I feel justified in classing them as fantasy rather than horror, a classification which I tell myself lets me exclude Charles Laughton's extraordinary *Night of the Hunter.* Instead I'm listing the film I regard as the last great example of Lewton's influence: not *The Haunting,* which is almost Lovecraftian in the way it makes an issue of not showing its horrors, but *Night of the Demon,* Jacques Tourneur's 1958 film. It was heavily cut on its original release, but a restored print is now available. Both Tourneur and Charles Bennett, the screenwriter, complained that their work was interfered with by the producer, yet only the opening reel (in which, *pace* Marvin Kaye, the demon is shown in closeup in all three versions that I've seen) compromises the structure of the film. Without that scene, the audience would be guided as gradually as the Dana Andrews character from skepticism through doubt to reluctant agnosticism. For me it's the most intelligent film on this process, and the most frightening, and the horror film I most love. I first saw it when I was fourteen, and before the opening credits were over I was enthralled by the introductory voice-over accompanied by Clifton Parker's great score over shots of Stonehenge. I still think Maurice Denham's drive through the spectral night is one of the greatest first scenes in all horror film, and by the time he encountered the demon I knew it was a classic. I must have watched the film perhaps a dozen times by now, and I'll watch it again. I discuss it more fully in the Penguin encyclopaedia of horror.

No Hammer films in my list, I see. Lee and Cushing are fine

actors, but Terence Fisher's remakes of Karloff films are otherwise inferior to the originals. Losey's *The Damned* is a considerable achievement but not, I think, a horror film, and Nigel Kneale's excellent Quatermass stories were never given as high a budget as they deserved, though the first two contain probably Val Guest's sharpest direction. To my great regret, *The Innocents* has been crowded out too, even though it is one of the very few genuine ghost stories in the cinema (far superior to the overrated *Uninvited*). So the fourth film on my list is *Psycho.*

A good deal of what's best about the film is Robert Bloch's, of course, including some of his neatest black jokes. But it is also Hitchcock's most densely constructed film in terms of images: the recurring journey into darkness (the opening track in from a cityscape into the darkness of a room leads to Janet Leigh's drive into night) becomes a plunge into darkness (the car into the swamp, Martin Balsam's down the stairs, Vera Miles' descent into the cellars; indeed, this recurrence seems to be the justification for the otherwise inexplicable unnerving track through the darkened hardware store toward Miles). The film shares with *Peeping Tom* a preoccupation with looking and with eyes, and the journeys into darkness lead into the black gaze (even blacker than the motorcycle cop's) of Mrs Bates, who stares at us out of Norman's eyes in the final seconds of the film (in the scene where, as Robin Wood points out, the audience has become "the cruel eyes studying you" which Norman earlier described as one of the horrors of being institutionalised). It is the most poetically organised of Hitchcock's films, and a triumphant vindication of genre.

If *Repulsion* rather than *Peeping Tom* joins it on my list, it was a difficult choice. *Peeping Tom* is Michael Powell's masterpiece, an especially witty and intelligent film, and disconcertingly gentle in its treatment of voyeurism and violence. I can only suggest rather lamely that its themes are dealt with in *Psycho,* and plump for *Repulsion,* the most terrifying film I've ever seen.

Some of Polanski's images of schizophrenia may derive from his experiences with LSD (as I imagine is the case with the hieroglyphics that print themselves out on the lavatory wall in *The Tenant*) but I think that hardly matters. When I see the rooms of Catherine Deneuve's apartment growing cavernous, when the walls grow soft and hands burst out of them, these things aren't happening to an actress up there on the screen, they're happening directly to me, and to object that we aren't asked to feel sympathy for the character seems redundant. I take Polanski to be one of the cinema's most distinguished specialists in horror, and I'd like to put in a word for *Rosemary's Baby,* not least because Marvin Kaye recently dismissed the book, of which the film is an exceptionally faithful (if sinuous) adaptation. "Try to find anything the least bit ambiguous about its sweet-young-thing-brutalised-by-the-bogeyman plot," Kaye challenges, but I don't think the ambiguity he seems to want is necessary: of course Rosemary's predicament isn't "solely in her mind", any more than is Irena's in *Cat People,* but surely by the time either of these films becomes unambiguously supernatural the psychological aspects have been explored—in Rosemary's case, the expectant mother's sense of losing control of her own pregnancy and confinement (eloquent word!), of becoming the property of experts, self-styled or otherwise. I'd suggest that if either film turned out not to be supernatural it would be much less of a film.

Hour of the Wolf is next on my list, for a variety of reasons. It uses generic conventions for deeply personal ends, yet it is one of the very few truly Gothic films (another being *The Saragossa Manuscript*), even using a possibly unreliable narrator; it is the culmination of the scenes of terror in Bergman's work—the opening of *Wild Strawberries,* the finale of *The Face,* various images in *The Seventh Seal*... For different but equally powerful reasons I might have chosen *The Shame,* except that I'm restricting myself to one film per director.

There was never any doubt that the next two films would be on my list—*Taxi Driver* and *Eraserhead.* If anyone wants to argue that *Taxi Driver* isn't a horror film, I'd be interested to hear their reasons. Travis Bickle is one of the cinema's most persuasively terrifying creations, and seems to me to underlie Scorsese's subsequent collaborations with de Niro, so that I continually expect the mask of Jimmy Doyle or Rupert Pupkin, already somewhat askew, to slip and reveal Bickle, eager for another crusade. Friends of mine have wanted the film to end as soon as the carnage is over, but I think the contentious ending adds to the film's power: Bickle is still on the streets, and the media's sanitised version of what he did even allows his lost love to admire him. "I'm over that now," he tells her, but his eyes in the rear-view mirror suggest otherwise.

As for *Eraserhead,* it is the most nightmarish film I know. There are films that deal explicitly with nightmare (*Los Olvidados,* for instance, or that admirable moment in *Tristana* where the clapper of the bell turns out to be something else, leaving the audience groping in their memories for the point at which the dream must have begun); there are films whose illogic comes to seem nightmarish (*The Brain Eaters,* allegedly related in some way to Heinlein, makes no sense whatsoever, and I found my inability to predict its narrative appealingly disconcerting); the nightmarishness of some may or may not be inadvertent (for instance, Corman's *Attack of the Crab Monsters* works surprisingly well for me, perhaps because it traps its characters on a constantly shrinking island with its defiantly unlikely monsters). The last films to trouble my sleep were *Los Olvidados* and *Onibaba.* But in my experience, no film other than *Eraserhead* records nightmare in such detail—the textures, the lighting, the meanings that flicker out of reach, the utter casualness of the outrageous. *Eraserhead* can be read as a metaphor about fears of birth, but I don't find that makes the experience of the film any more manageable. The only other films that affect me similarly these days are some of the work of Andrei Tarkovsky; for whatever reason, I was unable to watch a videocassette of *Stalker* for more than half an hour at a time.

One more film to go. I was tempted to include *The Shining,* not only for polemical reasons: I find it frightening, and Jack Nicholson's controversial performance (which some detractors have suggested, incredibly, was indulged against Kubrick's wishes) seems to me wholly convincing and impressively detailed. I see the objection that in the film, unlike the book, Jack Torrance starts out pretty deranged, but so did quite a few of Poe's characters, and after all, the novel specifically invokes Poe. However, on balance the film (which I discuss at length in the Penguin encyclopaedia of horror) just falls short of my list, from which it is ousted by *Videodrome.*

I'll own up to a personal interest in Cronenberg's film. On my first viewing it seemed more like a dream that was taking place in my own head, or rather one that already had taken place, for the film's narrative methods reminded me uncannily of those I'd used in my novel *Incarnate*—the moment when we see that James Woods and Debbie Harry are already in the Videodrome set, which throws into question the reality of all that has gone before; Woods slapping his secretary under the impression that he's slapping Debbie Harry, only to realise that he hasn't touched the secretary either... I've admired Cronenberg ever since *Shivers,* though I thought misogyny flawed *The Brood,* the horror film's equivalent of *Stanley and the Women,* unless one justifies Amis's novel as a study of a deranged narrator. *Videodrome* is Cronenberg's most adventurous film, and if the ending isn't totally satisfying, I take that to be a measure of his ambition. It is also the most verbally witty horror film I can think of; in some scenes there's hardly a line without resonance. A flawed masterpiece, perhaps, but nonetheless a masterpiece, and I see that my list ends as it began, with a film that refuses its audience the reassurance of conventional narrative. Here's to fiction that isn't reassuring—here's to the innovators.

Pulsating Posteriors and Submissive Misses or, Strapped for Cash

"Sent home from school, Jenny is put over her mother's knee for a spanking. After a few wallops her tight navy blue knickers are taken down. The tawse is then produced and the strapping plus the further spanking that Jenny receives in front of her school chum, Jane, leave us in no doubt that this naughty young miss will feel her punishment for some time to come!"

Blurb for *Fighting in School* (Janus, c. 1981)

"A sixteen-year-old orphan, Sylvie, is sent as a boarder to a special school where the *malaise Anglaise* is the rule and every misdemeanour is the excuse for baring female rumps and administering a sound spanking."

Blurb for *Education Anglaise*
(1982: released on British videocassette by Jezebel, 1995)

"Drive a spanking new Citroen ZX and get three of the best."

Full-page Citroen advertisement, *Observer,* 14 May 1995

"A good smack comes from paradise."

Greek saying

"Fear is kind of thrilling, isn't it?"

"Priscilla Waters" interviewed in *Janus Model Interviews*, volume 2

"Where do they get actors who can do this?"

Max Renn watching a videodrome tape

"A COMPLETE VIRAGO OF LIES." SO MR BARKER dismisses his employee Miss Granger's protests that she was unable to get to the DHL offices because she missed the train, thereby losing him a Rover deal worth £500,000. The stage is set for *A Caning for Miss Granger* in the videocassette of that name—a stage consisting of a minimalist office furnished mostly with a desk and some straight chairs. Mr Barker is a moustached fellow with a voice not unreminiscent of any number of officials played by John Cleese. Slim pinstriped Miss Granger sports straight immobile red hair and glasses, possibly her own. "This is a serious breach of company discipline that's been breached here," Mr Barker declares. How is he to convince the board she has been punished severely enough if he doesn't dismiss her? A further minute of improvisation manages to establish that she attended convent school. "How were you punished? Did they use one of"—says Mr Barker, producing the cane he keeps by his desk—"these?" Miss Granger admits they did, in yet another repetition of her solitary reaction shot and its accompanying camera shake. "I think we should commence battle then, don't you?" says Mr Barker, draping her across his knee. "Ah," she comments as she's spanked, and "Oh," to which her employer responds "Yes" and "Mm" before saying "Did the nuns punish you on your bare bottom? We'd better not disappoint the nuns, then." Once this is finished he sends her to don the school uniform he has thoughtfully—precognitively, one might say—left in advance on her desk. "The devil's tongue," he calls the tawse he then produces, "and you're going to experience this tongue right now," though the tawsing is so gentle it verges on the symbolic. He sips a malt whisky while she strips nude. "Are you embarrassed, Miss Granger?" he demands, to which she admits with mild conviction that she is.

There ensues a ten-minute caning, some of which does appear rather to startle her despite its relative moderation. All is then presumably forgiven, and she exits, having dressed. "Done it again, Reggie," he seems to murmur to himself as a punch line while he sits behind his desk and wags his cane.

The videocassette—a production of Paradox, one of several British companies filming videos within this genre—was submitted to the British Board of Film Classification in 2000, presumably on the basis that since the BBFC had started passing hard-core pornographic tapes uncut, such a tape ought to be indulged. Alas, the BBFC was not amused, and stated its reasons as follows:

"**A Caning for Miss Granger** was unacceptable because the use of a model dressed as a young schoolgirl in a sexual punishment scenario was in conflict with the R18 Guidelines constraint on depictions involving adults role playing as non-adults. Also unacceptable under the Guidelines is the portrayal of any sexual activity, whether real or simulated, which involves lack of consent. In this case 'Miss Granger' was forced to submit to a series of 'degrading or dehumanising' acts in order to save her job.

"The Board's Guidelines prohibit the infliction of pain or physical harm, real (or in a sexual context) simulated . . . The Board concluded that the work both promotes the idea that pleasure may be taken from inflicting pain upon another person and clearly shows, with some relish, actual pain and physical harm. In doing so it goes some way beyond what might be regarded as 'mild consensual activity'.

"The Board does not feel that the problems can be usefully addressed by cutting since the difficulty with this work lies not only in the great number of specific visual images, but with the overall theme of sexual pleasure being derived from imposing pain on a coerced victim. The work is therefore not suitable for classification."

I shall withhold my thoughts on this decision until the end of this survey. Ever since the Video Recordings Act came into force, requiring all videocassettes released in Britain to have been granted a BBFC certificate, small British production companies have been submitting videos of this description for scrutiny, but every one proved too much for our censor. Not that chastisement as an element in films appears to have been frowned upon; indeed, it has been celebrated in such places as the poster for *McClintock* and a television trailer for an Elvis season, which enshrined a severe encounter from *Blue Hawaii* (of which more later). But the idea of films whose bare, ah, -faced appeal is to those viewers who enjoy watching the administration of discipline continues to offend the BBFC, which means that few studies of them have been written except in publications or on Internet sites devoted to such games. So here for the relatively general reader are some notes and observations towards a history of the English schoolgirl chastisement film.

Before video there was 8mm., and the late Harrison Marks. What may have been his earliest essay in this field, *Late for School* (Janus Publications, 1977), is represented in *Spanking Special* number 2 (*A Martinet Photo Fantasy Special Beautifully Illustrated Plus Articals and Readers Letters,* the magazine describes itself breathlessly, and no wonder, on the cover). I say represented rather than simply illus-trated, since these are production stills involving a young woman whose single-minded look isn't quite able to conceal some amusement as she raises the school skirt of the plumpish girl she holds across her lap. In the film itself, exhibited for a while in a viewing cupboard at the rear of a Soho bookshop, the schoolgirl wriggles a good deal and eventually produces a series of grimaces while the woman delivers some would-be hefty pats to her bare buttocks, after which the miscreant spends at least as much time rubbing her bottom. In a second episode she's caned or at least tapped on her rear, to which the headmistress adds a playful slap as the girl at last flees the room.

While *Late for School* must await revival by the National Film Archive, other examples from this late dawn of cinema were preserved on video as soon as that medium became popular. Harrison Marks was the auteur of a trio released on a single cassette. In *The School Lesson* two rather senior schoolgirls are surprised at some mild mutual fondling by an apoplectic head-master, who canes and also mimes caning them; in *The Riding Lesson,* a squire discovers his daughter caressing her supposedly teenage friend, whom he spanks with more effort than effect before a riding crop is applied to the older girl's rear, causing no visible damage. Both men, as is often the case with male authority figures in these pantomimes, appear to be in grave danger of a heart attack. Not so the mistress in *The Gym Lesson,* who seems to devote most of her energy to not quite touching with a cane the behind of a pea-shooting girl, though she may give the accomplice a couple of actual smacks: hard to tell without a soundtrack.

Then (1981) came the advent of sound, and Harrison Marks was there. *The Prefect's Lesson* even boasts a voice-over by an unnamed narrator with a county accent, describing as we watch it how "Jane and I" throw Jackie Parsons, like them sporting a gym-slip and straw hat, on the school field and pummel her for her part in losing a hockey match. Enter the not especially fearsome Miss Clegginthorpe, who bustles them to the bearded Scottish headmaster and has, to put it mildly, improvised words with him. "Er, excuse me, er, headmaster, do you think I could see you for a mo, few moments . . . " Clearly this film, like many of its ilk, is of the school of One-Take Ed Wood. As the girls wait outside the voice-over laments "Blimey, that meant a whacking . . . I'd never had one before, but I'd heard from the other girls what was in store from Mr Granger . . . It was going to be awful . . . My bottom was already beginning to tingle with anticipation." By this line the culprits have been summoned to the office while Miss Clegginthorpe departs, Pinteresquely muttering. The voice-over then goes in for an alienation device if ever I heard one, whereby it explains what the dialogue it isn't quite covering up is saying, which means that the girl can protest in two ways simultaneously about having to lower her knickers. "Then suddenly I was draped over his fat repulsive knees. Was it a dream?" It might well be, since the headmaster rants at her without moving his lips and then moves them in a vain attempt to catch up with his lines while spanking her (though perhaps not her, or anybody, on the soundtrack). After not much of all this he canes her friend to the strains of the *Ride of the Valkyries*, an accompaniment perhaps intended to distract the audience from the unsynchronised quality of the sound effects. The caned girl has assumed control of the voice-over, but it's left to her friend to tell us that they leave the office silently, which they don't. As the headmaster lights up a fag she confides that to her surprise she later finds herself looking forward to the next session of punishment.

However true this might have been of the young actress, it's unusual for a character to say so. Most of these films are simply founded on the principle that some viewers of various genders find the chastisement of girls dressed in school uniforms sexy, and I quite see that a few of my readers may be offended or enraged by now, or (if they should criticise this essay for, say, *Sight and* Sound—I have in mind the review which appeared there of the first volume of *Shock Xpress*) may purport to be. Let's at least be clear that we're not talking about appeals to paedophilia. The films and related magazines habitually declare that all those involved are over eighteen years old, and I mean no disrespect to the long-suffering actresses when I assure my readers that the evidence is there for all to see and, I believe, is intended to be seen. (When the age of any of the schoolgirl characters is referred to, it used to be no younger than seventeen, although since yet another shift in British law, all the characters as well as the performers have to be at least eighteen years old.) Nor is the advertising nearly as misogynistic as the kind of description I remember outside the hard-core viewing booths in 42nd Street, where women were routinely described as "bitch". But isn't the subject of this essay (I hear myself asked) a genre which encourages violence against women?

That surely depends on whom the audience identifies with, and it's my observation that this is more complicated than it might seem. Back in the early eighties, the sex-shop backroom booth multiplied and eventually became a short-lived basement cinema club, the Spankarama, where my bladder one day urged me to the single toilet, effectively the Gents, since the audience packed into the small auditorium was almost entirely male. The toilet walls were covered with graffiti displaying the phone numbers of victims who were willing to be treated like the girls in the films and who, so far as I could tell, were as predominantly male as the audience outside. I cite this to share my confusion rather than to make a case, since almost none of the victims in the Spankarama programmes were male. (Most commercially released overtly sadomasochist films—the turgid *Exit to Eden* will do as an example—concentrate on male victims, perhaps these days so as not to be accused of political incorrectness, and a search of the Internet reveals that many videos exist in which men are disciplined, not always by women, but those are several other stories.) I note, however, that in his survey of Soho sex cinemas in the Winter 1982/83 *Sight & Sound,* Nick Roddick found that all the audiences were 99% male. Letters to the chastisement magazines suggest that the audiences for the home videos are more evenly distributed between the genders.

There remains, perhaps most importantly, the issue of consent. If we're to argue (as I suspect many of the readers of this publication feel) that the verdict in the Spanner case[1] was wrong—that it isn't the business of the law to interfere in whatever sexual activity adults choose to share—then it seems unreasonable to change the argument if the recipients of the treatment are female. I should have thought that films and magazines as specialist as these appeal to those consumers who already swing that way and who either have found a partner to share their tastes (at a party devoted to such fun, perhaps, or through some other means of contact) or take their pleasure in solitude. We may be more concerned about the young actresses if their consent to discipline, often quite severe, has to be assumed, even if it would seem likely that they watch examples of what they're letting themselves in for before they sign up. Such concern isn't always necessary, as I shall reassure the reader in specific cases in due course.

Nick Roddick found that this genre suffered from the worst technical quality of any in his survey, and in the early days of video the budget was certainly all there on the screen. *Fighting in School,* whose advertising can be found at the head of this essay, is typical in not even being able to afford credits. The camera, whose whirring adheres to the soundtrack, frames a sofa and the actresses and occasionally goes in for a closer shot. Whatever charms the film has derive from the performances of the duo, who appear to have established some rapport. "You don't like me," the daughter protests from across her mother's lap, to which the mother retorts "No I don't. You're an unpleasant little brat." There's a heartfelt quality to this response which suggests either the Method or some derivation from the lady's own experience. "Ow, ooh, that's not fair" and "Ow, it really hurts" complains Jenny, with scant effect on her mother but perhaps intentionally more on the viewer. Her friend Jane watches the latter stages with some fascination—"Not in front of my friend," Jenny pleads in tears[2]—before departing to figure in her own dimly filmed sequel, *Cane for Jane.*

By now videos were appearing with considerable frequency, and

[1] A British court case in which a group of adult male sadomasochists were convicted of breaking the law although their activities had been consensual.

[2] A nineties video is called *Not in Front of Her*, and we may note that titles often virtually sum up the scenario on offer—*You Two Again, A Disgrace to the Uniform* and *Sorry, Miss!* can, I assume, be imagined by the reader.

it may be that Janus decided to devote some of their profits to upgrading at least their production values. One result was the St Winifred's trilogy (or St Winnifred's, if we're to believe the name on a blackboard upon which a different bare-bottomed actress chalks the title of each episode). The films take place in a more capacious office than hitherto, sufficient to accommodate a bench occupied by the mortarboarded headmaster and Colonel Forbes, a school governor, and Norton, the head prefect, wearing black stockings with a suspender belt and knee socks. (Nothing like trying to please every member of the audience.) "Young girls actually benefit from a good flogging," the Colonel declares in *The Athletes' Lesson*. "It's good for them." Norton announces two miscreants, at which five troop in, apparently confusing the headmaster into warning them to "adjust yourselves intelligently and in a civilised manner." Blissett and Beddoes are accused of writing bad essays and wearing erotic underwear. Norton duly spanks them and is told by the head that "the punishment has been executed with great decorum and artistic style." It's the conviction with which he pronounces his lines which suggests they must mean something. The Criswell of chastisement, he tells Beddoes "I think you should be punished thoroughly, with anticipation and arrogance."

Words seem to fail him in *The Sixth Formers' Lesson*. It's left to Norton to tell off Lovat and Green, whom the zoom manages to locate after some stumbling about, for participating in a sit-in and reading *Playboy*, no less. "By gad, sir, if you'd put them in the army they'd have been shot," Colonel Forbes says. "Insubordinate young wenches." The historical interest of this short is its introduction of the slow-motion replay, slowed-down underwater sound and all.

Back comes the head, his lines in more disarray than ever, for *The Head Girl's Lesson*. "Little barnyard hussies behaving like tomcats" is his description of Slocum, the deputy head girl, and Norton, both of whom are found guilty of dallying in the woods with boys. "Your heinous crime has to be seen to be believed, Head Prefect Slocum, Deputy Prefect Slocum," he says without pausing, a man who knows what he's about even if nobody else does. "I see you're tattooed like an ancient bacon." I assume he can't really say that, but I challenge anyone familiar with the film to tell me what the actual phrase is. There was an utter lack of mirth at any of the dialogue of the whole trilogy in the Spankarama auditorium. All three shorts use as their soundtrack theme the Sanctus from the *Missa Luba*, perhaps so as to invoke Lindsay Anderson's *If*, although there teenage boys were the floggees.

Up to this point Janus seem to have had the field pretty well to themselves, but then along came Roué (a title which makes me feel old) to challenge them—indeed, it may even be that the St Winifred's trilogy was a response on the part of the Janus bunch. Not that *Jane and the Tutor* (Roué, c. 1981) had much going for it technically: gloomy photography, a wobbly video camera, jump-cuts where the camera operator stopped filming too soon . . . What it does display is a new insistence on convincing the audience that the rather sweet inoffensive young woman has invited the treatment she receives, by getting her under-rehearsed lessons wrong and by having written a letter mocking her convincingly humourless tutor. This had previously been a stratagem of commercial mainstream movies; for instance, the young teenager in *Blue Hawaii* falls foul of Presley by wishing that someone in the world would demonstrate they care about her (in a scene which rumour has it wasn't faked). Indeed, *Jane and the Tutor* isn't unlike *Blue Hawaii* either in reducing the unfortunate girl to sobs on screen.

The next few Roué films, all c. 1982, seem to be the work of real film-makers. *Rebel at St Angela's* gives head prefect Norton her revenge as a teacher, Miss Paget, who canes Jennifer, a slim blonde girl, at considerable length. The editing and selection of angles, and in particular the timing, are almost too professional; there's even, as a build-up to the main action, a series of flashbacks to a spanking by the headmaster whose face, sinisterly enough, we never see. *Room 2D* introduces a baby-faced young woman for even more of a caning, preceded by her encounter with a master whose English accent and general behaviour are, to say the least, theatrical. Even the most realistically performed chastisement shorts include some such unrealistic detail, and I'm inclined to wonder if these are intended to reassure those viewers who need it that the spectacle is still to some extent acted, if indeed it is.

The baby-faced girl returns as Carol Ellis in *First Week of Term.* (I have to refer to her in this unwieldy way because few performers are credited. I do recall Linzi Drew reducing the narrator of *The Prefect's*

Lesson to a display of hysterics with a few strokes of a cane and a great deal more anticipation of them in a short whose name escapes me, and we'll come to Lindsay Honey later.) She and her friend Brooks are variously punished by Alan Bell, the bearded editor of *Roué* magazine and enthusiastic producer of the videos. Brooks whines annoyingly, I have to say, and wails "It weren't me." The film (released in two parts) exemplifies a frequent ploy by which, if there are two girls, one is treated much more severely than the other. Brooks receives not much of a caning before she succeeds in weeping copiously, while her accomplice in drawing a phallic symbol on the Lord Mayor's car is severely spanked for twenty minutes (some of them admittedly made up of repeated footage, in one case not cut off soon enough to conceal repeated dialogue). She confines herself mainly to cries of "Ow" and "No", which soon becomes a bit dull—sorry, kid, after all that work. I was disconcerted to be told after the first version of this essay was published that the young lady (apparently a secretary at Roué Publications) didn't care for her movie experience at all—I hope she was well compensated.

Four O'Clock Report is more succinct, if to some extent inadvertently. Jennifer the rebel reappears, having perfected a screech of protest at the indignities visited upon her, as Virginia the hockey captain. She and Charlotte Lawson and Brenda, a Scottish new girl, wait uneasily outside the headmaster's office in a scene not unreminiscent in its mixture of bravado and apprehension of the equivalent episode in *If*. From the dialogue which he (not entirely accurately) quotes, I take this to be the film Nick Roddick cites as typical of the Spankarama programme, "a series of playlets in which young girls, generally dressed in gym slips and sensible knickers . . . are placed across the knees of middle-aged men and spanked, or made to bend over a table and whipped . . . The camera remains in fixed medium shot of the girl's bare bottom as it turns pink beneath the spanking (a colour rendered all the more lurid by the quality of the video)." Well, not quite or only all that, as I trust I've demonstrated already. Charlotte gets slippered for running down the corridor, and the new girl is severely caned, I'm told, for damaging in actuality a piece of antique furniture by jumping up after the first stroke, much to the dismay of the old roué whose flat was being used as a location. A fourth girl trudges into the office, but that's the end, apparently because the camera ran out of celluloid.

The latter girl does fall foul of *Uncle George,* who is played with gusto by Alan Bell. She's bent over a desk to have a ruler applied to the seat of her white knickers, a sexy image similar to one that survived the British censor to appear in the otherwise truncated *Education Anglaise*, a mainstream French tribute to the British genre. She crops up again in *The Girls of Effingham Hall* (not, I think, a Roué film, and an oddly titled one insofar as no more effing takes place than in any others of these pieces[3]), along with Lucy Palmer and a young woman who played a spanked secretary in a Roué production called *After Hours.* (Personally, I wouldn't dare to pinch a title from Martin Scorsese.) *Effingham* is a mild example of its kind, which (like *Jane and the Tutor*) signals its status as a fantasy by having the young women dress up onscreen as schoolgirls, but nevertheless it was a video of which the BBFC would have had none. Sympathisers with Lucy Palmer may find it comforting to see her being, for once, quite gently spanked and putting on a good show nonetheless.

As for the whiny Brooks, she was *The Tutor's New Pupil* before one of the more minimalist films in the genre, Roué's *Caned After School.* She plays an unnamed schoolgirl who is variously chastised by a master who keeps his face offscreen, perhaps in case it's too familiar, for doesn't his voice belong to Alan Bell? There is virtually no dialogue: in the first five minutes he says only "Stand up" and "Get ready for the cane." Maybe the intention is to involve the viewer as directly as possible, but I don't think it works quite like that. The actress begins to whinge before the action starts and continues throughout, a performance which, I fear, becomes irritating. Perhaps that's why this appears to have been the end of her movie career.

Alongside some of this, Janus returned to the competition with *Moral Welfare,* parts one and two. Of the three young women in these the schoolgirl character, Jassi Hafeez, is Asian. Uniquely for the genre, she stays fully dressed throughout. Perhaps more significantly, a still of the third girl (a punk) being spanked by a middle-

[3] Though I'm informed that occasional videos do turn hardcore in versions circulated abroad—shades of the old days when some films (*Witchfinder General*, for instance) had mild sex inserted for European release.

aged man was included by the Feminist Anti-Censorship Taskforce in *Caught Looking*, their anthology of images they found erotic.

Compared with the heartless efficiency of this film and the best made of its competitors, the next Roué video is rather endearingly ramshackle. This is *Schoolgirl Nieces* (c. 1983), starring a previously and subsequently unknown blonde girl and a brunette who talks like an understudy for some Southern comedienne. For a while it seems they're both called Jane, but the brunette proves belatedly to be called Sue. The budget runs to a pillow-fight in a bedroom as the first punishable offence, but not to more than one copy of the *Sun*, which is still being read by the aunt THE FOLLOWING EVENING, as a rare intertitle has it—maybe the film-makers are too delighted at having found a front-page headline saying simply **WHACKED**. A squabble in the front room gives the uncle a reason to slipper the girls mildly while they wriggle a great deal, a scene which illustrates the generic ploy whereby one character is lenient so that their partner has an excuse to be less so. THE NEXT DAY announces a curious shot of the aunt in her underwear bending over a table while she talks to the girls' school on the phone, and THAT AFTERNOON shows up the budget again, when a dull thud offscreen prompts aunt and uncle to assure each other "There's the doorbell." The girls act being spanked harder than is the case by their uncle, who leaves the real chastisement to his wife. By the end the film has more than delivered the goods, and no doubt caused its admirers to do so.

Soon Roué went into decline as a video production company. I recall being told by a young woman at the Roué number that one of the "two nice girls" in *Private Tuition* was "a bit plumper than usual". More than a bit, I fear. From the same period, *Private Lessons* is shot in hideous shades of orange and green and involves an alarmingly beaky schoolgirl. No doubt it was time for some more competition, which *Blushes* magazine set out to produce ("the greatest C. P. videos in the world, featuring the most nubile young girls") under the guiding hand of none other than Alan Bell. All of these films which I've seen feature him. In *Half-Term Punishments* he invites some friends around to his suburban house to spend a weekend disciplining several girls, rather like De Sade at his mildest restaged in Milton Keynes or wherever. In *Big Girls Do Cry* Mr Bell has just one niece to stay. *Sally's First Lesson* may be the first example of the genre to film an actress in school uniform in the street before she arrives at the indoor location. In one scene (a caning filmed in a take as long as any of Hitchcock's) Sally makes such a convincing fuss that her soundtrack is reused over shots of a different actress in *The Detention Room* (1984). This was the last *Blushes* video, and a description of the filming appeared in the magazine. "The young ladies involved (both 18 years old) were only given outline direction of the story line with no script. They didn't know what was coming next and the words and yelps are theirs. The result is very realistic, it must be, because it is real."

Perhaps after that there seemed to be nowhere to go for a while; years appear to have passed before the genre was revived in Britain, although dates are frequently unclear. I believe it was in 1989 that Vexfilms arose, advertising to the cognoscenti *Punishment PT* with "lots of navy blue knicker shots". No purchaser on that basis is likely to be disappointed, and others may be charmed by "Fawcett", a young woman with her blonde hair in bunches who grins while she tells her friend Johnson how nervous of their imminent treatment she is. "I thought you were looking forward to it," says her friend. Both wear high heels with their knee socks. After failing to impress their gym master they end up in the traditional position. While Johnson confines herself mostly to protests of "Ouch" and "Sir, not so hard" Fawcett giggles while being spanked and says "Oh, *sir*" and much else with great conviction. She's a star, and wriggles so much when she's about to be caned that the actor calls her Johnson by mistake. The second half-hour sees the girls strip off. "But why, sir?" Johnson asks, to be told "Orders are orders." Maybe, but it doesn't do much for those members of the audience whose interest in the material partakes of fetishism.

Lisa Must Be Caned (c. 1989, and perhaps from the same source) is unusual in naming its actress, Sophie Fennington, at least in the advertising. She takes three minutes of screen time to play tennis and walk to the house of Uncle Brian, a *Janus* reader who delivers a singularly unconvincing lecture in a strangled Monty Pythonesque voice, for which spectacle Sophie Fennington may have felt the need to compensate. "Uncle Brian, please don't smack me . . . I don't want you to smack me on my bottom, please . . . Not my bottom, Uncle Brian." That this is uttered in an accent very reminiscent of Alison Steadman's in *Abigail's Party* only adds to its appeal. Perhaps my essay will encourage someone to write a thesis considering the influence of Mike Leigh on the genre under discussion. Sophie Fennington is interviewed in the second volume of *Janus Model Interviews* (August 1992). To the question "Are you very proud of the amount of punishment you can take?" she responds "Yes, very." *Lisa Must Be Caned* may stand as evidence and offers a recherché use of a table-tennis bat as well.[4]

College Classics was a series that continued up to the end of the last century, but apparently not always under the same production team or even company. In *College Classics 1* (A Vexfilm Production for Tallion, © 1989), both the gym master and one of the two girls (French, a blonde) seem somewhat bored—she even jokes while being spanked. Another PT session, this one in the nude. "Take all your clothes off, otherwise you're expelled." The camera operator hardly bothers to frame shots, except for the occasional one centred on a pubic area, an image not exactly abhorred by the genre but mostly treated as beside the point. The colour borders on the emetic, particularly in shots which use a purple curtain as a backdrop. A trailer for *Punishment PT* is appended, including several mysterious shots of wriggly Fawcett brandishing a letter which doesn't figure in the film itself—perhaps the scrap of paper contains the whole of the written script.

College Classics 2 is a good deal more efficient than its predecessor. In a setting-up scene untypically serious for the period, Elizabeth Jenkins, ex-head girl, returns to school to persuade the headmaster to chastise her because the rules forbid his doing so to her errant younger sister. "You're a very determined young lady," he eventually declares. "You've persuaded me." The film has established an unusual amount of sympathy for her, which lingers through several pretty relentless disciplinary scenes, during each of which she tries to escape punishment. It's a convention of the genre that the penalty often seems out of proportion to the crime (to evoke the viewer's schooldays? to encourage identification with the

[4] I've heard her attitude described as submissive pride, which seems appropriate. The American Kiri (Kyrie) Kelly became famous for demonstrating it in the Nu-West film *Kyrie's Last Session*, which she found so severe that she gave up appearing in videos. When asked why she hadn't used a code word to call a halt to the proceedings she reportedly declared "Nobody can beat my ass hard enough to make me use a code word."

miscreant, or some version of the reverse?) The headmaster dons a mortarboard to perform the final caning. Elizabeth has to count the strokes and say "Thank you, sir" after each. "Twelve, sir, you bastard," she understandably cries at the last. There's a touching shot of her composing herself afterwards in her car to the strains of the Moonlight Sonata. This is another Vexfilm, and indeed her number plate contains the letters VEX.

The Moonlight Sonata can also be heard over the opening shots of *College Classics 3,* which is, however, more openly fun. French from the first one returns as Saunders, a brunette. Blonde Jenkins isn't the same actress as the one in the intervening film. They write insults on a blackboard and mess up table settings for ten minutes in what appears to be a restaurant or perhaps the school hall, until a master arrives to find the evidence of their behaviour and babbles to himself in a Birmingham accent. "Good gracious me, I can't believe this. I don't believe this at all. They've just got no respect for me whatsoever. I'm just going to have to sort these girls out. What am I going to do? Where are these girls?" is just some of what he says. "Good Lord!" he cries, much as characters in EC comics used to greet corpses on the move, on espying the girls from the window. Some interesting narrative disarray ensues, as French jumps out of a lawn chair to elude him only to reappear in it, and complains about leaving her shoes behind, at which they magically return to her feet. The anticipated spanking is enlivened by the odd line—"Let's get these down now, good Lord!" he says—and by bare-bottomed Jenkins' grin of pained surprise at an especially fierce series of slaps. It's Saunders, however, who can't contain a broad smile just before the end of being caned. This is a Tallion Video, and has as a tailpiece a trailer for *Tales of the Rod,* in which two young women hold out for £300 each to be disciplined. Is this documentary realism?

Around 1990 other production companies seem to have got in on the act. Lord knows who's responsible for *Headmaster's Study 1,* among the more static examples of the genre. A headmaster stumbles through his script and even looks past the camera for direction, apparently to have it confirmed that he should carry on spanking. The camera staggers about in search of angles while he chastises two Oriental girls, Ling and Jane, not least with a birch.

Ling (as Susie) makes the fun she's having more apparent in *Blakey's 7*, where Lindsay Honey, playing pop star Blakey Sputnik, gives her a lift in the street and takes her home to spank. He's better at ad-libbing than she is, but helps her past her fluffs; he even throws in what I take to be an in-joke about being famous for his pancakes. Huh? In the midst of being spanked she murmurs "I'd rather have you [inaudible] me than spank me now." "Fuck you rather than spank you? We don't want any of that messy nonsense," he responds, neatly summing up the underlying bias of the genre. Halfway through, the story turns unusually explicitly sadomasochistic for the schoolgirl genre when Susie agrees to be his slave. "Can I do anything I want to you?" he asks, to which she responds "Whatever you want" with an amorous look. Whatever proves to be a caning, more than halfway through which she admits "I do quite like it" with every appearance of conviction. For all the severity of the action, there's a sense of affection between the performers.

Sixth Form College is a Cheek to Cheek Production, beginning with a credit sequence in which a young woman walks away in slow motion, swaying her bottom, to a soundtrack unfortunately reminiscent of the tramp of the tyrannosaurus in *Jurassic Park.* The credits actually name the actresses: Nicky van Kiel, Sara Wilton, Emma Moore. Emma is threatened with a caning but by appealing direct to the audience for "anything else" gets let off with a mild spanking. "Ow," she says repeatedly with very little interest, a protest which sounds in the slow-motion replay not at all unlike a prehistoric roar. Her episode ends with an inset showing her on the cover of *Razzle* number 11. Somewhat at odds with the title of the video, Sara plays either a stewardess or an employee of a stockbroker. Nicola hoists her school skirt and bends over for the camera and says to the audience "Are you happy with that? I mean, is that the position you want me in now?" That's foregrounding the nature of the fantasy with a vengeance. "Do I have to have the slipper as well?" she later pleads with us, with about as much chance of a negative response as William Castle expected when offering to leave Mr Sardonicus in his toothy state. The film ends with out-takes of her getting her speech for the trailer wrong.

Trust *College Classics* to have more to offer. Number 6, a Spanking For Pleasure production from Paradox, involves a dark-haired young woman who acts her lines with such dramatic conviction that I shouldn't be surprised if she later made it to the big screen. She and her blonde friend play senior girls who scoff at the rules at their new school and boast that nobody can touch them. A strapping gym mistress overturns them one by one, though they struggle vigorously—an unusual scene, since in these scenarios it's almost always psychology rather than physical force that is used to overcome the recipients—and delivers a token spanking. The brunette has acted the rebel so convincingly that her humiliated look once she's sent to sit down is both touching and erotic. Beyond this scene the girls (whose names, so far as I can ascertain, we never learn) are more conventionally submissive while being paddled and caned, but the memory of their initial fire remains. It certainly left an impression on me.

The seventh film in the series subjects blonde Simpson and brunette Jenkins (not the actresses from the previous episode) to a ten-minute physical education session. They then rebel against Mr Adams and are duly bent over a vaulting horse to be spanked, Simpson emitting an impressive squawk which is amplified by the acoustic of what appears to be an actual gymnasium. Cue the headmaster, an actor I could swear I've glimpsed playing a minor role in some commercial movie, who sends the abashed master off before spanking the girls himself. Neither teacher nor pupils at this school appears to learn much, since halfway through the video Mr Adams is at it with Tompkins, a brunette ill-advised enough to let fall a packet of cigarettes while trampolining. This time it's Miss Gibbons, an unsmiling sports mistress, who catches him spanking his victim and remarking "Ha, ha, ha." He flees, leaving Tompkins to her mercies, hardly likely to be tender when the girl has pinched money from the mistress's car and secreted it about herself to be discovered. You might say the film displays a formal structure—you might, if you've seen as many of these movies as I have. It's a Spanking for Pleasure Production.

I take virtually all the films I'm discussing to have been shot around London, but *Class of '94* appears to want the audience to think it was filmed in Liverpool. There's a reference to that city, and two of the three girls display its accent. One (Lisa, I subsequently learned her name is) plays an unlikely head girl who sits on the edge of Mr Bruiser's desk and swings her legs while doing her best to get Parker and Jackson into worse trouble. Eventually they take a spanking revenge in a cat-fight so lacking in conviction that the head girl doesn't even bother trying to escape when the others let go of her to change places. She's delegated by Mr Bruiser to punish Parker, which she does with a will, though her announcement that she's going to cane her sounds about as fierce as a supermarket checkout clerk reading out a total. I don't mean to denigrate her lack of acting; in *Teacher's Torment* it's part of her charm, though in real life the teacher apparently runs an acting school. Here she's long-legged short-skirted Penny, who discovers Sir's collection of spanking videos while spending a weekend with him. Having been forbidden to watch one, she drops it in order to get the action moving. "Are you going to give me a spanking?" she pleads, apparently unable not to smile while attempting to look apprehensive, and it's impossible to tell whether she's acting or how much actual emotion she's trying to hide. "Please, sir, not on my bare bottom. Not my bare bottom, please." Who could resist such an appeal? The resulting scene has some of the lingering quality of the rubber-stamp episode in *Closely Observed Trains* (in which the provocative young woman was originally reminded, as I recall, "I told you I would spank you" but who in a BBC showing was warned "I told you I would mark your bottom"; I don't know what she says on the Criterion DVD). Red-bottomed Penny eventually climbs the stairs and announces from the top "I was just enjoying that, sir." After all this it seems mean of the teacher to use her having led him on as a reason to punish her again; after all, she only did it on behalf of the audience.

About then Red Stripe Productions entered the field. They and related parties were run by Ivor Gold, the Mr Bruiser mentioned above, who was knifed to death in early 2000, alas. His declared aim was to revive the psychological intensity and sense of actual punishment achieved by the best of the Roué videos, though using only young women who enjoyed such treatment. In one of his first sketches, *Burning Ambition*, blonde Dobson is so resentful of her A-level results that she conspires with brunette Hills to set fire to the school. We gather this much despite the camera, whose zooms rise to new heights of shakiness and which at the end of a scene fades back up from black halfway through more dialogue than it anticipated. Dobson has to vow twice to get her own back on Mr Pearson (Ivor Gold again) before the camera can find the lighter in her hand for a closeup. We next see Mr Bruiser-Pearson receiving with mild annoyance on the phone the news that the school has burned down. I appreciate this event couldn't have been staged, but might a couple of stock shots have improved matters? Still, by now it must be clear to the reader that the preamble hardly counts: only the action does. Mr B-P receives the girls in his office, or at least in a room with a sound keyboard in the background, and the difference between the actresses swiftly becomes clear. The more Hills is spanked, the more she acts, pouting and adopting a progressively more girlish penitent voice. Dobson, by contrast, gives a naturalistic performance unsettling enough for the next blunder in the staging to come as something of a reassurance, as Hills is sent into the next room to fetch a hairbrush only to walk not quite off camera and produce a clothes-brush. I hope that doesn't make anyone feel she deserves what she then gets. Me, I was impressed by and sympathetic to both young women, and reflected in the first version of this essay that one function of the brunette's performance might be to suggest that her colleague must also to some extent be acting. After all, the latter does stay in her fictitious role and speak lines appropriate to it despite severe distraction. She even says "Gosh", one of her upper-class traits that I'm told made her much in demand at parties.

College Classics 8 was also made by Red Stripe. This time Ivor plays a headmaster with no name, in colloquy with Mr Hill, a school governor and potential apoplectic who has just had an egg hurled at him in the schoolyard. Send on the girls: two blondes and a brunette, respectively Rifkind, Hurd and Clarke. (Let me hear no accusations of anti-Tory bias, however. *Punishment Platoon,* a video which falls outside the scope of this essay, concerns two young female army privates called Blair and Prescott. It's otherwise most notable for thrice using the exact same amused reaction shot of one girl watching her friend being spanked, as though the editor might be a failed student of Kuleshov.) When a season of chastisement films is screened at the NFT, perhaps these should open it, to encourage a political reading of the genre.

Hurd is an American at a British school, and disapproves vociferously of the spanking of her classmates. By contrast, Rifkind gets so bored with watching Hurd receive the same treatment that she doodles on the blackboard. Brunette Clarke seems to be having the most fun; there's even a close-up of her smiling at the camera while being spanked. Was she directed to play it like this, or is her personality irrepressible? Neither she nor Hurd can quite contain their amusement at the spectacle of Rifkind being strapped. When it's Hurd's turn she resists and struggles a good deal, but read on. Clarke suffers the fiercest strapping and yet, entirely to her credit, she can't hide a smile as she walks off camera at the end of the take. It seems poor Rifkind has to make up for her friend's frivolousness, but though she looks decidedly unhappy at the end of her own caning she has hardly adjusted her dress before she's asking "Can't I watch her caned, sir?" It seems ungenerous to send her off pouting before the American schoolgirl has to play the last scene. This lady also figures in Nick Broomfield's *Fetishes*, a Channel 4 documentary about S&M in New York, in which she reveals that she's called Maria and likes being disciplined enough to pay for it—indeed, she's in tears before she calls a halt to her own caning. The uneasy reader may be reassured that she is by no means alone in such enthusiasm: Eve Howard, owner of the American disciplinary outfit Shadow Lane, has been known to figure in their films as a tearful victim; Lucy Bailey, a British girl, recently wrote and directed a short in which she's severely strapped by a headmaster. Admittedly he canes her friend, but presumably the director is entitled to some perks.

Most of the foregoing was written in the mid-nineties. Much has happened since. I was able to interview some of the performers and view outtakes of several of the films (one of which demonstrated that the copious tears of the young woman in *Relative Punishments* had in fact been added with an eye-dropper), and was treated by Christa Faust to a commentary on a video in which she dealt with a whimpering young woman. Peter Straub thought my interest betrayed my Englishness (Pete Atkins, also present, kept mum), but other countries are productive in the field. Girls in American videos tend to be more immediately reactive, while those in Eastern European (mostly Czech) examples display unrelieved gravity.

Swedes say "Aie" as they're invigorated with a birch. I believe Australia may have quite a few titles to its credit: the only one I've seen is the extraordinary *Natasha Never Learns*, at the beginning of which we're informed that the parent who spanks and paddles the titular young woman is her real mother. That the lady's grasp of English rivals Tor Johnson's is a bonus.

We haven't space to notice more than a fraction of the British activity since the first version of this piece. Let me restrain myself to celebrating a few of the most memorable tapes while wondering if they and their like will ultimately migrate to DVD. I'll return later to Red Stripe. Two more companies with several tapes to their name are Strictly English and SMAX. Strictly English tends to issue films that are playful yet severe and that often trip over their own attempts at relative narrative complexity. *First Time* is the most charming, in which Carly, a young Northern woman, is shown excerpts from Strictly English tapes by their producer as an indication of what she can expect if she dresses up as a schoolgirl. She does, and makes her relish of her initiation clear. By contrast, SMAX productions have a stern surface. *Twins in Trouble* subjects identical twin schoolgirls (who have featured separately in other films) to a variety of punishments, and *As It Really Happened* reconstructs the treatment of a schoolgirl bully in the thirties by a headmaster who apparently wrote about it in *Titbits* magazine. The actress often seems close to tears, but the film closes with an out-take from her caning. "You might as well do it the best you can," she says, "'cos that wasn't your best—that was absolutely feeble." Both films are preceded by a declaration that "the actors, actresses and crew made this video of their own free will, and had a lot of fun making it". I have no reason to think otherwise.

No such overt reassurance was to be expected from Red Stripe. Though the cinematography may be rough at times (in *Phoning Home* not just a camera but the entire cameraman is visible in several shots) the seriousness of the performers never flags. *Sisters* epitomises this. Even allowing for conventions of the genre, the scenario strains belief. A schoolgirl is spanked by the headmistress and goes home to tell her elder sister, apparently her guardian, who insists on taking her back to the school to complain, only for the headmistress to point out that the senior was treated the same way when she was a pupil there. Perhaps we can suspend incredulity during the flashback that shows this, but it's followed by a scene in which both sisters are spanked and strapped for their temerity. This may sound and indeed be ludicrous, yet I for one found the headmistress ("Miss Brown", a Red Stripe regular) genuinely daunting, and the two girls' fear of her easy to believe.

"Miss Parker" is another schoolmistress who may be assumed to have enjoyed her years with Red Stripe. While she lacks the other lady's grimness she is at least as severe. In *Sorry, Miss!* she deals with a young woman usually called Emma onscreen and her friend apparently known offscreen as Essie. The latter (appealingly plaintive in this and other films) endures possibly the most spectacular punishments ever filmed by Red Stripe, even more impressively in *A Month in the Country*, where Ivor Gold rounds off an open-air spanking and strapping with a caning that takes the lady to her limit. (I gather that an annual American award for adult videos includes a spanking category; this would surely have won if it had been in competition.) Such is the enthusiasm of all concerned that nobody appears to have noticed the reflection of the cameraman in a window of the house behind, unless they weren't bothered. At one point a small plane flies over the scene, and it sounds as if the pilot may have lingered to convince himself what he was seeing. Miss Parker and brave Essie and Emma all return in *Bad Example*, one of the last Red Stripe films. Emma suffers gamely, but it's Essie who, as in *A Month in the Country*, argues and protests so as to invite extra. Faint-hearted viewers may want to remind themselves that the actress has chosen to do so and knows what it will bring her. Emma and Essie and four other girls make up a small class in the ninety-minute *Just Another Day at St Stripe's*, probably Ivor Gold's most ambitious production. The plumpest of the girls appears to achieve some satisfaction of her own while being strapped.

I realise that most of my readers are unlikely to have the chance to make up their own minds about such matters, if indeed they want to, as things stand. Some of the British films I've described have been released in America, but not necessarily under these titles or complete. The American editions seem to be the ones on sale in Amsterdam in pictorial covers. The irony continues to be that the only country where the films are officially banned, in the sense that in Britain videos without a censor's certificate cannot be legally sold, is the one where the bulk of them are made. At the outset I quoted the censor's reaction to one of the milder examples; we hardly need wonder how others I've cited would be received. Yet British magazines full of photographs of similar scenes, occasionally from one or other of the videos, are on open sale in many British news-agents, never mind dedicated sex shops.

That's one reason I renewed my prediction from the first version of this survey that in time these activities will find their way into, or rather back into, the mainstream. Directors such as Jiri Menzel, Carlos Saura and in particular Roman Polanski have celebrated them over the years, and the Korean director Jang Sun Woo devoted his 1999 film *Lies* to them. The British censor passed this film uncut, although all the on-screen discipline is real—apparently the characters, not just the performers, have to be seen to consent in order to escape censorship. Meanwhile the dedicated genre will continue to reach the cognoscenti, and it might be best if understanding of the issues involved preceded films such as I've described into the public eye. To that extent the delay imposed by the British censor may be beneficial. I do hope that these films and others of their kind are preserved for posterity, at any rate[5]. Then perhaps a detailed history can be written, not just this bunch of interested reminiscences.

That was my conclusion in the update of this article that appeared in the first edition of this book. The 2006 Canadian horror film *5ive Girls*, where several young women end up back in uniform at boarding school, includes a disciplinary scene that would have been at home in any number of the films I've cited. Articulate views of the scene by folk far more informed than me can be found online: I recommend Pandora Blake's *Spanked, Not Silenced* blog in particular. The British censor finally concluded that spank-ing porn wasn't necessarily unacceptable after all, and awarded R18 ratings to videos starring (among others) Amelia-Jane Rutherford, Samantha Woodley and Niki Flynn. The last-named lady even made one that's peppered with references to *The Wicker Man*. There (as if I needed one) is my justification for including this essay herein.

[5] Many of them are available online as downloads or on disc.

Floundering on the Bottom

IS THERE ANY MORE CONVINCING EVIDENCE OF the decline in standards than that Michael Medved is taken seriously in some circles as a commentator on film? Nothing about him has changed since *The Golden Turkey Awards*: the same unwillingness to let facts get in the way of his opinions, the same leaden humour, the same petulant tone of a child who has found that the world and other people's views of it aren't exactly as he wants them to be. I remember, less with affection than with a wince at the appropriateness of it, how in the early days of Channel 4 he dressed up as an ape with a tin head in order to introduce *Robot Monster*, to which film he'd added subtitles intended to nudge the audience into laughing, subtitles whose stupidity exceeded that of the film. The film was innocent: Medved is not. The turkey, a creature that gobbles incessantly and that continues to be active even when it has nothing above its shoulders, is his appropriate emblem. What I most disliked about his first book, *The Fifty Worst Movies Ever Made*, was the sense that he and presumably his fraternal co-author felt entitled to resent having had to watch allegedly bad movies in order to make money out of them.

Yet I believe there's nothing wrong with deriving as much fun as you can from inept movies. Given the amount of pleasure *Plan 9 From Outer Space* has afforded me, I number it among my favourite films. And I'll happily—well, maybe that's an exaggeration—watch on behalf of *Shock Xpress* (the original publisher of this piece) films that only its contributors and readers might brave. Maybe I'm acquiring a reputation for this activity, and that's why Douglas E. Winter sent me *Penpal Murders*, one of many films by Steve Postal of Florida (to be precise, P.O. Box 429, Bostwick, FL 32007-0428, phone 386-325-9356, email info@postalproductions.com). I shall attempt to convey at least some of the experience of watching this film.

The cassette is inserted. The machine emits a mechanical retching but fails to eject it. An FBI warning appears on the screen with a buzzing as of an enraged wasp woman, and gives way to the sight of a man in a Puritan hat screaming a great deal while being pursued by two people with mops over their faces. He wakes in bed with his hat on and screams some more. "Steve, you're having a nightmare," says his wife several times, establishing the Postal approach to dialogue and making the audience feel that the remark could equally be addressed to them. Steve goes out with his hat on to walk the dog, then comes home to feed the cat while someone switches a tape of Vivaldi's *Four Seasons* on and off with an audible click to provide soundtrack music. All this has taken four minutes, and then:

STEVE POSTAL PRODUCTIONS PRESENTS
PENPAL MURDERS
STARRING JAY BROCKMAN, JENNY TUCK, ANGELA SHEPARD
DIRECTOR OF PHOTOGRAPHY STEVE POSTAL
SCENARIO BY STEVE J. POSTAL AND GAIL A. POSTAL
WRITTEN AND PRODUCED BY STEVE POSTAL AND GAIL POSTAL
DIRECTED BY STEVE POSTAL

And then Steve, who we can deduce is played by Jay Brockman, screams a great deal while being pursued by two people with mops over their faces who now poke him with extra mops. All of the stuff before the credits has been a—surely not a selection of highlights from the film? Steve wakes in bed and screams "No" and "Get away" for thirty-six seconds until his hat falls off. After some more of this he declares his intention of taking a walk.

STEVE POSTAL PRODUCTIONS PRESENTS
PENPAL MURDERS

What's happening? Has the audience ingested some previously unknown psychoactive substance, or would that have been an advisable approach? Steve walks the dog, dragging Vivaldi after him. Perhaps it's unfair, even though I intend to continue doing it, to draw attention to the borrowed score: after all, the then recent Aikman Archive video of Murnau's *Nosferatu* sounded as though someone had grabbed the first couple of discs that came to hand, an organ recital and the latter half of Saint-Saens' Third Symphony. But I digress. Steve feeds the cats again . . .

STARRING JAY BROCKMAN, JENNY TUCK,
ANGELA SHEPARD

Presumably they're happy for their names to be repeated, since both Angela Shepard and Jennifer Tuck were vampires from outer space in the 1990 Steve Postal production of that title. Steve goes back to bed with that wretched hat on and argues with Karen about his penpal who is coming from California, and the audience wonders if they're making up the dialogue as they go along, and whether the mass marketing of the video camera has given rise to a new form of sadism. Not only does Steve Postal film the mugging of his performers in merciless close-up, but he tends to begin each shot before they've started acting and hold it after they've given up.

DIRECTOR OF PHOTOGRAPHY STEVE POSTAL
SCENARIO BY STEVE J. POSTAL AND GAIL A. POSTAL
WRITTEN AND PRODUCED BY STEVE POSTAL
AND GAIL POSTAL
DIRECTED BY STEVE POSTAL

So perish nearly fifteen minutes of my life. The cassette box threatens a running time of 110 minutes, and the fact that Jay

Brockman affects the most unconvincing stammer of all time makes each of his scenes feel not much shorter than that. Can the appeal of such a film be that, as with a good deal of contemporary horror writing and of poetry written for performance, every member of the audience can believe they could produce something at least as worthwhile and be right? Did Woody Allen film *Husbands and Wives* in the style of an unwatchable home video to prove to all of us who own a video camera that film-making isn't that simple? *Husbands and Wives* made me physically ill, and I kept my eyes shut for the last half-hour of it—indeed, after the press show half a dozen green-faced members of the Merseyside press gazed with dismay at the buffet. I'm not quite sure what effect watching *Penpal Murders* has on me, but I think it's time to read a book.

Here is *Science Fiction Stories* by Mark David Tingay (£8.50 from Aurora Books, a division of the Book Guild Ltd). The first story is "The Spore". I quote.

> The remains of a body skin was laid out on the grass, covered in blood, then as Anne ran up she screamed and pointed.
>
> Then as John looked up a mass of flesh was pulsating. When he saw this his first reaction was to run, but he was glued to the spot. Then, in a split second, the organism flew at John. He tried getting out of the way, but it was no good, the thing had latched on to him. As he stood there in total panic watching this thing start to crawl up his body, the thing expanded then leapt into the air. As the organism dropped down, its body at this stage was twice as large.
>
> (. . .) He shouted "Help me Anne!" She fainted on the lawn, and when a couple of seconds had passed the organism had finished devouring John and was crawling along the floor to Anne.
>
> When Anne awoke, she saw the thing crawling up her legs. She screamed, the thing started to devour her legs in a frenzied way. When she felt this, she died of heart failure. When the organism got no response, her structure was pulped and devoured in one mouthful as the thing was gobbling and chewing.

Let nobody say that some prose can't convey the same experience as some films. Just now I have the sense of a different kind of consciousness attempting to communicate with me. I must say I feel a little odd. Maybe the best place is bed. But *Penpal Murders* awaits, in my dreams and next day when I stumble, feet dragging and head lolling, into the room where the video is.

Steve and Karen eat another meal—maybe that's their fee—and argue some more. If Steve Postal's use of music seems to owe something to Godard, perhaps Warhol can be blamed for his apparent determination to leave every take in the finished film. But who is to blame for the dialogue? Here are, I assure you, the very opening lines of yet another argument:

> *Karen.* Here we are again—the big brain talking so profoundly and so early in the morning at that.
>
> *Steve.* Tough crap to you! It took you so long to say these things but it's not like you said them before. I could be sitting at the beach now with some curvy curvy-shaped brown-skinned girl who would talk to me with respect.
>
> [The reader is reminded to imagine all Steve's dialogue being spoken with a stutter.]
>
> *Karen.* Yeah, sure, you piece of I don't know what.
>
> *Steve.* Why do you say that? You ever hear the saying "The road less travelled was the better road"? Maybe I'll just travel down that road.

Alas, he stays where he is. Perhaps people really talk like that, and we're witnessing a new kind of hyperrealism. Perhaps people in Bostwick do, and Steve Postal's work will eventually spread the style as Bill and Ted popularised Valleyspeak.

We are now twenty-five minutes into the film. Jenny the penpal arrives, accompanied by Vivaldi. Perhaps the presence of three people in the film will improve matters.

> *Jenny.* Steve, it's me, Jenny.
>
> *Steve.* Jenny, is that you?
>
> *Jenny.* Steve, Steve.
>
> *Steve.* Jenny, don't move, I'll be right there.
>
> Steve walks ten yards.
>
> *Jenny.* Steve . . .

Karen. Jenny, is that you?

Eventually all three of them somehow manage to get into the house. Jenny is shown her room. Steve immediately has a birthday and holds onto his hat while he blows out the candles on the cake. Jenny acts by staring away from the camera and her co-stars, and who can blame her? The three make conversation, or rather I don't know what else to call it. Was New York crowded? Did Jenny get lost in Penn Station? Did she have trouble finding the train? How did she get from JFK Airport to the station? Was it easy for her to take a vacation? How did she get from the house to the station? Why is a neighbour chainsawing trees outside? Why is the house suddenly next to a railway? "With the sawing of the wood and those trains a person could go crazy here," says Jenny. I know how she feels. The birthday scene lasts ten minutes. Is the dialogue supposed to be awkward? I'm reminded of the problem Ed Wood set himself in *Night of the Ghouls* in trying to make a sham séance look more inept than the rest of the film. Are the Postal players making it up as they go along? In ten-minute bursts the film is hideously funny, but after ten minutes . . . Jenny sits in bed and brushes her hair. Karen gets out of bed and brushes her hair, and I find Mark David Tingay lying on the floor—not the young test technician from south-east London himself, you understand; just his book. Surely this will help me clarify my thoughts.

> Then after a couple of seconds, the block of ice was sinking beyond belief, then it fell deep down into the mountain's core. When the block of ice was falling very fast down this form of rounded tunnel, its presence was magnetic . . .
>
> Then the block of ice came to a stop. It had landed in a marsh, and the temperature was cold at the start, now at boiling point as the ice floated around in the marsh. The temperature was increasing with every second, then as the block lay there, it started to melt until John finally was floating on his own.
>
> After a couple of seconds, John came out of his ice cabin, then as he opened his eyes to see where he was, he had the shock of his life . . . He tripped and went under the water as he submerged again . . .

Maybe the end of the story makes everything clear.

> Then, as the ship came into dock, it roared then turned into a golden shade, with John as the top figure.

Are we witnessing the birth of a new use of the language? They laughed at Gertrude Stein, after all (and some of us still do). Are Tingay and Postal similar in seeing things they struggle to communicate? It occurs to me to wonder what Tingay tests as a technician. I think I'll go and lie down.

I dream of analysing *Penpal Murders* in terms of its sexual politics, but when I emerge from the toilet next morning I seem to have left my ideas behind. I climb back onto my cross and restart the tape. Karen takes the dog for a walk. Jenny sprawls on top of Steve on the couch and demands to know why he didn't sleep with her last night. She threatens to check into a motel because he doesn't love her but goes back to bed instead. Steve follows her into the room and, unless my mind is finally crumbling, they repeat the same dialogue. Karen comes home and falls asleep. Steve and Jenny go to bed together. He says "I'm not ready" four times, and "I can't do it because I've got the flu." Jenny takes a shower from the waist up. Karen brushes her hair and goes out, leaving them in bed together. God be praised, we're halfway through the film.

Steve types a script. Karen asks if he always stutters. She fails to find the cooking oil and eggs that are in the refrigerator and complains at, my God, length about it. She feeds Steve breakfast. He says "Leave my hat alone. Don't touch my hat. Leave it alone. Don't touch my hat." I begin to feel that Michael Medved and Steve Postal deserve each other. The dialogue then, well, it sort of

> *Steve.* Trees are more important than this house.
> *Jenny.* Why do you talk so slowly?
> *Steve.* Trees help me write.
> *Jenny.* What am I in your house? A slave? A toy? Let's get married.

Karen rings up to demand what they had for breakfast. Steve explains to Jenny how to call him on a pay phone—how. . . to . . . call . . . him . . . on . . . —when she goes shopping. He types a lot and crumples up each page of his script but alas, this is only fiction. Karen comes home and throws the pages about. Jenny rings up and invites him to dinner. "Where are you?" Steve says, and without waiting for an answer, "I'll be there in thirty minutes. That's half an hour." Perhaps we are to see the actors on location and with other people, but no, after a fade to black all we see are the same three wretches returning to the same wretched bungalow. Steve complains to Karen that Jenny was flirting with a cop and loses his temper, which involves breathing hard and holding onto his hat with both hands. (A variation on this style of acting may be seen in the 2002 British horror film *Long Time Dead*, in which at moments of especial drama various members of the cast clutch their heads.) Steve tells Karen to get in bed with Jenny so she won't go home. Karen does. Steve appears and tells her to get out of bed. He gets in the bed. Karen goes out. There are several shots of cows. Has Steve Postal been watching Eisenstein? Do I need my head examining? Let me turn to Mark David Tingay for relief.

> While they were looking around in the town they saw a "for sale" sign up one of the town's streets, so they knocked on the door, and asked for the guide.

Perhaps relief is not the word.

> Dr Samuals rushed over to the guide, in a frantic attempt to stop him from hitting the ground. But it was all in vain because the guide passed out and smashed onto the ground with a thump. As Dr Samuals and Mr Harding saw this, their first reaction was to hurry to his aid.

The Book Guild Ltd, of which Aurora Books is or was a subsidy, used to advertise: "Have you got a book that deserves to be published?" It can be found on the Internet at **www.bookguild.co.uk**, and I'm sure its list is worth exploring, though it no longer includes Mark David Tingay, alas.

> While they were walking, they got twenty feet down the preserved fossilised corridor, when they came across a stone wedged in the

sand. They couldn't believe their eyes, then as Mr Harding got close to it, the stone started to sink.

I know the feeling. Jenny takes a shower from the waist up and goes shopping while Steve writes. The cast takes turns to open the squeaky front door. Karen comes home and tells Steve that Jenny was making out with someone. Steve holds onto his hat and rages, followed by six seconds of him not acting. He strangles Karen while the dog wanders into shot. Karen escapes into the bedroom. He tries to strangle her by holding her shoulders. They switch to having sex. Jenny comes home and accuses Steve of being poor. He slaps her face. "You hurt my little nose," she wails. They have sex. Jenny kills Karen with a carving knife. Steve removes his hat and his stutter and laughs at immoderate length at Jenny and says "So you love me" several times. He strangles her and drops his hat on top of the corpses. And wakes up. I wish I could. He gets a phone call from Jenny and laughs a lot.

THE END

Steve types the end credits. German Shepherd Dog was played by Lady. Cats were played by Rusty, Susie, Whitey, Tiger and Teddy Postal. The story was based on the book *Penpal Murders* by Stephen J. Postal and Gail Postal. The British edition could be published by Aurora Books. The credits (on my copy, anyway) are followed by the last five minutes of a Florida movie set in a casino and starring Miles O'Keeffe and Dedee Pfeiffer.

Is Steve Postal entitled to look down on any other filmmaker? Well, actually, yes, although he appears to have decided that his films are comedies—he's selling them online "on retro VHS" as the "worst films ever made" (though the quotation marks presumably absolve him of responsibility for the view if not the films). He even credits Rudyard Kipling with the basis of one of them. Sorry, Steve, they aren't quite the worst, and Doug Winter is to be [deleted] for proving it by sending me *Street Soldier*. This is the work of Tim Anthony, who can or could be contacted for "the best in muscle movies" at P. O. Box 14738, Dayton, Ohio 45413. He should sell Steve Postal his camcorder.

The film stars Tina Plakinger and her muscles—a zoom staggers at her wearing a leopard-skin and wanders out of focus—and Tony Anthony, who poses for the camera while seeming unaware that the videotape has rendered him as green as the Hulk. His back view is flesh-coloured, but when he turns round again he becomes an interesting mixture of green and pink. Various other actors are listed—Debbie Dayo, Roger Revlon, Amber Rhoads, Otis Scales—but unfortunately whoever has typed the names on the screen has failed to grasp that longer names have to be split between two lines. We can only speculate about how the victims reacted to being listed as Phyllispadur, or Felix Niclsn, or Marshawalon, or Chucstewart. Maybe muscled people think of themselves that way. At last the credits tell us that the film is written, produced and directed by Tim Anthony. They have lasted six minutes while a synthesiser wails on the audience's behalf. Before long we may be sorry they came to an end.

Tony Anthony flexes his muscles for forty seconds in slow motion. Ninety seconds of stock shots of New York are accompanied by a rap in which a synthesised voice keeps saying "boogie". The film begins. A car with cartons perched on the luggage rack draws up and the driver exchanges some dialogue with a woman. I should like to tell you what they said, but despite several rewinds I've been unable to make out a word. The woman tells a man in a beret something incomprehensible and he gets in the car. Some people walk along 42nd Street and stare at the camera. A man with a microphone announces a fight beside a river. A woman in a leopard-skin who I take to be Tina Plakinger fights another woman while they try not to laugh. There's an interminable slow-motion shot, complete with noise bars, of the leopard-skinned woman pushing the other. She gets her down on the concrete and brandishes a knife. The other woman says something incomprehensible. She's then dead. Listen, you only have to read about all this, I had to watch it. The survivor joins some bikers and dunks a python in the river while music, if that's the word, drowns out their dialogue. A girl in a house talks incomprehensibly on the phone and then goes along the hall to tell a man with a green face something. Some men in a room say something about state's evidence. "You stick your nose into my business and I stick your nose in a turtle's shell," one tells another, and recommends fishing as a cure for nerves. He takes a turtle out of a box. "Learn to relax like him," he says, and the henchmen hold the man addressed down on top of the turtle. The turtle walks away. Good idea.

> All his arms and legs were paralysed. (Tingay, p.25)

You know, I'm beginning to wonder if Mark David Tingay could be a late surrealist. But back to *Street Soldier*. I tell myself that it's only a film, it's only a film. Some people with machineguns and other weapons hang around in a Manhattan street and discuss kidnapping before kidnapping a young woman who tries to look impressed. The owner of the turtle turns out to own a nightclub too, and talks to a woman about finding a contender for a fight while she does her best to look interested and to stay in focus. Did whoever developed autofocus for the camcorder ever dream what horrors they were bringing into the world? Tony Anthony walks about in a street and eventually enters the nightclub, where he throws various people about in a dark corner in order to get to the owner, who says he'll match him with the champion. "My name is Rodolfo Inaudible and don't you forget it," he says.

> As he spoke his face was disjointed and out of sequence. (Tingay, p.26)

The kidnappers gaze at their victim somewhere in the open and discuss something while the camera totters about in search of them. One of them uses a gun to poke the victim, who smiles. A plane arrives at an airport. A taxi driver picks up Tina Plakinger and drives her around some unidentifiably dull city areas for several minutes. She goes to a gym and works out with much use of her facial muscles, to a song which several rewinds have convinced me includes the line "The energy of a eunuch is the only way." Tony Anthony arrives and sweats a lot while he works out. Both performers acquire a greenish tint and tell each other, though not the audience, the names of the characters they're playing. The gym scene, in which they brandish their muscles for ten minutes, is presumably the hard core of the film, the kind of thing people send Tim Anthony money for.

Rodolfo Incomprehensible phones in search of a female challenger while one of his men hangs around in the background looking for someone to shoot with a machinegun. "So a couple of girls got killed," Rodolfo says into the phone. "That makes it more inviting." Tina and Tony run out of a lake in slow motion. Wind on the microphone carries away most of their dialogue, but not enough. We learn that someone called Mama Dog killed Tina's sister in the arena.

His friend had gone from his midst. (Tingay, p.31)

People in a nightclub dance. Fights are announced. Tony fights an opponent, mostly out of focus or offscreen or in slow motion with noise bars. The onlookers shout "Come on" except for those trying not to laugh. The fight comes to some sort of end that Tony walks away from. The master of ceremonies makes an incomprehensible announcement. Tina and Mama Dog jump about a bit and pat each other. Tina kills Mama Dog. Onlookers attempt to conceal their amusement.

A man wearing glasses who says he watched the fight phones Tony to ask him to rescue his kidnapped daughter. Tony and Tina turn green and discuss their relationship. They go out of focus and walk along a street in the company of some bits of rock songs. They visit a clairvoyant who tells them something. Tony meets a man with a horse and they discuss the kidnapping while the camera falls about. Tony calls someone, perhaps Tina, on the phone and drones at length about not needing their help. Tony and two men creep up on the kidnappers who are standing about under a river bridge. A kidnapper pretends not to notice that Tony is about to mime hitting him on the head with a length of pipe. Another kidnapper tries not to laugh. The kidnapped girl is told to escape. The man on the horse shows up. Shots are fired. People fall down. Tony and a kidnapper fight, taking care not to hurt each other. Tony tries not to laugh.

Then suddenly his legs gave away underneath him, as he was resting on the floor. (Tingay, p.36)

Tony phones the girl's father and goes out of focus. There are shots of New York streets. Tony wanders into one. The camera wobbles about inside a subway train. The camera staggers along some streets. Tony does something on a train. Tony walks up a stairway to a train and pretends not to see the camera. Tony gets on a train and reads something. It rains. Tina stands in a doorway to the sound of carnival music. Tony approaches and says something. Tina says "Can you handle a woman like me? I am the ultimate female, you know." Tony says something. The end. The credits all over again. An FBI warning, out of focus. Can I stop now?

You may wonder if Steve Postal or Tim Anthony could have a competitor at their chosen level of cinema. I believe they have: Doris Wishman, whose *A Night to Remember* is an experience beyond the grasp of my poor words, and one that actually achieved some sort of commercial release. You may subject yourselves to the film on an Elite DVD, and when you've recovered you can play it again with a director's commentary. They are consummately well matched. But enough—what's this the postman has brought me? My God, another package from Doug Winter...

So I said twenty years ago, but as so often, my writing has been overtaken by events. As evidence I append a review of *The Legend of Harrow Woods* from my column in *Video Watchdog*.

There will never be another Ed Wood, and fans of the ramshackle (especially of *Blood of Ghastly Horror*) might have feared that Ad Adamson was irreplaceable too. Not so. On the basis of *The Legend of Harrow Woods*, or *Alone in the Dark*, or *Evil Calls: The Raven Trilogy, Part I*, or whatever it may call itself next, I proffer the rickety palm to writer-producer-director-actor Richard Driscoll.

The film does indeed begin with an extract from Poe's "The Raven". In five lines whoever is responsible manages to mis-punctuate two of them and misbreak two as well. At least Allan is spelled right, though not in the credits. Before those Christopher Walken is heard reading a longer extract over a sepia sequence of a car driving into the wilds. Are the scratches on the film faked? If so, why does it actually break, skipping a word of Walken's reading? Does Driscoll have Tarantino's Grindhouse bill in his mind? A great deal else is swarming around in there, as we'll see. Playing horror writer George Carney under his thespian pseudonym Steven Craine, he marks the names of inspirations in a notebook. Lovecraft is in there too, and Machen. Perhaps they are somehow connected with the film. Carney types a single word at a desk and thinks of Kubrick while blood pours down the walls.

After the inexpensive credit sequence computer wizard Gary (Jason Donovan) tells professor Karl Mathers (Richard Waters) about the disappearance of the Carney family in New England, at which point a raven pokes its beak through the image as if it's searching for a reason to be in the film. The effect rapidly becomes as irritating as the clattery computer type that introduces (letter by l.e.t.t.e.r) every single extra on the disc. I say it's a raven, but given the film, a magpie would be more appropriate. Mathers takes a bunch of students to Harrow Woods for a combined birthday celebration and psychic investigation that will be broadcast online, and we may wonder if Driscoll has his little eye on another film besides *Blair Witch*. He recounts "the truth behind the legend": "the maiden Lenore" was burned there as a witch in 1843. Well, no, she's Elizabeth Selwyn (Patricia Jessel) in uncredited footage from the opening scene of John Moxey's *City of the Dead*. Look, magpie! Shiny stuff!

Birthday girl Anna (Kathryn Rooney) wakes up in Mathers' flat before the camping trip and is killed by Carney in the shower while Walken reads more Poe, and then she wakes in Mathers' tent in the woods. Surely Driscoll can't be taking on *Lost Highway*'s double awakening, one of the most terrifying moments in cinema. If David Lynch is his excuse for incoherence, it's not one; Lynch's films aren't incoherent. Next day Rachel (Sonya Vine) and Steve (Paul Battin) stumble on a scarecrow in the woods while somebody apparently fast-forwards the film on our behalf. We may thank them, but don't do it yourself or you may miss this exchange, which suggests that the magpie has found some Pinter:

Karl: Anna, can you keep a secret?
Anna: I'm already keeping a secret.
Karl: I think one's enough, don't you?

Anna: [long pause to camera]; scene ends

The investigators pitch camp outside Carney's cabin, where psychic Victoria Jordan (Eileen Daly) shows up and delivers, shall we say, an eccentric performance. Anna has a vision of Carney's brother Vincent (Robin Askwith) finding Carney's son under a table. "Come to daddy," he says and, adding to the plot, "Come to your real daddy." Here and elsewhere we may be driven to reflect that while you can rewrite prose if you get a belated idea, it isn't so simple with film. Part of the fascination is watching Driscoll struggle to reconcile the movie with his latest ideas for it, and who knows whether that's over even now?

Gary loses his online connection with the events and, as computer wizards do, thumps the monitor to restore contact. Anna potters about inside the cabin and finds one of Carney's books, which is titled *Murder at* [remainder off-screen] on the spine but *Welcome to the Carlton* on the cover. It's an apt symbol of the film. She has a vision of Carney in a hotel washroom, where he's told he's the manager by an attendant (Norman Wisdom). An exchange that Pinter might have written for Abbott and Costello ensues:

Carney: What do you know?

Attendant: Know what?

Carney: Yes, know what?

Attendant (meaningfully): I know what.

Perhaps the late Sir Norman may have improvised some of his dialogue, since he's immediately followed by Rik Mayall playing the exact same role with somewhat different lines while Carney threatens him with a rolled-up towel. It's clearly repeat time, since we now see the opening car drive again with some extra shots. Karl says Anna's lost—oh, no, she's back in the cabin by the tents where he just was, and we may wonder if the area has the magical properties of Dr Vornoff's house in *Bride of the Monster*, which takes far longer to walk around than its exterior suggests. Events appear to prove too much for Carney, who goes back to the washroom for a third take, this time performed by Eileen Daly in a mask. The scene turns into a stylised orgy; perhaps *Eyes Wide Shut* was in or on the air. Having seen Carney kill his wife in yet another vision, Anna declines to leave the woods; Karl apparently knows why, but isn't telling us. Various folk die gorily, and one has a Raven matchbook in his mouth—let nobody say Driscoll leaves loose ends. Anna finds the culprits in the cabin and then [**look away now if you don't want to know the twist in advance**] wakes up. Let me admit that I've left out a great deal; this review can only be a footnote to M. J. Simpson's epic 22,000 word account of the film.

The DVD also offers a 3-D version if you want more of a headache. Neither version is chaptered. The extras aren't as listed on the box. Some of the cast appear to be talking about a different film. Some are listed under their character's name, others under their own. Richard Waters says the film is quite original and then claims that both Lovecraft and M. R. James "went mad and died". This is rubbish of a different order, and he should be ashamed. A trailer for the film as *Alone in the Dark* can be found at **www.videosurf.com/evil-calls-the-raven-288011**, and you'll see Mayall deal the director a heartfelt slap.

In 2013, having falsely claimed that he'd paid David Carradine over £400,000 for unauthorised Carradine footage used in his film *El Dorado*, Driscoll was jailed for three years.

3: On Horror in Society

Turn Off

One reason my stories often deal with the theme of gullibility may well be that I'm gullible myself. When I read in my local paper that the effects of violence and obscenity in fiction were to be "hotly debated" at an "open meeting" in the Wirral Christian Centre, I thought that meant what it said. According to the headline, "Mary Whitehouse takes hot seat at clean-up TV public meeting." Mrs Whitehouse is the figurehead of the British pro-censorship movement. Perhaps it serves me right for taking headlines seriously, especially when another headline in the paper appeared to urge "Defeat diabetes meeting", but I don't think the situation was that simple, all the same.

One doesn't often get the chance to debate censorship with its sponsors. David Britton of Savoy Books (British publishers of Delany and Moorcock and Harlan Ellison®, among others) has good cause to be aware of that, since his science fiction shop in Manchester has been raided perhaps fifty times since 1976, when James Anderton, a lay preacher who believes he may be inspired by God to condemn homosexuals, became Chief Constable. Once David was sent to prison for a month for stocking Grove Press books. Recently the police seized copies of *Fangoria* and *Hammer House of Horror* from the shop. This kind of thing makes me uneasy, and so I welcomed the opportunity to observe the thinking that gives rise to it. I invited listeners to my film review to join in the debate, and went along to watch the fun.

By the time I found the Wirral Christian Centre, just above the Balls Road junction in Birkenhead, I was beginning to suspect it was visible only to the faithful. Several young people in luminous waistcoats were showing drivers where to park, and a policeman was at the door. I wondered if he was there to keep order, but perhaps he was a member of VALA. These are the initials of the Viewers' and Listeners' Association, and presumably are meant to sound like "valour" (above the stage of the meeting hall, where one might have expected to find a cross, hung a sword and a quill crossed behind a shield), but they sound rather like a trade name for a tranquilliser to me. Still, the meeting wasn't tranquil, nor (despite its Christian setting) was it joyful. Apart from Mrs Whitehouse's, there was hardly a smile in the place.

Her smile appears to be the product of a formidable set of false teeth. I don't say this to be offensive. She often denies that she is a media personality or that she projects an image of herself, but of course the denial can be part of the image she projects, and I believe it is: the image of a retired motherly schoolteacher, seventy-seven years old, just an ordinary lady surprised by her fame. But any successful schoolteacher is an actor and performer, unconscious or otherwise, and it seems obvious to me that she is using all of the techniques she learned in her job. What bothers me is that she won't own up to it, and I wonder why. Perhaps her age and ordinariness are too useful. When a group of Scottish teenagers cross-examined her on a television show and ruthlessly exposed the gaps in her thinking, even some of her opponents in the press expressed sympathy for her, though she would have known this was the style of the show when she accepted the invitation.

Here I should do some owning up. The man from National VALA (the name the organisation prefers to be called by in full) who introduced her to the audience asked casually if someone was there from the BBC. I'd mentioned in my broadcasts that I intended to attend, but I said nothing now. I wasn't there on behalf of the BBC, after all, and I didn't feel I had to be identified with the BBC on the basis of a weekly ten-minute broadcast. More to the point, if I decided to join in the debate, I would already have been identified as the enemy and therefore not worth hearing. A paranoid reaction on my part? Judge for yourselves.

Mrs Whitehouse took the microphone and began her statement. She'd been born near here (murmurs of approval from the audience). Though her opponents made her out to be against creativity, she had in fact taught art (laughter). Many people who thought they were hostile to her aims discovered they agreed with her when they learned what her aims really were. We were all reaping the consequences of the permissive sixties and of the selfishness of people who want to see and hear exactly what they like. The latest report on pornography had evidence that children as young as three and four were involved in hard-core films.

Now I'm sure most people would want to see that stopped, but I'm less sure what it has to do with the aims of VALA, except in a general sense. The point seems to be that children need to be protected, but to present paedophilia as being related to allowing children to watch horror films and hear bad language is questionable, to say the least. To be fair, I don't think that child pornography was cited as a step in the argument, perhaps because there was no argument. The citing of child pornography functioned rather as a way of exciting the audience, while Mrs Whitehouse thumped the table like the performer she claims not to be—exciting the audience to anger and receptiveness, I mean. In that state an audience is unlikely to demand argument, since every claim from the stage will seem more damning.

These grew more random and more specious. The increases in child prostitution and child abuse were quoted, apparently as effects of permissiveness. The rise in violent crime since the fifties was blamed directly on the development of television. Urban deprivation was mentioned, but not as a cause of violence: instead the claim was made that urban deprivation won't be cured "if pornography is allowed to eat away at people's characters." (Laughter, though only from me.) It was said to be easier for bishops to take a stand on political issues than on moral ones. Violence on television was convicted of numbing one's responses to violence in real life. At this point, intriguingly, Mrs Whitehouse invited her audience to admit that they sometimes enjoyed violence on television—"not," she added hastily, "that I do." Alas for that lost chance for honesty!

I could sense the general relief that she had bustled onwards to her next theme.

At least her points were becoming more specific and therefore more worth debating. Intriguingly, her objection to a scene in Dennis Potter's *The Singing Detective* in which Potter as a child watched his mother being seduced was that the view of what he saw was closer than his viewpoint (though surely the distance involved in camera placement can legitimately be emotional as well as spatial), and therefore the closeness could only have been meant to titillate. The word "bastard" was now being used in programmes shown when the family (that's to say, children) were viewing, and if this was allowed to continue "it'll soon be heard in the school playground." Well, it certainly was when I was a child. "If we let them [the BBC] get away with this kind of thing at family viewing time . . . " but the prospect remained undefined, perhaps because "this kind of thing" ("homosexuality, prostitution, verbal aggression") was too various for the effects to be summarised with recourse to facts. For a moment Mrs Whitehouse seemed actually to defend bad language, since she claimed that if it was no longer kept in reserve to express anger, only violence would be left. A point worth discussing, but she had already moved on. "There's so much more to all this," she said ominously, and in a remarkable coda she suggested that "anarchists" intended to destroy the language on which Christian society was based. "Destroy the word and you destroy the system," she warned. "All this [the call for censorship] isn't just a matter of taste, it's a matter of the whole structure of society."

Debatable, all that, I should say—but there was to be no debate. That seemed odd, because the reporter who had claimed beforehand that the issues "will be hotly debated" was identified from the stage as a founder member of the local branch of VALA. I must assume she would not have misled her readers unless she had been misinformed herself, but either case needs explaining. Instead of a debate, there was question time, but first VALA was treated to a hard sell by Steve Stevens, founder of the Festival of Light and member of the VALA executive committee: "obviously you're all here because you're concerned" (well, yes) led to the assumption that any of those present who weren't already members would join before they left. This assumption of agreement persisted into the question session, which was mediated by a minister from the Christian Centre and which proved to be more revealing than the organisers might have wished.

In answer to one supporter Mrs Whitehouse quoted an Australian study of violence on video. Some of my readers may remember the British report, "Video Violence and Children", widely used to whip up the panic about horror films on video, a report from which the Methodist and Catholic churches withdrew their support when they learned that the conclusions had been written leaving gaps for the research to be inserted later, and I wonder if the Australian report may be as eager to reach its conclusions. Mrs Whitehouse quoted the claim that the video sequence most popular among Australian youth is the one in which "the girl pulls off her father's head and eats it for a birthday cake." One of the more extraordinary aspects of the present censorship panic is that no matter how inaccurate or even plain fictitious a description of a (usually unnamed) film may be, it will be claimed as further evidence of the need for censorship. Now the scene Mrs Whitehouse quoted seems to be either a plagiarism or, I suspect, a misrepresentation of the episode in *Creepshow* in which an irascible patriarch returns from the grave in search of his Father's Day cake, and I think it's worth pointing out that the episode is meant and played as a black joke. Indeed, laughter (this time not only from me) greeted the synopsis Mrs Whitehouse quoted, but this was immediately quelled. "It's no laughing matter," said Mrs Whitehouse with a frown.

Otherwise the audience hardly needed to be told how to react. When a Church of England clergyman suggested that Mrs Whitehouse was acting as a propagandist for the Tory party just before the general election, since she'd stated at some length that only the Tories had included tighter control of broadcasting in their manifesto, his point was drowned by groans. Another dissenter was told by the mediator "Everyone has come to hear Mrs Whitehouse, not you"—a curious notion of debate. All the same, lengthy statements by members of the audience were allowed so long as they were supportive, while other speakers were required to restrict themselves to "one simple question only". Disagreements tended to be dismissed by Mrs Whitehouse on the basis that the speaker's point was "not thought through". Potentially the most fruitful confrontation was with a young man who'd fought in the Falklands and who wanted the reality to be shown. "Would you take your young children to the battlefield to see the dead and wounded?" Mrs Whitehouse demanded and, having extracted a reluctant no, said triumphantly "Then don't expect television to do your job for you." I might have asked whose job she wanted it to do, but the selection of speakers was becoming increasingly calculated: one attractive teenager, her face made old by hatred, was selected by the wielder of the roving microphone before she had even raised her hand. She wanted to know what they could do about blasphemy and sexuality in children's programmes such as *He-Man.* What indeed! "If you don't have promiscuity in your family you shouldn't watch it as entertainment," declared a speaker who apparently followed Mrs Whitehouse from meeting to meeting. "The BBC should be frightened of us," she shouted, but it occurred to me that an organisation which felt the need to exert so much control over a debate must be pretty scared itself deep down—maybe scared that the images of children and the family which it tries to use to discredit any disagreement wouldn't stand up to examination. (This concentration on what's suitable for family viewing means that VALA can't condemn theatrical screenings of films from which children are barred, but this can be used to make VALA seem more reasonable—for instance, Mrs Whitehouse wrote to the *Evening Standard* to deny press reports that VALA had commented on *Monty Python's Life of Brian*—while their friends in the Festival of Light can be relied upon to attack the films.) The very last question of the session mentioned censorship, to general restlessness and groans. "Ah, there's that word," Mrs Whitehouse cried. "That's a dirty word these days. You can use any word except that word." And so the evening petered out in silliness.

I bought several pamphlets published by VALA, and they saddened me even more than the evening had. Here is Mrs Whitehouse telling the Council of Europe Parliamentary Assembly that research denying a link between television and social violence is "inadequately financed and rapidly produced" (shades of "Video Violence and Children"!) Here is a claim that because a scene in the dramatisation of *I, Claudius* was not in Robert Graves' book, "if ever there was violence for violence's sake, this was it." (It is, however, to be found in Graves' sources.) Here is a standard form used by VALA members to monitor television programmes for violence, which includes the ominous instruction "Please list the advertisers DURING and immediately AFTER each [commercial television] programme." Here is an arts programme about Kurosawa monitored: "A film maker talking to another man about films he had made in Japan . . . A man stood against a wall whilst arrows were shot at him, he staggered away with all these arrows sticking out from various parts of his body,—very sickening for viewers to see." Here is an account of the Alistair Maclean movie *Fear Is the Key:* "First half hour non-stop fighting, car chase and abduction of woman threatened with violence. Rest of film included hits of heads, close up of dead man in a pit, three further fights, skeletons on a plane at the sea bottom, further shooting and goody and bad characters choking to death in bathyscope. Goody rescued and baddies arrested. Terrible example of violent driving." And here is part of an analysis of a programme cited in the VALA pamphlet *Television Programmes and AIDS:* "'Jesus' four times, 'shit' eight times, 'piss off' three times, 'wanker' three times, 'sod off' twice . . ." But I can't go on: the thought of these obsessed folk crouched before the television, pencils at the ready, is too much. I said I was saddened, and I am. Is it naïve of me to expect religion to be about largeness of vision? All I seemed to be offered that night at the Christian Centre was the spectacle of small minds snapping shut.

The Nearest to a Ghost

I

If you need to believe in ghosts in order to see any, I should have been overwhelmed by them when I was a child. Much of my reading conjured them and worse things up—the creature "with legs as long as a horse's . . . but its body no bigger and its legs no longer than those of a cat" which leaps through the nursery window in *The Princess and the Goblin*, the human remains and shapes far less than human which clambered into my mind out of the tales of M. R. James and his peers—and while it might be fun to imagine them by daylight, they grew clearer and more active once I went to bed. On a more benign level, though not necessarily more reassuring when remembered while the night-light flickered, my mother had assured me she'd seen apparitions of favourite relatives. That said, she was equally convinced that BBC radio broadcasts contained messages intended for her personally—all it took was for a character to have a name or a life that resembled hers—and so from a very early age I became sophisticated in sorting out what seemed from what was real. This sophistication deserted me once I was alone in bed, however, and it wasn't until my mid-teens that I ceased to be terrified of the dark, around or at the same time as my having been educated by Christian Brothers turned me into an atheist. I can't say which loss of fear caused the other. I do think that the prospect of encountering a ghost began to appeal to my imagination only once I was convinced I never would.

Since we all struggle not to turn into our parents, one reason for my skepticism may have been that my mother surrounded herself with the supernatural—not just Roman Catholicism but stuff that Catholics weren't supposed to believe in those days, about such things as black cats and walking under ladders. Her father had died before she got married, but he still sometimes dealt her a peremptory tap on the shoulder. Her mother was living with us when she died, and I was scared of going upstairs while the corpse was in her bedroom—scared not of anything the body might do, just of its presence. Soon after the funeral my mother saw the old lady standing in a nightgown at the top of the stairs, and found the nightgown crumpled on the landing when she went up. I wasn't there to see, and having spent much of my childhood rationalising her imaginings, I wasn't disposed to believe. By that age I may have been too busy putting the extremes of my imagination into prose form.

I've written about my relationship with my mother elsewhere, in the foreword to *The Face That Must Die* and a more self-contained version of the piece. Suffice it here to say that she may have had some intermittent sense of her own mental problems, insofar as she often threatened to come back to haunt me if I had her put into any kind of care when she grew old. Desperation at that stage made me abandon her instead, reducing her to a state in which she was taken into hospital to die. The Saturday after the funeral I drove with her ashes to the family grave in Huddersfield, only to find there was nobody to tell me where the plot was. The single time I'd visited it was for my grandmother's funeral twenty years earlier. I decided to come back on a weekday when there would be someone to consult, and went for a stroll before returning to the car. The apparently aimless stroll took me by the shortest possible route to the point where I stopped and found I was standing beside my mother's family plot. As I saw the grave and the headstone were untended I was overwhelmed by a surge of grief which I felt was not my own.

It vanished, and gave way to mine, as I scattered her ashes on the grave. Perhaps in some sense she did haunt me after all. Beneath her name on the memorial the inscription reads HOME AT LAST.

If this was a haunting I hadn't sought, the ones I did seek proved less responsive. Not long after I began to review films for BBC Radio Merseyside (still doing so twenty-seven years later at the time of writing*) my then producer Tony Wolfe decided to involve me in a series investigating the local supernatural. *Lands Beyond the Day* was its name—my title, if hardly a reason to boast. Tony met the diocesan exorcist, the Witchfinder General as we nicknamed him, and John Owen (anthologised by August Derleth as Frank Mace) interviewed Singing Sid Ordish, Litherland's leading trumpet medium. My wife and I journeyed to Newton-le-Willows to meet Leonard Jones, a psychometrist who held a kitchen knife of Jenny's and gave her the name of an old relative which she had to phone her mother to learn was accurate—an impressive performance by the psychic but, I thought, too wild a talent to be of much application. Leonard Jones also painted psychic paintings reminiscent of the work of Ferdinand Léger, and in the course of his occult research had fallen foul of a Mancunian coven, after which encounter he'd fallen downstairs. At least that must have been more dramatic than the plight of the Amityville priest who, having visited the bogus haunted house, seems to have needed only to come down with a virus to convince himself the devil was after him.

It remained for *Lands Beyond the Day* to visit a haunted location. This was Everton Library, where the tale went that an attendant had hanged himself some decades earlier. (Hauntings of workplaces generally seem to involve suicides or at least the rumours of them, suggesting that employment isn't always as desirable as it's supposed to be.) Cherry Newton, a friend, and I talked our way with a BBC tape recorder through the library one night—its cellars, its attic full of books, the latter commoner in libraries then than now—and did a good job of scaring each other for the tape. Once, below the street, we heard a cough. I returned the tape to the radio station,

* After thirty-eight years they saved themselves the price of a pizza and let me go. More regrettably, they celebrated Liverpool's year as City of Culture by doing away with *Artwaves*, the arts programme very ably compiled and presented by the excellent Angela Heslop, who also conducted most of the interviews. No doubt it was too elitist—that is, it and she had standards.

and next day it was played back to me. The last few minutes of our commentary had been replaced by silence, broken only by a cough. I confess to finding that pretty scary, but a skeptic who took part in the discussion which brought the series to an end reminded me that the tape had been out of my hands.

I've visited two famously haunted places on my own behalf. Robert Aickman and I were among a party who travelled to Chingle Hall near Preston, where a disabled guide told us some stories but showed us no ghosts. (The artist Martin McKenna and his girlfriend had a more memorable time there recently, when their guide dropped dead before their eyes.) Robert's signature is presumably still in the visitors' book, and that's my scrawl adjacent to it. More disquieting than Chingle Hall is Plas Teg, and it deserves at least a paragraph to itself.

Plas Teg (Fair Mansion) is a Jacobean mansion in North Wales, on the A541 between Mold and Wrexham. Its ghosts, according to the booklet the owner publishes, not to mention the television documentary in which she talked about them to Colin Wilson, are many. Nowadays visitors are given a guided tour, but when we first visited the house one could wander at will through the renovated sections. The first bedroom Jenny entered she immediately emerged from, dismayed by the atmosphere in it, and this room proved to have been used as an execution chamber, not least by Jefferies when he was a circuit judge. Upstairs, the Great Chamber has a witch mark carved within the fireplace, above which is a hideous painting by Snyder, a pupil of Rubens, of the Medusa's head from which crawl insects as well as snakes. A recent canvas that hangs in one of the bedrooms shows a naked male body whose inverted head leans backwards towards the viewer, its face erased, and a study of an inverted head from the neck down beside it, exhibiting distress. I'm at a loss to understand why I find this picture so disturbing. Whatever time of year it is, several of the upstairs windowsills are strewn with dozens of dead flies for no reason the owner of Plas Teg can explain. While visiting the mansion with J. K. Potter and his partner Susanne, we discovered a framed sampler in a basement storeroom. Above the motto on the sampler was the number 777; below, the Seal of Solomon. The motto was Aleister Crowley's: "Do What Thou Wilt". I think it safe to say there is something odd about

Plas Teg. I should have liked to spend a night, but the owner preferred to do without the publicity, and so I've never stayed in a haunted house.

I don't mind thinking that I live in one, though. Jenny has often sensed a presence in the bedroom next to my workroom on the second floor (third if you're American), and years ago, while staying with us, her sister Penny was convinced our children had come up behind her in the room when they were downstairs. Not long after this incident we were burgled. It appeared the criminals had made their way up the house, taking all Jenny's jewellery on the way. Something had frightened them in the bedroom I've referred to, however, because they'd fled so hastily they had left the jewellery there. I may not believe in ghosts, but I'm grateful to them, and not only as a writer.

So I have no more definite ghosts for you—not at the time of writing. In due course I may be one, however, and then I'll know if they exist, though perhaps I won't believe that either, won't know how to distinguish between any afterlife and my last dream. Maybe you, my posthumous reader, can help by trying to invoke me. Maybe by reading this you already have. Is that me behind you? Is that my breath, if lungs less substantial than rotten leaves can breathe, on the back of your neck? Is that shadow that flickers across the page all of my hand that I can summon up? Is that glimpse at the edge of your vision, that object which flutters like a windblown scrap of litter caught on a twig, trying to shape itself into my face? Is that sound you almost heard the best such a mouth could produce in the way of a voice? Don't you know how important it is that you understand its message? This may be the nearest to a ghost you've ever been. That's certainly how I felt as I wrote the foregoing.

II

The above piece first appeared in 1997. Now I must add the following, written about a decade later for *All Hallows* and not previously published. It slightly overlaps the previous account.

Age brings ghosts. Some are memories of friends, and some are thoughts of one's own potential ghosthood. Although the gravestone that stands guard outside the guest room next to my office remains a polystyrene prop—a relic of a Granada television production of my biography—at times my mind turns to the matters it prefigures. Of course funerals are for the living rather than the dead, but unless I utter a dying cry of faith, I don't expect my ceremony to be too religious. Two friends arranged to end theirs with jokes: Phil Rogers' coffin vanished to the tune of the Radetsky March, while the curtain music at Harry Nadler's funeral was the Indiana Jones theme, prompting those at the back of the church to wonder if they were about to be mown down by a giant boulder. Perhaps I should plump for the Cuckoo Theme, or is that already overused at wakes for Sons of the Desert? My present instinct is to share some serious favourites, though. J. S. Bach's cantata *Ich Habe Genug* (the Hans Hotter recording)? Richard Strauss's *Four Last Songs*? A late Beethoven quartet? The *Missa Glagolitica*? Perhaps not the last, since the *Agnus Dei*, with its chilly responses that sound like the voice of the void, is as disturbing as sacred music gets in my experience; Lovecraft might have approved, and Aickman did. As for my epitaph, I very much hope to leave "Find the golden light" on the stone and perhaps on a bench overlooking a favourite view (somewhere up on Thurstaston would be ideal). None of this should be read as evidence of a death wish. I've too many tales still to tell, and now I have ghost stories that I don't think I've made up.

I've been a practising sceptic since at least my adolescence—just about the time I started writing seriously, in fact. You may retort that if I were a real one I wouldn't need to practise. Being educated by Christian Brothers is a good way to lose any faith in the supernatural, for me at any rate; if God existed (so my theory went) he wouldn't have allowed them to get away with half that they did in his name. That aside, I'm drawn to rationality, perhaps as a result of having lived with schizophrenia in the family throughout my childhood and later decades. I'm a James Randi man, not least because I find the likes of Uri Geller not just unconvincing but useless. Martin Gardner and John Sladek are great debunkers too, and I've tried now and then to be worthy of them. I pointed out absurdities in *The Amityville Horror* as soon as that grab bag of second-hand material was published, and I impaled the Highgate vampire slayer on the stake of his own book, a jerry-built collection of dialogue and scenes from British horror films of the early Hammer era, differing from edition to edition. Of course I write supernatural fiction, but that relates to the aesthetic pleasure of terror, not to a conviction that these events could really happen. Still, perhaps the pleasure may involve an unadmitted desire to encounter the supernatural, in which case the reader should keep it in mind throughout this piece. At the very least, though, our house has strange tales to tell.

Let me begin with one of the oddest, even if it doesn't appear to be of the same breed as the rest. As the President of the Society of Fantastic Films, I contribute a couple of elements to our annual festival in Manchester. Apart from playing auctioneer, I provide DVDs for one strand of the programme and write the notes about them. In 2004 Jenny and I had hardly returned from a fortnight in Petra on Lesvos when we had to drive off to the festival. I loaded a carton with the discs I'd listed, all in their cases, and reached the hotel just in time to deliver them before the programme began. The first to be shown was *Terror in the Haunted House*, a standard minor Gothic enlivened by subliminal images, but when I looked in on the showing I discovered that the organiser of the 16-millimetre programme was showing a copy on film. The weekend was duly enjoyed, and on Monday morning I retrieved the carton of DVDs, only to learn that *Terror in the Haunted House* was missing. No doubt it had been mislaid because my copy had proved to be redundant, and I ordered another copy from Amazon. Soon it arrived, and I took it to the room where our DVDs are stored in alphabetical order. There was my original copy in its case, correctly filed on the shelf.

How curious is that? At the very least it means I neglected to take to the festival the only DVD of a film I didn't know that someone else had brought on celluloid. I would suggest that it's quite a coincidence. Still, it's hard to relate to the rest of the strangeness, except that the DVD room is at the top of the house, three floors up. That's where most of the tales are located, nearly all of them in the guest room next to my workroom.

We became the owners of this house in late 1983 and took up residence in early 1984, after some building work was done. In the intervening months I often walked over from our old house to check on its state (a practice that gave me the idea for "Where the Heart Is" when Kathy Cramer commissioned a haunted-house tale), and several times I sat in the dark in the room that was to become mine. Now it has a window built out onto the top of a two-storey bay, from which my desk overlooks the river, but then it only had quite a small window. Nonetheless I didn't experience any unease. I was making the place familiar, and I enjoyed the feel of the deserted house. I do belatedly wonder if I had any subconscious notion that its darkness needed for some reason to be confronted.

Jenny and her sister Penny were the first to have a sense of a presence. On one of Penny's visits our then young children crept up behind her in the guest-room, but in fact they were downstairs, and nobody was there. I was happy to hear it but politely interested rather than convinced. I was rather happier about the next incident—indeed, we all were, though certainly not immediately. Soon after moving in we returned home from a family picnic to find that we'd been burgled. It appeared the criminals had made their way up the house, taking all Jenny's jewellery with them in a bag. Something had frightened them in the guest-room, however, because they'd fled so hastily that they had left the jewellery there. We had an alarm system installed, but perhaps the presence on the third floor is enough. Whenever we go away for any length of time Jenny makes a point of asking it or them to look after the house.

I should describe the room. It's about sixteen feet by fourteen and a half, with a view across the Mersey towards the Liverpool waterfront through a side window in the longer wall, while the rear window beneath a skylight overlooks our large back garden. Against that wall is the water tank for the house, although it wasn't in there when the first incidents took place, and an old dressing-table with a mirror. There's a wardrobe, its door inset with a mirror, against the side wall, and two bookcases beside a radiator on the wall that the room shares with mine. The room also contains a double bed and a few stray household items. One odd, though surely not supernatural, phenomenon is that in the dressing-table mirror the wardrobe appears to merge with the wall. In fact it is simply difficult if not impossible to distinguish the edge of the wardrobe from its shadow, a condition that persists even on the sunniest day. If I were writing a story I might describe it as resembling a barely open entrance composed of shadow.

The word is now out that the room may be haunted. Reactions differ. Some visitors have yet to encounter anything. Poppy Z. Brite was daunted by the prospect, but in the event she merely thought she dreamed that something touched her face as she lay in the bed. Our son's friend Robin felt someone sit down by him on it, twice. Jenny can't sleep in there, because it makes her feel as if she's sharing the room with a demanding child. Our son Mat has had the impression that something was hanging across the room, while our daughter Tammy seemed to sense something outside the door. Keith and Martie from Holland stayed overnight, and at breakfast Martie asked Keith if he'd meant to put a Stephen King book in their suitcase. It was an edition of *Needful Things*, I believe, but not one we had. He denied all knowledge, and when they went to look the case was empty. Of course I may be to blame for some of these incidents, because by now I've had more experiences in there than anybody else has mentioned, and I've let folk know.

I'll save the worst for last. First came the coins, about four years ago. I noticed two new (in the sense of current) pennies on adjacent shelves of the first bookcase, but when I looked the next day there was another on the next shelf down. Since then they've turned up all over the room, at the last count a dozen altogether, which I've arranged in a pattern on top of a disused television to see if they shift. Perhaps they could all have been shed by living guests, but not long after the first few coins appeared I was treated to a closer display of their antics. I'd just opened the curtain at the side window on a sunny afternoon, and turned to hear and see a penny land on the floor between the door, the wall and the bed. The space measures nine feet by just under five, and the coin lay flat pretty well at the intersection of the diagonals. I was impressed.

That's a good word for my reaction to my first encounter after dark. I snore, perhaps not as much as I used to, given nightly applications of Snorodont or whatever the spray is called. For a while, until she told me not to, I tried to give Jenny nights off by sleeping in the by now famous room. One night I was drowsing, though by no means asleep, when something sat beside me on the bed, on the side towards the skylight. If we had pets I would have thought it was a kitten. I found the sensation interesting but unthreatening, and turned over, at which point it came and sat in front of me again. I was duly convinced of its presence but not alarmed, and went to sleep.

We're almost at the unresolved finish. I've taken to following Jenny's example and asking anything that's there to keep the house safe whenever we go away. In the summer of 2004, on a sultry night before we left for Lesvos in the early morning, I looked half-naked into the room and made the request. As I turned away, something the size of an adult hand but no heavier than cobweb was laid on my bare shoulder. I found it reassuring on the whole.

Jenny and I had discussed befriending the room by spending the night up there together. During one of my attempts to let her sleep without my snoring I wakened at about two in the morning to discover that she'd decided to try the experiment. It was only when I opened my eyes and reached for her that I realised the silhouette next to me, its head on the other pillow, wasn't Jenny. I tried for a very long time to move and cry out. Apparently I achieved the latter. In our bedroom on the floor below Jenny heard me make some kind of protest, but I've often exhorted her not to wake me if I'm having a nightmare, because I believe these dreams contain their own release mechanism, and I resent being taken out of them before the end. Jenny headed for the toilet on the middle floor, and when she returned I was still making the noise. Perhaps I was dreaming, in which case it had to be the longest nightmare, measured in objective time, that I've ever experienced. It consisted purely of lying in the bed I was actually in and trying to retreat from my companion. I admit to never having been so intensely terrified in my life. After minutes I found myself alone in the bed. I made myself turn over and close my eyes, but had a strong impression that a face was hovering very close to mine and waiting for me to look. Meanwhile, downstairs, Jenny felt an intruder sit beside her on our bed.

Our only other uncanny event since then took place elsewhere, while we were staying with friends in their impressively venerable house. It's seventeenth-century or earlier, three storeys high, and even has a priest's hole. There's also a local tradition of the Green Lady, who is best not encountered—but as Jeremy (who has written a history of the area) pointed out, such tales tend to be found where priests were being concealed and may have been invented to scare off the inquisitive. It's relevant, though.

On the Saturday they had friends round and much wine and cheese was savoured. At one point I played Nim (an Oriental strategy game that I learned from *L'Année Dernière à Marienbad*) with their friend John. Jenny then commandeered the several dozen cocktail sticks and built an impressive structure with them. She adjusted it so that it was symmetrical and very solid. It stood while we carried on drinking, while their friends eventually and severally departed with much opening of doors, while we dined at the same table with Apryl and Jeremy. At some point someone said that it would be fun if we found in the morning that the structure had been moved intact to the opposite end of the table.

In the morning we were up first and I worked on my new novel while Jenny went down to make us mugs of tea. She cleared away wineglasses from the table and then brought the mugs through, closing the door so as not to waken our hosts. As she retrieved the mugs from the table she remembered last night's remark and saw that the structure hadn't moved. She says she thought along the lines of "Oh, Green Lady, you've let me down. You didn't do anything. . . "

At which point, as she puts it, the structure exploded upwards and strewed itself across the table and the floor. She says she laughed with surprise before the actuality of what had happened caught up with her, and then she turned very cold indeed. I saw her a few seconds later, and I believe it. She showed me the devastation, and as I turned the light on, it fused. She wouldn't let me leave her until the others came down. So it seems that if their house wasn't haunted before, it may be now. As well as welcoming guests in our house, perhaps we leave them behind us elsewhere.

The Strange Case of Sean Manchester

"WHAT KIND OF PERSON WOULD BE THE BEST for the job of vampire killer?" asks Ellen Datlow in *The Year's Best Fantasy and Horror*. Her answer is Pat Cadigan's excellent story "The Power and the Passion". I imagine that one quality which Ellen admires in the tale is the way the narrator reveals more about himself than about vampirism. This at least it has in common with *The Highgate Vampire*, Sean (now Seán) Manchester's account of his experiences with vampirism. I refer for the moment to the first edition of the book, which considerably expands his original account of the saga, published in *The Vampire's Bedside Companion* (edited by Peter Underwood, Leslie Frewin, 1975).

"No one, named or unnamed, bears any responsibility for what I have written," the first page declares. This sort of candour is to be found throughout the book, and there's a similarly inadvertent aspect to the puff by Paul Spencer Vickers, of the Department of English Literature at University College, London (a graduate student, apparently, who then taught there for a while): "I found the book fascinating in its subject matter and magnificent in the quality of its prose. Sean Manchester's literary style is refreshingly reminiscent of the Gothic genre." Reminiscent, certainly; or as Manchester puts it in his foreword, "I commit pen to paper in what is hopefully the last frenzied flutterings of a force so dight with fearful fascination that even legend could not contain it." Having met him twice on television, where I was invited as the voice of reason, I can confirm that no frenzied fluttering is visible.

The early pages continue to be reminiscent—"Circumstances have brought me to many a strange, unchartered place in my endeavours as an occult investigator... the threshold of a vast, shadowy world... I am already beginning to wonder if the whole adventure were not some part of a frightening, fragmented dream—a nightmare in which the door between us and another world was almost ripped off its hinges... " This sort of thing may just be decoration, but we can hardly use that as an excuse for the pages which attempt to define and prove the existence of vampires. These start soberly, quoting history and dictionaries, but when they try to demonstrate why a vampire can't simply be an artificially preserved corpse the writing can no longer contain its enthusiasm: "When the stake pierces the heart, fresh blood will jet and spurt forth in all directions as the quivering, writhing body shudders to a halt." At this point the style seems to have spent itself for a while, and tries to be sober again: "Another point that all scientific explanations overlook is that when a vampire is exorcised it will emit a blood-curdling scream and, where many years have elapsed, will turn immediately to dust," an attitude to science and scientists worthy of von Däniken (whose ideas Manchester suggests were prefigured by *Quatermass and the Pit*). Can he really be suggesting that folk borrow material from Hammer films to include in their non-fiction books?

It would perhaps be unreasonable to expect too much hard information from a writer who admits "It was while being bathed by an attractive nanny at the age of seven that I learned of the blood-sucking undead". At least, he does in the first (1985) edition, which was the one I received when I ordered a copy of *The Highgate Vampire* to review in *Shock Xpress*. In a letter to the publishers of that august tome, Sean Manchester protested that a "completely revised and updated" version was about to appear, though he seemed most put out that any version should be analysed by "a pulp fiction writer... a bizarre and singularly appropriate reviewer... a hack like Campbell". Also received by the publishers before the piece appeared were letters from local history writer, artist and researcher Barbara Green ("I think you should in all fairness to Sean Manchester, have someone to do the work who will employ resious[1] research on the subject" rather than "a paperback writer of fantasy horror stories") and Keith Maclean of Reading ("Ramsey Campbell is not exactly Shakespeare and his major motivation is undoubtedly to make as much money as possible . . . What do you think would have happened to Sarah if it were not for Sean Manchester?") and a postcard from "BG" (". . . a fiction writer with no understanding of the real occult has no right to review this type of work"). It is certainly my duty to report that the attractive nanny has vanished from the 1991 edition, when Sean "was still being transmitted onto television screens in millions of homes across the country and staring out from magazine covers at home and abroad." I shall do my best to note other major differences.

Still, a book should at least exhibit internal consistency. There isn't much of that in either edition. The author first became convinced in 1967 that there was something amiss in Highgate Cemetery when, after two sixteen-year-old convent girls watched bodies rise from the graves (an experience that prompted them to "continue walking in eerie silence"), an employee of an acquaintance of Manchester's saw someone standing behind a locked gate, "an expression of basilisk horror on his face" (or, in *The Vampire's Bedside Companion*, "an expression of terror"). Why the sight of someone looking horrified inside a graveyard should have made the young man (who later joined the army) and his girlfriend flee isn't clear, but in the space of another four lines the intruder in the graveyard has become "the thing" and then "the spectre". Sean Manchester elects himself to investigate and makes his way to the "large, pulsating heart" of the graveyard. From this a path leads directly to the gate beyond which the intruder was standing, which might suggest to the careful reader that his appearance beyond it was of no great significance. However, the soon-to-be soldier climbs over the wall near the gate one night, presumably rather than use the path to it, and sees a dark shape. For no reason he can think of he recites the Lord's prayer aloud and jumps back over the wall, rather as the Karnstein's manservant does in Roger Vadim's 1960

[1]Surely not a mistype of "resinous"?

version of "Carmilla", *Et Mourir de Plaisir*. I hope he did well in the army.

Denied the chance of visiting the cemetery at night with someone who had seen the someone /thing/spectre, our investigator lets the case drop for two and a half years and concentrates on other matters, until by chance he meets Elizabeth Wojdyla, one of the convent girls. She is anxious to speak to him and displays all the symptoms of anaemia and somnambulism. She tells him one of the experiences that have been troubling her: "Midnight had struck . . . Something is outside my window . . . My arms and legs feel as if weights have been attached to them . . . I see the face of a wild animal with glaring eyes and sharp teeth, but it is a man . . . The face is gaunt and grey . . . There is a strange, falling sensation and I remember no more . . . " Now, if an eighteen-year-old brought me that story I should say she'd pillaged several fictions about vampires, but apparently Manchester takes her more seriously. Some weeks later her boyfriend Keith (a tall young man of Scottish descent whose help is to prove invaluable) phones him for help because she is "being overcome by something". They both observe two small holes in the side of her neck. Three days later Keith writes him a letter—"The full horror of the situation is too much for her to accept at the moment", he writes—and feeds her broth. "Take a look at this," Manchester tells him, and hands him a photostat of an extract from *Dissertatio de Vampyris Serviensibus*, Duisburg, 1733, which Keith slowly reads aloud. Slowly shaking his head he adds "Can such things really be? Can they?" and is persuaded by our investigator to seal the door and window of Elizabeth's bedroom with garlic and a crucifix, write the first fourteen verses of John's gospel on a piece of paper and slip it under her pillow, and sprinkle the room liberally with holy water while reciting the Creed three times at the top of his voice, among other activities. In case she's alarmed or thinks they're crazy Keith doesn't tell her why he's doing all this. For about a week she is "especially restless during her sleep", but then the fever goes away, and so does our investigator, though not without taking some photographs of Keith waving a Bible at her and of her smiling at the camera while poking a hand towards the lens "in her bedroom towards the end of her nightly visitations".

In February 1970 the *Hampstead and Highgate Express* publishes an account of three sightings of a figure inside the same old gates. The writer (unidentified, at least in the book) of the account "can think of no other explanation than this apparition being supernatural". Perhaps six years of daylight take their toll, since the entire paragraph has disappeared from the 1991 edition of *The Highgate Vampire*. The letter-column of the newspaper then breaks out in a rash of sightings, all of the writers being identified only by initials. Someone who didn't write to the press was supposedly attacked by a tall figure with the countenance of a wild animal—a description which, Sean Manchester admits, "was somehow not altogether unfamiliar". Indeed. At the end of the month Manchester decides after much soul-searching to tell the paper that a vampire is abroad, and is contacted by the sister of a twenty-two-year-old woman "whom", he declares, "I shall call Lusia". Why Manchester should conceal her real name isn't clear, since the book prints a photograph of her, emphasising her cleavage, on the cover and repeats it inside, above the caption "beautiful and innocent as a child"—not, admittedly, in the 1991 edition, where she is depicted only by an actress and in a painting and is simply "called Lusia". How mysterious![2] The introduction explains "Though very necessary to the first edition, which would have lacked impact and credibility had the wealth of illustrative material been absent, the bulk of photographic evidence has now been expurgated in the interest of good taste." Still, the 1991 edition does offer a photograph of Rosemary Ellen Guiley, author of *Vampires Among Us*, smiling at the camera while "being shown photographs of the decomposing vampire by the author in the summer of 1990".

[2] No longer so mysterious, since more material has risen from the grave. Before either edition of the book there was *Witchcraft*, for which Sean penned "The World of the Vampire" (vol. 2, no. 8, 1973, pp. 52–5). The article sports a photograph of him so youthful that his first name has yet to sprout its accent. More significantly, it includes the familiar photograph of Lusia, but identified as Jacqui Frances, "a pretty 22-year-old blonde". In this version of events she's the person who sees the figure with the "look of basilisk horror on his face". We must assume that the vampire is so powerful that he is able to infect the very narrative with his ability to shift shape. Ms Frances says that the figure was driven away by the "large silver crucifix" she wears. Oddly, both in the magazine and the first edition of the book, the item she wears is not a crucifix. It is the Iron Cross—the German military award.

Elizabeth Wodjdyla shows up in this article too. She's "a 21-year-old Polish immigrant", which is curious, since at this point in the book just two and a half years have passed since she was sixteen. Though in the book she's living with her boyfriend, here her brother notices the marks on her neck at breakfast. In the article it's her boyfriend who protects her with vampire repellents, apparently being familiar with the drill. Sean seems not to have intervened, and wonders "Did she fall victim to her own imagination?" We may wonder something close to that ourselves.

However, let us return to Lusia, who has started to go in for sleepwalking and two marks on her neck. Soon her sister Anne leaves Manchester a note: "She is now at the front door and undoing the locks . . . You know where she will be heading." Off they all troop to the pulsating heart of the graveyard, where Lusia heads for an iron door and collapses. Our investigator decides on an official vampire-hunt, but alas, freelance vampire-hunters are beginning to get in the way, possibly because Manchester has referred in the *Hampstead and Highgate Express* to staking and decapitating the vampire just after dawn between Friday and Saturday. Despite his declared aversion to publicity, Manchester then plans to appear on a television show introduced by Eamonn Andrews, but things go wrong during the shoot outside those cemetery gates: the camera director falls over; the wind howls and screams; the generator wires lash the ground. It's a pity that Professor Quatermass couldn't have been summoned to investigate this kind of thing, along with the booming vibration at the heart of the graveyard. Nevertheless the programme, including full instructions for destroying vampires, is broadcast on the eve of the vampire hunt, and to our investigator's surprise a crowd worthy of a football match arrives at the graveyard, including "all manner of freelance vampire-hunter", not least one Alan Blood, a history teacher from Chelmsford or Billericay with an interest in the black arts. Manchester, together with one hundred official assistants, gamely ventures to the iron door and has himself lowered through the roof of the tomb. He finds three empty coffins and blesses them, but the vampire must be shy of publicity. All Manchester can do is continue the official investigation, and has himself lowered through the roof again in August. One of the coffins has gone.

Nothing will do except that he take Lusia to the iron door and use his hypnotic powers. "You should never have come here," she says in a deep voice, but obligingly walks to the doors of a nearby vault. Here he and his three hand-picked assistants find a monstrous black casket in much better conditions than the others, and we must imagine for ourselves why he didn't notice this beyond the iron door on the night of the vampire hunt and how it has been transported to its new home. Inside the casket is something gorged and stinking with the life-blood of others, burning red eyes, long sharp teeth, you know the kind of thing. Our man poises a stake over the heart. "Is there no other way?" an assistant says, though we aren't told how much they sound like Michael Gough in the Hammer *Dracula*, and in *The Vampire's Bedside Companion* our investigator responds "We can try. We can try" (or, in the book-length version, "Probably not, but we can try. We can certainly try!" while shaking his head from side to side). He senses the vampire's dreadful aura of triumph, but decides against hammering the stake. Instead he hangs around until sunset and performs an exorcism and decides that bricking up the tomb with garlic in the cement will do. Lusia sobs on his shoulder and hugs him with all the strength she has left, having dropped a Bible that falls open at the words "For the blood is the life."

You may wonder whose tomb it was. So did I until I found our investigator's first account of the Highgate business. In the Underwood book, though some distance from the chapter Manchester contributed, the fourth photograph shows the very man brandishing a crucifix outside "the vault where the suspected dead was eventually located" and looking young enough to play an altar-boy. The sixth photograph shows us the same vault "after the ceremony, bricked up and permanently sealed". The vault is clearly identifiable in the fourth image, which is oddly absent from both editions of our man's own book. It's the tomb of Charles Fisher Wace of Camden Road, who died in 1872. He was a meat trader.

However, we are less than halfway through the book. Once again overcoming his dislike of publicity, our investigator appears on a national BBC television show about the Highgate Cemetery events, though he finds it "difficult to focus his mind" on the questions he is asked by the interviewer. Watching the programme reminds him that he neglected to hammer in the stake. Meanwhile a mail order clerk, one Barry Edwards, explains that at the time of the sightings in the graveyard he and the Hellfire Film Club were filming an amateur vampire movie there. Our investigator hasn't much time for amateurs, of course, nor for the objection that human canines can't leave vertical punctures on a neck: "During my various lecture tours and talks on the subject, I have satisfactorily demonstrated—using a live model—that the canines can in fact sink into the jugular vein on the neck." In any case, perhaps vampires have hollow teeth, and besides, his critics fail to mention that werewolves become vampires after death, and we should also remember that there is anti-time just as there is anti-matter, not to mention that the atomic weight of the vampire's body can be raised above the level of the earth's vibrations, though "this is looking at it scientifically". So much for science.

The BBC programme rouses more amateurs. Some wander through Highgate Cemetery banging on tombstones with stakes and shouting "Come out vampire, we are coming to get you." Our man's adversaries begin to proliferate: David Farrant, who lives in a coal-cellar and who has the temerity to found the British Psychic and Occult Society, apparently in opposition to our investigator's British Occult Society, before (according to Manchester's account) he is convicted of interfering with corpses and sent to Blunderstone Prison; John Pope, a fire research assistant from Barnet who tries to raise Dracula in a Transylvanian hotel room ("I wish he'd throw away all this rubbish and find himself a girlfriend," his father, once an RSM, apparently said); Jean-Paul Bourre, a black magician who dresses "predictably in black from head to foot". Also abroad are a whole bunch of Satan-ists, "the vampire's living emissaries", who desecrate an Anglican Church in Islington. The Reverend Pauley of that church calls in our investigator, and over a bottle of Napoleon brandy they agree that Manchester should exorcise the church (why him, rather than the diocesan exorcist, isn't clear). Lusia is brought along to the exorcism, and before long she needs to be hypnotised, sending our investigator to Highgate Wood. There he seems to see a robed figure in an old pavilion, and when he returns in daytime with an assistant and a camera he finds signs inscribed on the floor. Lusia is brought along to be hypnotised and utters remarkable utterances—"must go to the old house" and so forth. At least, she does in the 1985 edition, but in the revised version she says "I must find the old place" and is significantly less loquacious. Our investigator decides it's time to return to the cemetery, "indeed to the undead tomb itself", for apparently a house which used to cast its shadow over the (pulsating) heart of the cemetery was occupied in the early eighteenth century by a nobleman who was brought to England in a coffin, after which there were tales of "hobbs, ghaists and daemons" and a grey giant that walked through walls. No doubt Nigel Kneale came across these tales while researching

Quatermass and the Pit. Our investigator has two workmen reopen the bricked-up Wace tomb (in the 1991 edition, though not in the first one, after "permission was obtained"). What is his surprise on discovering the coffin has gone! In the 1985 version the workmen seal up the vault again, but not in the later edition. Could this have anything to do with a photograph of the vault taken by John Gay in March 1991 and held in the English Heritage collection of images of the cemetery? The photo shows that the vault isn't bricked up but secured by a pair of doors[3]. Still, perhaps it has simply taken six years for someone to grasp that resealing the tomb isn't necessary if there's no vampire within.

Two years later he finds the missing coffin, in a house at the edge of Highgate where "whatever walked the broken staircases, walked alone." The building has been "yawning ominously" at passers-by. Surrounded by clichés, he and a clairvoyant (Veronika) and a skeptic (Arthur) enter the building, which the residents of the adjoining Jewish old folks' home call the House of Dracula. They probe the darker recesses with enthusiasm and try to settle down for the night, only to suffer a further onslaught of clichés. Close to midnight they attempt to fuel themselves with sandwiches "freshly cut that same evening" that prove to be "covered in mould, as if they were weeks old" in the 1985 edition or, in the 1991 version, "covered in mould and crawling with maggots as though they had been left for months"—no doubt the six-year gap is somehow to blame. Veronika announces that the tenant won't let them leave. Perhaps it is fed up with being mislaid by our investigator. He gives Arthur a cross, and the trio sit outside in their car and fill the window spray with holy water, seemingly from inside the vehicle, though in the 1991 edition someone appears to have spotted that anomaly. Manifestations cause Arthur to cry "I'm off" and be so. Manchester runs after him and gives him another cross, but they are assailed by an apparition "nearly impossible to describe", hence not described at all. More apparently fed up than ever, it allows them to go next door to the old folks' home for some buckets of water. An

[3] In the entry for 17 February 2012 on his blog (http://therightreverendseanmanchester.blogspot.co.uk/) the Bishop celebrates the life of Jean Pateman MBE, former chairwoman of the Friends of Highgate Cemetery. "We knew each other and continued to stay in touch by correspondence until quite recently." I'm assured that if you mention Seán's name on any of the tours the Friends give of the cemetery you can be sure of a reaction.

old lady looks somewhat astonished. Back outside Hill House or whatever it's called, Manchester chunters for a page and a half at Arthur—more than that in the reprint—while an apparition forms behind him. "What does it all mean?" says Arthur, and in the 1991 version "Is all this really necessary?" Veronika falls asleep. The sun comes up. Before heading for the basement of the veritable temple of a dark force which has permeated the very wood and stone with living evil they see Veronika home, but the vampire has also nodded off. They drag the enormous black casket upstairs and out of the house, and Manchester poises the stake. "In God's name strike!" cries Arthur. Terrible roar from bowels of hell, sluggish flow of inhuman slime and viscera, etc. Arthur tries to use the camera but has to turn away (in the 1991 version, "after several frames had been taken"). The old folk next door are presumably catching up on their sleep. The house is subsequently demolished to make way for flats, but the Bodgers who live there speak of "a presence"[4].

In 1981, while filming a documentary about vampirism, our man is called back to England by a telegram. Animals are being drained of blood in Finchley in what the local paper calls "the sinister midnight rabbit kill". Clearly one of the vampire's victims is on the rampage, and the best thing for our investigator to do is to climb over the wall of Highgate Cemetery at night with Sylvaine Charlet, an actress. Nothing comes of this visit, but before Sylvaine returns to Paris they attend a masquerade at a stately home, since she likes to dress up. Here, by a lake during a firework display, our investigator thinks he sees Lusia dressed in white, a scene so cinematic I'm surprised that nobody—Roger Vadim, let's say—has used it in a vampire film. Then he meets Lusia's sister, who tells him that Lusia died "almost seven years ago from a form of leukemia" (or, in the 1991 revision, "from a blood disorder some years earlier").

Our investigator locates her and her activities in the graveyard in

[4] At least, those are the accounts to be found in the two editions of the book, but once again an early version forms from the mist—Sean's article "The Haunting of Hell House" (an oddly familiar title) in *New Witchcraft*, volume 1, number 4, 1975 (pp 51-5). Strange! The neighbours call it Hell House, not the House of Dracula, and they aren't identified as Jewish. In this version our intrepid adventurers don't even have time for a sandwich, let alone a rotting one. How could our narrator have forgotten such a striking detail? And in the book, how could he possibly have failed to recall that Veronika heard voices chanting her name? "It knows my name," she cries, and for some reason I can almost imagine Julie Harris saying the words. Still, while it may know Veronika's name, our author is less sure of their companion's. In the magazine he's called Dennis, not Arthur.

New Southgate where she was buried. Here a boy was lured out of a park nearby and bitten by a "lovely lady all in white" who can be none other than Lucy Westenra—than Lusia, I mean. Our man visits her grave, where "a jagged fork of lightning lit the freshly inscribed letters on the stone ahead". In order to avoid publicity he adopts the name of George Byron, recalling a family legend that he is the great-great-great-grandson of Lord Byron. Before long he is forced to disguise himself in order to campaign against a council plan to develop part of the graveyard, and gives a television interview among the graves. Spike Milligan is the first to sign his petition, which Byron plans to deliver to the Prime Minister, having ridden along Downing Street on his horse Thunderbolt. After posters appear advertising him as a council candidate under his assumed name his phone is tapped and Special Branch officers are cautiously polite as they interview him in his room full of vampire repellents. He is astounded to be subjected to such an interview. He is also troubled by dreams of Lusia "caressing her silky skin in rhythm" and licking her lips until he raises a stake and she uses it for "a ferocious masturbation which leaves her spurting blood out of every orifice at the moment of orgasm"—so troubled, indeed, that in the 1991 edition she is reduced to "swaying to and fro, making a hissing sound" and "everything becomes a blur". Perhaps things are getting on top of him, not least the local newspaper reports of the council election under the headlines "Vampire Slayer Fighting Election" and "I'll Oust the Living Dead, says Candidate." He is unsuccessful at the election, but forgives those who didn't vote for him—"Their heart was not in their sword when the day of battle arrived"—and, at least in the 1985 edition, quotes Kipling's "If" to himself.

It remains only for him to deal with Lusia. He takes her sister to the grave and tells her "The night is full of her voice calling my name." Nevertheless Anne won't let him dig up the corpse, and so he is beset by various manifestations; indeed, in the 1991 edition he has managed to remember that one night a woman he took to be Anne turned out to be Lusia and bit him. Later in that version she appears as a vaporous substance with two burning eyes and harangues him at length. "Why do you oppose me? Do we not desire the same thing? Faugh! It sickens you, does it?" is a sample of her seduction technique. (Kim Newman has pointed out that vampires seem to enjoy making anagrams out of their names; perhaps the Highgate species infects its victims not just with vampirism but with bygone language.) This rouses him to invoke the vampire at the grave during the hours of darkness. Having performed various rituals he strips naked, feeling like "a schoolboy on his way to meet his first real date" (or, in the 1991 edition, where at some point he dons purple vestments, "like a forlorn lover about to encounter the object of his passion"). After a good deal of Wheatleyish conjuration he is rewarded by the appearance outside the magic circle of a spider the size of a cat. A still from the Hammer film of *The Devil Rides Out*, showing the charmed circle that protects our heroes from just such a creature, has vanished from the second edition of the book like a vampire at dawn. He shoves a stake through the centre of the spider. "Something wet and glutinous oozed stickily as I pressed the stake still further." I refrain from a Freudian reading of the entire scene. The spider turns into Lusia's corpse, which he holds until dawn, at which point he returns the quickly decomposing remains to the ground, presumably by digging up the grave.

While *The Highgate Vampire* was originally published by the British Occult Society (and the revision by Gothic Press) the sequel, *From Satan to Christ*, comes from Holy Grail. The sequel is less a book than a prolonged contradictory footnote. Our man has usually been able to trace any attempts to discredit him back to Satanists, not least David Farrant of the coal-cellar and of what Manchester calls the symptoms of someone with an identity crisis. Having dressed in a robe and carried a nine-foot cross through the West End and fed his followers on Hampstead Heath with fish and bread, Manchester is called upon to save one Sarah from Satanism. The book says she has "a child's heart in the body of a woman," and a good deal of the latter, emphasising cleavage, is visible on the cover. While at primary school she used to preach to the neighbours about their shortcomings, but became disillusioned with the church after the parish priest tried to give her a French kiss and his successor ran off with a nun. On leaving college with an Arts degree Sarah decides to move to London in search of a coven.

Meanwhile Manchester is hard at his mission of rescuing stray sheep, which apparently began in the sixties. The Satanists are too busy to have become aware of him: David Farrant stands in the Hornsey election as the Wiccans Awake candidate; John Pope (the ex-RSM's son) consults Farrant for a ritual to use against David Crawford, organiser of the Bedford branch of the Brotherhood of the Ram, and later tries to join the Orthodox Temple of the Prince but receives a letter calling him "a fly on the backside of Occultism". Where our investigator obtained this letter and much else besides is unclear, but perhaps it has something to do with Sarah, who has joined the Croydon Order of the Star and Snake.

We are told this was run by Mark Pastellopoulos (the Great Beast, or Lucifer, or son of Mercury) and Samantha Courtenay-Devonshire, who preferred to be addressed as the Whore of Babylon. Sarah is initiated in a temple with black candles and a statue with a goat's head and an erection, but doesn't realise she's involved with Satanism. (One tip the book offers is that you can recognise Satanists by their untidiness.) Luckily she encounters our investigator, whose aversion to publicity has prevented the coven from hearing about him, and he recognises her peril from the weird, discordant music on the stereo in her flat. (He himself is given to improvising on the saxophone and playing *Metamorphosen* on the piano, not simultaneously but no mean feat either.) He confronts Beast and Whore at Sarah's birthday party, where the guests dress as vampires and ghouls and so on, and our man comes as Lord Byron. Eyes blaze and voices grow cold and snarling while our investigator ripostes, the Beast unlocks his chubby fingers and rolls forward on the sofa and sweats a lot. Our man is unable to prevent Sarah from undergoing an impregnation by a demon, but the ritual apparently doesn't work, although in the original version of this review my mind must have been clouded by some demonic influence, causing me to misread Manchester's hypnotic prose. Here the book trails off; Sarah marries our hero; David Farrant has a last confrontation with him in a wood before they "each dissolved into the night's shadows in opposite directions". The final pages, however, warn us not to fail to recognise the Messiah, so perhaps all is not over.

If these books are less fun to experience at length than to read about, this can't be said of the illustrations. The Satanists seem to have been happy to be photographed; we have David Farrant at his devilish altar in Highgate, Sarah stripped to at least the waist for a ritual, and the Satanic coronation of John Pope. The first edition of the vampire book offers a "remarkable picture of Lusia somnambulating", for some reason shot from floor level, as well as a buxom wench throwing out her chest in the pulsating heart of the graveyard, some freelance vampire-hunters, a large black casket, Caroline Munro and our investigator (wearing a Marvel Comics badge) discussing vampirism "before an astonished audience" at a horror film convention, our investigator surrounded by vampire repellents, our investigator with his box of accoutrements, our investigator's official portrait displaying his esoteric shield which boasts three bats, our investigator on his horse Thunderbolt, and much else. Most striking of all is "a representation of the vampire in its final moments of dissolution", which is nothing of the kind; it is an early makeup by Dick Smith, featured in *Famous Monsters of Filmland*, for an American television production of *Dorian Gray*, and perhaps that is why it has vanished from the reprint. (Forry Ackerman displays the actual item on YouTube at **www.youtube.com/watch?v=IsjSYlWQxaI**.) Closer to the image films have led us to expect is a picture of "the decomposing vampire—moments after exorcism", which in 1991 has multiplied into "pictures showing the vampire in stages of rapid decomposition which were televised in 1990". Perhaps such things take five or six years to develop. It is striking that the balder of the two images in the 1991 edition has been superimposed onto a different background, even more obviously if you compare the fuller version of the original photograph in the 1985 book. But enough. I should respect Sean Manchester's aversion to publicity.

Seán still has books in him. 1997 saw *The Vampire Hunter's Handbook* (in which one chapter bears a motto quoted, with no discernible aversion, from this very essay of mine). Admittedly it's the one about David Farrant and an identity crisis. The *Handbook*'s author asks us "Who knows what went through [Farrant's] mind as he listened to my improvised harmonic structures, accompanied by a perspiring rhythm section, in that dimly lit venue for modern jazz aficionados?"

Who indeed. We are told of Michael Ranft's "book of the chewing dead in their tombs", and that James Frazer "recommends" decapitating vampires in *The Fear of the Dead in Primitive Religions*. I really wonder if the noted anthropologist advised the reader to do anything of the kind. And Seán ushered in the new century with *Carmel*, a sequel to Stoker's *Dracula* narrated by James Harker. Harker encounters the Count de Ville, just as a character of mine did when I was eleven years old. The Count is of course who we suspect, and proves capable of uncanny actions: "Reaching inside my jacket for the silver container that held the sacred wafer, the Count simultaneously swooped back into the dimly lit chamber which might have served as a private chapel in a previous age." We learn that if someone stutters this proves "that he has not become one of the nondescript undead". Harker teams up with vampire hunter Lord Mamucium (yes indeed, one of the Latin names of Manchester). "Imagine my horror when he pulled a decapitated head from the carrier bag he was holding—and asked: 'Do you recognise it?'" I assume this isn't among the autobiographical elements—there are many—of the book. Mamucium delivers quite a few lectures in the course of the novel, most significantly one that suggests the Nazis persecuted Jews "because they were kindred in so many ways . . . Most Nazi leaders were, in fact, Jews" (along, we are assured, with Jack the Ripper). There's a good deal more of this kind of thing, and we may conclude that the rich vein of deadpan humour Seán's work previously offered has run thin. Perhaps our author is better kept out of mischief chasing vampires. May he carry on—in print, at any rate.

4: On Some Writers

Tim Powers

PROVIDENCE, RHODE ISLAND. HALLOWEEN 1986. My family and I were there for the World Fantasy Convention. One night, after some intensive partying with the Turtles and their lovely doves, I set out to give my wife Jenny a tour of Lovecraftian Providence. It had certainly been some party, because I found myself wholly unable to recall the route on which Richard Tierney had once guided me or even to locate any of the historically lamplit streets on the hill. In the early hours we straggled back to the Biltmore Plaza, the convention hotel which seemed to have been under construction since the last World Fantasy Convention there and which was rumoured to conceal a complete floor uninhabited by human guests; and as we crossed the lobby, a figure approached through the gloom to murmur some kind words about my writing. Because of his unassumingness, I didn't realise until I read his name badge that he was Tim Powers, no less. When I admitted with some embarrassment that I hadn't read *The Anubis Gates*—though it was on my shelf of books to read—he advised me, I believe, not to expect too much.

Reviews and word of mouth had led me to expect quite a lot of the book, but the author of a masterpiece can afford to be self-effacing; and, having read the book not long after I returned to

England, I'll stake my reputation on that description of it: a masterpiece of science fantasy, to be precise.

At least, I claim that's what I'm being, but the precise definition of science fantasy has never been agreed. Peter Nicholls came up with an attractive one: "the kind of fantasy science fiction readers prefer". I was about to suggest here that it is a grey area where fantasy and science fiction overlap, except that far from being grey, it is often gorgeously multicoloured. It occurs to me that its great strength is its scope. In Tim Powers' case, very much as in Fritz Leiber's, it gives his imagination room to develop, and I for one would be much poorer without the awesome inventions of both men.

Once upon a time, *The Anubis Gates* would have been called a romance. It is one in all the best senses. Besides his enviably fluent imagination, Powers the writer offers great emotional range. Leiber comes to my mind again (as so frequently when I think of key works of the fantastic): years ago he identified the appeal of the weird as the inextricable interweaving of wonder and terror. That is to be found here, and more: in the context of a breathlessly paced adventure, Powers achieves extraordinary scenes of underground horror, of comedy both high and grotesque, of bizarre menace, of poetic fantasy. So varied a pile of riches might be expected to topple in all directions, but still another talent Powers has made his own is the ability to plot. All the profuse imaginings which make up *The Anubis Gates* are kept in balance and control by a structure of Byzantine complexity. The man is astonishing. As my friend Jonathan Carroll might say, I hate his ass.

Well, I think I've stood between you and the first page of his novel long enough, and besides, if I reflect any further on the book I imagine I'll end up rereading it to repeat the pleasure—in fact, I'm sure I shall. Welcome, then, to the gates into the labyrinth inside Tim Powers' head. I count it a privilege to have met and read him.

Terry Lamsley

GENEROSITY IS ITS OWN REWARD. IN MY EXPERIENCE that is all too often true when it comes to reading unpublished fiction, an experience from which I flinch these days. At least unpublished work may prove to be worth publishing, however; but we may assume of almost anything self-published that it has done its weary rounds until at last the author, maddened by its latest reappearance as a yet more tattered revenant, decides that astounding the world is worth any cost of publication. Alas, most bookshops avoid such books, and so, unless they promise to be sufficiently comic to reward the outlay, do I. You may therefore imagine my dilemma on being confronted, at the 1993 Ghost Story Society convention in Chester, with a pile of Terry Lamsley and the author in attendance.

I picked up a glossy paperback and gathered that it was published by the author, and illustrated with photographs to boot. Could I have replaced it on top of the heap under the gaze and the genial but, for all I knew, brave smile of its author? Another factor decided the situation for me: Buxton, which I observed was the setting of some of the tales, was where I met Jenny, my wife and one true love, at a convention of the science fiction sort—indeed, in the very crescent that was illustrated. What embarrassment might not have been worth, nostalgia was, and so I stumped up a few pounds and had *Under the Crust* gracefully autographed.

It was probably nostalgia that led me to sit down with the first story soon after my return home, but a much more immediate emotion caused me to ring up Steve Jones, then my collaborator but now sole editor of *Best New Horror*, to tell him in some excitement that I'd discovered a new author who was a must for our annual. Was I responsible for alerting our old friend Karl Edward Wagner too? I should be happy to think so. Karl used a different tale of Terry's in *Year's Best Horror*, at any rate, and our editorial triumvirate must have helped notify the cognoscenti of the emergence of an important author, because the next World Fantasy Awards had Terry Lamsley on the shortlist in no less than three categories, by gum.

I was in New Orleans for the presentation, and happy to be asked to attend the banquet so as to accept on Terry's behalf. In my brief speech I said that Terry was the kind of new talent Karl had been most delighted to support, and so I would like to accept the Best Novella award for "Under the Crust", the title story of Terry's book, in memory of Karl as well. I'm only sorry I couldn't have surprised Terry with his inscribed bust of Lovecraft at the next Chester gathering; I'd gone down south to present Poppy Z. Brite with a British Fantasy Award. Sorry, Terry, but she's prettier than you, and I got a kiss as well.

I shake myself and grow sober. Terry Lamsley was born in 1941. His early childhood was spent around Maidstone, his teens in the North of England. In 1978 he moved to Buxton. Convinced that the atmosphere of the town deserved celebrating in ghost stories, between December 1991 and July 1992 he wrote a group of them, as a response to the decaying of the centre of the town. They were collected as *Under the Crust: Supernatural Tales of Buxton*, which Lamsley published in collaboration with photographer and book designer Michael Patey-Ford under an imprint, Wendigo, invented for the occasion.

The book is a major debut. The first story, "Two Returns", displays Lamsley's talent for spectral imagery in its opening scene. As a figure glimpsed at the far end of a dark station platform vanishes into what might be a doorway "his arms and legs appeared to fold into him, like blades returning to the handles of a knife." While the economy of effect is reminiscent of M. R. James, the apparition is admirably original. Manifestations of it pursue a retired schoolteacher home, drawn by research he conducted into the history of his house. In "Living Waters" Druidic survivals that Christian practices have imperfectly subsumed take shape in the spa water and begin to overrun the town in forms a lesser writer would have rendered unintentionally comic, but Lamsley's imagination doesn't falter. These tales have the traditional ghost story's sense of an ignored past, but in "Killjoy" there's no hint of it. Doz, a solvent-sniffing teenage schoolboy with a fondness for violent (though pointedly not horror) videos is dogged by a progressively incomplete tramp, who begins by having a silhouette that changes "in small ways" but who soon does without eyes. While the reader may make a guess at the tramp's identity, it isn't as simple as it seems. "Something Worse" studies a family, the Saltrees, who become obsessed with life after death. The accent on psychological detail, and the restriction of supernatural effects to a very few subtle manifestations, recall de la Mare and his successor Robert Aickman. "Tabitha after Life" is a darkly comic tale in which a spectral spinster offended by the class of the other ghosts haunting Buxton becomes involved with somebody not quite as dead. "Under the Crust" turns the Peak District landscape around Dove Holes, in particular a rubbish tip, into a vision of hell more closely related to surrealism than mediaevalism.

While *Under the Crust* was a remarkable debut, *Conference with the Dead* (which I take to have been known as *High Peaks of Fear* and *The Outer Darkness* at different stages of its gestation) is finer still. Its roots are in the great tradition of the field. "Blade and Bone", for instance, is entirely worthy of M. R. James, not only in its reticence but also in its willingness to horrify, a quality about which some of the antiquary's admirers maintain a silence that seems almost embarrassed. The tale sends the luckless Ogden Minter on the sort of antiquarian quest M. R. James's protagonists pursued. There's an admirably unnerving touch when on learning that Minter has been talking to a character who we gather at this point was spectral, the manageress of a cafe doesn't recoil but laughs uproariously. Minter's enquiries attract a revenant from the days when trespassers were tortured, and the story ends on a grisly turn of phrase.

Like James's spectres, Terry's are memorably inhuman and by no means shy of using the banal devices of modern life to manifest themselves: see "Screens", for example, in which a murderer returns through the medium of a blurry video that hints at where he went just before his death—not, we are led to believe, on an ordinary holiday, given the companions he brings back with him. James himself might have shuddered away from this tale and from "The Toddler", where the results of an episode of sixteenth-century licentiousness manifest themselves today, but the prose is no less reticent than it is suggestive; even when Lamsley goes as far as this he maintains his taste.

"Someone To Dump On" proves with the great simplicity of utter confidence that the classical ghost story can still work; it triumphantly revives a classic trope of the genre, the ghost that goes unrecognised as one until it's too late. "The Break", set in a seaside resort overrun with confused old people, conveys the nightmarishness of which childhood can seem to consist as powerfully as any piece of fiction I have ever read. "Running in the Family" is also concerned with childhood and its perceptions of an alien world gradually revealed, as the young narrator learns that her father is not a Russian and her mother is not her mother, and becomes psychologically involved with a ghost that can't stop running. I would furthermore count Terry as, along with M. John Harrison, Peter Straub and Lisa Tuttle and practically nobody else, an inheritor of the influence of Robert Aickman: such tales as this and "The Extension" suggest the affinity to me with their strangeness and the poise with which they are narrated. In the latter story the son of two killers returns to their home, only to discover that they were involved in more than murder and that the past has the power to reclaim him. "Inheritance" is as dark as the book gets, maybe as the genre gets: it would do as an unrelenting study of paranoid schizophrenia, believe me, but it asks us to decide whether that or the supernatural is least reassuring. By contrast, the title story offers the largest helping of the humour and irony which underlie much of the best of the genre, though even this leads to a bleak coda. In "The Outer Darkness" the obsession of two men with the woman they both loved when she was alive leads them to follow her into an after-life as skewed as at first sight it looks banal. As for "Walking the Dog", it will serve to introduce the reader to Terry's growing originality. It would once have been called science fantasy, presenting as it does the symbiotic relationships between a voracious alien being and the various unfortunates employed to feed it. Despite his fidelity to his genre, he is triumphantly like no other writer.

In these two books Lamsley established himself as an inheritor of all the qualities of classic English supernatural horror fiction: wit, detachment, an economy of effect bordering on the poetic, a seemingly effortless originality. In 1997 *Conference for the Dead* received an award for best collection from the International Horror Critics' Guild. Since then he has published a third book, *Dark Matters*, which shows no sign of running out of talent or ideas, but has recently grown less prolific. May he continue to produce and prosper.

American Psycho

I EXPECTED TO HATE BRET EASTON ELLIS' NOVEL. I'D been made aware of its early history, which seems to be as follows. In December 1989 Ellis delivered a first draft of *American Psycho* to Simon & Schuster, who had paid him an advance of $300,000. At an internal meeting some months later, members of staff were outraged by a sample chapter. George Corsillo, who had designed the covers of Ellis' two previous books, refused the assignment. In October that august journal Time extracted and regurgitated choice cuts from the novel so as to deplore them as "the most appalling acts of torture, murder and dismemberment ever described in a book targeted for the best-seller lists". On 14 November Simon & Schuster announced that although copies had been printed they had decided not to publish after all. It isn't clear whose decision this was; rumour suggests some paragon of Paramount Pictures, which owns the company and which, of course, released *Friday the 13th*. (Martin Davis, the chairman of Paramount, commented "Compared to this book, *Friday the 13th* would be endorsed by the Vatican.") Less than two weeks later Vintage, the paperback division of Random House, had bought the novel.

Predictably, much of this outraged both the liberal and the censorious. The president of the Authors Guild described the withdrawal of the book as "a black day for American publishing", and the Horror Writers of America wrote to Simon & Schuster, rebuking them for censorship. Personally, I wouldn't mind suffering a kind of censorship that brought me two advances for the first edition of a book, not to mention a great deal of free publicity before publication. Meanwhile, the Los Angeles coordinator of the National Organisation for Women set up a telephone hot line on which callers could hear some of the more outrageous scenes read aloud. If only the Christian Fundamentalists had treated my books similarly instead of just burning them! Ellis, however, told Reuters that he was shocked by the condemnation of his book—"It looks like outside hysteria is reaching into the publishing industry"—and I wonder if he is missing the point as much as many of his readers seem to have.

I'd suggest that the readers have more justification, insofar as by the time most of us get around to the book we're likely to have been prejudiced by at least some of the above. There have been similar disagreements in publishing before—for instance, female staff members at Grafton objected so strongly to Thomas Tessier's *Finishing Touches* that the book was denied a hardcover edition in Britain—but none so well publicised. In my case I'd also read several extracts from *American Psycho,* admittedly quoted out of context by the press but so disgusting that I couldn't imagine a context that would justify them. Alongside these were the comments of Sonny Mehta, the chap who commissioned *New Terrors* from me and now president of Vintage ("... a serious book by a serious writer... a significant writer writing in a documentary manner about a particular segment of American society") and comments by Ellis himself, in an interview that would have been enclosed with the Simon & Schuster review copies: "I don't think it's a novelist's job to give little moral lessons... sequences that were very upsetting to write but [which] felt real and honest and true... very clear there is a moral tone to the book [which] lies in the direction of the author abhorring this kind of behavior." (In the context of this book it's unnerving that Ellis appears to think of himself in the third person.) More recently we've had the managing director of Picador claiming that "we are not promoting the book—we are not seeking to add to the hype." Well, few things look better on the balance sheet than free publicity, but I suspect that some readers of *Fear* might respect the book more if its publishers had taken a lead from *The Wasp Factory* ("the lurid literary equivalent of a video nasty") and quoted some of the hostile comments—from *Time,* say, and Martin Davis—on the cover. Admittedly *American Psycho* sounds like two Robert Bloch novels run into one, but the title is hardly enough to suggest that much of the book reads like unrestrained Shaun Hutson.

I mean that literally, and not as a sly dig at Shaun. On a panel some years ago Shaun described how Star Books had persuaded him to tone down the violence in *Chainsaw Terror,* reissued as *Into the Night* (the book in which a character called Ramsey gets done in with a claw hammer). The death of one victim, Amy, was considerably more prolonged, and the cut is denoted by three dots. Several chapters of *American Psycho* consist of precisely the kind of material Shaun suppressed, and in at least as much detail. Does this mean that an author can get away with it so long as he and his publishers lay some claim to moral seriousness?

Well, not any more. Fiction whose violence is comparably explicit and relentless has been published as pure unashamed horror: for instance, Richard Laymon's "Mess Hall" in *Book of the Dead.* The irony is rather that by pretending to comment on a society in which consumerism and the pressure to compete lead to amorality and mayhem, Ellis' novel ends up looking at least as much like a product of that culture as the material it seeks to criticise. Shaun has said that his own most graphic books were written in order to satisfy the tastes of the audience which saw horror in terms of the video nasties (and presumably as a substitute for the nasties once the videos fell foul of censorship). Ellis, on the other hand, suggests strongly that horror on video is part of the problem by having his psychopath rent de Palma's *Body Double* several dozen times as an aid to masturbation, though nowhere does he acknowledge the similarities of scenes in his book to some of the sleaziest post-*Psycho* horror films—*The Toolbox Murders* and *Bloodsucking Freaks* among others. Perhaps this needn't mean that Ellis seeks to set himself above the horror genre, but the packaging certainly does; with its cover design by the Lloyd Ziff Design Group and its author photograph for *Männer Vogue*, the book becomes one more example of the brand-name chic which it monotonously criticises. Of course all fiction—all art—is a product both of the individual and of the culture within which it is created, and this seems to be my cue to talk (as John Gilbert, the editor of *Fear*, requested) about censorship. But first . . .

American Psycho isn't a book I especially want to defend, not least because I have less and less time for prose which gives me no pleasure as prose. Selecting a page of dialogue at random I find this: "Van Patten asks . . ." "McDermott follows . . ." "McDermott suggests . . ." "I correct . . ." "Van Patten says lewdly . . ." "I murmur . . ." "I exclaim . . ." "Van Patten cries out . . ." "I shout . . ." "I suggest . . ." "She asks coyly . . ." "I ask back, coyly . . ." "She whines . . ." "My voice trails off . . ." (and no wonder). This is from one of the book's better scenes, in which the psychopath and some of his friends spend several hours arguing on the phone over where to dine, and I quote it at such length because this kind of overstatement is typical of the book. It is of course told in the first person, and I suppose one could argue that Ellis discourages imitation of his character by making him write badly, but I'm not about to try. Approximately the first two hundred pages of the book consists of scenes like this, in which characters described largely in terms of the brand names they're wearing do nothing at great length (in particular paying for, and failing to eat, increasingly unlikely meals), and the more cynical among us might wonder if all the publicity had the function of assuring the reader that the book eventually hots up. For myself, I found the first half cumulatively funny, while the scenes of violence (the kind which, in splatter fiction, tend to make me wish the author would grow up) are the ugliest and most depressing I have ever read.

If that is the book's justification, it isn't much of one, particularly for a book just three pages short of four hundred. These scenes do ring true as psychotic fantasies, which the book suggests at least some of them are, but both they and the length of the novel offer excess and not much else—indeed, the length looks like an attempt to compensate for a lack of plot and insight. If none of this is a reason to admire the novel, nor is it a reason to ban it. I'm increasingly convinced that censorship is a method used by a culture to deny what it has itself produced, and *American Psycho* is in every way a product of its time.

Time moves on, and so does culture. Who remembers (for

instance) D. Scott-Moncrieff's horror collection *Not for the Squeamish*, sold under the counter on Charing Cross Road after the Second World War? I predict that once the free publicity fades, Ellis' novel will be quickly forgotten, not least because I suspect that most hard-core splatter fans (even if they don't lose patience with the book's pretensions) lack the attention span Ellis appears to expect of his audience, while few other customers are likely to finish the book. In other words, most people are perfectly capable of censoring for themselves if they are allowed to do so, and in the case of *American Psycho* it looks as if they may be given the chance. Perhaps it really is a failed serious novel, or perhaps it is an attempt to market a level of violence beyond the scope of the commercial cinema—a development which my bookseller friend David McClintock, recalling Lovecraft, dubs the "tickle your innards" school of writing—but in any case it seems to me to spend most of its time pretending that its psychopath has nothing to do with the author. Either that means it has less to tell us than Ellis imagines or more than he might like. Let the public decide, and have this opportunity to be honest about itself.

S. Hudson

medved, (med´ved), *n.* a lesser flea; hence, a parasite on an insignificant species. *v. i.* **medved,** *pa. t.* and *pa. p.* **medvedded,** to play the insect. *adj.* **medveddy,** insect-voiced, insect-brained. [Origin obscure: **med**iocre **ved**ette (one who observes the motions of an enemy) and **med**dling **ved**ette have been suggested.]

I MAY WELL NEED TO REMIND MY READERS WHO Michael Medved was. Some years ago he and his brother wrote *The Fifty Worst Movies of All Time,* which was followed by *The Golden Turkey Awards,* or so memory tells me. I glanced through both books. What I disliked most was the sense of medveddy resentment which kept declaring itself, as though the writer begrudged the amount of time spent in watching bad films (as well as films by Eisenstein and Resnais) so as to make money out of complaining how bad they were. Indeed, the books are so clearly the product of a lack of enjoyment and humour that not infrequently they have to invent details to mock. This contempt for the material was even more apparent when Michael Medved introduced a British television season of some of the films, to which numbingly unfunny subtitles had been added, presumably to tell the audience when to laugh. For me the highpoint of the season was the sight of Medved costumed as an ape with a tin head. I recall that in one of the books he expressed regret that the cast of a film which he lampooned had never seen a penny out of it; I very much hope that he paid them a portion of his royalties.

There's nothing wrong with having fun with eccentric books and films. I quite like to share my experiences of odd and obscure fictions, and I intend to do so in this column now and then. Given the augustness of our journal *Necrofile*, let me vouch at the outset for the accuracy of everything I quote.

Here is *The Hounds of Horror*, by S. Hudson (New Horizon, Bognor Regis, 1984)—Hu*d*son, please note. It is a rarity. You will learn why. The sketch on the cover depicts three almost identical scraggy dogs' heads which appear to have been gorily severed but which seem not much more than annoyed by the experience. Let us look within.

The author is nothing if not classical. He states his theme in his foreword: "This story is a sample of what could really happen. The number of large dogs, such as alsatians and Dobermans that are kept as pets or guard dogs, at anybody's whim or fancy is growing every day, a dog licence is laughable as a means of control."

Perhaps this robs the opening of some suspense: "Geoffrey Sanders was wandering about in his back garden, enjoying it, relaxing, enjoying the many years of loving care he had put into it . . . " He blows his nose. "Taking his handkerchief away afterwards, his nose still seemed to be running." In fact he has a nosebleed, and two weeks later, rubbing his nose with a finger makes it bleed again. Topper the Alsatian licks the blood off his hands and turns savage and has to be locked out of the house. When the dog runs away Sanders reports it to the police and shakes his bandaged fingers under their noses. Soon Topper attacks some sheep and then some police. "There was no doubt [a policeman] had felt Topper's teeth and vicious claws a few times." Then a child "was found dead and partly eaten", and newspapers carry the headline "Man eating alsatians loose." Meanwhile guards at a government establishment hear growling and whining which appears to be a signal for their Dobermans to attack them and jump over the perimeter fence.

All this and more is reported with a sobriety reminiscent of

Lovecraft at his—reminiscent of Lovecraft, anyway. Then the dogs, "obviously looking for more recruits, attacked an alsatian breeding kennel with tooth and claw, ripping it wide open". The pack is now some thirty strong, "taking into account the one or two dogs that had joined the pack voluntarily", and by chapter three it's more like two hundred. It's time for a set piece.

"It was Wednesday lunchtime, between twelve and one p.m., just like many lunchtimes that had gone before and would follow after. The location, the junior school, that is children up to eleven years of age at Yewtown." A kitchen worker is careless. "This day, due to pressure of work, or wanting to finish early; and it had happened the day before as well; the kitchen worker propped the door open as she had done in the past, before the dog menace, ever since she had worked there." A "very large collie-alsatian cross" slips unnoticed by her legs, and after she has locked the door and gone away it turns the key with its teeth. "Immediately dogs, large dogs in the main, predominantly brown, some with black or white or both markings, one or two almost all black . . . " I hope you will forgive my elision in the interests of pace. "For a few minutes there was a scene of horrible and terrible carnage" in the dining hall: "a scene of indescribable horror and carnage." Nonetheless, S. Hudson tries. "One small child almost reached the kitchen door. A large shaggy brown dog, jaws slavering, bounded up to one of the tables scattering food, plates, dishes and cutlery in all directions down on to the child . . . " That might indeed tax a writer's descriptive powers. Let me bound ahead to what a party of rescuers finds. "There was blood, bones and flesh and stomach scattered all over the place, among the upturned chairs and tables, the plates, dishes, knives, forks and spoons, mixed together with the potatoes and vegetables, dishes of sweet that had been scattered by the attack. No second look was needed to see there were no survivors." Undertakers and County Coroners' officers clear away the remains, and "every man working in there was at first violently sick".

Clearly it's time for action. The British government asks both America and Canada to send over their best wolf hunters. "As soon as the planes touched down the hunters disembarked attending to the unloading of their baggage personally. It was noticed they all carried rifles which they kept slung over their shoulder all the time."

Their leader is Tex Lane, a Canadian, who proposes to "find out what rules and regulations those dogs stick to, then I will do the same". "The men standing around listening loudly agreed." "The reporters were next. They approached in a body." Tex Lane deals with them and takes the hunters to look at the scene of the carnage—"They could not get into the school, but looked through the windows"—and then, after taking up residence in a country mansion, "the hunters in ones and twos gradually drifted off to their beds".

During the night they're wakened by a canine uproar. Tex "scrambled into a few clothes" in time to watch the hunters' dogs see off a savage pack. The hunters help. "Their aim, in most cases, was unerring, resulting in each case with one less marauding pack dog... The rest fled with their tails between their legs and as they made their escape one of those was brought down by a very accurate long shot."

In the morning Tex interviews Sue Rigton, the teacher who saved some of the children at the school. "She made the telling interesting, covering every little detail." Perhaps you have guessed that a relationship develops, though only on the far side of more than a quarter of the book, pages from which I'll quote just a few lines. "[The hunters' dogs] were off without hesitation with their noses down in full cry." "That was the ruling force at the time and vice versa." "The caretaker had seen, slipping through the shrubbery, first one large dog, then another and another and so on at intervals. He immediately realised what was happening." "A gory battle swayed backwards and forwards in the confines of the quarry... The general appearance of the site was, as in others, an indescribable scene of carnage, blood-soaked, gory, pathetic really, something that should never have been."

When a nuclear power station is attacked Tex and his men are picked up by a fleet of helicopters—"five or six of them, if helicopters in numbers were called 'fleets'"—and Sue Rigton joins the party. "'I am equally as capable as any man... Give me a gun and I will prove to you that I am capable. I didn't spend all my childhood on a farm, in the bush, without learning to take care of myself.'" Once at the power station she is taken aback by "two horribly mutilated half eaten bodies of men... a gory, revolting sickening sight" but soon recovers. "She was one determined little lady and would insist on equality. Tex and the other men admired and respected her, her woman's intuition might come in handy although there was no disputing the fact, however they tried to ignore it, she was a woman, and an attractive one and it was natural to try and protect her."

They press on. "Peering around a wall pillar, Tex first, then Susan looking under his arm resting on the pillar, they could see five large dogs . . . snarling, tearing and scratching at the door of the room which housed the material suspected of being radio active contaminated." "The dog suspected of being Topper turned so it could be better seen." They do away with a bunch of dogs, but Topper escapes, to be pursued into some woods. "Susan wondered what Tex could see, especially as they were jogging."

After a while they come upon a hut and look inside it. "There was a couple of rustic chairs, a rustic table and a couple of rustic bunks." They decide to have a snack. "'Just one other thing, before I forget it,' said Tex, 'I am going to lock the door as a precaution.'" Needless to say, they're besieged. "Both Tex and Susan were very level headed, neither were given to wild flights of fancy, imagining what would happen, were the dogs soon going to get them, nothing at all like that." All the same, "the most frightening part was, several dogs were working on one particular place, not as in the habit of dogs, to move from place to place, while trying to get out, or in, of an enclosure or building, worrying at a place here or a place there". (Do I detect the influence of Samuel Beckett on the author's style?) "Tex fired quickly as he saw a brown nose at the door." The dogs concentrate on biting chunks out of the hut, until Tex and Susan "were really up against it now. The dogs had them with their backs against the wall. They were spinning and turning, firing into one wall and then another." In such a state of confusion anything is possible, and before long "in his wild gyrations round the floor Tex dropped his gun".

Lots of dogs get in but are shot. "Suddenly everything went quiet. It was weird, unearthly, an anti-climax." Surely not. It occurs to the couple or to the author that they can use the furniture to block up the holes and as a shield. More dogs come in. "This was the end, something must have happened to the relief party, they had broken down or had an accident." The couple "fought hard, each using a piece of wood as a club and their guns". The relief party arrives in the nick of time, and Tex sets off after Topper. Susan jogs after him. "He was alert spotting Susan as soon as she came in sight . . . With his extraordinarily acute sense of hearing he heard her coming. He carried on keenly searching the ground for any tell-tale marks as she approached." Off they go up a hill. "They must go on now and hope that the daylight would last." At the top they are confronted by a page of landscape description which I really think I must leave as a treat for anyone who finds a copy of the book. Topper and about thirty dogs cut them off, and Susan falls over the edge of a sheer thousand-foot slope "with a terrible thud of finality. Tex was rooted, it could not be Susan, lively vivacious Susan, with all that spirit knocked out of her."

There are still seven pages to go, and it would be churlish of me to spoil the suspense. Add *The Hounds of Horror* to your want lists now and have Lloyd Currey list it. It doesn't deserve the oblivion in which it is poised to fall.

SHAUN HUTSON

Heathen, by Shaun Hutson. Little, Brown, £14.99. Published on 24 September 1992.

1

Shaun Hutson.

Hutson for Horror.

Hardcore Horror.

His new book is *Heathen.*

Little, Brown will promote it massively in Britain.

They will describe him as "the man who writes what others are afraid even to imagine".

So said the *Sunday Times.*

Heathen will be seen as the ultimate horror.

2

The sentences tend to be short.

And the paragraphs.

And the chapters.

3

Does brief mean terse?

You decide.

"'I thought there was something wrong . . .' Jackie Quinn began. Then, as she looked at Donna, she realised that there was. Something terribly wrong.

"Donna stepped away from the door, allowing Jackie into the hallway.

"'Donna, what's wrong? What is it? You look terrible,' Jackie said quickly, shocked by her friend's appearance . . . "

4

Here is a longer paragraph, describing a man who has just jumped fifteen feet off a staircase.

"The cuboid and navicular bones in his foot had simply disintegrated under the impact and, so huge was the force with which he fell, the left fibula had snapped, part of it impacting into the talus at the top of the foot, the other part tearing through both the flesh of his shin and also the material of his trousers. A jagged point of bone projected from the leg like an accusing finger. The man screamed again as he toppled to one side."

Descriptions like this are what Hutson is known for.

It comes on page 101.

Pretty late for the first such scene in a Hutson horror.

The publishers say it is a mainstream book, but Hutson is loyal to his image.

5

And to his images.

Donna, the widowed heroine, smiles thinly on page 12.

And on page 22 she smiles thinly again.

And page 30.

Not to mention 52.

On 53 she "allowed herself a thin smile".

Eight pages later "she too smiled thinly".

It must be catching, because now a policeman is doing it as well.

But Donna reclaims the expression on page 62.

On page 75 we find her "managing a thin smile".

Her sister has a go on page 87.

At least Donna hesitates on page 114 before doing it again.

She doesn't pause before smiling thinly on 122, however.

And here's an attacker picking up the habit on page 148.

While on page 161 her husband's solicitor does it.

Donna consolidates her record for it on page 173.

On page 201 she goes for the world record.

And on page 229.

And 281 too.

Even the policeman who smiles thinly on page 309 can't overtake her now.

On the other hand, Hutson writes "He shuffled his fingers together like fleshy playing cards" just once.

In this book.

He must be proud of the image, because he used it in *Nemesis* too.

6

Here are some more sentences from *Heathen*.

"His eyes bulged madly in their sockets, like bloodshot ping-pong balls threatening to burst from his skull."

"Donna turned as Ryker came at her, avoiding his clumsy attempts to grab her."

"Other trains, some also newly arrived, stood emptily by platforms, their passengers long since departed."

"The door was starting to split from its merciless battering."

"Julie threw back the cellar hatch and came hurtling forth like a maddened trap-door spider, brandishing the hammer."

"Charlie Chaplin waved to anyone who cared to look up, frozen forever in that pose."

"Donna licked her tongue across her dry lips."

7

Heathen is about the Sons of Midnight, a superhuman occult group which Donna tracks down.

She seems pretty superhuman herself.

She is thrown out of a high-speed train in a tunnel.

Her attacker is "pulped" by the wall and the train, but Donna grabs the frame of the window in the door she has just been thrown out of.

A rescuer pulls the door shut, and Donna's feet are dragged through the weeds beside the track before he lifts her in through the window.

How has she ended up holding on to the outside of the door?

Pretty damned occult, if you ask me.

And all she has to show for her experience are ripped stockings and a few scratches on her shins and ankles.

But compared with the thugs the Sons of Midnight hire, she's a wimp.

They punch people "with incredible force".

And use guns to poke people in the face "with incredible force".

One of the thugs is shot through the bridge of the nose, the bullet "taking out an eye as it exited".

Two sentences later both his eyes are "still staring wide in shocked surprise".

That's nothing compared to the surprise of the reader.

Another, Kellerman, is shot point-blank through the calf with a .38, while a hammer hits his crony Ryker in the mouth before cracking his skull above one eye and mangling one hand.

The next day both men are able to drive cars in pursuit of our heroine, and together with their leader Farrell they trap her in a waxworks.

Perhaps only the Three Stooges could do these scenes justice, or the one where Farrell sprays Donna's cottage with the contents of a full clip from a sub-machine gun before reminding his colleagues "We need her alive."

But then Hutson's seems to be a world where things don't work as they should.

When Donna drives her Volvo over "a gentle crest" at seventy miles an hour the car leaves the ground for "precious seconds" before "finally crashing back down to earth".

When she makes a phone call, the units on her phone card are deducted before the call is answered.

When she shoots a villain in the stomach at "point-blank range" with a .38, the bullet continues "ploughing through intestines" but only manages to travel "close to his spine", where it lodges. A second bullet, presumably at the same range, hits him in the shoulder.

A ring on an electric cooker manages to be "almost white hot". Maybe that's an effect of the unusual conditions under which the air in the "hot and clammy" kitchen is "warm and dry".

Yet Hutson seems to want to be precise.

The book contains almost as many time-checks as a speaking clock.

And we're told the speeds of bullets, distances between a torture victim and an electric ring, a count of bullets as they leave a gun, the wattage of every light-bulb, and all the names of the people portrayed in the waxworks.

"Sean Connery, George Lazenby, Roger Moore and Timothy Dalton stood around Paxton as he searched."

"Danny Kaye, Liza Minnelli and Judy Garland looked on blankly."

And so on at intervals for fourteen pages.

Perhaps this is a new kind of atmospheric writing.

8

Sometimes the prose includes words horror writers are apparently supposed to use.

"As if from nowhere, Ryker and Kellerman appeared from the shadows. Like two spectres rising from the umbra they rose up before the women."

"Staggered" might seem more appropriate, given what they suffered the previous day from the gun and the hammer.

Here is Donna confronting two of the superhuman occultists.

"'Who are you?' she asked, seeing the pallid skin that hung in festering coils from their faces."

And here are some sentences from a fictitious book about them, supposedly written at least as recently as the middle of the eighteenth century.

"Som would kill the unborn child or chilldren of women and

som ript open their bellys to take the child as offering. The skull of that child would always be theres . . . All these Evils are set down in great and Anciente Bookes called Grimoires . . . "

In his very last letter H. P. Lovecraft commented about a pulp writer: "What sort of insanity gets hold of some of these birds . . . when they try to represent the diction of an age which after all is, historically speaking, essentially modern? . . . See what a mess of quasi-Tudor bunk the author had . . . 'booke', 'worlde', 'bodie and soule'. . . "

Still, it wouldn't be quite fair to apply this to Hutson's invented text.

The second edition of the *Oxford English Dictionary* maintains that the world "grimoire" was first used in 1849.

That must be a mistake.

9

Of course *Heathen* has a plot.

The grimoire of the Sons of Midnight keeps them immortal.

Donna's late husband has infiltrated the club and stolen the book.

His solicitor brings her a posthumous letter.

Her sister brings it when she meets Donna at Euston.

More than two hours later Donna still hasn't opened it, and "the obvious thing seemed to be to retire to bed."

That must take some self-control when you're convinced your husband has been murdered.

She does take time to load her Smith and Wesson .38, her Beretta 92, her .357 and her Charter Arms .22.

And she runs her index finger over the envelope.

Smiling thinly.

Then she goes to bed, though not before running her fingertips over the envelope.

10

It contains the key to a safety deposit box.

You might expect the box to contain the grimoire.

No, just the address where the grimoire is hidden.

But not where at that address.

Of course Donna's late husband was the author of fifteen massive bestsellers.

If the Sons of Midnight have infiltrated "every branch of the Media, Politics and the Church" and "they have members everywhere" and "no one can be trusted", why is he wasting her time with this rigmarole when he wants her to destroy the grimoire?

Perhaps that is how authors of massive bestsellers think.

11

Heathen has a twist in the tail.

If the above had not made nonsense of the book, this would.

Hutson says he gets more cynical with every book he writes.

Indeed.

Pete Atkins

ONE SCARY SCINTILLATING SCRUPULOUS SCOUSE SCRIBE

BLAME BASCOMBE'S. THAT WAS ONE OF THE VERY few shops in 'sixties Liverpool where one could find books of fantasy and horror, not to mention science fiction—magazines as well, both second-hand and new. It stood on Smithdown Road, about a mile from Penny Lane, that coleopterally celebrated site, and close to a public park named the Mystery. We shall return there later. Mr Bascombe was the shopkeeper, an oldish man who seemed to smell of pulp paper and whose skin increasingly displayed the colour of that material. He might be seen to flinch from naked flames, and once, through the dusty window, I seemed to glimpse him crumpling like a mass of pages as he passed deep into the dim interior. I was one of his frequent customers for books that, at the time, I was convinced could be found nowhere else. Some of my visits yielded none. Decades later I learned why: another Bascombe regular was Pete Atkins, and many were the tastes we share, as the sharp-eyed reader may discover.

Perhaps sometimes I almost saw Pete fleeing the shop with a tattered issue of *Weird Tales* in his clutch, or peering out between the American paperbacks bearing half-crown stickers on the rickety shelves that occupied the darkest section of the shop, away from the counter with its jars of sweets, but we didn't meet until the eighties. As to where and when, rumours accumulate, and I think it's entirely appropriate that, aging bugger that I am, I can't with any certainty recall our first meeting: it seems as if we've always been friends. It didn't take him long to become an honorary uncle to Tammy and Mat, regaling them in restaurants with his version of Chucky from *Child's Play* (for this and other reasons it's amazing that some of our favourite eateries still let us in), consuming chilli peppers on a dare from Tammy, riding roller coasters in Blackpool with Mat because neither Jenny nor I could be coaxed. Thank heaven Szechuan cuisine hadn't then caught on in Britain, or he might have been challenged to drink the chilli oil (knowing Pete, he'd have done it too). Alas, once he began to write for Hollywood he went to live in that part of the world, and now our get-togethers involve crossing the ocean.

For quite a few years Pete was an honorary American—that is, he adopted the style. Rock singers frequently do, and of course Pete has been one of those, and I'm only sorry that I've yet to hear his band or see a performance by the Rolling Darkness Revue. It's less usual for writers on this side of the ocean to seek to sound American, though Eric Frank Russell did for decades—the editor of *Astounding* thought Russell read more like an American than most of the native contributors—and Pete Crowther often gives his own literary voice a Yank. In Pete Atkins' case the change of nationality has been completed, even if in person he sounds less mid-Atlantic than our friend Clive Barker, whom he followed to Hollywood. Indeed, when he appeared as a barman in *Hellraiser 3* his voice was apparently insufficiently American for the context, and so someone else's emerges from his mouth. I believe that sometimes he wakes in the darkest hours to feel that voice bumbling like an insect between his lips, and coming out with words he hopes he'll never understand.

The *Hellraiser* franchise brought him into films, of course. Trust a Scouser to blag his way in, assuring the producer of the first of the series that he'd already written screenplays. That said, he has an instinct for playing the movie game that I suspect I'll never match. Once he and Dennis Etchison took me to a meeting in Los Angeles to discuss a proposed television horror show, where I floundered and demurred when asked to synopsise some tales of mine as potential material. That Pete is equal to such meetings and all the demands of making movies is apparent from his film work, not least his Wishmaster creation, a memorable monster. He brings more than professionalism to the screen: a love of myths, for instance, and the ability to create his own as well as drawing on the great tradition of the fantastic. Who else would have thought of including an echo of Cocteau's great *Orphée* in the second Cenobite film?

However—as with most writers who have spent time in the Hollywood sun—his finest achievements are in prose. There are no budgetary restrictions on language, after all—no compromises with casting, no restrictions on locations. In particular no special effects in the cinema are capable of embodying the products of his luxuriant imagination, even given recent developments in CGI. *Morningstar* revitalises the vampire theme before the novel even begins (with its subtitle alone, *The Vampires of Summer*, the kind of phrase that encapsulates so much evocative suggestiveness that some of us would risk applying to the Wishmaster for the secret). You might describe the book as supernatural noir if that wouldn't omit all the gorgeous colours of the prose. *Big Thunder* uses an even larger canvas (or—if we want to think in terms of imaginary cinema—where *Morningstar* is in Cinemascope and Technicolor, *Big Thunder* goes to IMAX). It's both a pulp tale in the very best sense—after all, Hammett and Chandler and Lovecraft and Clark Ashton Smith were pulp writers too—and a great tribute to those chunky magazines. It's also such a cornucopia of the fantastic that a lesser author could easily lose control of the material, but (to cobble yet one more metaphor together and pinch some alliteration from another pulp star, Bob Bloch) Pete is in charge of his menagerie of myth, ruling the ring with his wickedly witty whip. His most recently published novel *Moontown* shines with an uncanny light that illuminates terrors we might have thought we'd left behind in childhood (although we devotees of horror may be glad to find we haven't). I only wish that Mr Sponge and Mr Scrotum, those forgotten masters of visceral slapstick (splatstick, you might call it, or perhaps you'd rather I didn't) had reappeared at the finale rather than just being advertised on a poster. I'm sure they had guest roles in one of Tubby Thackeray's rarer films—was it *Tubby's Tuberous Tangle* or the legendary unreleased *Tubby's Tentative Tendrils*? At any rate, I hope to encounter them again. They deserve at least a short story to themselves.

Speaking of short stories (I say as a sly ruse), I introduced Pete's first collection, *Wishmaster and Other Stories*, in 1999. It deserves to be back in print—indeed, to be embedded in a bigger book of his. Much of what I said back then was this:

Let me begin with the afterword to "Aviatrix". The title is indeed a beautiful word, though when I said as much to a group of drinking buddies the furthest left of them said with unassailable seriousness that maybe some people used to think "nigger" was. That none of us had any evidence of that was apparently no reason why it should be denied equal standing with facts. I've often wondered if the list (of words not to be used by Scouse public servants) that inspired Pete's tale forbade the use of the term "dominatrix". These days the public libraries in Liverpool sport notices declaring that racism is unwelcome therein, a worthy enough sentiment but, put like that, capable of tempting the contentious to ask loudly at the counter for a copy of *The Swarthy Crewman of the Narcissus* (to be on the safe side, make that *Crew Member*) or the score of Debussy's *Comical Dance of an Ethnic Doll* for piano solo.

I don't mean to imply that Liverpool is exceptional. I can't resist the opportunity to cite another shining example of correctness. Back in the nineties, members of the Society of Authors received a glossy brochure from the Invisible Children Conference, at which "150 key image makers" (invisible indeed, since none of them was identified) "argued for a change in the way disabled people are portrayed". Among the images listed as unacceptable were Richard III, Douglas Bader, Clifford Chatterley, Long John Silver... Anyone naïve enough to think I'm making any of this up may apply to me for a photocopy of the document. Horror and fantasy were well represented in the list, of course: Dr Strangelove, the Beast from *Beauty and the Beast*, the Morlocks, Captain Hook, the X-Men, the Time Bandits, the Mask, the Hunchback of Notre Dame, Freddy Krueger... Presumably all one hundred and fifty key image makers resembled Mr Magoo (also on their docket) in being too shortsighted to notice that Freddy was never a cripple. It seems I'm one myself. If I take off my glasses I can't read these words on the computer screen, but I can still see that the Invisible Children inventory is bollocks. Enough! Turn to "Aviatrix" and chase away the foregoing with a piece of fantasy that knows it is, and a fine example too. I find its sense of awe very moving, as the best tales of terror are.

"Milk of Paradise" and "Faithless" are early tales, and I imagine their author regards them with a mixture of paternal pride and a necromancer's fascination with what he has managed to raise from the grave, curiously incomplete objects that perform strange tricks with ungainly charm before abruptly vanishing. They are more than excused by all the technique he's learned since—here are several deft examples of that most difficult of fictional forms, the short short story, of which "For Your Immediate Attention" may not be in your copy of the book—God help you if it is. As for "Dr Arcadia", it is perhaps the most astonishing performance—witty, sometimes openly comic, yet poignant and visionary too—in a book full of wonders that led me to expect even more surprises in the future from my fellow Wacker.

Some showed up in *Spook City*, Angus Mackenzie's anthology of Liverpool tales for PS, where Pete confirms his Dicky Sam identity with admirable thoroughness. "Eternal Delight" confronts us with a squirmy apparition as vivid as any of Clive Barker's and combines gruesomeness with stylish Scouse humour to produce a flavour unique in my experience. It even celebrates the kind of emendation of official signs we're used to in Liverpool, and ends in an explosion of Liverpudlian anarchy to a Mersey beat. I suspect John Lennon would have been rocked. "Here Comes a Candle" is a companion piece to "Aviatrix", taking on revisionism. Distorting fairy tales to appease contemporary squeamishness simply invites revenge from their dark side, and the monster that appears in the final paragraphs is by no means unlike the kind of illustration we used to see in books for the young. (I'm reminded that an edition of *The Princess and the Goblin* published in the 1970s didn't just delete the unnerving illustrations by Arthur Hughes but censored George Macdonald's text as well, rendering it less grotesque).

While trawling the Internet to make myself seem more informed

I saw some curious transformations overtake Pete and his tales; the Atkins Crunchy Morning Start breakfast cereal appeared by the magic of Google, followed by a favourite foodstuff of FatSecret Members: the products of Morningstar Farms, apparently part of some versions of the Atkins Diet. (I'm more concerned about that secret fat and how it's hidden from the world, but perhaps it's better not to know.) At last I found what I wanted—an interview with Pete. I hope he'll forgive me for reviving the comment that Paula Guran used to epitomise his view, because I believe it does so very well still: "My two favourite authors in the field are Arthur Machen and Algernon Blackwood. Now both of these gents are—trust me—more than capable of making you check the lights and lock the doors but frankly that's the least of their skills. The inculcation of metaphysical awe is their ultimate aim . . . "

No wonder he wrote "The Mystery", the most recent of his tales in *Spook City*. While the Mystery is indeed a park in Liverpool, it's also the perfect word for Pete's underlying (can I say favourite?) theme. The story is founded on several Scouse legends or traditions—guess which are real—but it leads us into the startling vistas of his imagination. It demonstrates that his true territory is that infinite one, the dream. So does "Between the Cold Moon and the Earth", for my taste the most extraordinary of his *Spook City* quartet, and in my view a masterpiece. The mirror that is "just too tired" is one of many splendidly turned phrases I envy in his work, but the final stream of poignant incantatory prose may well be his finest writing to date. I'm happy to tell you it had me in tears.

Well, I think I've embarrassed Pete enough. Let me just say he's a great friend and a genial chap with whom I've shared many an adventure and a meal (sometimes synonymous). It's my pleasure to welcome him and his delightful wife Dana Middleton back to these shores—they're too seldom here. Buy them a drink and perhaps Pete will tell you all about the lobster puppet Billy No-Arse. If you're dining he may even demonstrate.

Bob Shaw

Bob Shaw was a friend of mine and a writer of considerable talent. If those aren't reasons enough for me to speak of him in *Necrofile*, I can add that I encouraged him to contribute two horror stories to anthologies of mine—"Love Me Tender" in *New Terrors* and "Cutting Down" in *Fine Frights*. I'll return to them in due course, but here are my memories of him and his delightful wife Sadie, as near to chronological order as I can cobble together.

Jenny and I first met the Shaws at Two Rivers in Weybridge on the Thames. This was Dave and Ruth Kyle's house while they were living in Britain, and a splendid pair of hosts they were. In the very early seventies they put up with most of the Liverpool Science Fiction Group, not to mention our hangovers, for an entire weekend. Other guests drifted in from various parts of the country, and I still remember the awe I experienced on hearing that Bob Shaw was imminent. I'd read and much admired his science fiction novel *The Palace of Eternity*, a visionary book that also features aliens quite loathsome enough for Lovecraft, and his short story "Light of Other Days", which I'd convinced myself had gained itself a Nebula award—I obviously felt it should have. Bob being Bob, he'd hardly arrived before proposing an exodus to the nearest pub. Jenny and I rode in his and Sadie's car, which struck me as being as immense as I would have expected from a writer far more famous and significant than me. In the pub I'm sure any conversation I made was deferential and worth forgetting, as I've done.

Years passed, and Bob and I exchanged greetings at various science fiction conventions, usually in the bar. Bob's salutation would almost always be a low-voiced pun or quip in his inimitable Belfast accent (so inimitable that when early in our friendship I rang him up with an attempt to mimic it he congratulated me on my Scottish brogue). During this period he and Sadie and their children moved to the Lake District—to Ulverston, Stan Laurel's birthplace. It's a small town which they were soon to leave, apparently because its size kept Bob too close to the temptations of his drinking buddies and the pub. The Shaws ended up in Warrington, half an hour's drive from Merseyside, and for the rest of their lives we saw a good deal more of them.

By then I'd coaxed "Love Me Tender" out of Bob, my instincts having told me that he could write horror. Later that year (1979) he published *Dagger of the Mind*, which sports some gruesome flayed apparitions and the nightmarishly static clientele of a boarding-house invaded by an extraterrestrial influence. Given the delays inherent in publishing, I assume that book was already written rather than owing any of its horror to my approach. Bob's two short tales for me are science fiction too, but resemble Robert Bloch (whom he admired) or EC comics (which I don't know that he read) in their macabrely punning titles and their insistence that whichever character suffered the payoff of the tale should have done something to deserve it. Once he told me that felt horror fiction should be this kind of moral tale. I don't know whether our friendship led him to spice any of his later work with horror: I'm thinking especially of the last lines of the prologue of *Fire Pattern* (a novel he wrote in some haste to ensure he produced the first science fiction rationale of spontaneous human combustion). As for his fondness for puns, sometimes it could lead one to find them where they hadn't been intended: he was quite piqued to learn that Jenny had assumed he'd called a book *The Ragged Astronauts* as a jokey reference to *The Ragged-Arsed Philanthropists* (which we understand to be the suppressed title of Robert Tressell's socialist novel). At times he seemed to regret being so appreciated for entertaining science fiction fandom with his humour that he'd received two Hugo Awards for fan writing—I know he wished he could have won one for his fiction, as he deserved.

I suspect the subject of the morality of horror fiction came up during one of our discussions in a pub, quite possibly Stanley's Cask, just a short walk (or, at Bob's insistence, a drive) from my house. With its bare floorboards it wasn't the kind of pub Sadie cared for, though she liked pubs well enough, and so when the Shaws stayed overnight with us rather than drive drunkenly home, it was where the men adjourned to the next morning. Little was said there that couldn't have been said elsewhere, though Bob did once muse aloud that since Sadie never left an odour after using the toilet he wondered whether she could be an android. We often took the opportunity to talk about writing, and Bob admitted that he envied my having a wife who read my work. Once he asked me what I would do if I sold some film rights for so much that I would never again have to depend on my writing for income. I said I'd try to take more time over my prose—Bob said he would give up writing.

All the same, we weren't so different. One reason I'm doing my best to present him objectively is that I see a good deal of myself in him, and I'll suggest that many if not all of my readers who are also writers may. If we can find a way of avoiding our current project while persuading ourselves that we're writing, many of us will. Even writing this column is an excuse for stopping work for the day on an especially difficult chapter of *The Pact of the Fathers.* Gentlemanly always, Bob would write a thank-you letter to Jenny after a stay at our house, but I do wonder if as well as showing courtesy this helped him feel he was writing. (My own wariness of this trap is why I'm such an unsatisfactory correspondent to friends, and the reason why I try not to let email take up too much of my time.)

Eventually it became apparent that Bob's career as a writer was at least as shaky as mine, then and now. His novel *Ground Zero Man* had been sniffed at by his publishers on the grounds that it wasn't a science fiction novel, which he had a contract to write, and had only been accepted for a lower advance. *The Fugitive Worlds,* the third book of his Overland trilogy, was rejected by a publisher of the first two volumes because it supposedly differed too much from them. A feminist editor made him rewrite a good deal of *Killer Planet,* a science fiction novel for youngsters, to make the young girl in it a more positive model for female readers. (Bob was fond of quoting the editor's marginal note on the scene in which the boy hero pilots a spacecraft to a dangerous landing with the girl as his passenger. "What is she doing now?" the editor wanted to know, to which Bob's answer was old-fashioned and terse.) He may have told me some of this one summer day at a picnic table in the back garden as we saw off a three-litre wine box together (the kind of drinking only women would do in a Kingsley Amis novel, and I wish those of my readers who don't know which one the pleasure of finding out). Still, what's a writer to do? Carry on writing, of course, and he seemed to be doing that successfully until early 1991, when Sadie was unexpectedly hospitalised. The next day she died of liver failure.

Bob blamed himself. At the funeral he had to be supported along the aisle of the church, and I doubted that he would survive long. In fact he survived for almost five years, but mostly that was all he did. He produced a small amount of new work, including a guide to writing science fiction, for which I believe he sold the copyright outright (an indication of how desperate he was), and the first of a planned series of sequels to his 1977 comic science fiction novel, *Who Goes Here?* This was *Warren Peace,* and Jenny's and my copy bears the inscription "Hoping that the jokes herein are not too familiar". Sadly, the problem is that they are not only too few but separated by wodges of the worst and most ponderous writing Bob ever published. Indeed, John Clute's *Interzone* review of the book is a memorably painful one, which can't quite conceal its determination to be as kind as possible under all the circumstances. Bob's working method may not have been helpful—he would revise each chapter of a novel as it was finished before starting the first draft of the next—but what writer can presume to tell another how to write? At times I thought of suggesting to him that instead of struggling to cheer himself up he should attempt a memoir of Sadie, but I never got around to intruding. I still don't know if I should have, though I would have tried if the fine example of Brian Aldiss's *When the Feast is Finished* had existed. Telling the immediate or recent truth can certainly be a way of overcoming writer's block, in my experience.

Other problems may have made it harder for him to work. In order to avoid bankruptcy he had to sell his and Sadie's last house and rent a smaller one. He contracted bowel cancer and underwent a colostomy operation, though this did lead to a glimpse of the old Bob: having discovered that the colostomy bag was the perfect place to secrete cannabis for importation, he declared that he looked forward to being asked by a Customs officer what was in the bag. "Just some shit," he would have enjoyed responding. I appreciated the gag, but I must admit I didn't subsequently share a joint with him.

In his last year he married Nancy Tucker, a fan he'd known while Sadie was alive, and moved to America. I know Nancy took a good deal of care of him. Nevertheless many of us felt that when he died in early 1996 in Warrington, having flown there for a brief visit, he had returned to say goodbye to his old haunts in the knowledge that he was dying. His funeral was held there, at the same church as Sadie's, after which his good (now, alas, late) friend Henry Newton arranged a wake. It was the kind of fun Bob would have wanted it to be. Much was drunk and many stories told of him by friends. A display of his work reminded us of his achievements as a writer, but the tales reminded us of Bob the man. I see I've flinched from printing any of his puns, so let me end with the one I read out at the wake. It's from the copy of *Orbitsville* he signed to me: "to Ramsey Campbell, the critic who has shown me the most Mersey." I hope any groans that greet this will be affectionate. They certainly were at the wake.

JOHN BRUNNER

AND AFTER MEMORIES OF BOB SHAW, SOME OF John Brunner.

I wrote last time about having been in awe of meeting Bob, even though I'd seen print for years. My first encounter with John was not long after my entry into both fandom and being published. Pat Kearney, my first publisher (in his fanzine *Goudy*), took it upon himself to introduce me to authors he knew at my first convention, held at Easter 1962 in Harrogate. Such was my sense of my own lowliness that I never dared to speak to Tom Boardman, the guest of honour, even though he'd sent me an encouraging editorial letter four years before, while E. C. Tubb and Michael Moorcock struck me as possessing the stature of Easter Island statues. Having been advised that I wrote in the manner of Lovecraft, Mike leaned down from the height and boomed that he didn't like him. Perhaps such encounters provoked me into drinking even more beer, only to deliver myself of the vari-ous results into the sink in my room that night, en-suite bathrooms being a thing of the future for fandom. The results were waiting to confront me the next day, and had to be poked doggedly down the plughole with a souvenir convention pencil before I reeled forth from the room. A vast Chinese lunch to which Pat Kearney managed to entice me proved to be a fine aid to recuperation. I don't think pallid Campbell in his sombre suit and nondescript shirt and tie and (as August Derleth had it) beetling horn-rimmed spectacles met John Brunner in Harrogate, but soon I did.

Years passed. Word circulated that I had a book to my name. Science fiction conventions were yet to admit panels on horror to their programmes, but I found myself invited onto a panel of new writers at an Eastercon. Who were the other red-faced gawky victims? Perhaps someone may recall more about this than I do, though Lord protect us from a photograph. All I remember is that the moderator of the panel was John Brunner. I believe I was already aware of him. He was at the height of his extended youth, urbane, satyr-bearded, keen-eyed, with a voice so clear and precise that, along with his pedagogical manner, it struck terror into at least one member of the panel. Can he really have asked where we got our ideas? I'm sure that's an impression my mind tried to erect in retrospect as a defence. I suppose he enquired into our working methods, and I babbled in response that in order to generate a tale I went either for a walk or to the toilet, true enough then. "One way or another," I declared with the unconscious humour of the desperate, "I produce something." I'm glad to say that is the extent of my memory, except for a sense of having imitated a sack of potatoes in my chair for the rest of the interminable event.

No doubt I slunk away from it as swiftly as I could, though I seem to remember John telling me—it would have to have been with a good deal of kindness—that I'd done well, or some such phrase. I imagine I avoided him thereafter as the loftiest witness of my ignominious performance, but not too many years later I realised he was at least an acquaintance. His fondness for puns even worse than Bob Shaw's helped to humanise him, as did his inviting me to join him and his wife Marjorie for breakfast at a later Eastercon—Buxton, I believe it was, in 1968. I enthused about his novel *Stand on Zanzibar*, which won the Hugo Award, and a mention of the influence of John dos Passos on its method led Marjorie and me into a discussion of that writer. "Yes, yes, dear," John intervened, perhaps with a laugh, "but we're talking about *me*."

One suspects that he may have been a difficult person to live with. Show us a writer who isn't, comes the cry. Well, maybe, but with John it was sometimes public. Jenny still recalls hearing him snap from the stage at yet another convention "If my wife is in the audience can she bring me my drink, please?" A female fan whose anonymity I shall respect stayed overnight at the Brunners' house and found John proposing to share her bed. "It's all right," he assured her, "Marjorie knows." Before long much of British fandom did, but it only added to John's reputation, based on his often turning up at conventions with yet another younger woman, generally darker-skinned than he. Perhaps this was literary research, since he wrote several effective novels from the viewpoint of Max Curfew, a black South African.

I mentioned his puns above, for which he also had a reputation, and not only in English—at Eurocons he translated his own speeches and joked in the other language too. (He was one of the very few people of my acquaintance who I believe understood all the elusive allusions of Nabokov's *Ada*.) His English puns were often the kind one saw coming but couldn't avoid, and John rarely committed them to print. I do have a postcard from him dated 13 February 1989, however:

I hit on a title the other day which I have no use for but might serve you for a horror or terror collection. And I can't bear to sequester unshared puns . . . A STEP IN THE FRIGHT DIRECTION? If you use it, I'll settle for credit* and a few copies for my shelf. (Did I mean that? Shouldn't I have said my<u>self?</u> No, I'm shtill too shober to shtart shlurring my shyllablesh . . .)

And the inclusion of something by me!

On the other side of the postcard, and on the rest of the correspondence I received from him, John has stamped a quote from Heine: "Where books are burned, in the end people too get burned." By now—indeed, years earlier—our relationship had rearranged itself, when he became another of the science fiction writers I invited into *New Terrors* (or, as Marc Laidlaw retitled it, *Newt Errors*). John sent me a tale from a series which had run in *The Magazine of Fantasy and Science Fiction*, this one having been rejected as too bleak, I think. That was the general reaction to a later story, "The Clerks of Domesday", which I grabbed for *Fine Frights*. It wasn't then apparent to me that I was one of the few editors still publishing his work, and I only gradually became aware of the desperation he was concealing whenever we met at subsequent science fiction conventions and he enquired whether I was buying for any new horror anthologies. His situation was that virtually all his books—fifty of them? sixty? more?—were out of print, and nobody wanted to revive them.

In some of my darker moments I imagine I resemble poor Frank Belknap Long in destroying whatever talent I may once have had while convincing myself I'm improving as a writer; at others I'm afraid I may end up like John. A prominent British fantasy and science fiction editor told me how saddened he was not to be able to republish John's backlist, but sympathy pays no bills. Recently the same editor has been sad about me. It's grimly ironic that John should have viewed horror fiction as the route to take when it was already starting to collapse under the weight of too much rubbish, and I feel both complimented and dismayed that in an interview he said my tales had helped him see the genre could be used for social comment. That had been his aim for much of his career, and perhaps too few readers wanted it, for all that it had earned him a Hugo. Perhaps his curse was that he was able to see and to foresee the worst—he was fond of recalling that one of his tales had predicted computer viruses—and had no patience with readers who complained about fiction that showed what was wrong but failed to tell them what to do about it. His books tended to be didactic, but other science fiction writers lecture their readers more relentlessly and have hordes come back for more. Maybe the secret of those writers is to be right-wing.

John—the composer of the Campaign for Nuclear Disarmament's marching song—would never have pretended about that or, I believe, anything else. Some fans may have been daunted by the breadth of his learning. (Our daughter once commented that John was the only person she knew who would have told us over dinner how many Popes were named Urban. This was in a Portuguese restaurant on Jersey, where he also gravely informed a waiter who asked us if we'd enjoyed the food that the Portuguese had been too busy creating Henry the Navigator to excel in their cuisine.) Nevertheless he did his best to keep some of himself to himself, even though his private state was worsening. Marjorie had died, to be succeeded by an Oriental lady, Li-Yi, and their relationship was so volatile it sometimes revealed itself in public spats. His blood pressure was mounting. For a while he used cannabis to keep it down, only to find that smoking the drug began to bring panic as an inevitable side effect. He was prescribed other medication, but I understand from friends we had in common that the unwanted effects were at least as bad. In 1994 I had two late-night calls from him.

Some of the content remains too personal to set down here. In the first call he describes himself as living in a horror story. His voice is slow and shaky, and he seems to have difficulty in remembering his phone number. "I would love to hear from friends," he finishes. "I'm scared." I admit that when I played back the tape the next day I didn't respond, having decided, however cravenly, that he might be embarrassed to acknowledge the call. The same went for the later message, where his voice is far more slurred. "John Brunner is living through a genuine horror story," he says, and much else before "Ramsey, I am terrified. I'm desperate. I must have help." I was by no means alone in receiving such calls, and I gather those of his friends who lived closer intervened as best they could. He still maintained his public persona when he was able, and was in witty evidence at conventions. But it was at one such—the 1995 Worldcon in Glasgow—that he suffered a heart attack at a party for members of Science Fiction Writers of America. The next day he was dead.

I wish I could say that his work lives on, and I suppose it does, at least in second-hand catalogues and on collectors' shelves (though at his last conventions he had started to despair of the dealers' rooms, from which books were being ousted by all sorts of less literate stuff). But *Waterstone's Guide to Science Fiction, Fantasy and Horror* (published by easily the most enterprising British bookshop chain) lists a solitary book by John in print, *Stand on Zanzibar*. It's far short of a fitting memorial. *Weird Tales* celebrated him by showcasing his work in a special issue not many years before his death, and I know he was pleased with that. Perhaps his work will be revived in an edition aimed at the cognoscenti, as the short fiction of Dick and Sturgeon has been. But oh that all the writers who deserve it should be supported when they need it! A fantasy, I know, and unworthy of John. I recommend my readers to seek out his tales of fantasy instead. He wrote some good ones.

K. W. JETER

K. W. JETER IS ONE OF THE MOST VERSATILE AND uncompromising writers of imaginative fiction to have emerged from the seventies. Despite these qualities, he is beginning to attract the appreciation he deserves.

In his afterword to Jeter's first novel *Dr Adder,* Philip K. Dick complained that "the [science fiction] field has been growing weak . . . a stale timidity has crept over it." Indeed, and no doubt that's one reason why *Dr Adder* went unpublished for twelve years. Having myself been told by publisher after publisher that my second novel was unpublishable, I can imagine how much more dispiriting it must feel to be informed that one's first novel is. Jeter could hardly be blamed if he had decided to spend the rest of his career manufacturing commercial fiction, however sad the spectacle might have been (as it was, for instance, in the later books of John Franklin Bardin). But Jeter seems to have continued to listen to the inner voice that prompted him to write that novel, and I suggest that his tenaciousness deserves not only our admiration but our gratitude.

A new writer can gain an audience by giving one that already exists more of what it seems to want (always assuming that the audience hasn't changed its tastes by the time the writer's work sees print), while a writer who gains fame by having something of his own to offer may succumb to the temptation to retain his audience by imitating his successes. But there are also audiences for writers whose appeal is their unpredictability, and those audiences are likely to be the most loyal—that is, once the publishers have let them know about the work. Alas, too many publishers seem to regard unpredictability as a cardinal sin, and punish it by packaging it as conventionally as possible, a good way of alienating its likely audience.

I suspect that Jeter may have suffered from this attitude in the past. I blame the packaging of some editions of some of his books for my failure to read his work until I was asked to write this introduction (though the reading, let me say, was far more of a pleasure than a task). Imagine the mutters of dissatisfaction at editorial meetings (the places some editors always seem to be when writers phone) and sales conferences! What sort of a name is K. W. Jeter, anyway? He won't even use his first names to make it sound less jagged. What kind of a writer does he think he is? Science fiction, except he wrote some kind of mad thing set in Victorian England that might fit in the sci-fi section of the bookstores, only he's written all these horror books as well that don't even read like Stephen King, and just to make it worse, his sci-fi novels aren't enough alike that they could be packaged as a trilogy... "Metaphysically related"? If there's any of our sales people who use language like that they can look for work somewhere else...

Meanwhile, it seems to me, Jeter becomes increasingly true to himself. *Dr Adder* contains echoes of Philip K. Dick, not to mention a walk-on by the man himself, but its vision is even bleaker. *Pace* Aldiss and Wingrove in *Trillion Year Spree,* I thought the book contained humour, admittedly unusually chill. The humour of *Infernal Devices* is more variegated and sometimes uproarious, but even this book has less to do with what I take to be a kind of informal trilogy of wild Victorian science fantasies (Jeter and his excellent friends Tim Powers and James Blaylock trying to outdo one another in inventiveness) than with his own dark themes. All this I say as a preamble to suggesting that Jeter's vision is most fully expressed in his horror fiction: at any rate, for me it is his most powerful work.

Given my field, that may sound biased, and perhaps it is. All the same, *Soul Eater* reads to me like the work of a writer made even more eloquent by horror—not always the case with writers who begin their careers in science fiction. The novel wrests the theme of transmigration from the Dennis Wheatleys of the field and turns it into a metaphor for the psychic cannibalism of family life: no knee-jerk Manichaeanism here. It's an unsparing novel, towards both the reader and the nominal hero. (For the record, let me admit that if I had read it before writing *The Influence,* my own novel would probably have been stillborn in my notebooks.)

Again, it seems to me that the bracing grimness of a novel like *Dark Seeker* (for instance) must come from deep in its author. An editor once complained that in a novel of mine, everything was menacing, but perhaps it goes without saying that I don't regard it as a weakness: it certainly isn't in Jeter. Novels such as *Dark Seeker* are not for the faint-hearted, and especially not for those readers who look to horror fiction to put everything right for them at the end. *Dark Seeker* contains some of the finest scenes of terror I've read for years (I think particularly of the nightmarishly vivid episode of the policeman and the corpse), and it further explores the territories Jeter has made uniquely his: those parts of the mind that come into play when the night, both temporal and of the soul, is darkest, and the city that is brightest and most dangerous then. That's the territory where Jeter abandons the reader of *Mantis,* having lured them towards the "acceptable" solution to the mysteries of the book, the psychological sinuousness of which is worthy of the darker novels of Thomas Hinde (*Games of Chance, The Day the Call Came:* don't let them be absent from your shelves). *Mantis* also contains what might be Jeter's statement of his intentions: "People aren't supposed to talk like this, to say out loud the things they know are true . . . you can't go back after that, to that safe, sad, pretend world you used to live in. You can only keep going forward, no matter where it takes you."

All of which brings us by however tortuous a route to the present novel*, and another unpredictable twist in Jeter's career. Les Escott, the man behind Morrigan Publications, remarked to me that it's the first of Jeter's horror stories to be set in the past, but I wonder if in fact it is set there: my instincts suggest that Jeter wouldn't offer us

* *In the Land of the Dead.*

even that much reassurance. Perhaps the precise setting in time doesn't matter, for in this book Jeter raises social realism (an element in all his horror fiction) to the level of the fantastic—of that kind of fantasy that illuminates reality rather than trying to take its place. While the book is entirely recognisable as his work—see, for instance, the scene with the corpse and the safe—it suggests that there are levels of his creative personality that he has only begun to explore.

Let me end by declaring that reading his four horror novels consecutively has convinced me that Jeter's is one of the most impressive bodies of work in my field today. Sometimes reminiscent of *noir* fiction but far darker, oppressively intense and hallucinatorily vivid, deeply felt and unflinchingly honest, these books are what I believe contemporary horror fiction should be. I hope the Morrigan edition may help to spread the good news.

Alan David Price

YOU HOLD IN YOUR HANDS AN EXTRAORDINARY book. I pause for the essence of that sentence, if not the whole of it, to wriggle caterpillar-like from between the pages, its movement made irregular by the inequality of its segments, and onto the cover to fatten itself there. If you gaze long enough at other phrases you may glimpse their eagerness to display themselves on the exterior—perhaps you may feel some settling themselves under your hands on the cover. Remember that we are involved here with the supernatural, for this is a book about vampirism.

I've read quite a few admirable ones—from the turn of this century, Poppy Z. Brite and Kim Newman come immediately to mind—and avoided many more on the basis of having found so many that I've tried to read forgettably derivative. As a writer of fiction I've discovered little to say on the theme, unless that's what *Ancient Images* is about, although I did write the Dracula Society a marching song:

> We are the marching vampiroids!
> Yes, we're the marching vampiroids!
> We devote ourselves to Vlad
> 'Cos we're essentially trad—
> That's us, the marching vampiroids.

Agreeing before I'd read this book to write the introduction therefore might have given me several kinds of problem. Suppose I had to pretend to be enthusiastic about a friend's work? Alan David Price and I are old friends from the sixties. We're competing at growing grey and bald now, but then the contest was for length of hair. Many was the night we walked home out of the centre of Liverpool, deep in discussion of the film we'd just watched—perhaps the new Antonioni, or maybe *Sting of Death*, in which Igor, the scientist's misunderstood assistant, breeds a giant jellyfish in the Everglades so as to wear it on his head and sting to death those who mock him. Sometimes it was an argument about philosophy that echoed through the empty streets, from beyond which might be heard a distant chorus:

Observe the marching vampiroids!
Indeed, the marching vampiroids!
Though we have no use for splat
Except the kind that makes us fat,
We are the marching vampiroids.

But it was most often art—let's not mince our capitals, it was Art—that was the subject of our nocturnal debates. I still recall the night when Alan despaired of the cinema—can it have been after a viewing of Losey's *Accident?*—and went on to despair of all fiction. Me, I knew it was worth writing, and nothing has stopped me yet, though that night may have been when Alan convinced me a tale of mine, "Reply Guaranteed", was no good—convinced me sufficiently that I withdrew it from my second published book, *Demons by Daylight*[1]. There's a lot to be learned about both of us from that anecdote, not least that Alan was committed to waiting until he was sure he had something to say as a writer, while I was already addicted to the process, compelled to pen anything that came to mind: stories, novels, reviews, polemics, introductions, marching songs . . .

Here come the marching vampiroids!
We draw the line at haemorrhoids!

[1] I was wrong, and it will be returned to its rightful place in the forthcoming definitive PS edition of that book.

You'll never find us drinking plasma
Because it only gives us asthma—

Well, you get the idea. (Usually I'm quick to resist the incursion of American usage into English, but the above rhyme works better if given a Yank.) For years Alan had assured me he was working on a book of vampire fiction, and I'd begun to wonder if it, like *Last Dangerous Visions* and T. E. D. Klein's second novel, would remain forever legend when he rang to let me know he'd found a publisher. How could I not agree to write a foreword? Let me dissimulate no longer. This is as original a vampire book as I have read, and I hope the Dracula Society will agree with me once their members have feasted on the book, even if they have to keep their ears (are some of those pointed?) alert for a dawn raid by a man carrying a valise laden with stakes or wearing an ankle-length garment with dozens of slim inner pockets. Perhaps a verse will help keep up their spirits:

Regard the matching vampiroids!
We're still the marching vampiroids!
We're neither psittacoids nor fish,
But we antagonise the Bish . . . [2]

However, to the tales that follow. The first of them succinctly demonstrates that vampirism is to have many meanings herein. The Lugosi story begins by ringing true and goes on to be truer than fact. "The Man Who Wrote the Openings . . . " says what every writer knows, that inspiration is a curse, a parasite that battens on us and the lives around us. The tale is eager to sidle into metaphor, and Alan's fiction often opens unexpected entrances to other dimensions of prose. Sometimes the story seems to challenge the reader to discern the vampirism it contains: in "Big Head and Loud Voice" the vampire is surely religion. I don't want to give the impression that the book contains no overtly supernatural tales, though. "The Forcers In" sounds like a title Algernon Blackwood might have invented, and the story's powerful sense of myth would be at home in a Blackwood book. In "Stub" blood is shed by the innocent, while in "The Re-Possessed" the vampire is capitalism, and in the Portu-

[2] Alternatively:

And we must say it's quite a tonic
To lampoon someone Byronic . . .

guese tale it could (shades of Leiber and Ackroyd!) be architecture. "Sybilmeet and Retreata", an onion of a fiction, may convict fantasy of decadence, but it is followed by a bunch of fantasies—never presume to predict this book. Though "Deconstructing Dracula" shows what a thesis Alan Price could write, it is also a persuasive episode in the endless life of Stoker's Count, and "A Bali Tale" is a particularly effective, not to say wholly original, supernatural horror piece. No fantasy except maybe the narrator's is to be seen in the gruesome reminiscences of John Terse, followed by a dark comedy of ageing in which the knowledge of a lifetime is drained away by its own weight. "At the Edge" discovers the poetry of vampirism and celebrates its depths. "Fog Heart" (also the title of a fine novel by Thomas Tessier that spent years wandering the wilderness of contemporary horror publishing) finds vampirism in birth and in the grey depleted post-war years that downgraded Englishwomen. "Munch's Vampire" is a meditation on that image, and very much the kind of tale I would expect from its author. "My Elongated Scar" is a lonely monologue from which meaning bleeds, and it gives me the chance to praise the author's variety of voices. Last and most impressively substantial, "Blood Libel" confronts the risk this book has already taken once, of setting fiction in a concentration camp. With its considerable range of effect and metaphor, not least those rooted in the German fairy tale, it's a far better summation of the aims and achievements of the book than this introduction has managed to be.

The novella and its fellow tales triumphantly vindicate Alan David Price's choice of theme, and his determination not to be content to recycle or imitate. He joins those few writers who have persuaded me there's still life in vampirism. Aficionados—Hammer Film fans in particular—should be delighted to learn that the author lives in a place called Bray Towers, and I invite them to raise their voices in a final rousing chorus:

Salute the marching vampiroids!
Hurrah, the marching vampiroids!
And you must strike off every head
If you'd be certain that we're dead,
For we're the marching vampiroids!

Poppy Z. Brite

I RISE FROM MY GRAVE BEFORE YOUR EYES, OR AT least my column returns from the limbo it inhabited since the demise of *Necrofile*. (A final issue may yet see print: if so, this will be announced on my website.) Does the genial Anthony Sapienza, editor of *The Spook*, realise what he may have brought upon himself by reviving my monologue? I shall begin gently by celebrating a permanent edition of a similar column and other non-fiction by Poppy Z. Brite.

In an instalment of the earlier incarnation of my column, I wrote: "Poppy is already a better writer—more lyrical, more sharp-eyed, surer of her characters, at least as fond of language but more precise—than I am." Before I turn to *Guilty but Insane*, her non-fiction book, let me present a few earlier reasons for my enthusiasm.

I first became alert to her prose when Steve Jones and I read "His Mouth Will Taste of Wormwood" for *Best New Horror 2* ten years ago. It (the story, and for all I know our use of it) was the first of many Poppy controversies I'm aware of. Yes, we noticed that the story was a riff on Lovecraft's tale "The Hound"—her calling a character Howard, as Frank Belknap Long once did, acknowledges the source. But in the clarity of the imagery, in the (I use the adjective deliberately) incomparable evocation of the morbid atmosphere of New Orleans, in mating the decadence of the turn of one century with the club scene of another, the tale is far closer to itself. Whereas most fiction with its roots in Lovecraft reads far too much like imitation, my own first book certainly included, "His Mouth" has an immediately recognisable voice.

The lushness of its prose is found throughout her first collection (*Swamp Foetus* to its friends). Reading more than a couple of the stories at a time is as heady an experience as I imagine absinthe to be. Indeed, some of the individual pieces are too intense to need the company of others. Besides "Wormwood", personal favourites include "The Sixth Sentinel", a spectral tale both shuddery and erotic; the extraordinarily terse and bleak "A Georgia Story"; "The Ash of Memory, the Dust of Desire", a tale of urban supernatural terror worthy of a place beside, but quite unlike, the best such work of Fritz Leiber or Harlan Ellison®; perhaps most impressive of all, "Calcutta, Lord of Nerves", a story that takes the unpromising prospect of setting a narrative in the world of George Romero's living dead (a task I myself shirked, feeling that Romero had said all there was to say about it) and transforms it into an extraordinary metaphor, both (often simultaneously) gruesome and beautiful. Among quite a few quotable lines it offers one that suggests a principle underlying much of her work: "There are beauties too terrible to be borne." Nevertheless she devotes some of her considerable imagination and skill to depicting them, and in this tale imagines a Calcutta at least as vivid as any of Lovecraft's accounts of places he dreamed of visiting.

Swamp Foetus also contains "Angels" (written 1987) and "How to Get Ahead in New York" (1991), two adventures of her young duo Ghost and Steve. They're central to her first published novel, *Lost Souls*, and so is her gift for lyrical horror, epitomised in the prologue. It's worth noting that the most gruesome episode, the end of the birth scene, is presented with reticence, hardly a method the average splatterpunk would use—rather the technique of a writer who knows when it's more shocking to stop. I suppose *Lost Souls* is one of the reasons people say she wants to shock, as if this were a questionable aim for a horror writer or any other kind. Here it's the shock that freshness of imagination brings, a quality that also makes this a powerful vampire novel, a rarity in my experience. Another objection I've encountered is that all the characters are under thirty and use drugs. My memory suggests that Scott Fitzgerald's characters were of an age and generally drank, and I maintain that Poppy has pinned down a generation too.

She continues in her second novel, *Drawing Blood*, and perhaps with greater lyricism. This is especially apparent in the prolonged erotic episode in chapter thirteen, one reason why she has been accused of having "an unhealthy fascination with gay men, particularly oral sex between males". That's a quote, but I've seen other similar comments. To me they make precisely as much sense as accusing my fiction of "an unhealthy fascination with heterosexual couples, particularly their treatment of children". Perhaps that's a quote too, if one I've yet to see. Forgive my obviousness in pointing out that the comment about Poppy scarcely bothers to disguise its assumption that gayness is unhealthy. Me, I'm not aware of being gay, but the episode in *Lost Souls* is as seductive as any erotic scene I've ever read.

None of the foregoing quite prepared her readers or, notoriously, her publishers for the starkness of her third novel, *Exquisite Corpse*. It slightly resembles James Ellroy's *Silent Terror*, in which two serial killers commit murders as love letters to each other, but is considerably more extreme—indeed, it's the only fiction other than *American Psycho* that has made me shut my eyes at times and steel myself before reading on (though parts of Poppy's Crow novel *The Lazarus Heart*, written as *Framed*, came close). Her new spareness distinguishes most of the tales in *Are You Loathsome Tonight?* (her second collection, ignominiously renamed *Self-Made Man* in Britain—my suggestion was *The Phantom of the Okra*), but doesn't preclude lyricism (one of many images I'd give much to have written: car radio static "like the sound of the desert clearing its throat"). Especially spare is her novella *Plastic Jesus*, which was almost a novel. This is one of her treatments (along with "Arise" and "Entertaining Mr. Orton" and "A Georgia Story", among others) of a recurring theme, the separation of a creative duo and its aftermath. I take the spareness to be another way she's found to tell the truth. That's certainly the case with *Guilty but Insane*, an uncommonly honest book even by her standards.

Let me not begin too dauntingly. Some of the book is just fun, however keen-eyed the prose: a reminiscence of Dublin (where a taxi driver once spent the entire journey to the airport talking to me about James Joyce, and where the late Bob Shaw taught me how to enjoy Guinness, by ordering two pints so that the second reached the correct temperature while you drank the first), a sketch of New York (where a glimpse of puked noodles may be read as an omen of her recent Parisian adventure, a chunk of black comedy to be found on her website), an evocation of Amsterdam that is also a succinct guide for the cannabis tourist, and I hope nobody's surprised to find New Orleans and Mardi Gras given pride of place. One of her accounts of the city also venerates decadence and in passing epitomises one aspect of her work: ". . . beauty and decay have always gone hand in hand." This has never been clearer than in her memorial to William Burroughs, of which more later. There's also a touching tribute to the late Mike Baker and some compliments for, by gum, me. Let nobody imagine they've made me more enthusiastic about her work than I would otherwise be. Several episodes of her titular column offer useful tips for writers, and in one case a peek in her notebook.

Am I making *Guilty but Insane* sound too uncontroversial? I'd better rouse myself. One essay addresses the question of whether horror writers should criticise one another. My answer is yes, on the basis that they may be expected to know what they're talking about (better to have informed criticism, I'd say, than the ignorant kind that so often besieges us). That's not to say all do, and the comment by a writer in Mike Baker's journal *Afraid* that set Poppy off sounds less like criticism than someone trying to be controversial for the hell of it while not quite owning up. (I'm in favour of people speaking their minds, but that ought to involve making sure they're worth hearing.) "There are some good female horror writers, but . . . Poppy Z. Brite [is] not among them"—to which my response would be that there always have been more than is generally recognised, often even by their peers, and Poppy is by no means the only one enriching the field.

I promised controversy, but not for its own sake. Her celebration of "The Poetry of Violence" isn't that; it's about looking hard. It first appeared in an anthology about screen violence, where it nestled close to a diatribe against such stuff by Mary Whitehouse, who I imagine recoiling in horror from the company in which she found herself. Readers unfamiliar with her name should take a look at **www.mediawatchuk.org**, where they will encounter folk such as David Turtle and Miranda Suit and read reports with headlines like **Boy, 13, held over child porn**. (The organisation does agree with Poppy in using "media" as singular.) A similar fount of fun can be found at **www.capalert.com**, which cites as an instance of "Wanton Violence/Crime" in *Lara Croft, Tomb Raider* a "great fall". Perhaps the writer had in mind *Humpty Dumpty, Tomb Raider*.

Some commentators will undoubtedly be lying in wait for Poppy's remarks about sex: I hope they'll have the grace to be amused by her study of the replies to a sex survey (sliced mushrooms?? Kitty Litter??). An essay that could have been the afterword to *Plastic Jesus* marries off Lennon and McCartney: Mr Sapienza asked me to refer to Liverpool and the Blue Meanies somewhere, and I can't think where else to smuggle them in (except by calling Mary Whitehouse a Blue Meanie, or at least a blue-rinsed one). If they skim Poppy's observations on child sexuality (originally published in a butchered form as "Behind the Oval Offspring"), determinedly hostile readers may find themselves some ammunition but will miss how thoughtful the piece is. But the book's core of frankness is her examination of her own sexuality, not without some rueful humour at the expense of possibly her most famous statement. Embedded in the essay is her contribution to *Dick for a Day*, an anthology that was exactly what you think. In the frontispiece to *Are You Loathsome Tonight?* she gets one, courtesy of the always inventive J. K. Potter.

Can something have two cores? There's as much frankness in the final pages, about pain and drugs. Elsewhere she praises the "measured honesty" of an autobiographical account, which certainly contains no more than hers does. I've some idea just how measured hers is—I read rawer versions in our correspondence. During one of the worst of the periods she describes, she took the time to write me several very supportive emails, though I was suffering from nothing worse than writer's depression. That's bad enough, as some of us know, but I wasn't aware of her state when I wrote to her about mine. Hers was so extreme that, as she put it, she was unable to reach the essential quiet place inside that a writer needs. I reassure myself that she found it again in order to produce this piece and later ones.

I've left one of the finest until last—her tribute to William Burroughs. Those already outraged by her work will no doubt fall on this, and perhaps on me for praising it, as though I care. It is an erotic memorial to Burroughs in the shape of his corpse. In the remarkable accuracy of its images and the lucid beauty of its prose, in its demonstration that any subject can yield itself up to art in the hands of a sufficiently gifted artist, it renews my faith in my own medium. It vindicates her stance that art should never be subject to limitations, and is one of many reasons to snap up *Guilty but Insane* before it goes out of print. But does the book reveal the secret of the Z? My lips are sealed, nay, stapled. Masked with night and armed with language, Poppy will continue to leave her mark in blood.

Much has happened since I wrote this piece in 2001. Poppy abandoned the Gothic for the mainstream, writing the G-man and Rickey series of novels about New Orleans restaurant life. These came to an abrupt end when a publisher's editor attempted to impose a Hurricane Katrina theme. My old friend is now Billy Martin and makes art, absurdly inexpensive too—check it out online.

Richard Christian Matheson

Relative contemplates model.
Respects childhood mentor.
Rapid clear messages.
Record consummately macabre.
Reinvents classic moulds.
Restores confidence munificently.
Rallies cinematic methods.
Retina captures moments.
Registers century's madnesses.
Recasts calvaries modernly.
Relevant comments mesmerise.
Reveals concealed mysteries.
Reawakens clammy maledictions.
Reappears clutching monsters.
Reinvigorates comatose minds.
Rouses carotid matter.
Raises chilly merriment.
Realism creates magic.
Resounds cadences magnificently.
Relishes colourful metaphors.

Rhetoric courses mellifluously.
Replicates cruel malevolence.
Redeems cacodemoniacal maniacs.
Rationality conveyed meticulously.
Rare courageous mentality.
Represses censorious manipulation.
Resultant candour magnificent.
Results cure melancholy.
Readers crave more.
Reviewers can't mock.
Read closely, mindfully.
Repays careful musing.
Rejects clichéd modes.
RIP, cloned material.
Rather classy, methinks.
Represents creative meticulousness.
Regenerates critics' mirth.
Reputation: champion marabout.
Really, cool magician.
Regards cult modestly.
Reflects cultural mainstream.
Renders categories meaningless.
Remarkable chameleonic metamorphoses.
Raw cathartic mayhem (red cascades madly)
reinforces cerebral meanings (remember, created *Mercenary*,
releasing consciousness monstrously).
Rejoice! Celebrate, mankind! Revel, cheery mob!
Rivals can marvel, rue charm, mastery.
Repercussion: crestfallen mimics.
Reborn celestial manitou?
Rewards confound me.
Restrain—calm myself . . .
Reason ceases—mine . . .
Ramsey Campbell—murderer?

LOVECRAFT: AN INTRODUCTION

HOWARD PHILLIPS LOVECRAFT WAS BORN IN Providence, Rhode Island, in 1890, and died there in 1937. Except for a short-lived marriage which took him to New York, he always made Providence his home. In some ways he was a lonely figure, convinced of his own physical ugliness, but he corresponded with numerous friends, many of them writers of weird fiction: August Derleth, Donald Wandrei, Robert Bloch, Clark Ashton Smith, Frank Belknap Long, and Fritz Leiber were among them. He signed himself "Grandfather" to his younger correspondents, and as teenagers Bloch and Derleth benefited from his criticism when they began to sell stories to *Weird Tales*, the pulp magazine which published most of Lovecraft's work in the field. His criticism of his own work was harsher, and during the last years of his life he believed that almost all his tales were failures, not even worth preserving in book form. Since then, however, he has emerged as the most influential horror writer of this century to date. He is also probably the most controversial, and so I'd better state my view at the outset: I believe Lovecraft is one of the most important writers in the field.

He is most famous for inventing what has come to be known as the Cthulhu Mythos, in itself enough to antagonise some of his detractors. Lovecraft never referred to it by that name—with typical self-deprecation he dismissed it as "Yog-Sothothery". Nor is it likely that he ever said what he is most often quoted as saying: "All my stories, unconnected as they may be, are based on the fundamental lore or legend that this world was at one time inhabited by another race who, in practising black magic, lost their foothold and were expelled, yet live on outside ever ready to take possession of this earth again." For a start, many of his stories are certainly not based on this idea, and even those which belong to the Lovecraft Mythos (the term I prefer, for whatever that's worth) don't conform to this essentially Christian model of evil versus good. Indeed, in 1935 he wrote "Nothing is really typical of my efforts . . . I'm simply casting about for better ways to crystallise and capture certain strong impressions (involving the elements of time, the unknown, cause and effect, fear, scenic and architectural beauty, and other seemingly ill-assorted things) which persist in clamouring for expression." In the same letter he advised his correspondent to "avoid actually recognised myths such as vampirism, reincarnation, etc.", and praises writers he himself admires for creating "a sort of distinctive awe of their own". All of which helps to explain how the Lovecraft Mythos came into being—as a stage in Lovecraft's attempts to create a perfect form for his preoccupations and for the weird tale.

Of course many writers are driven by their dissatisfaction with their own work and by the hope of doing better next time. In Lovecraft's case, when his last illness put an end to his fiction he had written virtually every kind of weird tale there was to write. He wrote a couple in his mid-teens, but the work for which he's known began in 1917 with "The Tomb", a ghost story about "a dreamer and a visionary" whose obsession with the past and with death causes him to find companions in his ancestral vault. Indeed, at least ten of Lovecraft's stories are relatively delicate fantasies, often based on his dreams, and ten years later he wrote a novel, *The Dream-Quest of Unknown Kadath*, in the midst of his most famous horrors. Recognisably Lovecraftian horror began in 1917 too, with "Dagon", in which the narrator is cast ashore on an island raised by a submarine earthquake and glimpses a giant survivor of the race which built a monolith there—froglike and fishlike, yet "damnably human".

Now this is precisely the kind of material which Lovecraft's detractors use to demonstrate his supposed inadequacies as a writer, in particular his tendency to suggest rather than show. (In 1923 he wrote to Frank Belknap Long "I am not so much thrilled by a visible charnel house or conclave of daemons, as I am by the suspicion that a charnel house exists below an immemorially ancient castle, or that a certain very old man has taken part in a daemonic conclave fifty years ago. I crave the ethereal, the remote, the shadowy, and the doubtful . . .") But it needs to be said that "Dagon" is an early minor story, of greatest interest as a first draft for both "The Call of Cthulhu" and "The Shadow over Innsmouth". Clearly the visions it hints at meant a good deal to him.

In 1921 he wrote "The Nameless City" and introduced the *Necronomicon*, that best-known of forbidden books. The title, which he later translated as "An Image of the Law of the Dead", came to him in a dream. Abdul Alhazred, the name of the author, was suggested to Lovecraft when he was five years old as a suitable name to call himself while playing Arabian Nights games. The book was the first major image Lovecraft invented as a symbol of terrors and wonders larger than the human mind could grasp. On one level the whole point is the sense of breathless anticipation and of "dread suspense" Lovecraft sought to convey to the reader, and soon he would devote much of his creative energy to shaping entire stories to that end.

The products of these efforts are enviably various: "The Outsider", perhaps a metaphor, however inadvertent, for his own feelings about himself; the dreamlike vision of "The Music of Erich Zann", the sole Lovecraft tale which the late Robert Aickman liked; the subterranean horrors of "The Rats in the Walls", perhaps Lovecraft's most powerful achievement of what he called "loathsome fright"; the sense of relentless doom in "The Shunned House" . . . Then, in mid-1926, he wrote "The Call of Cthulhu", and horror fiction was never quite the same again.

"The Call of Cthulhu" blends science fiction and an invented occultism to communicate a sense of awe and terror and in particular the enormity of the unknown universe. It is wholly original and yet rooted in the work of authors Lovecraft admired, particularly the hints of other dimensions which Blackwood conveys in "The Willows" (Lovecraft's favourite weird tale) and the complicatedly suggestive structure of Machen's "Great God Pan". It is also yet another beginning for Lovecraft but, sadly, the furthest many of his imitators progress.

The following year he wrote "The Colour out of Space", which subsequently he always regarded as his best work. Almost the opening line of "The Call of Cthulhu" is "We live on a placid island of ignorance in the midst of black seas of infinity", and "Colour" develops that theme. "It was just a colour out of space", but it is Lovecraft's purest symbol, the strongest expression of his sense that the universe, and anything living out there in the dark of space or time, is indifferent to man. Yet the terror of the story is only a stage on the way to the awesomeness of the finale. For me "Colour" is Lovecraft's masterpiece, and the single best introduction to his work.

But he was continuing to experiment. Among his other tales of the period are "Pickman's Model", which reads like a tribute to the cruel humour of Ambrose Bierce, and *The Case of Charles Dexter Ward*, the most Gothic of his stories, which sustains a superb build-up of supernatural terror at novel length. (Two other novels which he had planned to write, *The Club of the Seven Dreamers* and *The House of the Worm*, exist only as titles; but with Lovecraft, sometimes the title is enough to awaken the imagination.) He was also revising stories for clients, so extensively that most of the stories (for instance, those signed by Zealia Brown Bishop—"The Curse of Yig", "The Mound" and "Medusa's Coil") are virtually all his work, unlike the stories published as by Lovecraft and August Derleth, which were in fact written by Derleth.

"Yig" and "The Mound", and perhaps "Out of the Eons", signed by Hazel Heald, sometimes approach Lovecraft's own standard, but in other cases it seems he was devoting too much time to indifferent material. Still, perhaps this let him recharge his batteries, because his own work continued to progress. "The Dunwich Horror" (1928) is probably his most substantial fusion of science fiction and the occult, while "The Whisperer in Darkness" (1930) and *At the Mountains of Madness* (1931) show him to be moving closer to science fiction. In the latter pair, in fact, curiosity and exploration are overcoming terror. Even the aliens in *Mountains of Madness* are scientists, no longer incomprehensibly monstrous.

But Lovecraft's self-doubt was catching up with him. He so much disliked typing that he never prepared *Charles Dexter Ward* for publication. When *Mountains of Madness* was bounced by *Weird Tales* he took the rejection as a sign that he was all but written out. I assume Michael Moorcock had this kind of thing in mind when he claimed that Lovecraft "regressed into an attitude of permanent defensiveness", but if this were wholly true then Lovecraft would surely have stopped writing; the real truth about a writer is to be found in his work. In the last years of his life he wrote several fine tales of terror—"The Shadow over Innsmouth", "The Thing on the Doorstep", "The Haunter of the Dark"—but his best late story, the awe-inspiring "Shadow out of Time", displeased him so much that he mailed the handwritten manuscript to Derleth without even keeping a copy. "My work dissatisfies me extremely," he wrote to a correspondent, "& of late I have destroyed much more than I have saved." In March 1937 he died of intestinal cancer after a winter of agony. The last things he wrote were a long unfinished letter to a correspondent and, a scientist to the end, observations on his own symptoms.

Perhaps few people other than readers of *Weird Tales* would ever have heard of him if it hadn't been for August Derleth and Donald Wandrei, who created Arkham House to publish his collected works and showed the world that there was a market for horror in hardcover. (Sheldon Jaffrey's *Arkham House Companion* is an excellent guide to the first fifty years of that publisher, while S. T. Joshi's *Sixty Years of Arkham House* is even more substantial.) By the sixties Lovecraft and his mythos were becoming widely known and widely imitated, and that is the source of a problem. It's easy to convince oneself that by imitating the apparent excesses of some of Lovecraft's writing one is adding to his imaginative achievement—I certainly thought so when I was a teenager and writing my first book—but that misses the point. His stylistic tricks—the runs of adjectives and images, the extended fantastic metaphors—are generally part of the construction of the story, without which they aren't worth imitating; as Fritz Leiber says, Lovecraft's language is orchestrated. And when lesser writers like myself began to elaborate the Mythos, explaining what Lovecraft had only suggested, we simply turned it into another stale occult concept of the kind it had been meant to replace.

It is a tribute to the power of his work that Lovecraft has survived any amount of inept imitation and continued to influence writers as excellent (and as different) as Thomas Ligotti and T. E. D. Klein. In striving to write fiction which would make positive use both of his talents and of his limitations (in particular his difficulties with creating characters), he developed near-perfect structures for the horror story. As with Machen, his determination to convey awe gives his tales a quality too seldom found. His work unites the British and American traditions of horror fiction; it unites the realistic and the fantastic, the personal and the cosmic, the occult and the scientific. No wonder he is worth rereading when there is so much to discover.

What would he have made of his posthumous fame and influence? He might have been dubious about the way writers like myself married off his monstrous creations and reduced them to occult or scientific banality and in general left nothing for the reader's imagination to feast upon, but I think he would have been happy to have influenced such fine writers as Ligotti, Klein and Fred Chappell. What he would have made of his tales giving rise to role-playing games I dare not speculate.

In his final letter he describes how, on one of his last expeditions before his illness began to overcome him, he was joined by "two tiny kittens" (cats being his favourite animal) in the midst of a hitherto unexplored forest near Providence. As he emerged from the forest after sunset they disappeared among the trees. I should like to think that in his final moments he may have dreamed of being accompanied by them on the "voyages of discovery" he planned. He deserved a final vision after having left us with so many and never appreciating that he had.

R. R. RYAN

BACK IN 1983 THE EXCELLENT AND FAR TOO unprolific T. E. D. Klein asked his "three best-read friends"—R. S. Hadji, Thomas M. Disch, and Karl Edward Wagner—to contribute to "The Fantasy Five-Foot Bookshelf", a two-part article recommending works unlikely to be familiar to the, as Ted had been dismayed to find, largely ill-read readership of *Twilight Zone* magazine. The article deserves reprinting, guaranteed as it is to send all but the most arduous collector in search of treats as obscure as Francis Xavier Faversham's *The Rising of the Gorge.* Two of the recommendations did see new editions: *The Hole of the Pit,* which I was delighted to include in *Uncanny Banquet,* and *The Death Guard* by Philip George Chadwick, granted its first paperback in 1992 by Roc, with an introduction by Brian Aldiss. This was on Karl Wagner's list of thirteen best science fiction horror novels, and a powerful book it proves to be. Even more than his fellow list-makers, Karl favoured rarities. The work of R. R. Ryan, a writer he especially championed, is well-nigh impossible to find, and so the inclusion of a book of hers on his sf horror list (*Freak Museum*), another on the supernatural horror list (*Echo of a Curse*), and a third, *The Subjugated Beast,* among the non-supernatural recommendations, must have produced more frustration than enlightenment. I've now read them and almost all Ryan's other books the very copies Karl owned. Was Karl right to elevate her work? Was I, to write an entry on her for David Pringle's *Horror, Ghost & Gothic Writers?*

The answer to the second question must be yes. If Guy N. Smith and his follower Shaun Hutson deserve an entry each, so does Ryan. I admit to mixed feelings about that justification. Years ago Steve Jones compared Jack Sullivan's *Penguin Encyclopaedia of Horror and the Supernatural* unfavourably with the *Encyclopaedia of Science Fiction,* insofar as one could look up just about any science fiction writer, no matter how trivial or inept, in the latter and find at least a listing of their work. There was talk of a companion volume on horror; instead, this has been subsumed into the fine but partial fantasy encyclopaedia of Clute and Grant, which means that anybody wanting to make themselves aware of most if not all of the writers who have worked in the genre during our century will need the Pringle book. What this may not offer, perhaps by design—I've yet to see a copy—is any indication of their relative worth. I suppose that like an organisation of writers in the genre, such a book would find it difficult if not impossible to exclude people who have brought the field into disrepute. Still, I was able to hint at my reservations about Ryan in my entry on her, and I'd like to develop them here in a further attempt to rescue the author from legend.

First of all, who was R. R. Ryan? The British Library identifies her as Rachel R. Ryan, but in the publisher's advertising the author is referred to as male. The prose style seems feminine, and on the whole the female characters are drawn with more conviction than the male. Richard Dalby, who wrote a brief entry in the Sullivan *Encyclopaedia,* assumed the British Library to be correct but now isn't so sure. I wouldn't dream of being surer than Richard without evidence, of which I've none. Let me confine myself to considering Ryan's work, and assume her on the basis of it to be female*. All the books were published as library fiction by Herbert Jenkins. Some library readers must have been made of stern stuff.

The Right to Kill (1936) establishes her method and preoccupations. "Should women, in certain circumstances, defy the law?" the advertising asks. It is the scarcest of Ryan's books; even Karl didn't own a copy, and I owe my reading of it to the generosity of

* Since then James Doig has made out a strong case that the author was in fact Evelyn Bradley (a man), but his grandson David Medhurst argues strongly that Ryan was in fact Denice Jeanette Grosvenor-Bradley, his mother (Evelyn's daughter).

Dwayne Olson. Central to it are Mary Bootle, a nurse, and Robert Litherland, a policeman (surnames that strongly suggest a Merseyside connection). Litherland goes off to the war, having left Mary pregnant. An army friend of Litherland's attempts to rape her, and she kills him in self-defence, only to be blackmailed by his crony Prentice Lawler. Her daughter Fay is born and grows up, to fall in love with Garth Rimrose, Litherland's young colleague in the police. Then Litherland and Rimrose come calling on the Bootles to investigate the murder of the blackmailer...In its almost operatic contrivance and its clammy sense of moral confinement, not to mention the awkwardness of some of its prose, this first novel is typical of Ryan's work. "This story presents a problem," it or perhaps the publisher announces at the outset, "and must not be considered a justification."

Death of a Sadist (1937) shows similar concerns and a real sense of evil. Trevor Garron, an introverted bank clerk, filches two hundred pounds from the accounts, only to fall foul of Selwyn Maine, his manager. (The manager's first name may be intended to recall George Selwyn, the famed eighteenth-century sadistic voyeur, or perhaps Selwyn & Blount, publishers of the *Not at Night* anthologies.) Maine is the sadist of the title, who takes advantage of Garron and of a defaulter tenant, Edna Ferrar. Garron ultimately kills him, but Edna is convicted of the murder. The ending is unexpectedly bleak.

Ryan's writing is strongest in conveying, reticently but oppressively, the psychological sufferings of the victims. Elsewhere it lurches into sentimentalism. As Garron falls in love with Edna, "happiness began to flower in his breast. Its incipient bud had long lain dormant in the dark of his nature; needed but a modicum of emotional sunshine to encourage the lovely bloom which now enchanted him . . . " Yet a policeman interviewing Edna finds "there was something absent, ice-like, invisible, about this girl which left him cold, even a little repelled". Whether or not the overstated romanticism of the first passage is meant without irony, such chunks of prose—to be found throughout Ryan's work—are generally called into question by other elements of whichever book contains them. It's reasonable to assume the contrasts are those of the author's personality, and intriguing to imagine a readership as happy with Ryan's willingness to be relentless and disturbing as with the gush. At times, unfortunately, Ryan writes like someone needing to convince herself that she's an Author. "Unknown to any she leapt again and again from her exiguous bed, jarring her body in a mad desire to wreck the purpose of her womb."

Devil's Shelter (1937) is an early modern Gothic, written when the paraphernalia of the old dark house could be expected still to work. Divina Mason, an actress, sets out to drive from London to Newcastle but breaks down on the Yorkshire moors. The mansion in which she takes refuge during a thunderstorm proves to be an asylum, and worse. The butler who admits her says "Excuse me, I am dumb." A dog howling as it is beaten is in fact a man. Patients are mutilated to subdue them. If the institutionalised sadism may seem to prefigure world events—indeed, Divina reflects that the asylum is a microcosm—the book (hardly uniquely in the popular fiction of the day) also expresses casual anti-Semitism. A Jewish pharmacist driven to imagine himself as an Aryan scientist may be an ambiguous figure, but there's no ignoring how a thoroughly English character presented as admirable gives a casual Nazi salute. Midway the novel becomes more of a thriller, with a gun concealed by a portrait above a dinner-table, and produces a sane hero to help Divina escape; but it's the nightmarish first half, and scattered such episodes in the second, that stay in the mind.

Freak Museum (1938) is located in central London. Bridget O'Malley, impregnated by a boyfriend who then dies, is lured by the Mary Magdalen Guild to their nursing home in Climax Street, a hospital which turns out to serve the adjoining museum. Her baby either dies or is surgically deformed, and she is incarcerated in the museum, where she encounters various grotesques and is exhibited under hypnosis as one of them. An artist, Passport, eventually sees her plight and attempts to rescue her but is trapped himself. Like *Death of a Sadist,* this book keeps a minor character in reserve as a deus ex machina, but here the child who performs this function simply causes further deaths. While it seeks to horrify the book is ruthlessly effective; its later attempts to humanise some of the inmates slacken the momentum (though an encounter in which Passport discusses literature with the Elephant Woman is almost matter-of-fact enough for surrealism). The underlying notion that the owners of the museum have trapped the protagonists so as to use them to politically extremist ends is murkily expressed, but seems to be dear to the author, who also suggests that the world outside the museum is at least as freakish and regressive. It's a pity she regards "Negro" and "nigger" as interchangeable terms.

The Subjugated Beast (1939)—"frankly a thriller", the half-title announces—begins with a short history of the Rock family, generations of which committed murder and even cannibalism. The tale is narrated by Kyrie Rock, last child of the line, who will inherit on condition that she lives with her uncle Paul, a researcher into abnormal psychology, and his mysteriously disturbed wife. The book artfully sustains the uncertainty of how the Rock history is to invade the present, and a mounting mood of horror, but shows signs of hasty writing. The first-person narrative allows Ryan to indulge in a statement of opinion not unreminiscent of Robert Bloch. "Much, if not all, of this so-called modem psychology is utter nonsense, achieving nothing, proving nothing and profiting humanity not at all."

Echo of a Curse (1939) is Ryan's most ambitious book, which attempts to combine social realism and the supernatural in a narrative apparently based on "a Balkan story conveyed by word of mouth from one person to another". Mary Rodney marries a war hero, Vincent Border, only to discover he is a drunken sadist. He also claims kinship with a lycanthropic exhibit in a travelling fair. At the height of a domestic struggle, Mary curses her unborn child. Twins are born, one displaying traits of the monstrous side of the family. A normal child is substituted for the monster, which returns as an adult to wreak revenge, but Vincent, drawing on powers he derives from a rite known as the Black Commune, attempts to overcome it. While the book has powerful scenes of domestic violence and threat, some of its fantastic elements lack conviction: not least THE INEXPLICABLE, the sideshow monster, always referred to in capitals. Had Ryan belatedly encountered Lovecraft's work? "Eldritch" appears in the text, and the monster grown to adulthood masks itself by no means unlike one of Lovecraft's aliens trying to pass for human, while THE INEXPLICABLE (whose capitals might be Ryan's attempt to outdo the italics Lovecraft used so sparingly, and the name her version of the Unnameable) is "something out of the foul, forbidden world which Chambers believed to ride parallel with ours and which was inseparable from the unimaginable vast in whose enormity we are lost". I think this passage shows she was out of her depth with the cosmic, and the mundane elements of the book—household arrangements, bus rides—are never integrated with its macabre themes, a difficult trick to bring off. Perhaps that's why she confined herself to the claustrophobically domestic in *No Escape* (1940), her most coherent novel.

The narrator, Gerald Day, meets a young woman, Adela Beevers, on holiday and marries her, only to discover that she is so "narrow and terribly tight" that the marriage goes unconsummated. She also suffers from gastritis and self-pity, both chronic, and such are her demands on him that he becomes unable to move out of earshot. He spends much of the book planning to murder her, often in terms very like the domestic situation of *Echo of a Curse*, and eventually gives in to the compulsion, but his guilt proves even more insistent than her need for him. If the book ultimately turns romantic, this sharpens rather than compromises the portrait of obsession maintained almost until the last page. As a story of everyday horror it is often oppressively convincing. It is also so much more confidently written than her other books that one might suspect the use of a house name or else a theme so personal that its expression appears to have silenced her as a writer.

It was a short-lived career, and one which, without Karl Wagner's enthusiasm, might well have been forgotten. I have to say that her work may have seemed more impressive if one came on it unprepared—as Karl apparently did—than when it has to live up to the reputation Karl gave it. Nevertheless for several years, and apparently to little or no critical notice, she was one of the earliest twentieth-century British novelists to specialise in the horrific, and as such should be noted. To any of my readers dismayed by the rarity of her books, however, I would suggest there are more important gaps to be filled on the five-foot shelf.

Robert E. Howard

In October 1976 my American agent Kirby McCauley asked me out of the blue to write the introductions to two books of Robert E. Howard's tales of Solomon Kane, and to complete three unfinished stories. In some ways it was an odd time to ask. My first novel had just been published, to mostly bad reviews and far worse sales, and I was about to start my second. Nevertheless Howard was one of the few writers of American sword and sorcery, as distinct from the Tolkien variety, whose work I admired, along with the tales of Fritz Leiber, C. L. Moore and Karl Edward Wagner, and the idea of helping resurrect Howard's British adventurer appealed to me. In order to do the work, and to make myself appear as well-informed as Howard, I read up the historical background. Some of my research may be worth regurgitating here.

The latter years of the sixteen century were times of voyaging, of discovery, of men and exploits that became legend. The known world was growing; Cortez had discovered and destroyed the Aztec nation, Pizarro had conquered the Incas, Hernando de Soto had reached the Mississippi. Much of the world was still unknown, and many felt its call.

These were also years of religious strife. In France during 1572, fifty thousand Huguenots were massacred for their faith; in Spain, the Inquisition dealt out torture and death. Clearly, it was an age of fanaticism.

Injustice and exploitation were, as always, widespread. Spain looted the South American civilisations, but her treasure ships were themselves looted by the English in acts of piracy. The people of the West Indies were exploited; African Negroes were enslaved, with the approval of the church. Elsewhere, too, poverty flourished. Even in 1619, children were dying of cold in the London streets. In England, corrupt towns and neighbourhoods in decay were common, as was idleness; work was regarded as a consequence of the Fall, and hence not to be thought of as honourable.

Is it any wonder that Robert E. Howard created a Puritan hero? Not all Puritans of that time were dour fellows who devoted their lives to objecting to details of church practice and disapproving of other people's pleasures. Consider Richard Norwood, author of a journal written in 1639-40. He had run away to sea, soldiered in the Netherlands, voyaged in the Mediterranean, and associated with Sir Henry Mainwaring, who shortly turned pirate. He had been shipwrecked, and attacked by pirates; he had suffered plague and imprisonment. His journeyings have been described as "a physical search for celestial happiness," but if this sounds more peaceful than Kane's restless wandering in search or in pursuit of evil, Norwood shared one crucial trait with him—paranoia, a diagnosis Howard frequently applies to Kane. "All things seemed in their kinds to be my enemies," wrote Norwood of one such experience. "It seemed then to my apprehension to proceed from indignation, wrath, and as it were a gnashing of teeth against me."

Many famous Puritans, not least John Bunyan, have been discussed as pathological cases. Perhaps this underlines their courage rather than detracts from it, and Kane has the courage to trust his instincts. "A true fanatic," Howard writes of him in *Red Shadows*, "his promptings were reasons enough for his actions," although he "was not wholly a Puritan, though he thought of himself as such." For most of its adherents, Puritanism was a compulsion. Often it led to rational statements of the creed—Puritan autobiographies were common—but conversions to the faith (which consisted of "knowing, feeling, and obeying the truth") were frequently the result of terrifying visions, of harrowing self-examination, of paranoia and hallucinations. Let me not presume too much about Kane's background, however. Howard said only "Solomon Kane I created when I was in high school, at the age of about sixteen, but... several years passed before I put him on paper. He was probably the result of an admiration for a certain type of cold, steely-nerved duellist that existed in the sixteenth century."

His rapier was not the sort to which Errol Flynn has accustomed us, nor would his fencing have been so rapid. Kane's blade would have been diamond-shaped in section, and perhaps more than four feet long; the rapier of that period was blade-heavy. (Blades were shortened for lightness around 1650; about 1670 the section was divided, giving the triangular short-sword blade.) In fencing, opponents generally faced each other rather than turning side on. There was relatively little delicacy; hacking with the blade's edge was more common than thrusting (though Kane favours subtlety and the use of the point). One might use a dagger in conjunction with the rapier, as Kane sometimes does. Incidentally, Kane's rapier need not owe its "unadorned" guard to Puritan severity; one trick of swordplay was to insert one's sword-point amid the decorations of the opponent's cup-guard and disarm him.

The musket which Kane sometimes carries was a cumbersome weapon, slow to use. It may have weighed as much as twenty pounds; its barrel was four feet long. It was designed to penetrate heavy armour, but Kane uses it, when at all, as a bludgeon. His pistols would probably have been snaphaunces—a forerunner of the flintlock, but lacking its safety feature of the half-cock.

So much I feel justified in adding to our picture of Kane, but much else remains mysterious. In the course of what untold adventure did he suffer "scars made by Moslem whips in a Turkish galley"? And what was his connection with Sir Richard Grenville, "long fallen by my side"? For those readers unfamiliar with his tale, here is Grenville in brief.

A cousin of Sir Francis Drake, he was an obsessive voyager. He planted the first English colony in America in 1584. Ten years earlier, he had planned a voyage to discover Terra Australis, a surmised continent in the southern hemisphere; but Queen Elizabeth refused him the license, on the basis that it was not the time to challenge the Spanish Empire, and granted it to Drake three years later.

No doubt the story of the *Revenge* appealed to Howard. In 1591, a squadron of six English vessels was sent to wait at the Azores for the Spanish treasure fleet, only to be attacked by twenty galleons of the Spanish navy. Five of the vessels ran, but Grenville fought for fifteen hours, even though sickness had left only ninety of the crew of the *Revenge* fit for action. While the *Revenge* was riddled with eight hundred cannonballs, it sank two Spanish ships. The Spanish recognised his valour, and offered him terms of surrender: he and his officers would be held in honourable captivity for ransom, his seamen would be given safe passage to England rather than sent to the galleys. Even this was not enough for Grenville, who seems to have been as much of an atavism as Kane; apparently preferring death before dishonour, he ordered the *Revenge* blown up. He was overborne, and died on the Spanish flagship of his wounds—or, legend has it, chewed fragments of a wine goblet to end his life.

As to Kane, even his dates are conjectural. Commentators have assumed that "Solomon Kane's Homecoming" takes place in 1610 on the basis that Bess, dead seven years, is Queen Elizabeth; I did. But is this likely? One historian describes the Queen as "a huge boulder in the path of Puritanism, unavoidable, insurmountable, immovable." The Puritan ideal was to make oneself clear to the common people; Elizabeth was hostile to preaching, and more hostile to "prophesyings"—meetings of ministers to discuss the Scriptures—which she saw as a political threat. On matters of church reform she refused to support the Puritans. Many Puritans blamed her advisers rather than the Queen, but not so Kane, to judge from his reaction to her name in Howard's section of "Hawk of Basti." It seems unlikely that he would later say "Woe that I caused her tears." Besides, Queen Elizabeth was buried not by the sea but in London, in Westminster Abbey. Bess is one more mystery Kane keeps to himself.

At least we can hazard a chronology, deduced by Glenn Lord from clues in the tales and in Howard's correspondence. "Skulls in the Stars" seems to take place around 1560. Already Kane has seen the Spanish Inquisition, though not in any of the stories. "The Right Hand of Doom" finds him still near Torkertown in England, but he finds it "hard to remain in the land of my birth for more than a month at a time." In "Red Shadows" (the first published Kane story, which appeared in the August 1928 *Weird Tales* as "Solomon Kane"), we discover him in France. In the interim he may have been "a captain in the French army for a space." His pursuit of evil takes him from France to Africa, whence he sets sail again.

We hear nothing of him until he appears in the Black Forest in "Rattle of Bones." Perhaps meanwhile he has sailed with Sir Francis Drake, and has had the encounter described in "The One Black Stain"; in the next Black Forest story, "The Castle of the Devil," he has been to sea. He returns to England, and a dying man's words send him on a search that lasts years, leading him eventually to the west coast of Africa and beyond, to the city of "The Moon of Skulls."

In "Blades of the Brotherhood," piracy appears to be flourishing; perhaps this is later than the defeat of the Spanish Armada, so that Kane has already sailed with Grenville. After this brief return to England, we find him next in Africa. On the West Coast, in "Hills of the Dead," he encounters vampirism; he meets an old acquaintance from his seafaring days, Hawk of Basti; Grenville appears to him. As he wanders east, he comes upon a city of the inhuman, in "Wings of the Night." Further east, menaced by "The Footfalls Within," he learns an ancient use of the magical staff he carries. Still deeper into the jungle, he discovers the survival of an ancient civilisation—"The Children of Asshur." He makes his final appearance, still cloaked in brooding mystery, in "Solomon Kane's Homecoming."

Readers may like to know where, in the posthumous collaborations, Howard ends and I begin. In "Hawk of Basti" his last line is "Then calling to a man who had the appearance of a chief, he ordered him to walk between himself and Kane." "The Children of Asshur" is all his up to the end of section III. "The Castle of the Devil" is the shortest fragment, ending with Kane's comment to John Silent: "Your speech is wild and Godless, but I begin to like you." I read the fragment while waiting to meet Jack Sullivan, the critic of supernatural fiction, at the Staten Island Ferry terminal, and before he arrived I'd scribbled notes on the blank portion of the last page, and knew all about the Baron and his deadly obsession and how Kane would defeat him.

Rereading my contributions now, I'm surprised how thoroughly they resemble the work of someone other than myself. I won't presume to say they read like Howard, but certainly I was in creative sympathy with him rather than forcing myself to imitate him. In retrospect, it was a good time for me to attempt the task. I imagine that in these squeamishly correct days most writers, me included, would be uncomfortable with putting further pidgin English into N'Longa's mouth, although where would such a character have learned better English in that century? These collaborations are the closest I ever came to being a pulp writer. Because I respected the job I enjoyed it, and I hope Howard's admirers will not find my prose too out of place beside his.

II

How strange the world of films is! I mean not those aspects of it that attract the buzzing of the media, but the way it touches the lives of us lesser mortals, capriciously and unpredictably. John Collier has a tale—"Cancel All I Said"—that says much about this in few words. Like almost all of Collier, not least the splendid *Defy the Foul Fiend*, it is worth searching for. I can't recount any experience as daunting as befalls the characters in Collier's story—not yet, at any rate. Still, I think I have a column's worth.

Back in 1976 I completed three tales of Solomon Kane left unfinished by Robert E. Howard. The work was very perceptively reviewed by Richard Tierney in *Necrofile*. I expected nothing further of the project except more royalties than I've seen (at least from recent editions). Imagine my surprise, then, when Milton Subotsky expressed interest in my writing a Solomon Kane film.

This was in 1978, and dim in memory. I recall that we met for lunch in a London hotel, but not the meal or much of the conversation—mostly my own awkwardness. Subotsky proposed that the film should be based on at least some of Kane's adventures in Africa. He said he liked to pay writers only a token advance, the rest of their fee acting as encouragement for them to deliver. Presumably I mumbled in approval or resignation, because before we parted we shook hands on the deal. Off went the papers to Carol Smith, then my British agent, nobody's now. Soon—too soon—I wrote a screen treatment and sent it to Milton.

Recently I found the carbon among some old papers, hence this column. I've shared my juvenilia with the world—why not my early stumbling into film? It must be clear by now I have no shame. Here's how the carbon looks.

SOLOMON KANE

(story treatment by Ramsey Campbell)

A man rides through a bleak Southern English landscape, searching. His close-fitting black clothes make him look even taller and more gaunt; a wide-brimmed black hat shadows his eyes. He wears rapier, dagger, pistols and musket. This is Solomon Kane.

Cries for help lead him to a dying manservant. "Puritan," the man hisses, recoiling.

"I mean you no harm. Who has done this to you?"

"Le Loup and his robbers . . . they are killing my mistress . . . "

Kane rides wildly to a great house. Ruffians dressed as Puritans bar his way. "You are too late, Puritan," one sneers as a woman screams above. "You must wait your turn."

Kane fights his way through them and up through the house, where others of Loup's men fail to overcome him. Loup, who is tall and gaunt as Kane, is torturing a young woman, Lady Elizabeth. After a duel Loup escapes, locking the apartment door against Kane, though not before Kane has scarred his face.

Kane learns that Loup has killed her brother for half a treasure-map, the remainder of which she holds. It was willed to them by their father, who gambled away the rest of their wealth.

Disguised as Puritans, Loup and his men have been plundering houses. They must have got the idea from the Puritans, she says bitterly. She blames Kane doubly for having let Loup escape.

Kane pledges his honour to bring her the treasure intact. Eventually his fervour convinces her. She shows him her map, which he commits to memory. All geographical directions were on Loup's half, but she recalls that the route began at a port on the Slave Coast of Africa.

We next see Kane landing there. A Spaniard tells him that a tall scarred Frenchman landed some days ago and went into the interior. He shakes his head: no man goes alone into Africa.

Kane tracks Loup to a village in the interior. In sight of the fires of the village, he is struck down by a massive figure.

He regains consciousness trussed up in a hut. Beyond the doorway Gulka, the massive savage who captured him, is sacrificing a man before the Black God, a huge ape-idol with a man's face, its teeth bared like an ape's. Looking on are an immensely fat man, obviously the chief, and Le Loup.

Kane is not alone in the hut. An aged but sprightly black, adorned with magic fetishes, squats in the shadow of the doorway. He gives a long slow wink. "Englishman, listen: I help you, you help me."

He is N'Longa, the witch-doctor. Loup has turned the chief against him, by convincing him that guns are more powerful than N'Longa's magic. N'Longa will release Kane so that he can retrieve his guns, which must still be lying wherever Gulka struck him down.

Before N'Longa can release Kane, Gulka seizes them. Loup is triumphant; he'd told the chief that N'Longa would reveal his treachery if they left Kane alone. The drums had sent word of Kane's coming. The chief agrees to let Gulka torture N'Longa, who has magical knowledge of the whereabouts of the treasure. Loup points out that Kane can save him.

Once he is tied to a stake N'Longa yields up the secret, only to find that the chief means to let him burn. N'Longa sends his spirit to reanimate the corpse of the sacrifice, which puts out the fire at N'Longa's feet, then kills the chief by touching him. The corpse gives Kane a long slow wink and releases him. Seconds later it falls inert and N'Longa's body revives.

In the confusion, Loup escapes. Kane dashes back to his guns, only to be confronted by Gulka, whom he kills.

N'Longa tries to dissuade him from pursuing Loup, who is heading for worse perils: the dying city of Negari, the treasure guarded by the dead. When Kane is adamant, N'Longa gives him a voodoo stave as protection. Kane is dubious of accepting any magic object, but can't bring himself to refuse.

Following the directions of N'Longa and the map, he has to climb to a plateau. Here he encounters black guards who escort him to a chasm crossed by a narrow bridge of rock. A city is visible on the far side. They try to kill him for not bearing gifts. In killing their leader on the bridge, Kane loses his balance, but manages to save himself in mid-fall by clutching the top branches of a tree.

By clambering along the tree he reaches a ledge, and from there a cave. He is now on the side he needed to reach. The cave leads gradually upward, ultimately to join artificial, faintly luminous passages. These open secretly into the city of Negari.

One secret entrance gives onto the throne-room of Queen Nakari. She has a warrior slain for not bringing Kane from the bridge; her eyes gleam at the killing. Then she commands the other stranger to be brought before her. It is Loup.

When he is searched they find his map. Only treasure would bring a man to this land, she says. Sensing her desire for him, Loup persuades her to give him an escort to find the treasure. With a crafty look at him she instructs the warriors to bring Loup and the treasure back safely to her.

Kane searches for an exit that will take him toward the treasure. Secret entrances give him glimpses of the city, most of it in ruins. He sees a slave market where native women and children are sold. Two guards catch sight of him and chase him through the passages, into one where the walls have caved in. Here he gets the better of them, then has to cross a deep crack in the passage.

Beyond this, through a secret entrance, he reaches the dungeons. In one cell he finds an ancient man, the last of the race of Atlantis, the last high priest. The Atlanteans built this city and eventually interbred with their slaves. Now the city is decadent; the people are unable to leave, and resorting to savagery; the only thing that holds them in check is the skull of a renegade high priest, to which they make sacrifices each full moon. As a tremor passes through the city, shaking dust from the walls, he curses the city and its inhabitants: the earth will rise up against them as the sea rose against Atlantis. He dies, murmuring of the sea.

Beyond the dungeons Kane finds a large door, heavily barred, which leads out of the city. It takes effort and ingenuity to move the bar from its sockets. He has just done so when guards appear. Ominously, instead of pursuing him out of the city, they bar the door.

Still, he is nearer to his goal. He manages to kill some small game, since he lost most of his provisions in the fall from the bridge. As twilight falls he builds a fire for cooking.

Near sunset, two unnaturally pale natives join him. They neither speak nor gesture, only wait. The sun has almost vanished when a vulture perches above them. They are vampires.

At sunset they attack. A musket shot cannot stop them, nor Kane's rapier. Then he hears N'Longa's voice: *The stave!* Kane manages to stab first one vampire, then the other, through the heart with the voodoo stave. At once they crumble to dust.

Still holding the stave, Kane hears N'Longa's voice: *You eat now, then sleep. You are safe*. When he sleeps in spite of himself, N'Longa tells him in a dream that tomorrow a warrior from Loup's party will come fleeing. Loup is miles to the north and has found a village massacred by vampires. Kane must not kill the warrior, only make him hold the stave.

In the morning Kane is ambushed by the warrior, but manages to stun him. Then reluctantly he places the stave in his hands. The man recovers consciousness and greets Kane with a long slow wink.

N'Longa guides Kane along short cuts which were not on the map. He has the ability to scent game or perhaps to lure it to him. That night they eat well. Later, Kane wakes to find them encircled by vampires, but N'Longa creates a circle of fire which drives them back.

At noon the two men reach the city, among hills honeycombed with caves. The ancient buildings, built of great stone blocks, are in ruins. Vultures perch on them. The city was old when Negari was built, N'Longa says.

They search for the treasure. Eventually Kane notices, beneath the rubble on the floor of the largest building, a metal ring almost obscured by dust. They manhandle heavy slabs of rubble away from it and find a trapdoor which leads to a vault. In the vault is the treasure, gold dulled by dust and time—but a crack in the vault has let in several vampires, who are sleeping.

As the men retrieve the treasure the vampires wake, glaring. They are powerless until sunset, N'Longa says. But as the men leave, laden with treasure, a vampire seizes N'Longa's ankle and will not let go. Other vampires block the exits. By the time the men escape it is sunset; vampires swarm out of the caves beneath a gibbous moon. The rattle of treasure brings them to the city.

N'Longa calls down a flock of vultures on them, then sets fire to the dry grass within the city. The vampires die silently in the flames. As the men flee dazzled into the hills, spears surround them and Loup disarms Kane.

Now that he has a gun, he has the upper hand—but he is disarmed before he can use it. The warrior whom N'Longa possessed is executed on the spot for deserting; his executioner thrusts the voodoo stave in his own belt.

Queen Nakari condemns Loup to death. Kane, who has not betrayed her, she offers a throne beside hers and a share in her dreams of empire. She is desperate to found a dynasty and bring new life to the city. Kane refuses. "You fool," Loup rages, "you might have saved both of us!"

In the dungeon Loup wishes for his guns, which must still be in the city. Kane asks if he knows where. "Will you pray them here?" Loup asks bitterly. Their situation seems hopeless—then Kane sees that the guard is the man who took the voodoo stave, which is still in his belt.

Kane pleads with the guard to give him the stave. The guard makes to snap it in half, but holding it sends him into a trance. Soon N'Longa winks. Before he can release Kane, several warriors come to take the victims to the sacrifice. It is the Moon of Skulls.

In the temple Kane sees Loup's musket and pistols close to the altar. So does N'Longa, but the ceremony begins at once, as the moon's rays creep closer to the enshrined skull; there is no chance for him to reach the guns. Kane holds up the ceremony, calling down the wrath of God on the city, while N'Longa sidles to the guns. He throws the musket to Kane, who shatters the skull.

Chaos ensues. Dust rains down from the walls as tremors begin. Most of the people flee in terror. Loup retrieves his pistols; he and Kane battle the warriors. Kane reaches the treasure, only to be attacked by the Queen, who is herself run through by Loup. Loup fingers the scar on his face. "The treasure is still to be won, and we have a score to settle, Kane."

As they duel, the earthquake begins in earnest, but Loup will not desist. "If we must die here, let us die like men!" At the end of a prolonged duel, he has Kane at his mercy, but is swallowed by the earthquake.

N'Longa has rescued the treasure, and leads Kane to safety. They look back at the final collapse of the city.

N'Longa leads Kane back as far as his village, where he returns to his own body. The warrior is now in awe of him and guides Kane to the coast, from which he makes his way to England.

Having delivered the treasure to Lady Elizabeth, Kane refuses to take payment or to stay. "I am a landless man. I come out of the sunset and into the sunrise I go, wherever the Lord doth guide my feet . . . " Maybe dissolve to final shot of him on horse, speech continuing as voice-over.

How would you have responded to that? Here's how Milton did.

Dear Ramsey,

I am sorry to have taken so long before reading the SOLOMON KANE outline you sent me. I am still working on the screenplay of THONGOR and hated to take time out from it.

I don't think the outline is yet a proper structure on which to base a film. Some of it is right, I think, but we don't as yet have the logical connections and motivations for the action.

I won't be able to be more specific until I have re-read the stories and put in about a week's work on the structural outline. Then I think I will be able to send you suggestions that will make sense. For example, I now think that the key to the motivation of the entire action has to be religious—something particular to the Puritan religion. We might start with a scene showing Kane in action, but turning out to (with all good intentions) have done something wrong, which he then feels he must expiate. If the thing that he does wrong is something that unwittingly helps Le Loup get at Lady Elizabeth, it could properly motivate his trip to Africa. That's why I suggested updating the film to the end of the Civil War, because in war people can do things thinking they are doing good, which turn out to be evil. As I read your outline, I more and more felt that the missing motivations throughout should be religious and

> moral beliefs—Kane's, N'Longa's, Queen Negari's, etc. I miss the magical and mythical elements which could make the incidents of the story bigger than the events themselves.
>
> This is all very vague, but I can't be more specific until I put in some real work on the outline. I won't be able to do this for about 2 weeks. Please bear with me.

It seems to me his letter proves that Subotsky had more of a sense of the cinematic possibilities of Kane than I had. Alas, I didn't hear from him again. I believe that financing fell out from under his Thongor production, leaving him with a large bill for Eastern European special effects, a situation that may have deterred him from attempting any similar film. Years later it was rumoured that he planned to revive the Kane project with a script by the screenwriters of *The Monster Club*. Perhaps the world is as well off without that production as without the Campbell version.

Stephen King

I

I KNOW TWO HOTEL ANECDOTES ABOUT STEVE King. One is my favourite souvenir of Baltimore, where the hotel staff were either entering into the spirit of Halloween or aiming to give members of the World Fantasy Convention the welcome that seemed appropriate. The lady at Reception who obviously suspected Steve of not being able to pay for his hotel booking because he didn't have a credit card was dressed, as I remember, as a pumpkin. I can think of no better introduction to a weekend of fantasy than the spectacle of the most popular author in the field being suspected of insolvency by a lady pumpkin. That's one anecdote; the other comes from Birmingham, England, where Steve King nearly was.

(*o god that room in the Imperial mustn't think about it talk about something else*)

He was to be guest of honour at the British Fantasy Convention in 1978, until the surgeon intervened—or rather, until the aftermath of a vasectomy did. I shall leave the details to your imagination, not least because I don't want to put off any potential subjects of the operation, which I believe is a good thing. I should know, having had two of them. (I'm sure I'm wrong to think that to make certain the second time, the surgeon used a chainsaw.) However, there's no truth to the rumour

(*rumour doesn't sound like room don't think about the room that changed*)

that Steve and I ever thought of collaborating on a vasectomy novel, especially not if the Guild of Master Vasectomists makes it worth our while not to do so. A pity about those wasted titles, though: *The Unkindest Cut, The Ball Is Over, Scragging the Scrotum, Nobbled in the Nuts, Deferens Deferred, The Testy Testes, Sacrifice That Sac*... But I was talking about Birmingham and Steve King as the guest who never was.

I can't now lay my hands on the appreciation of him that I wrote for the programme booklet, but I believe I suggested that King is to the present what Matheson was to the fifties, *'Salem's Lot* rediscovering the logical terrors of *I Am Legend*, the Overlook Hotel threatening to overtake Hell House as the least desirable venue for an overnight stay (high praise indeed from me at the time, *Hell House* being the last work of fiction that actually made me wish I hadn't stayed up late reading it to the end). I also claimed, I think, that part of the secret of Steve's success (besides his gift for storytelling, whose equal I have yet to find in contemporary fiction) might lie in the way his fiction holds up a distorting mirror to popular themes: The Ameri-can Novelist Returns Home in *'Salem's Lot*, The Artist Struggles With Alcoholism in *The Shining*, The Ugly Duckling Strikes Back in *Carrie*, Local Boy Makes Good in *Cujo* and *The Dead Zone*.... Of course by this stage the distortions are so severe as to be dismaying, but surely that's one of Steve's most remarkable achieve-ments—that he manages to reach so many readers by giving them (in Hitchcock's words) what they think they don't want*, telling them what they would rather not admit they know. That, incidentally, is one factor that distinguishes good horror fiction from escapism. It's also more worthwhile than simply appealing to the side of the reader that wants to gawk at car accidents. There's considerably less of the latter appeal in Steve's work than he sometimes lets himself be persuaded there is, and far more of the nobler stuff.

If the sincerest tribute one can offer another writer is to imitate him, perhaps I should point out a couple of tributes of mine. *The*

* What other popular novelist would risk titles such as *Misery* and *Desperation*?

Parasite was written in the spirit of discovering whether I could learn from *The Shining*, as Peter Straub told me he had—whether I could achieve large-scale supernatural effects, full frontal terrors. I think mine was only a moderate success, and so a few years later I designed "Down There" as a tribute to Steve and his work. What imp of the perverse distracted me from noticing that the story's chief fatality was called Steve? Freudians no doubt will make of that what they choose.

I was involved in one other tribute to Steve King, and if one believes the stories, that one

(*just a story just a ghost story just a mistake people ought to overlook o god overlook*)

is still going wrong, lingering like the phone numbers Steve has scattered through his home town (I've lost count of how many ex-directory numbers I've rung only to be told tartly that no, this is no longer Stephen King's). But surely the stories are a joke, just like the prank that gave rise to them.

The idea was, you see, that when Steve arrived at the Birmingham hotel he should discover that he was booked into room 217. But there was no suite of that number, and certainly nothing less than a suite would do. So, like Kubrick in his film of the book but for quite different reasons, we decided to have the number changed on the door of the suite. Then Steve's vasectomy grounded him, and the number wasn't changed, and so nothing could have happened at the hotel, could it? Surely any rumours meant that the hotel staff were trying to outdo the British Fantasy Convention in imagination, however un-British that might be. Why, the hotel records don't even show the name of the guest some people claim booked the suite.

Whoever was to change the numbers must have told his colleagues why. Several of them read Steve King, but what's surprising about that? Does a bear shit in the woods? The chambermaid who claimed she was making up the suite for Mr Bachman

(*the man who would be king no the man with no face o god*)

certainly was a fan of Steve's, and so can't we conclude that her admiration and imagination got the better of her? Perhaps the thought of entering a bedroom that was to have been Steve's proved too much for her, or the thought of venturing into the bathroom of a suite that had almost been 217. She must have been thinking about that, for she says that as the door to the corridor closed slowly behind her without her having touched it, she was sure she caught sight of the number 217 on the door.

She told herself not to be foolish, she says. She made herself go quickly into the bathroom to prove that there was nothing—made herself do so even though the shower curtain hid the whole of the bath. She heard her footsteps click over the linoleum like the ticking of a clock that was counting the seconds it took her to reach the curtain. The fluorescent lighting gave a small buzzing twitch as she closed her hand on the edge of the chilly plastic. She took a breath that tasted of new soap, and then she snatched the curtain back.

The bath was empty. That was such a relief that she had to support herself with one hand against the damp tiles above the bath. She only just restrained herself from mopping her forehead with one of the fresh towels she was supposed to hang up on the rail. She laughed at herself then, and told herself she'd stay off books that scared her for a while, read Shaun Hutson instead. She switched off the bathroom light and went along the hall to the bedroom, to change the sheets.

She couldn't get hold of the doorknob at first; her fingers slipped. She wiped her hand on her uniform and tried again. This time the doorknob turned, though it was wet. It reminded her that the tiles above the bath had been damp even though the last guest had checked out of the suite days earlier. Then she realised that she'd noticed something else without being aware at the time that she had. There were wet patches on the hall carpet—patches like footprints leading from the bathroom to the bedroom.

They must have been made a while ago. If they'd only just been made there couldn't have been much to the feet that had made them. All at once she decided not to go into the bedroom after all, at any rate not by herself. She bit her lip and said a prayer and let go of the doorknob. Just as she let go, she felt the doorknob turn the rest of the way.

Something on the other side of the door was turning it. Before she could run down the hall, which was only a few paces long and yet the outer door seemed so far away, the bedroom door swung open, and

(*no god no not the drowned woman just a story i promise i won't read anything like that again only the Bible*)

when the hotel staff heard her screams, a carpenter had to unscrew the hinges before they could get into the suite, she was huddled so immovably against the outer door.

She was in the Birmingham hospital for weeks. When she started talking to her visitors they learned that she remembered nothing since she'd unlocked the door of the suite that wasn't 217. She seemed happy enough, especially once a nurse gave her a Bible, and nobody might have known what she thought she saw beyond the bedroom door if the hospital public address system hadn't happened to page a John Smith. She began to scream then

(*o god the dead zone carries on never flags never flagg*)

and cower against the pillow, and babble until they thought she would never stop.

Whatever she saw in that room, surely she couldn't have seen all she claimed: a dying young girl whose death seemed to reach for her and draw her into the dark, a cellar trapdoor yawning as the dark fell over it and a voice called from below "Come down," a man in a white jacket who told her she'd always been the chambermaid, a man wearing an anorak whose hood seemed to contain nothing but blackness and two glaring eyes, someone reaching up to his own face with a spade-claw hand, a closet creeping open to let out a sound of vicious growling, a head in a refrigerator, the mouth stuffed with feathers. . . . All that, and a voice saying "Always more tales"? Could any door conceal so much?

If a door really opened, we try to reassure ourselves, surely it was only in her mind. But that explanation is by no means as reassuring as it seems. Whatever happened in the hotel suite, it was more than imagination. Something beyond imagination was needed to make her listeners see in their own minds all the words she babbled, *in parentheses, printed in italics.*

Perhaps she was simply making a tribute to Steve King, beside which mine seem amateur and clumsy. Still, I did my best. Here's to Steve. Let's raise a can of Bud to him. Long may he continue to open doors in the Gothic structures of our minds.

II

And this was what I wrote for the PS edition of *Pete Sematary*.

THE WIND FROM THE BURYING GROUND

My first reading of *Pet Sematary* turned into a nightmare. I was somewhere above the Atlantic in the depths of the night. That was the situation, not the dream. I'd bought the novel to read on the flight home from Chicago, where I'd attended the 1983 World Fantasy Convention. I was more than halfway through the book, I think, and loath to put it down, but an in-flight dinner and a glass or two of wine had taken their toll, and I slipped the book into the seat pocket, intending just to shut my eyes for a minute. I don't recall the unnerving dream I had, but I vividly remember starting awake with a sense of returning to the nightmare that was the book.

Don't take that as a complaint or any kind of negative criticism. It's rather that the book had reached me on some profound level that most fiction leaves untouched. Part of the issue may have been that our son Mat wasn't much older than Gage in the novel. If fear is one reason why we write horror fiction (and it's difficult to see how it wouldn't be, unless the fiction is dishonest)—if we write it because we're uncommonly aware of and subject to fears—then parental fear is likely to seize us even more fiercely than it affects most folk. As writers we may find different ways of dealing with it; Steve King and I seem driven to imagine the worst onto the page (in my case, a couple of years earlier, *The Nameless* encapsulated some of my terrors about Jenny's daughter and mine), while James Herbert went the other way, sparing children in his stories once he became a father. However, I don't think parental panic is the only source of the power of *Pet Sematary*. At the core of some of King's most disturbing tales—certainly here—is a sense of malevolent chaos.

It shows up in "Crouch End", his highly individual contribution to Lovecraft's mythos, where chaos erupts in a London suburb. It inhabits the hotel room in "1408" and the bad place in "N.", and it infects every mobile phone in *Cell* (where once again, significantly, the continuing threat is to the protagonist's young son). I would argue that it is one of King's major themes and contributions to our field. The short stories I've cited have the intensity of genuine nightmare, and *Cell* balances its apocalyptic vision with a remarkable account of the psychology of a handful of survivors, but *Pet Sematary* is the darkest of them all (or used to be, although the climax of *Revival* is inescapably terrifying, and lifts the theme to a new height of cosmic terror). Two years after it *Pet Sematary* was published, its author regretted that it "just spirals down into darkness". I don't think it's so simple, and I'll presume to suggest that in any case that wouldn't invalidate it as a work of art. Sometimes, perhaps, a writer is so aware of the process involved in writing a piece that it defines his own view of it. At those times, reader, trust the tale.

This one is about death. Of course much horror fiction is. To what extent the field reduces death to a generic convention is a subject for another essay—a substantial one. I would argue that, as in many other areas, horror isn't unlike comedy in its treatment of the theme; both often present taboo subjects in a sufficiently stylised way to let us feel able to approach them. Certainly some horror stories, prose or film, belittle death, but I can't think of any that trivialise it less than *Pet Sematary* does. I feel especially justified in saying so because while I was rereading the novel to help me write this introduction one of my oldest friends died unexpectedly (in February, the month the book cites as most fatal). I was looking forward to discussing this very book with him, along with much else; indeed, I catch myself still doing so. That's the kind of loss we must all experience, and one of many truths the book confronts.

Death is present virtually from the outset in the form of foreshadowing. I'm often reminded of Nabokov's dictum that you can only reread, not read, a book (at least, I would suggest, any good one). In *Pet Sematary* details that may resonate as you continue reading first time round become considerably more ominous on reacquaintance. On the very first page we have Church's unnerving restlessness, and in the third chapter Jud Crandall both cautions the Creeds about trucks on the road and talks about fixing Gage up, having just promised to tell his big sister about the pet cemetery. Much more has gone on even in these three short chapters: they've introduced us to several of the major players, who already live and breathe with that enviable vitality King gives all his characters. Here even more than in most of his tales, their humanity intensifies the horror.

In interviews Steve has suggests that horror defines by contrast what is normal or desirable, and one quality the book affirms is acceptance. If you can't acknowledge the realities of ageing and death, you end up "in a small room writing letters home with Crayolas". Ellie's first day at school gives her parents a sense of their own mortality, but is her father's panic at the thought a reaction too far? It's closely followed by his attack of undefined terror on Gage's behalf, and before long we may suspect that his tragic flaw is an unacknowledged inability to accept that even as a doctor he's helpless in the face of death. Failure to come to terms with death and the suffering that may precede it is epitomised by his wife Rachel in one of King's most vivid depictions of marital conflict (which is also caused by a breakdown of acceptance—by the mistaken assumption that within a marriage "it was possible for one mind to really know another"). Perhaps she's expressing what Louis, for all his rationality, dare not articulate.

Victor Pascow, the student Louis fails to save, is the harbinger of death at its most unconquerable. As he expires he gives voice to Creed's doomed future and, as he grows incoherent, becomes a spokesman for chaos (rather like the phone in room 1408). He will return from the grave just as ambiguously to set about making the nightmare real. His apparition blurs all the boundaries—between dream and reality, between life and death, and the one that marks the point at which the burial ground begins to influence Creed's life, an issue that stays disturbingly unresolved. Perhaps this influence has no part in Norma Crandall's collapse, although she suffers that on Halloween, but at the very least her attack is one of the omens that swarm through the novel, and an event that helps send Louis on his awful mission. We should also note the chill wind that greets him when he crosses the fatal road to deal with the family's dead pet (Church, a name that surely adds meaning to the cat's transformation into something diabolical). It's a wind that will grow stronger, whatever we take it to be.

Beyond the pet cemetery lies a place of ancient dread. The boundary between them is ambiguous—insurmountable except when it chooses not to be, and perhaps revealing more of its uncanny nature in Creed's dream. The other place flouts natural laws and psychological ones too, not to mention generic conventions: it's warm at night when it should be anything but; it brings a sense of contentment and exhilaration, not fear (at least not until the place lets the pretence slip, most disturbingly when a hood seems "to surround a blankness"). Its power is sufficiently insidious to quell doubts or at any rate distract from them. Once Louis has made use of it he's in its thrall.

"It was as if, after the short and placid stupidity of his life as a neuter, Church had rediscovered his real nature in dying." That's a strikingly vivid image of the naturalness of death (even if, as in this case, accidental), and the account of the cat's return, like Jud's tale of the revival of his dog, conveys the uncanny quality of resurrection as well as any treatment of the theme I've ever encountered; it may well have been one source of my nightmare above the Atlantic. The first of the novel's funeral scenes allows King to address death and its aftermath very fully and lets Rachel talk about it at last, feeling as if she has "sicked up something that's poisoned part of me for years." This section is surely the heart of the book, one consolation it offers. Past that we do indeed descend into the dark.

This effect is emphasised by a technique unique to our author in this field, as far as I know—a kind of pre-emptive foretelling of doom. There's a hint of it in "The Mist" ("I haven't seen my wife since then"), but it's crucial to *Pet Sematary*. ". . . some ten weeks before a second heart attack would kill her. . . " ". . . who now had less than two months to live . . . " Near the end the repetition of a solitary word—"Almost"—tolls like a bell. The sense of doom is only emphasised by the false futures that invade the narrative, since they might have been. For instance, while Louis Creed's first dream of working at Disney World may seem innocently benign, its later revivals are heartrending. At the last it turns into a meditation on death.

The dark half (as you might call it) of the book begins with the sentence "It's probably wrong to believe there can be any limit to the horror which the human mind can experience. Like an insight earlier in the novel—that sometimes "since it was its own inviolable self and would not break down, you simply passed terror intact, like a kidney stone"—this reads like a riposte to one of Lovecraft's famous observations, perhaps "The most merciful thing in the world, I think, is the inability of the human mind to correlate all its contents." While Lovecraft was reaching for a sense of cosmic terror, King is committed to psychological precision. That's the opposite of sentimentality, none of which I can find in this book. I'm applying D. H. Lawrence's definition—"the working off on yourself of feelings you haven't really got". There are certainly expressions of emotion that are uncomfortably raw, but that isn't the same thing at all. Indeed, the scenes that don't involve the supernatural are unrelentingly realistic—see the funeral scene in chapter 36, for instance. As for the disinterment, a staple of horror fiction ever since Poe, it's thoroughly reinvented in this novel. Like all the best fiction, it makes us look again at things we've taken for granted. All too often opening a grave is put across as not much of a task—I'm reminded of *The Brides of Dracula*, where Marie Devereux's vampire appears to have been buried about six inches deep, the better to help her pop up—but in *Pet Sematary* there's no shirking on realism. Indeed, the scene conflates gruesomeness and poignancy in a way I've very seldom encountered.

The uncanny dread that the novel has been gathering reaches its height in Jud Crandall's zombie reminiscence and especially in Creed's second walk to the burial ground, when his inner turmoil (unsparingly observed) leads him there. At times the narrative seems to recoil from his experience, introducing for the first time other viewpoints, none of which can save him. The wind has risen and won't be quelled. Moments beyond the barrier recall Lovecraft (the unfamiliar constellations) and Machen (the shapes in the rock), but the intensity of panic is peculiarly King's. It's followed by the brutally succinct final section of the book.

Does the terseness of these chapters suggest that the author wanted to leave his horrors behind? In an interview he told John Connolly ". . . our son Owen, who was 18 months old, ran for the road while we were flying kites one day, and I heard one of those trucks coming, and I tackled him like a football player. I brought him down so, unlike Gage Creed in the book, he lived. But I thought to myself—and again, this is the impulse a lot of times with these things—I'm going to write the worst thing I can think of, and that way it won't happen. So I sat down and wrote *Pet Sematary* and as bad as I imagined it was going to be, the book turned out worse . . . "

The worst thing? The late Thomas Disch suggested that Gage

ought to have returned in the way Church does, walking but dully dead. Surely the book has already dealt with this by letting Creed foresee it, and instead the story follows another logical course, where the malevolent chaos that lies mostly dormant in Church becomes unbridled in Gage. The finale does read like a prolonged cry of rage and grief—in fact, Creed utters one—but I'd venture to suggest that it brings its own built-in reassurance. The fantastic has possessed the narrative, just as it possesses Gage, and we may comfort ourselves with its extravagance if we can. Or perhaps not, in which case I propose this alternative. By showing an unnatural survival after death, the book implies (the "definition by contrast" I ascribed to King earlier) that there may be a natural one—some kind of after-life. Perhaps the darkness of which Steve convicts the book can't entirely put out the light after all, and his optimism shows through even if he doesn't notice.

I'll end on, I hope, not too irrelevant or intrusively personal a note. When Jenny and I started going out together she was at a teacher training college in Hereford. I went to visit her one weekend in 1969, and the train halted for some minutes just outside the station—at least, I thought it had until I realised that the carriage I was in didn't reach the platform. By the time I disembarked Jenny had gone, having assumed I wasn't on the train, and I wandered the campus in search of her. We didn't meet for four hours, when she met the next train from Liverpool. At least we had the rest of the weekend, and rounded it off with a double bill of Roger Corman's Poe films, Jenny's choice and a good sign that we were right for each other. All the same, I sometimes think our afterlife will consist of those four hours, except this time we'll spend them together and they'll last for eternity—our last dream, from which we'll never need to waken. At my age such thoughts become increasingly common, and nothing in *Pet Sematary* does away with them. Even if Steve may not care for the book, he can be proud of it. It's a dauntingly honest and authentic piece of work—a great horror novel.

Robert Aickman Remembered

"WHAT A SELF-IMPORTANT, SELF-REGARDING so-and-so Aickman was! Can he really have been as unlikeable as he seems?" Thus Roger Johnson in *Ghosts and Scholars,* issue 25 of that most M. R. Jamesian of journals. He'd been inflamed by a passage Don Herron quoted from a letter from Robert Aickman to Donald Sidney-Fryer: "I . . . cannot pretend that I do not know what you mean when you say that the range of both Henry James and M. R. James is smaller than mine." Aickman went on to paraphrase the comments he made about M. R. James in his introduction to *The 4th Fontana Book of Great Ghost Stories:* ". . . one becomes aware as one reads of the really great man . . . all too consciously descending a little, to divert, but also still further to edify, the company." Nevertheless Robert reprinted "A School Story", explaining that he found it "free from this defect. The Provost knew about schoolboys."

Two points are worth making before I go on: first, that Aickman may only have been more honest than many of us would be if invited to agree that our work was superior to work we didn't particularly admire; second, that we often most dislike in others what we resist admitting about ourselves. Aickman told Sidney-Fryer that he found "an excessive distancing" in James: "the reader is not meant to feel too involved. This, needless to say, is an intensely

English attitude!" May we assume that Robert was less than happy with the blurbs that compared him to James and praised the "feline detachment" of *Dark Entries?*

I leave that question unanswered and return to Roger Johnson's. Hugh Lamb responded "Definitely not" and suggested that I might have something to add. Let me gather my reminiscences of Robert into as chronological an order as I can.

I first met him when I was nineteen. Kirby McCauley, as part of the second European trip we took together, had arranged a post-luncheon appointment for us at Robert's rooms in Gower Street. Exactly as Michael Pearson puts it in the publisher's note that introduces Robert's book *The River Runs Uphill,* "I was acutely conscious of being in the presence of A Great Man." I was at the peak of my painful shyness with strangers, and may have uttered no more words than were involved in ascertaining whether I might smoke, then a habit of mine. (I was given an ashtray without comment.) At any rate, Kirby did much of the talking, and Robert most of the answering. At this distance I recall very little other than his dainty allusion to the fate of King Zog of Albania.

Ten years passed, and brought the first World Fantasy Convention, where I was among the judges for the World Fantasy Award. I note with sadness that all the nominees for the Life Achievement Award that year—Aickman, Long, Wandrei, Wellman, and the winner, Bloch—are now dead, and recall that the prize for short fiction went to Aickman's "Pages from a Young Girl's Journal". I accepted on his behalf, and ferried it back to England to present to him.

He was now living in the Barbican, an apartment complex whose functional exterior concealed, in Robert's case, a home from an altogether more genteel age. He chortled politely at Gahan Wilson's bust of Lovecraft, and served me glasses of cream sherry. (Subsequently he had the bust separated from its stand, and after his death only the base bearing the award plaque was found to have survived. He was, to put it mildly, no admirer of Lovecraft, or indeed of any fiction he regarded as horror.) I must have conquered some of my shyness by then, but I believe Robert helped. Hugh Lamb once rightly said (I may be paraphrasing) that having a conversation with Robert always reminded you how much you yourself knew. Whatever art of conversation has been lost, Robert was one of its masters.

Next year—1976—he was guest of honour at the British Fantasy Convention in Birmingham. As the only person there who'd met him, I was made responsible for him. Perhaps by then we knew each other well enough for me to have been able to perceive him as a pale chubby fellow with the worst teeth I've ever seen in a living mouth. I showed him to his room and returned at the appointed time. He emerged in a suit, not togs generally favoured at conventions even in those bygone days, and declared "I am at your disposal." I introduced him to a number of suitably respectful people, some of whom accompanied Jenny and us to dinner at an Indian restaurant. When the horror writer David Riley ("The Satyr's Head", "The Lurkers in the Abyss") revealed that he'd stood as a candidate for the National Front, Robert quizzed him about Oswald Mosley. Later various of us escorted Robert to someone's room party. I was the first to call it a night, but gather that Robert and Jenny and the anthologist Richard Davis shared a mug for drinking white wine, glasses being scarce. I'm told Robert declared that all men were looking for their Jenny and that I'd found mine.

Next morning he appeared at breakfast in a shirt and sweater. Ken Bulmer approached to tease him about having lightened up and received a lethal glare. Perhaps Robert was getting himself into an appropriately grave mood to deliver his guest of honour's speech that afternoon. Alas, there is no transcript, but my memory suggests that his talk drew on the philosophy of his Fontana introductions and on the essay he wrote for Gahan Wilson's *First World Fantasy Awards* anthology. Afterwards he admitted disappointment with the audience reaction. "They don't want standards," he told me. Presumably his sitting through every item on the programme—something Fantasycon attendees had already ceased to do—confirmed this verdict. To my surprise, of the films shown he preferred *Night of the Living Dead* to *The Leopard Man,* whose reticence and delicacy I would have expected to appeal to him.

By now Robert and I were exchanging letters frequently. "What a fascinating correspondence we are having!" he wrote. Sadly, I no longer have his letters, which failed to survive moving house, and so I can't recall if it was just before or just after the convention that I wrote to invite him to stay for a weekend, in our Liverpool house very like George's in *The Doll Who Ate His Mother*, including the rabbit.

Either his train was early or I was late. I found him standing outside the barrier and proffered my hand, which he took with, I thought, a brevity close to reluctance. When I proposed a bus ride home he acceded without demur. Of the ride I remember only asking him (for the purposes of the novel of *Dracula's Daughter* I was about to write) where one might have found fog by the Thames in the era of the tale—Whitechapel? He betrayed no disdain at my lack of research. "Stepney," he said at once, and so it was.

We'd invited friends to dine with him: Stan and Marge Nuttall, John Owen. For some reason Robert took a dislike to Marge, even though Jenny formed the view that in general he preferred the company of women. When Marge suggested that the texture of Jenny's chicken tikka might not be authentic he sprang to its defence. Whether this disagreement was the source of the dislike I have no idea, but during a lull in the conversation he asked Marge if she was wearing a wig (which she wasn't, in case the reader wonders). After dinner the conversation focused on artistic matters. Asked his opinion of Iris Murdoch, Robert said only that while it might be too much to expect contemporary fiction to have uplift, at least it shouldn't take away from life. Rebecca West he declared had written the nearest things to masterpieces of literature our century was likely to produce. *Rosemary's Baby* (the novel) he thought "a good shocker". As to films, he enthused about Leni Riefenstahl, *Das Blaue Licht* in particular. *Ugetsu Monogotari* and (later, after I'd commended it to him) *Picnic at Hanging Rock* drew his praise; he agreed that it was reminiscent of his own tales, especially (he said) in the scene where the teacher appears in her underwear. A mention of *Don't Look Now* provoked his ire—"offensive to du Maurier, to the ghostly and to Venice in particular." He was contemptuous of Donald Suther-land's accent, which he found calculatedly international, and outraged by Sutherland's sex scene with Julie Christie. When John Owen suggested it might have been put in for commercial reasons, Robert responded with a look that rendered words superfluous. Indeed, dislike often roused his passion; other detestations he expressed while I knew him included the magazine *Private Eye* and the Anthony Shaffer play *Sleuth*, although he only chortled upon learning that I liked Penderecki's opera *The Devils of Loudon.*

(Let me return parenthetically to Leni Riefenstahl. In his autobiography *The Attempted Rescue* he devotes a chapter ("A Distant Star") to her and cites *The Blue Light* as his favourite film; "when it was new I saw it again and again." It may well have influenced his strange tales, in particular "The Visiting Star", but his account of the film is stranger still: he has Vigo learning of the blue light when he watches all the men of the village attempt to scale the mountain with ladders, and Vigo later climbs the mountain in their company but reaches the summit alone. In Aickman's version it's Vigo who finds the cave despoiled because "the villagers have called in experts", and the film ends with him roaming the mountains and vainly calling Junta's name. I don't think any amount of re-editing could change the film so radically, and must conclude that this vision was to some extent Aickman's own—a vision it conjured up for him, and no less valid for it.)

Sunday gave me time to play him Korngold's early opera *Die Tote Stadt.* "Mr Aickman, you simply must hear it," a lady had told him, and he was grateful for the chance. At intervals he took out a notebook and made a memorandum, either quoting the libretto or recording an error in translation. Also found worthy of a note was my admission that submitting "In the Bag" to the *Times* ghost story competition (judged by Kingsley Amis, Patricia Highsmith and Christopher Lee) had brought me no success. Jenny had the impression that there was something he hadn't forgiven Amis for, perhaps not just for being (as Robert put it) a wine snob. I reflect that they were both in love with Elizabeth Jane Howard. All the same, he vigorously defended the finale of *The Green Man* from her objection that an exorcist had to believe in exorcism for one to work.

Monday found us picnicking in Lancashire, having been driven there by the Nuttalls. Later we visited Chingle Hall near Goosnargh but saw none of the reputed ghosts. Robert felt he and I should sign the visitors' book, and perhaps our autographs still haunt it. On the same trip we failed to find an abandoned waterways terminal Robert had been given to believe was somewhere in the area.

Alas, that was our last meeting. We continued to correspond regularly until he wrote to apologise that he would no longer be able to keep it up, having been told "not really to my surprise, that I have cancer. At present I am oppressed by the mere vulgar symptoms." What can one say on such occasions? We assured him he would be welcome to stay whenever he liked, but it's hardly surprising that he neglected to take up the offer. A year or so later he died, leaving me and Jenny with memories we wouldn't be without. Jenny feels he should have given us a sign from the other side by now, since he was such a believer in the supernatural. I'm just as much of a skeptic, and yet I sometimes have a sense of being observed by him, especially if I swear immoderately to myself when there's nobody else to be seen.

So was he as terrible a chap as Roger Johnson thinks? About as much as I am, I'd suggest. I'm the better for having had him as a friend and as an example. Once he commented to Kirby McCauley that there were no longer any vivid men. That was certainly untrue in at least one instance while he was with us.

CLIVE BARKER

I

"THE CREATURE HAD TAKEN HOLD OF HIS LIP AND pulled his muscle off his bone, as though removing a Balaclava."

Still with me?

Here's another taste of what you can expect from Clive Barker:

"Each man, woman and child in that seething tower was sightless. They saw only through the eyes of the city. They were thoughtless, but to think the city's thoughts. And they believed themselves deathless, in their lumbering, relentless strength. Vast and mad and deathless."

You see that Barker is as powerfully visionary as he is gruesome. One more quote, from yet another story:

"What would a Resurrection be without a few laughs?"

I quote that deliberately, as a warning to the faint-hearted. If you like your horror fiction reassuring, both unreal enough not to be taken too seriously and familiar enough not to risk spraining your imagination or waking up your nightmares when you thought they were safely put to sleep, these books are not for you. If, on the other hand, you're tired of tales that tuck you up and make sure the night light is on before leaving you, not to mention the parade of Good

Stories Well Told which have nothing more to offer than borrowings from better horror writers whom the best-seller audience have never heard of, you may rejoice as I did to discover that Clive Barker is the most original writer of horror fiction to have appeared for years, and in the best sense, the most deeply shocking writer now working in the field.

The horror story is often assumed to be reactionary. Certainly some of its finest practitioners have been, but the tendency has also produced a good deal of irresponsible nonsense, and there is no reason why the whole field should look backward. When it comes to the imagination, the only rules should be one's own instincts, and Clive Barker's never falter. To say (as some horror writers argue, it seems to me defensively), that horror fiction is fundamentally concerned with reminding us what is normal, if only by showing the supernatural and alien to be abnormal, is not too far from saying (as quite a few publishers' editors apparently think) that horror fiction must be about ordinary everyday people confronted by the alien. Thank heaven nobody convinced Poe of that, and thank heaven for writers as radical as Clive Barker.

Not that he's necessarily averse to traditional themes, but they come out transformed when he's finished with them. "Sex, Death and Starshine" is the ultimate haunted theatre story, "Human Remains" a brilliantly original variation on the doppelganger theme, but both these take familiar themes further than ever before, to conclusions that are both blackly comic and weirdly optimistic. The same might be said of "New Murders in the Rue Morgue", a dauntingly optimistic comedy of the macabre, but now we're in the more challenging territory of Barker's radical sexual openness. What, precisely, this and others of his tales are saying about possibilities, I leave for you to judge. I did warn you that these books are not for the faint of heart and imagination, and it's as well to keep that in mind while braving such tales as "Midnight Meat-Train", a Technicolor horror story rooted in the graphic horror movie but wittier and more vivid than any of those. "Scape-Goats", his island tale of terror, actually uses that staple of the dubbed horror film and videocassette, the underwater zombie, and "Son of Celluloid" goes straight for a biological taboo with a directness worthy of the films of David Cronenberg, but it's worth pointing out that the real strength of that story is its flow of invention. So it is with tales such as "In the Hills, the Cities" (which gives the lie to the notion, agreed to by too many horror writers, that there are no original horror stories) and "The Skins of the Fathers". Their fertility of invention recalls the great fantastic painters, and indeed I can't think of a contemporary writer in the field whose work demands more loudly to be illustrated. And there's more: the terrifying "Pig-Blood Blues"; "Dread", which walks the shaky tightrope between clarity and voyeurism that any treatment of sadism risks; more, but I think it's almost time I got out of your way.

Here you have nearly a quarter of a million words of him (at least, I hope you've bought all three volumes; he'd planned them as a single book), his choice of the best of eighteen months' worth of short stories, written in the evenings while during the days he wrote plays (which, by the way, have played to full houses). It seems to me to be an astonishing performance, and the most exciting début in horror fiction for many years.

II

Here's a blurb from a fantastic story. Most of twenty years ago, at John Lennon's old school in Liverpool, parents are so dismayed by a school magazine that they take it away from their children. A student at Liverpool University attacks Conrad's *Heart of Darkness* for not describing "the horror, the horror." "What does Kurtz do," the student wants to know, "fuck chimps?" Police in Manchester sieze copies of a film magazine that contains stills from a new British horror film, *Hellraiser*, and police in London insist that a science fiction bookshop remove a window display advertising the film. Fellow writers mutter that the writer and director of the film owes his success to having sold his soul to the Devil. His name is Clive Barker, and he is irrepressible.

He's thirty-six years old, but in person seems even younger and more energetic than he looks in photographs. When he talks about his work he unfolds his hand toward his listeners as if he's making them an offer. He seems to have preserved his boyish innocence and enthusiasm and capacity for awe while acquiring the professionalism to put them to their fullest use. We first met twenty years ago. I'd been invited by Clive's English teacher to lecture at Quarry Bank High School on the subject of horror. Teachers grimaced while I talked about the theme of venereal disease in the tales of Arthur Machen, but one schoolboy was leading the laughter and applause. Clive claims that he was bespectacled and overweight, but I remember him as he is now, wiry and bright-eyed and impatient to be astonished. He has been impatient to astonish ever since.

He was born in Liverpool in October 1952, and lived with his parents and younger brother near Penny Lane. He had imaginary friends and loved fantastic fiction, but many children do. Perhaps the normality of his life made him impatient with what he calls "the tyranny of the real." Fiction that mimics reality doesn't interest him, since "we already have to *live* that stuff."

He was eleven when his mother produced his first play, enacted by a Boy Scout group. His impatience with traditional school productions of Shakespeare led him to write "plays about magicians and dragons and mad Nazis . . . and they were pretty popular." His dissatisfaction with the Quarry Bank magazine caused him to publish *Humphri*, an alternative school magazine which featured a nude sketch and which came in the form of loose sheets in a plastic bag. Later he attended the University of Liverpool, but preferred to work outside in theatre and mime with some of his fellow students. "I never took much notice of my courses. I was biding my time," he says.

He worked for some years in the theatre before moving to London in 1977, where he wrote comedies and Grand Guignol. One play, *Colossus*, requires a ship to sink on stage. In 1981 he read Kirby McCauley's anthology *Dark Forces* and was surprised by the range of the horror fiction it contained. "The options are wide open," he realised, and began to write horror stories in his spare time. "Let's see how far we can press this."

At the end of eighteen months he had written a quarter of a million words, which he called *Clive Barker's Books of Blood*. For an unpublished writer to put his name above the title looks presumptuous, but Clive knew that nobody had written fiction quite like this before. Most radical is his outrageous optimism, by virtue of which his characters encounter "the capacity for the monstrous in the world" but neither seek to destroy it nor are destroyed by it, rather emerging transformed. A tourist becomes part of a giant built out of the bodies of Yugoslavian villagers (*In the Hills, the Cities*); an intelligent cancer makes its lair in a seedy cinema and assumes the forms of John Wayne and Marilyn Monroe in order to trap its victims, but fails to impress an overweight lady (*Son of Celluloid*); Poe's ape becomes the hero of its own tale (*New Murders in the Rue Morgue*) . . . This kind of unclassifiable extravagance isn't easy to market, and when the collection was published in 1984 it was split into three thin paperbacks. They were received with a resounding absence of reviews, and went straight onto the horror shelves in bookshops, but they had already gained an underground reputation from people who had read them in manuscript. Soon Stephen King was claiming "I have seen the future of horror, and its name is Clive Barker."

Clive seeks less to horrify than to excite. His excitement is infectious, and together with the efforts of his agent, the formidable June Hall, has set him on a ladder whose top is not in sight.

Hi first novel, *The Damnation Game*, in which a character spends the entire book decomposing, was submitted for the Booker Prize, but Clive was already heading for the movies. His dissatisfaction with the way his scripts were filmed took him to New World, a company noted giving first-time directors a chance. The result was *Hellraiser*, which begins in a large room full of a man who has been torn apart with meathooks, and goes on to explore what happens to him next. Before it was released Hollywood was making offers—to write and direct *Alien III* or continue the *Friday the 13th* series—but Clive was off in search of something new enough to interest him.

More recently it was *Weaveworld*, in which he makes love to the fantastic. When an old carpet is unwoven, it releases an entire world of the imagination remembered in legends and fairy tales (which, for Clive, include the Bible). The spectacle includes a policeman who turns into a dragon, the sex life of planets, the angel which guarded the Garden of Eden and which lurks in the ultimate desert . . . Publishers have paid appropriately huge advances, and the Royal College of Art was commissioned to produce a handwoven carpet to publicise the book.

"There are no limits," says the poster for *Hellraiser*, and that goes for Barker too. Of course this means he will antagonise people. Pamela Armstrong, a BBC chat show hostess, commented "Presumably some people like this sort of thing" in a tone that suggested she was holding the subject between finger and thumb and looking for the nearest dustbin. Not everyone at the Brighton World Science Fiction Convention appreciated Clive's jokes about dead babies. Though the British Board of Film Censors is said to have admired *Hellraiser*, it surely can't be long before Clive himself draws the attention of the censorious—not that this is likely to do anything other than charge him afresh. The openness he brings to everything he attempts suggests that we have hardly begun to hear from him. What he asks of other people's horror films also sums up his ambition: "Whatever you want to do, *do it*." I believe he will.

PETER STRAUB

SO THE TERRIBLE TRIO MEETS AGAIN—PETER AND Thom and me. Before I attempt to put my thoughts on *Shadowland* in order and find words worthy of the book, let me reminisce.

It was Thom Tessier who brought us together when he was my first British hardcover editor, at Millington Books, which issued me in several plain black wrappers. One merit of Millington was that its offices on Southampton Row faced Peter's Bar, which became something of a meeting-place for writers of the fantastic and macabre (Manly Wade Wellman and Karl Edward Wagner are surely among its ghosts, sharing a table). I rather think it was there (though Peter remembers it differently) that Thom introduced me to a writer friend of his at one of our bibulous preambles to an eventual lunch, sometimes too belated to reduce the wages of conviviality. If that initial meeting wasn't in Peter's Bar, later ones certainly were, and perhaps my memory of the precise location of our first encounter has been driven out of my head by the persistent echo of the first words I blurted at Peter: "I've just read it."

"What?" Peter reasonably said.

"*Julia*."

"Uh huh," said Peter, or words to that effect, as one would. I had indeed, and by coincidence, just read his first supernatural novel, about which I proceeded to enthuse, rather spoiling the effect by declaring that Mark's breakdown in the park at the end of the book had much in common with an LSD trip. "I wouldn't know," Peter told me, politely enough; no doubt he felt I was either assuming too much about him, who'd had no truck with psychedelics, or revealing too much about my own indulgences. The conversation faltered until Peter mentioned that he'd read Millington's first book of mine, *The Doll Who Ate His Mother*. There was then an awkward—one might say prolonged—silence.

Well, we writers are awkward creatures, bumbling social incompetents who may be far more articulate on the page than in person and who need only the least excuse to withdraw into ourselves: that's me, at any rate. Soon Peter and I learned to pretend in each other's company that we were nothing like that, and got on famously. In time I met his delightful wife Susie, and enjoyed their hospitality both in London and New York. As Thom and I, and especially Peter, increased our writerly fame, we often met at conventions—at the British Fantasy Convention, then located in the slowly but spectacularly decaying Imperial Hotel in Birmingham, or at the convention's American counterpart, the World. I tried unsuccessfully to entice both my drinking buddies into an anthology, *New Terrors*, but otherwise I don't think much of our conversation concerned our own writing; it seems that if you talk about it you don't do it, and vice versa. Nevertheless we must have sensed or deduced in one another our own need for reassurance, and before long it showed up in our intermittent correspondence.

It was reassuring to learn that a writer so much better than I needed just as much support. Perhaps Peter has forgotten, but I vividly remember the letter he sent me shortly after completing *Ghost Story*, which he described as a big bird which stubbornly refused to fly, and as a book with maybe one good scare in it. Readers can choose their candidates for that description from among their favourite moments. Success, whether commercial or artistic (in Peter's case, both), doesn't do away with self-doubt; it may even create a fear that the success is undeserved. That may sound like self-indulgence to those who don't experience it, but I suggest that if we weren't so hypersensitive we wouldn't be writers. It took a great deal of sensitivity as well as control to write *Shadowland*.

Which means I've tricked myself at last into trying to do justice to the book, although if anyone with that volume in their hands needs an introduction to Peter's work (an unlikely situation, it seems to me), they should obtain a copy of *Wild Animals*, which collects his first three novels together with an admirably insightful preface by the author himself. Still, here I go, having run out of delaying tactics. Two readings of *Shadowland* have convinced me that if the magic of this book will be difficult, maybe impossible, to describe, it is at least unassailable.

I mean the storytelling, to begin with: the apparently effortless (an adjective guaranteed to wring a wry smile from almost every author) complexity, the joy in narrative play, which astonished us in *Ghost Story* is both taken further and refined here. Unlike Coleman Collins, Peter is never "lost within his own powers". But as well as being its achievements, magic and mystery are the themes of the book, and the very ambiguity of its view of them combines them. It manages to contain both the seedy unsatisfactory occultism one finds in the work of M. John Harrison and the tortured ritual path to self-knowledge hinted at by Georges Chevalier (*The Sacred Magician: A Ceremonial Diary*), and to suggest that they are aspects of something else. Like so much of the best work in our field, the entire book seems a metaphor for something it couldn't otherwise describe.

It is also, though by no means uniquely, quintessential Straub. Here I falter, remembering the unlucky poet in David Lodge's *Changing Places*, whose urge to create was destroyed by a computer which listed the words he used most—but I believe Peter is aware of the themes he has made his own. Loyalty is one, and the dangerous ecstasies of war, and the banal evil of creativity turned inward. Many of the characters appear in different guises, in later books too. "Mystery is always duplicitous, and once you know its secret, it is twice banal." To what extent can we trust this definition and the character who utters it? That seems to be one of the questions to answering which Peter has devoted his career.

Some final thoughts before I entrust you to him. In his afterword to *Mrs. God* he says that though he admires Robert Aickman he isn't like him, but I see one similarity: both writers use the fantastic as an aid to—even a way of—thinking about the world. *Shadowland* is perhaps the first of his books that could have been written only by Peter: the work of a writer who is developing his talent to the full by enlarging his genre in the direction of the mainstream. Unlike some who claim that process for themselves, he never denies his roots in the genre, which would be much the poorer without him. Enough! I can hold him and his book down no longer. It's a wild flight and a fine one, and your imagination will be enriched by it. We adults need fables and fairy tales too, to remind us we can fly.

DENNIS ETCHISON

I FIRST MET MY FRIEND MR ETCHISON AT THE 1979 World Fantasy Convention in Providence. I was already in awe of him. He, or maybe our agent Kirby McCauley, had submitted two stories for my anthology *New Terrors*, both of which had struck me—I blush to admit this—as too experimental for the book. (One was "The Walking Man", and may be found in the Etchison collection *The Dark Country* by anyone who wants to be appalled by my poor judgment.) I eventually used "The Spot", by Dennis and the shadowy Mark Johnson, whose sharing of initials with the Etchison pseudonym Jack Martin seems unsettlingly suggestive. The Etchison letters to me had been more literate and formal than I could manage, and I had the impression of an intellect that might be barely approachable in person. No wonder I felt overwhelmed that Saturday in the Biltmore Plaza, a hotel which always seems to be under construction, when Mr Etchison sent Barbara Wagner as his emissary to invite me to his table in the bar.

I shuffled over and shook hands and took a seat, and we sat in judgment on each other. It was only much later I learned that our nervousness on meeting a writer we admired had been mutual. As I recall it, our conversation was guarded and tentative and a bit stiff, both of us being afraid to put a thought wrong. Dennis, on the other hand, claims to remember insulting me, saying he hadn't expected the sensitivity he found in my fiction to be contained by such a hulk of flesh. Me, I find it hard to imagine Stocky from Stockton passing such a comment, since he has as little between his chin and collarbone as I have. Maybe our thickness—you could roll us together and make three Christopher Priests—is one reason why we became friends.

Another is that I know one real Dennis is the jovial character who has, it seems, a genius for imitating just about any voice he hears (though he refuses to imitate me to my face) and who, together with Pete Atkins and Karl Edward Wagner, is one of my children's favourite adopted uncles, buying them sweets and jokes and sharing with Matt a taste for fruit machines and pinballs. Jokes? You've perhaps blinked at that, not having noticed many in the man's prose. But don't let that deadpan fool you. So controlled a writer, and one with a vision of the world as bleak as his, needs to be able to joke.

Of course sometimes the joke is on him, especially when his last name acquires an extra N, most recently throughout the tributes to him in the programme of the British Fantasy Convention. Or has that consonant which has haunted him throughout his career a message for him and the rest of us? In mathematics it denotes an unspecified amount, in religion and the occult it signifies a name that should not be spoken. Let me leave the subject to grow stranger in the reader's mind, as so many of Dennis's tales bloom in the memory. I was talking about jokes and Dennis's vision of the world.

It wasn't clear to me which of those, if not both, I was inhabiting when I first stayed with Dennis in his house on a bend where every time his car backs out the lives in the vehicle are delivered into the care of any higher power there is. I'm not thinking so much of the brunch to which he ushered me one Sunday, where I chose a meal called Mexican Surprise which more than lived up to its name throughout a bookstore signing I sat down for numerous times that afternoon, but rather our jaunt which rounded off the week. Dennis proposed that we and Steve Jones and Jo Fletcher, who were now also picking their way through the luxuriance filling the interior of the Etchison bungalow, go down to Ensenada for the weekend, by which time the party included several students of Dennis's from UCLA, and friends of theirs too. Life does tend to contort itself around Dennis, which may well be one reason why he exerts so much control over his prose. In deference to my grey hairs, I was driven in a Lincoln Continental by the composer David Gibney, who gave me medication for my still surprised innards and another kind for my brain. Steve and Jo were stuffed into Dennis's car, avoiding bits of wire that dangled from the dashboard, and other vehicles set off independently. Sometime after midnight we crossed the border into Mexico, having left the Etchison car somewhere behind, and hours later I wakened just enough to stagger to bed.

The sun rose, and so eventually did I, to discover that the Etchison contingent had broken down on the far side of the border and gone back to Los Angeles for repairs, presumably to the car. So here I was in a country where I didn't speak the language and surrounded by people I'd never met before in my life. At times I have a sense of inhabiting my own fiction, but just then I felt as though I'd been dumped into an Etchison plot. Pretty soon someone proposed a trip into town for a drink, and no voice was louder in support than mine. We found a hotel bar and listened to a mariachi band, and one of the party elected to teach me how to drink tequila—a test which, to his visible bemusement, I passed, alcohol in various forms having on occasion touched my lips. Then someone else—I recall no names—produced some psilocybin from her handbag.

I don't mind admitting that these mushrooms are my favourite psychedelic, but to consume them in a public place where the Federales might walk in at any moment struck me as less than tempting. I might almost as well have indulged, though, because the experience of waiting for the effects to manifest themselves on those who had was nearly as nerve-racking. After a while one of the party began to express his desire for the young woman who had supplied the drug. More precisely, he declared in what I thought was rather a loud voice that he wanted to fuck her, and insisted that I wanted to fuck her too. I pointed out that I was married, and English, and ground my teeth and kept my eye on the door in case it should admit armed police or the Etchison party. In the depths of my mind there might even have been an unworthy suspicion that Dennis had cancelled his arrival, maybe as a prank. But less than days later, really only hours, he and his guests appeared, and a good deal of time passed before I learned that some of the people I'd been sitting with he'd hardly known at all.

By now you, patient though you may be, are perhaps wondering what this ramble has to do with *Darkside.* Would I waste your time? Wouldn't you expect obliqueness from Campbell writing about Dennis—oblique creatures, both of us? Actually, all I'm trying to do in this piece is live up to his example, and now I realise that nothing I can say about *Darkside* is worthy of delaying your experience of reading it.

Or perhaps this introduction seems too personal. My response to the novel has to be, because I recognise how autobiographical some of it is, which is one reason I find it so moving. Autobiography is one of the sources of its moral concern, but that quality ought to be apparent to any reader. It's a quality you may expect to find throughout Dennis's work, including his novels based on films, books written with a seriousness rare in that kind of work, though why shouldn't novels derived from films be as legitimate a form as films derived from novels? All either needs is an artist who cares about his work, and it would be redundant to say that description fits Dennis.

One further point may in time need to have been made. The film *Flatliners* was released several years after *Darkside* had been published, and indeed after Dennis's script based on the novel had been circulated in Hollywood. While the film has its merits, Dennis's treatment of the theme is more imaginative, more affecting and more meaningful. It is the work of a writer driven to tell the truth. As for Dennis, he is one of my best friends, and a better writer than I am. All of his books deserve to see an edition at least as permanent as this, and in the days of Scream/Press several did.

The first was *The Dark Country,* for the title story of which I presented Dennis with the British Fantasy Award for best short story of the year. The circumstances were an Etchisonian tale in themselves, or at least the kind of deadpan joke reality too often plays on him. Though the award should have been presented at the Birmingham fantasy convention, I was forbidden to do so by the committee, which had become estranged from the British Fantasy Society, whose award it was, and so the ceremony took place in the back garden of David and Sandra Sutton. All this is incidental and not very interesting, except that the way Dennis was denied his moment of glory in front of the audience which was waiting to hear who had won the awards seems frustratingly consistent. Etchison is still far less appreciated than he deserves to be, and it was certainly time that Scream/Press awarded him some permanence.

And yet for a period in his twenty years of writing he was appearing alongside Stephen King, in alternate issues of *Cavalier.* What must the readers have made of the oblique and allusive Etchisons which appeared in (continued on page 90) fragments between the nude ladies primly covering their pubes and the body-brief ads, Big Flash, Scuttles and Sling Shot (. . . a tornado of perfection . . . big idea with brief action)? Perhaps they didn't know enough about the conventions to which horror fiction is expected to conform to be deterred by his unpredictability.

I can only think it's that quality which has denied him the fame accorded to so many lesser writers. In those days of supermarketing labels it's dangerous for a writer of HORROR FICTION to break the conventions. Maybe it bothers some readers that some of his tales pursue their themes beyond what would be the conventional punch line, while some do without a punch line entirely. You have my word that he is offering more than hidebound horror fiction does, not less.

Etchison is a poet of loneliness and alienation, whether in the big city or on the freeway. "You Can Go Now", "The Nighthawk", "It Will be Here Soon", and "Deathtracks" are four of the most poignant fantasies (which means anything but escapism) of our time. On the other hand, his transplant trilogy is one of the most chilling achievements in contemporary horror I can think of; in particular, "The Dead Line" manages to live up to the most horrifying first line ever written. Etchison has little time as a writer for the manufacturing of atmosphere, and why should he when he can even (in "The Pitch") make a description of food terrifying? Who else in this too often reactionary field has forged so far ahead and kept on while so few people noticed? Now at last (I concluded my introduction to *The Dark Country*) the power and range of his work is on display too strikingly to be ignored.

Dennis Etchison is the finest writer of short stories now working in this field, and the rest of us ought to learn from him.

James Herbert

I

"James Herbert," Stephen King writes in *Danse Macabre*, "is held in remarkably low esteem by writers in the genre on both sides of the Atlantic." I was one of the writers he had in mind. A thorough reading of Herbert's work has convinced me I was wrong, and I've begun to wonder if Herbert is disliked by some writers because he challenges the class bias of English horror fiction.

English horror fiction is almost entirely middle-class, either in its overt attitudes or its assumptions. As the world outside this perimeter becomes increasingly difficult to ignore, writers react in various ways: Dennis Wheatley blamed everything that threatened his way of life on Satan, Basil Copper retreats consciously to the Victorian era and writes, as one reviewer aptly put it, "as if he lived in a timeless void of writing". Compared with the American tradition, English horror fiction is singularly lacking in working-class characters, and too many of those it presents are caricatures: for example, Brian Lumley's criminals (one of whom manages to call a character both "guv" and "recluse") ring as false as Russell Wakefield's. All too often the working class in English genre fiction seem based on versions of the working class received from English genre fiction. Not so with James Herbert, whose first novel *The Rats* (1974) is based solidly in the real world.

In this novel a mutant strain of rats bred in the East End of London emerges from a derelict house to hunt human beings. The threat is eventually contained by government intervention, though not, as the sequel *Lair* makes clear, for very long. Herbert himself was born and bred in the East End, in a street which had been left half derelict by bombing, and which was overrun by rats. The protagonist of the novel, a teacher called Harris, has a background that resembles Herbert's. "How colourful," an art student remarks about Harris's East End background; perhaps it was this kind of comment that encouraged Herbert to show the area as it really was.

The Rats announces at once that he won't be confined by the conventions of English macabre fiction. The first chapter is a sympathetic portrait of an alcoholic who has become outcast because of his homosexuality, while the fifth portrays one of several derelicts who meet on a bombsite. This latter chapter has a savage power that recalls *Last Exit to Brooklyn,* and as in Selby's novel, aesthetic objections to the savagery are beside the point: it would be dishonest of both writers to try to soften their material so as to spare the reader. In Herbert's case, given that he was working in the mid-seventies in a genre often dictated to by the audience's expectations, his refusal to mince the squalor is all the more admirable.

The rats "were the system", Herbert said in an interview for *Fangoria* magazine. "That's why it was open ended, the system still goes on." They clearly also represent neglect personified. "What disgusted him more," Harris the teacher reflects, "the vermin themselves—or the fact that it could only happen in East London?" But Harris continues "It was no good becoming overwrought with authority, for he knew too well that apathy existed on all levels . . . Wasn't that what Original Sin was supposed to be about? We're all to blame . . . " That the book can discuss its underlying themes so directly without becoming pretentious—a trap into which several contemporary American writers in the field have fallen—is one of Herbert's strengths. The hint of Catholicism is developed in later books, while the flaws of "the system" are explored in more detail in his next book, *The Fog* (1975).

The fog is a bacteriological weapon, stored underground when its development was discontinued, released by explosives during an army test. Herbert uses the situation of a potentially nationwide disaster for two purposes: to show its effect on ordinary people and how they respond (as in the science fiction novels of H. G. Wells and, later, John Wyndham) and to illuminate flaws in the Establishment, particularly in terms of the way they deal with the crisis (a tendency in Herbert's writing which recalls the Quatermass stories of Nigel Kneale). In Herbert's world, however, the "ordinary" person is generally lonely and often deeply flawed. Portraits of loneliness are central to almost all his novels (some of the most extreme appearing in the early chapters of *The Rats*), and the typical Herbert hero is an outsider who develops a strong, usually sexual, relationship in the course of the novel.

Where *The Rats* had its characters doing their best to cope with a crisis, *The Fog* shows its characters invaded by the threat, a "fog" or gas which causes insanity. (In this it resembles Charles Platt's pornographic novel *The Gas*, but Herbert's novel is altogether more controlled.) The book has been criticised for the consequent scenes of violence, and Stephen King quotes Herbert as saying that his approach in writing it was "I'm going to try to go over the top, to see how much I can get away with" (a comment reminiscent of Straub's statement that he meant *Ghost Story* to "take the classic elements of the horror novel as far as they could go"). But *The Fog* contains remarkably few graphic acts of violence, though two (one in a gymnasium, and the other in the bedroom of a Chief Superintendent of Police) are so horrible and painful, at least for this reader, that they pervade the book. Herbert concentrates rather on painting a landscape of (occasionally comic) nightmare, and most of the human episodes are of terror rather than explicit violence: the pilot of a 747 goes mad at the controls, and in the most disturbingly ironic scene a would-be suicide who has thought better of making away with herself is caught up in a lemming-like exodus from the seaside town of Bournemouth. Herbert triumphantly reverses the usual method of building terror in a novel: where traditionally this is achieved by a gradual accumulation of events, *The Fog* is all the more nightmarish for its breathless pace. Its final image (prefiguring that of the film *Alien*) is, appropriately, of restful sleep.

The Fog was a bestseller, but Herbert's next two books show that he won't play safe. *The Survivor* (1976)—later filmed, insipidly and obscurely, by David Hemmings—is the pilot of a 747, the only person to survive its crash, who proves to have been sent on a mission by the spirits of its victims. Though the book rises to heights both of horror (an infernal scene in a college chapel) and ecstasy, it's weighed down by too much spiritualistic discussion, as hindering to Herbert as it was to Algernon Blackwood. Perhaps at the time Herbert's preoccupation with the afterlife, or his doubts about life after death, were so great that the theme got the better of him. For most of its length *The Survivor* (an ironic title) is among his bleakest books, not least because the pilot's lover has been killed in the crash.

Fluke (1977) returns to the subject of the afterlife, but with great stylistic and narrative confidence. Of all his books, this divided his admirers most sharply; none of his books conforms less to the expectations of his fans. Fluke is a man reincarnated as a dog, much to the dismay of Herbert's British publishers, who would have preferred the dog at least to be rabid. It was Herbert's only first-person narrative so far, and it may be this unaccustomed voice that reveals new qualities—a greater generosity towards his characters, an unexpected lyricism. Significantly, it's his favourite among his novels. Not that the book is inconsistent with his other work: again the protagonist (in many ways the typical Herbert hero) is sent on a quest whose outcome proves to be ironic. A greater belated irony may be that the entire book-length monologue goes unheard by its chosen audience, a dying tramp. However, this image of extreme loneliness gives way to a finely suggestive last line.

His next book *The Spear* (1978)—an action thriller about neo-Nazism and the resurrection of Himmler—is more immediately commercial; nevertheless it's courageous of Herbert to address the theme of British fascism through a genre which, like sword and sorcery, attracts fascist mentalities. (One of the most blatant statements of this appears at the end of Dennis Wheatley's non-fiction coffee-table book, *The Devil and All His Works,* where Wheatley declares that anti-apartheid demonstrations are the devil's work and that it is the job of the governments to govern.) *The Spear* scores as a thriller, especially in its set pieces (a Herbert speciality, perhaps most skilfully and expressively employed in *The*

Fog), but its anti-fascist message was clear enough to earn Herbert the hatred of the National Front, the British fascist party. Because the supernatural is only hinted at in the course of the novel, the climactic manifestation is the more disturbing.

Herbert sees *Lair* (1979), the sequel to *The Rats,* as a relaxation after *The Spear.* It attacks the apathy of officialdom with renewed vigour, and contains one of the most terrible death scenes in all his work, the death of a priest who is losing his faith. This points forward to the more explicit horrors of *The Dark.*

The Dark (1980) is necessarily his most violent novel. Whereas the possessing force in *The Fog* was unmotivated, the dark is evil embodied and deliberately invoked. The book is about the rejection of God, whatever God may be. Proving the non-existence of God is seen as the ultimate insanity; rejection of faith leads straight to breakdown and the asylum. *The Dark* conveys a greater sense of helplessness than Herbert's earlier work; the little organised response to the threat is largely ineffectual. It's to his credit that he doesn't use the theme of possession as an alibi for his characters (which is to say, to allow the reader to feel that evil has nothing to do with us). The novel's most terrifying scene, an outbreak of football hooliganism, hardly needed possession to explain its cause.

The Jonah (1981) restates this theme in passing: a character dismisses the supernatural as "something people have invented to suit their own tiny minds, something that helps them put troubles and misfortunes into tiny little boxes". As in *The Spear,* the supernatural is kept largely offstage until the final chapters. The "jonah" is a policeman haunted by something that brings disaster to those involved with him and which he finally confronts while investigating drug smuggling. It's an oddly contradictory book: one character gives a speech against drug abuse so impassioned that it's reasonable to conclude (particularly since her partner in argument hardly gets a word in) that Herbert endorses her feelings, yet a later description of an LSD trip is as lyrical as it is terrifying. Presumably Herbert's imagination is stronger than his doubts. Still, *The Jonah* is his most lightweight book.

Shrine (1983) is an overtly Catholic novel, about a child who claims to have had a vision of the Virgin Mary, but who is in fact inspired by the Devil. The first half of *Shrine* is as compelling as any of his novels, and leads to a stunning set piece that is rounded off by a breathtaking supernatural image. Untypically, the second half slows down enough to let the reader spot inconsistencies: symptoms of possession which the reader can't help but recognise seem to trouble the religious characters far less than they should (though this might be one of Herbert's objections to the way the Catholic Church responds to the child's visions). Once again, Herbert uses the conventions of the genre more responsibly than many of his peers: there is no suggestion that the child herself is evil. Despite its flaws, *Shrine* is deeply felt, and clearly was a book Herbert had to write; some of its effects show a new deftness and subtlety. Some readers have found the final apparition ambiguous, but presumably Herbert is being true to his own doubts.

Domain (1984) is one of his most vividly imagined novels. It pits man against mutant rat in a London devastated by nuclear bombing. As in several of his novels, there are vignettes of character at the moment of disaster; those in *Domain*, and the insights they convey, are especially bleak. A scene in which characters try to clear an escalator piled with corpses has a nightmare absurdity, while the novel's sense of suffering is appropriately more intense than that of any of its predecessors. One chapter in which an injured man is dragged back from drowning is as disquieting as anything Herbert has yet given us. *Domain* is really only nominally a novel about the rats; it's a clear-eyed view of a future that may be uncomfortably close, a praiseworthy attempt to give readers what they may not think they want. It seems to have been too uncomfortable for the American editor who worked on the book and who suggested omitting some of the character vignettes. Herbert, already at work on his next novel, told him to go ahead as a preamble to telling him and the publisher where to go, and so some chapters from *Domain* have appeared as self-contained stories in America.

Moon (1985) is a suspense novel which is gradually invaded by the horrific. Its theme recalls that of Thomas Harris's *Red Dragon*—in both novels the protagonist is able to help the police track down serial murderers by sharing their mental processes—but Herbert pushes the psychic theme further, to an especially disturbing conclusion when the process becomes mutual and the murderer to whose consciousness the psychic Jonathan Childes is intermittently linked begins to feed off Childes' own memories of atrocities which Childes has vicariously experienced. Herbert's sojourn in the Channel Islands lends the book its setting. As the island is invaded first by Childes' visions of atrocities and then by the murderer herself, so the book is invaded by terse savage chapters from the mainland, the most disorientating of them no more than a sentence in length. The growing horror is kept under severe restraint until the very end, when psychical and physical horror meet in a finale whose outrageousness both delivers what the novel has been threatening throughout and passes beyond it into a kind of spectral surrealism.

The Magic Cottage (1986)—which would have been called *The Enchanted Cottage* if Hollywood hadn't got there first—is a personal favourite of the author's. As in *Fluke,* the first-person voice makes for relaxed narration, but the book abounds with details which suggest that it will repay a careful reading: the names of characters—Flora Chaldean, Eldrich P. Mycroft, the Reverend Sixsmythe—sound as if Herbert is both having fun and scattering enigmatic clues through the book, so that when the narrator Mike Stringer claims that "when luck is on your side numbers don't come into it", this reader's immediate reaction is to look suspiciously at the phone number of the estate agent handling the cottage—Cantrip 612, a six and two more sixes—and to begin to wonder about that name Sixsmythe. After all, the book is sufficiently playful to accommodate a walk-on out of *Fluke.* Even without all this, the ambiguities are plentiful. In particular the magic of which the cottage proves to be a focus is presented as a powerful but neutral force, much like the mushrooms which sprout in place of the cottage at the end of the novel. Though the book contains its share of warnings about the allure of the occult it also celebrates its appeal to the imagination, and so the scenes of magical confrontation are unexpectedly, if entirely appropriately, reminiscent of Bulwer-Lytton, "The House and the Brain" in particular. Despite its gentleness or quite possibly because of it, *The Magic Cottage* also builds up a considerable sense of horror, though underlying this effect there generally tends to be a deeper meaning. There's even a scene of batty birth to appal conservationists.

The Magic Cottage can be read as an expansion of the last line (also the last chapter) of *Moon. Sepulchre* (1987)—with its subtitle "A conflict of evils" and its epigraph "There are no absolutes"—reads like a further exploration of the moral ambiguities of its immediate predecessor. It's perhaps the grimmest of Herbert's novels which begin as thrillers and turn nastier; though at least one of his imitators has accused him of toning his books down in order to court a wider audience, that is clearly not the case here. While the central relationship between the crazed psychic Kline and Halloran, the man apparently chosen to protect him from kidnapping and worse, is as ambiguous as the protagonist Halloran himself, the darkest sections of the book trap the reader in the minds of several monstrous characters, as disturbing an experience as it evidently was for Herbert to write them. The book is something of a return to the raw horror of his early books, but it may be said to reach back further, however inadvertently or coincidentally. Of all Herbert's novels it's the one which most recalls the pulp horrors of the thirties: in passages of writing ("They did their best to ignore the squishy gurgling of the sinuous island as it heaved itself from the water"); in its use of an ancient Sumerian evil; perhaps most strikingly, in the titles of chapters—"Return to the Death Hut", for instance. The scene in which the heroine is tied up and whipped by an obese hairy bodyguard offers a combination of bondage and horror the like of which has scarcely been seen since the days of the spicy horror magazines.

After *Sepulchre*, *Haunted* (1988) is yet another change of direction and simultaneously a further exploration of earlier themes. It's possible to mourn the non-existence of the BBC film which would have been based on Herbert's original script, but then, had the film been made we might not have had the novel, his most atmospheric to date; we would certainly not have had the séance scene, which was written to bulk out the novel and which is one of his most affecting set pieces. Also particularly effective, as in *The Magic Cottage*, is the image of the haunted building whose fabric gradually betrays what it hides. Herbert's return to the area he first explored in *The Survivor* is all the more welcome for the greater control he brings to the material, and especially for his increasing ability to communicate a sense of supernatural terror. What else the book conceals I leave for its readers to discover.

Creed (1990) is his best book since *The Magic Cottage*, and it strikes me as one of his most personal. In some ways it sums up aspects of his work to date: it rediscovers the eroticism of his early books, and revels in its macabre set-pieces—a nightmarishly comic episode in which paparazzo Joseph Creed is pursued across a London pond by a paddling Nosferatu, a demonic masked ball, a descent into the bowels of an especially hellish rest home. It also stars his sleaziest protagonist yet, who nevertheless compels the reader's reluctant involvement. Like *The Magic Cottage*, it feels relaxed, though in fact the circumstances under which it was written were hardly conducive to relaxation. It easily incorporates gags aimed at the fans of the genre (there's even one about *The Rats*) and an intermittent commentary by the author himself, which seems almost Victorian. This willingness to comment, and the serious theme underlying all the gags, suggests to me that *Creed* may be read as a kind of statement of the author's beliefs about his genre—his creed, dare I say. Mind you, in an interview in *Fear* Jim declares that the book is his *Abbott and Costello Meet Frankenstein*, so perhaps he may give my interpretation a raspberry. Let me content myself by saying that I believe it is a perfect companion volume to Steve Jones' book devoted to him.

Herbert writes bestsellers, but he doesn't manufacture them. Rather than compete with his imitators in terms of escalating violence (a trap into which such as John Carpenter and the EC comics of the fifties have fallen), he has opted for restraint. His sex scenes are sometimes prolonged, but they range from the tender to (particularly in *Shrine*) the grotesquely comic to an accumulation of awkward detail which is the opposite of pornographic. Some of his novels contain no sex at all. It may be his Catholicism, or the puritanism that seems to underlie *The Jonah*, which leads him to suggest that any kind of sexual deviation is bound for grief, but in other ways his work is less reactionary than much of the genre. While he sometimes stumbles stylistically, there's a developing sense of language in his effects. In *Danse Macabre*, in the course of an appreciation of Herbert, King describes him as coming at the reader "with both hands, not willing to simply engage our attention; he seizes us by the lapels and begins to scream in our faces. It is not a tremendously artistic method of attack, and no one is ever going to compare him to Doris Lessing or V. S. Naipaul—but it works—he is what he is and that's all that he is, as Popeye would say."

To be fair, King has more to say for him than that, yet I wonder if some of King's readers may have gained the impression that Herbert's work is cruder than in fact it is. Herbert is an unmistakably English, and unmistakably contemporary, writer who refuses to conform to what's expected of him or to stop questioning what he sees and feels.

I look forward to many more surprises from him, not to mention some of the most attractively designed novels in the British bookshops. He designs them himself.

II

And this was what I wrote for the Centipede Press edition of *The Fog*.

OUT OF THE FOG

Writers aren't responsible for their imitators. Lovecraft can't be blamed for the eldritch hordes that gibbered hideously in grotesque versions of his voice after his death. (Yes, I was one, at sixteen years old.) M. R. James is not the leader of the musty mob that mistook antiquarianism for the appeal of his work (rather than his genius for conveying horror in a single glancing sentence or even a phrase). Stephen King had no control over the swarm of gerunds that gave their names to books after *The Shining*, let alone the small towns that grew monstrous in the wake of *'Salem's Lot*. And James Herbert isn't answerable for the ambitions of the herd of horror hacks that hastened after him, brandishing entrails and severed limbs and every body part that they could find in their limited imaginations. While there is still a sorry band of writers with apparently no goal other than to be more disgusting than one another, Herbert was never among them or at their head. One surprise *The Fog* holds for any reader who comes to it on the basis of its early reputation is how restrained the novel is (not least by comparison with books that had already preceded it—*The Exorcist*, for instance, or *Hell House*).

There's a famous exchange during the American Senate's enquiry into horror comics. Senator Kefauver asks William Gaines whether he considers a cover with a woman's severed head on it to be in good taste. "Yes, sir, I do," says Gaines, and explains why (the frame of the image excludes the sight of the bloody stump). No such restraint for us Brits! The cover of my New English Library paperback of *The Fog* gives us a woman's hacked-off head, ragged neck and all. It's considerably more graphic but significantly less effective than the equivalent scene in the book. Less is more, and Herbert knows it. If only the gorehounds did, and tried learning from the classics of the field.

James Herbert did. *The Fog* belongs to an honourable British tradition. In a terse essay on the novel he acknowledges its precursors—*The War of the Worlds*, *The Day of the Triffids* and Nigel Kneale's Quatermass serials. The latter led Hammer Films to develop another science fiction horror film, *X the Unknown* (which they originally planned as a Quatermass tale), and the chasm that gapes at the start of *The Fog* to release a cataclysmic threat is reminiscent of that too. Both Hammer and Herbert frequently deal with the eruption of the monstrous into placid reality, but Hammer never hit us with an image as vast as the disappearance of an entire village. Even more than in *The Rats*, his only previous novel, Herbert seems to be announcing from the outset that nothing is safe.

Much else that recurs in his work is established early on. There's the resourceful but flawed protagonist, reluctantly heroic and suspicious even of his own heroism, not to mention of the establishment he works for. There are the vignettes of desperate lives, deftly and tellingly sketched. Their relentless clarity doesn't preclude compassion. It's worth recalling that Jim's favourite novel is *The History of Mr Polly*, a very specifically British account (like Jim's) of the downtrodden. There's the erotic frankness, rare in the field at the time, which sometimes surfaces in unexpected and disturbing ways: the sexual charge our hero Holman experiences while grappling with his deranged girlfriend, for instance. The gymnasium scene remains excruciating, all the more so for its reticence, and the final image is echoed (scream and all) in Gregg Araki's apocalyptic film *The Doom Generation*. Charles Platt's pornographic novel *The Gas* can easily be read as a riff on the glimpse of an orgy in *The Fog* and indeed on the threat in Herbert's book.

Let me celebrate some individual scenes and techniques. *The Fog* is so cinematic a book that the lack of a film version remains inexplicable. The novel even uses montage: several chapters intercut fragments of episodes to considerable effect (building tension in the third chapter, and much more with the premonitory sketches in the eighteenth, the resolutions of which add to the power of a grand finale). Besides displaying the fates that overtake the characters—from the gruesome to the poignant—the montages further undermine any sense of security the reader may have. Anything at all may happen to the victims of the fog, and the book even breaks into slapstick ahead of the time of the genre—it was years before Sam Raimi's love of the Three Stooges brought it to the *Evil Dead* trilogy, and longer still before the *Final Destination* films married horror to the ingenuity of Buster Keaton and Harold Lloyd. By contrast, one disconcerting glimpse in the fog simply shows us Londoners trying to get on with their everyday lives—abnormal precisely because it's so normal. It's an index of Herbert's witty way with horror. Still, many of today's readers may be most alarmed by the episode involving the GPO Tower. We could wish Jim hadn't been so inadvertently prescient.

It has long been my argument that the best horror fiction has mystery at its core and never quite reveals or fully explains it. That's certainly the case with *The Fog.* While the scientific explanations are detailed and (certainly for this layman) convincing, they don't entirely sum up the nature of the catastrophe. Why does the fog take refuge inside a cathedral? The scene may be reminiscent of the first Quatermass serial, but it has its own unnervingly numinous quality. Has the fog a kind of sentience, and what is its allure? At times it suggests a mythic element, which seems to call for some kind of knight to confront it. However reluctant, Holman is that hero, and only as intermittently courageous as a modern champion is likely to manage. Like a true existentialist, he chooses what he has to be. All the same, he gets called valiant once, which is more than most of us earn.

I was amused recently to find Steve King and myself linked with Jim by an Internet pundit as "modern horror writers—purveyors of gratiutous, meaningless horror fiction—not serious authors in the true literary sense". Well, at least we aren't accused of being gratuitous—"gratiutous" must mean something else entirely—and anyone who uses language like that has no business accusing his betters of being meaningless. The funny chap gets one thing right, however. Modern horror is what we're about, and horror needed to be brought up to date if it was to continue to be relevant. Few living writers did so as thoroughly as James Herbert. The vision of *The Fog* is as pertinent now as it ever was. Let Brighton and World Horror celebrate him! Just be glad the convention's not in Bournemouth!

THOMAS LIGOTTI

I DON'T KNOW WHEN I HAVE ENJOYED A COLLECTION of an author's horror stories more than the book you now hold in your hands, if hands they are [*Songs of a Dead Dreamer*]. I'll go further: it has to be one of the most important horror books of the decade. His work alone (though in fact, of course, not only his) would justify the existence of the semi-professional magazines—*Nyctalops, Eldritch Tales, Fantasy Tales*—that have published him, for Ligotti is one of the few consistently original voices in contemporary horror fiction, one of the few whose work is instantly recognisable.

He belongs to the most honourable tradition in the field, that of subtlety and awesomeness rather than the relentlessly graphic. At times he suggests terrors as vast as Lovecraft's, though the terrors are quite other than Lovecraft's. He's capable of writing tales as dismayingly horrifying as any of his contemporaries—"The Frolic", for example—yet even there one finds a hint of more than horror, an extra dimension of awe. Others of his tales—"The Troubles of Dr. Thoss", "The Greater Festival of Masks", "Dr. Voke and Mr. Veech"—read like dreams prompted by memories of M. R. James, dreams stranger than anything the good doctor ever wrote: perhaps the dreams of the consciousness glimpsed behind one of Ligotti's most elaborate stories, "Dream of a Mannikin". Despite faint echoes of writers he admires, however, Ligotti's vision is wholly personal. Few other writers could conceive a horror story in the form of notes on the writing of the genre, and I can't think of any other writer who could have brought it off.

In "The Consolations of Horror" (a companion piece, published in *Dark Horizons* 27, to "Professor Nobody's Little Lectures"), Ligotti defines the consolations of the genre thus: "simply that someone shares some of your own feelings and has made of these a work of art which you have the insight, sensitivity and—like it or not—peculiar set of experiences to appreciate." In his case the consolations also include an elegant and witty style, an inimitable imagination, a willingness to expand the genre, and a timelessness which ought to mean that his fiction will be read with as much pleasure a hundred years from now. May this book bring him the acclaim which he certainly deserves.

DONALD R. BURLESON

ONE TROUBLE WITH BEING A WRITER IS HAVING friends who are. I confess that while my view of unsolicited material sent to me for an opinion or a blurb grows more unwelcoming with age, a request to comment on the work of a friend can pose a special problem. If I don't like what I've been asked to read, what am I to say? Can I really assume that if they pleaded for an honest opinion they meant that more than I would?

But perhaps they requested an introduction, of which I've written a few. Suppose their lovely wife has already dedicated a poem to me, how can I refuse? I say that simply in order to send my love to Mollie Burleson by way of this preface. The entirely pleasant truth is that I've enjoyed the stories in this collection [*Beyond the Lamplight*] as much as I've enjoyed the company of the Burlesons over the years, which is to say considerably—indeed, so much that I lingered over relishing the contents while the publisher, the amiable Scott Aniolowski, was too polite to send me a fax or a letter or telephone message demanding that I get a move on. But here is the introduction at last, and hence the book. The latter at least was worth waiting even longer for.

Where do I begin? Every page is a nest of enviable images. The opening tale declares many of Don's best qualities: the economical sureness of his scene-setting and of his conjuring of eeriness, the unerring sense of place, the deftness of characterisation, the powerful suspense, all this achieved in much less space than it would take most of us (I refrain from a jealous grinding of teeth). Is "The Interview" placed first to remind us that Don is a literary critic? Later, in "School Closings", he may be seen to joke about this, but the whole book goes to prove that a critic can write fiction worthy of the authors he admires.

And what range! I take some of the tales to derive their simplicity from his knowledge that here is yet another genuinely original idea—"Mulligan's Fence", "Frosty", "Peripheral Vision" are just some based on notions I wish I'd had. He's happy to animate familiar objects and dare us to laugh in the face of so much vividly imagined detail: "Hopkins House", "Brownie". More daring is required of the reader when Don turns gross: "The Wind at the Top of the Tree" is perhaps the mildest introduction to this tendency of his, after which the reader may risk "Down in the Mouth", a compelling tale whose title I wish I'd commandeered first. I'd warn gently against reading this in the same sitting as "Milk" or "Uncle Neddy's Chair", though even these are outdone in loathsomeness by "Gums", who is the most repulsive street character I can recall encountering in fiction. It's as well written as anything in the book, though; indeed, it boasts one of my favourite Burleson images, of the backs of shops "turned to each other in the dark like lovers fallen out of love". Together with "Melons", the least fantastic and most distressing story in the book, "Gums" demonstrates that Don can compete with any splatterpunk.

After all that we can be grateful for his humour, however grisly, which "Hair of the Dog" certainly is. There are jokey images in "A Little Place off Elm Street", and perhaps a wryness about the title, while "Reflections" and "Leftovers" will test the gruesomeness of the reader's sense of mirth; possibly even "The Swimmer" and "Now You Know", because how much of the pleasure of horror involves a simultaneously appreciative shiver and laugh at the grotesqueness of the imagination? "Stopping at Crazy Frank's" is a comic nightmare, but perhaps the best joke is the ingenious dual structure of "Christmas Carrion". Carry on indeed. The ghastliest pun is "Family Dentistry", the title and the tale.

More delights! "Kokopelli" echoes Lovecraft faintly but offers its own frissons, while "The Treehouse" tops Lovecraft's "The Tree", and didn't I once write something like "Mikey Joe"? Not as well as Don has. Commentators have been kind enough (to me, that is) to compare "Ziggles" with my stuff too. That may be a reason why it's among my favourites in the book, but others need no such additional reason: the wonderfully chilling "P.O. Box 108" and "Snow Cancellations"; "Walkie-Talkie", with its poignant sense of loss shading into terror; "The Walker", a familiar theme, perhaps, but beautifully handled; "The Missing Book", which may depict the senility of who knows how many of us bibliophiles amid the detritus of a life. Lucky Joyce Carol Oates, to have the remarkable "Sunflower" dedicated to her! But I believe my absolute favourite is "Jigsaw", a brilliant piece which interweaves senility and the supernatural. I wrote a jigsaw story once, but it wasn't nearly as good as this.

In sum, *Beyond the Lamplight* is as generous a midnight feast as I've been presented with in many a full moon. No lover of the macabre should be without it. May it charm the aficionados and demonstrate to the newcomer how much imaginative nourishment our field supports.

5: On Ramsey Campbell

How I Got Here

WHEN DOES A MEMORY BECOME THE MEMORY of having had one? I seem to remember that before I started school I was able to recall lying in my pram. It was parked in the sunlight by the coal shed at the back of the house. Another recollection lasted longer: sitting on the sofa in the front room of that small house in suburban Liverpool while my mother read aloud to me from a *Rupert Bear* annual. These weren't comics in the usual sense, because the images didn't include speech balloons or captions; instead a paragraph of narrative was printed at the foot of the page, while each drawing was accompanied by a simpler version in verse for the less literate. My mother's small forefinger—I suspect it must have been tanned with nicotine—underlined each word she read. For some years I remembered the moment at which I grasped how the symbols she was indicating related to her speech. Either immediately or at the next session I began to read the book aloud to her. I believe I wasn't yet two years old.

Reading *Rupert* gave me my first taste of terror in fiction. One of the many presents I found in a bulging pillowcase at the end of my bed at Christmas 1947 was a copy of *More Adventures of Rupert*. Since the stories include "Rupert and Koko", in which the little bear befriends a black boy ("How funny his black face looks on the white pillow!" Rupert's mother exclaims, while the verse reads "Their bedtime comes along too soon / For Rupert and the little coon"), I don't think it would be published now. The tale that haunted my nights, however, was "Rupert's Christmas Tree", in which Rupert acquires a magical tree that decamps after the festivities and returns to its home in the woods. Perhaps this is meant as a charming fantasy for children, but the details—the small high voice from the tree, the creaking that Rupert hears in the night, the trail of earth he follows from the tub in his house, above all the prancing silhouette that inclines towards him the star it has in place of a head—are surely the stuff of adult supernatural fiction. I think I got my start in the field right there, and many of my preoccupations must derive from my early childhood.

For years I believed that my first memory dated from when I was three years old. I suspect that's because of its understandable vividness. I recall little about my father up to this point, although I have a random memory of his telling me that early in the morning you could see ladies' fingers in the sky—I imagine he meant clouds turned pink by the dawn. He used to take me out on Sundays, and on the only occasion that has stayed in my mind we walked across the line at the end of a platform at Broadgreen Station instead of using the pedestrian bridge. When we came home he told my mother, to her horror. They had a hearty argument above my head that ended with her ordering him out of the house.

The front door contained nine small panes of glass, reaching from chest level to the top of the door. My father blocked the door from outside as my mother tried to close it; presumably they were struggling for the last word in the argument. My mother's hand went through one of the panes. I remember her dripping bright red blood and crying out that he had deliberately closed the door on her hand. The sight of blood except for my own has distressed me ever since. A neighbour—Gladys Trenery from next door—looked after me while her husband took my mother to hospital. I suppose they humoured her to calm her down, but at the time I thought they were accepting her version of the incident. Since my father had fled, I tried to set the record straight. What did I know about it? I was only three years old. I don't think it's fanciful to relate one of my recurring themes—the difference between perception and reality—to this.

I forget the aftermath, but years later my mother said that she had subsequently asked me in front of my father if I wanted to go out with him again. How could I have said yes when it might have led to another such scene? It feels as if that was the last I saw of my father, though it may not have been. Certainly relations between my parents grew steadily worse, until soon they met hardly at all. One reason must have been that my father (who was in his late forties, my mother having been thirty-six when I was born) felt robbed of his only son.

Divorce wasn't easy in the 1950s, not least because my mother was a Catholic. I accompanied her as she trudged from lawyer to lawyer in a futile quest for legal aid to help her make a case for a divorce on the grounds of mental cruelty, of which she provided a lengthy written account. Apparently I would have been circumcised for medical reasons when I was three months old, but my father objected that it was "a devilish pagan custom performed by Roman Catholics to gratify their sadistic tendencies". I gather that my parents ceased to sleep together four years after I was born, one reason apparently being that my father took to making macabre threats during or after sex. My mother wrote that "he ran the side of his large hand back and forward across my throat, as though with a knife; he then pressed lightly on my throat with his two hands; his heavy body was on top of me so that I could not move—he said in a deliberate, cold voice: 'What a nice little throat you've still got.' "

Soon her failure to obtain legal aid convinced her that the lawyers were conspiring to thwart her, perhaps on instructions from the police, since my father was a policeman; many people in Liverpool (which she hated) were in on the secret too. A popular song of the time, Billy Cotton's *Friends and Neighbours*, was guaranteed to anger her every time it was played on the radio (specifically for her to hear, she was convinced). After her death I found her notes for a novel she was planning at the time, in which her neighbours were given fictitious names and classed according to their attitudes to her—"snoopers", "kind but afraid for themselves", "were nice but obviously worked on", "passer-on" (of gossip about her, presumably). Sometimes her view of them infected me, and I remember once shutting my eyes with disdain as I rode towards and past a couple of them on my childhood scooter, to a crash I was apparently too introverted to foresee. By now my mother detested the house for its smallness, and frequently told me how much better her family home in Huddersfield had been. She insisted that my father had tricked her into living in our house by promising it would be temporary, though in fact she had written to him shortly before their marriage that she would live there always. They kept each other's letters, and I found them after they died[1], which raises several questions. When did my mother repossess her letters to my father—after his death, or did he return them to her? Why did he keep them, and what does that say about his feelings? Why did she keep even the few of his she kept, given how she constantly said she felt about him? The answers are dust.

For most of my childhood my father was heard but not seen. My mother told me things about him, referring to him solely as "him" in a tone of loathing: though he was a policeman he dressed like a tramp, he spoke several languages but made no use of them, he wrote letters in my name and hers to the *Christian Science Monitor* (religion therefore being one of their early conflicts, and his use of Americanisms to me another), he'd got her lost on a fell in the Lake District during their honeymoon (an incident that she grew to believe meant he'd tried to kill her), he'd once substituted tooth powder for salt in the cruet and poisoned the family except for himself, he came downstairs in the mornings and damaged the already dilapidated furniture, he blew his nose with his fingers in the bathroom sink (for years she would go in the bathroom every night as soon as his bedroom door closed and I would hear her ritual cry of disgust), he'd thrown a toy of mine in the fire when I was making too much noise with it, she'd given up the love of her life (one Harold Broadbent) for him . . . He left her housekeeping money on Fridays, and she cooked his breakfast last thing each night and left it on the table. Now I imagine him coming downstairs in the mornings to be faced by congealed fried egg and bacon seven hours old in the chilly kitchen with its stone-flagged floor (hardly surprising if sometimes he went and kicked the furniture), but then his unseen presence was infinitely more powerful than anything I

[1] I quote at length from their correspondence in "Coming to Liverpool" in *Spook City*, also published by PS. This essay will be reprinted in *Ramsey Campbell, Certainly.*

might be told about him. For nearly twenty years we didn't meet face to face, although he continued to live in the house.

I used to hear his footsteps on the stairs as I lay in bed, terrified that he might come into my room. Sometimes I heard arguments downstairs as my mother waylaid him when he came home, her voice shrill and clear, his blurred and incomprehensible, hardly a voice, which filled me with a terror I couldn't define. (Being a spectator to arguments made me deeply nervous for decades, though since becoming a parent I'm much more likely to intervene or take sides.) If he was still in the kitchen when it was time for her to make my breakfast she would drive him out of the house; presumably it was unthinkable that I should share the table with him. Once I found I'd broken a lens of my glasses as I'd put them down by the bed the previous night, and my mother convinced me that he'd sneaked into the room to break it. Worst of all was Christmas, when my mother would send me to knock on his bedroom door and invite him down, as a mark of seasonal goodwill, for Christmas dinner. I would go upstairs in a panic, but there was never any response beyond a mutter of refusal.

I mustn't give the impression that my entire childhood consisted of nothing except terror, even if it was an underlying motif. You may not notice how strange your own childhood is while living it, at any rate for a while. Because the house at 40 Nook Rise was the only place I'd lived, I saw nothing remarkable about it. It was part of Wavertree Garden Suburb, an idealised community built in the first decade of the twentieth century alongside Thingwall Road. My father's family had moved to the house from Glasgow, and may well have seen it as idyllic; my mother had lived in a much larger house in Huddersfield, and it's no wonder if she found this one claustrophobic. So did I when I last returned to it not many years ago; reality had overtaken my perception of it and its surroundings after decades of failing to do so.

As a child I thought it was the size it ought to be, and the back garden seemed immense. It contained two apple trees I used to climb, and a silver birch. To the right lived the Trenerys, to the left the unmarried Misses Cropper. The territory beyond the end seemed close to boundless; it contained allotments on the right and the garden of the Forrest family beside them. Brian Forrest was some years older than I, and talked to me over the privet hedge. He must have seen a Western, for he often said "Ay, señor." More than once he invited me around to play with him, but my mother wouldn't hear of it; she didn't care for him or almost any of the neighbours' children (though Hazel Carline escaped her opprobrium). I don't think she knew that when I was three or so, some of the older girls called me into one of the arched passages that led between the pairs of houses and asked me to show them my penis (or as one of them put it, my little feller). There would have been precious little for them to ogle, but that wasn't why I fled.

I was apparently four when I started attending Christ the King Roman Catholic School. I believe my mother gave me the notion that I would impress the teachers by being able to write. Imagine my chagrin at being told that I was holding the pencil the wrong way! I learned the approved grip quickly enough and have used it ever since. Indeed, that middle finger is growing numb with decades of writing and typing.

Before long I made an acceptable friend at the school. She was Pauline Godfrey, who lived in Abbeystead Road, perhaps half a mile from my home. We often played together, but I think it was usually at her house; my mother was so ashamed of ours that she tried to keep people away from it, my friends included. One day Pauline and I decided to go for a walk without telling anyone. On Thingwall Road a man in a front garden asked where we lived. "Don't say down the drain or I'll spank you," he added. We insisted with enthusiasm that we did, and I for one was disappointed when he didn't carry out his threat. (I'd had just one spanking at the age of four from my mother, and was shocked by how much it hurt, but soon tried in vain to provoke a repetition of the experience.) No doubt these days the man would be arrested as a paedophile or at the very least harassed by vigilantes. We continued onwards to Queens Drive, a dual carriageway, and made our way up it to Childwall Fiveways and along a second carriageway to rejoin Thingwall Road at the far end. It was a whole afternoon's adventure, and I think we gradually realised how much panic we might be causing, but our reappearance hand in hand seems to have assuaged the worst of our parents' wrath. I can't help visualising us in terms of an advertising poster common at the time that displayed such a pair of innocents.

In the first stages of the disintegration of the marriage my parents used me as a go-between. I was six when my father bought tickets for my mother to take me on holiday to the Lake District, but when I gave her the tickets my mother tore them up and threw them at his feet. Me, I'd been looking forward to the holiday. The next day we enacted the identical scene. Instead she insisted on saving up to take me to Grange over Sands, where she'd stayed on her honeymoon, or Southport, where her widowed mother had moved from Huddersfield; sometimes we stayed with her sister and brother-in-law in Yorkshire. It was in Southport that I discovered my taste for the weird.

I believe I was seven by then. In those days it was common for general stores to sell books and magazines. One summer day in Seabank Road, one of the broad side streets of the Victorian seaside town, I saw a magazine in a window. The cover appeared to depict a bird-like creature cowering in terror of two monstrosities—huge human skulls for heads and very little in the way of bodies—approaching it across a black desert. If the cover looked like that, what extraordinary things would the magazine contain? At seven I wasn't allowed to find out, and so the image and the name of the publication—*Weird Tales*—haunted me for years. A decade later I identified the issue for November 1952. The cover shows a vulture perched on some bones with two admittedly evil-looking human skeletons in the background. It seems to me that back in 1953 my mind was already bent on improving on the terrors I encountered and rendering them even more grotesque.

Perhaps I preferred visions to everyday terror. Apart from my home life, schooldays were taking their toll, or my mother's nervousness on my behalf was. She was especially bothered, I think, by having seen the headmaster slap some unfortunate's face for talking to a friend in line while parents watched from outside the schoolyard. Had I begun to suffer from nightmares? I know she was unhappy because I had a tendency to roll my eyes in public, but I doubt that she chose to take me to a child psychiatrist. I suspect that our doctor advised that she should.

She was always hostile to psychiatry and psychoanalysis. One reason was that in the heat of at least one argument my father had threatened to have her sectioned under the Mental Health Act, and on another occasion he'd invited neighbours to come and look at his "mad wife", but I suspect that her aversion may have dated from before the marriage —why, we'll never know. The child psychiatrist can't have changed her attitude. She was especially suspicious when he took a rectal smear, perhaps to check for evidence of child abuse. When she demanded what he was doing I explained it was a smear, to which he responded "You'd make a good detective." Of such odd moments is fiction made. My medical records show that he estimated my intelligence quotient as 160, and that the psychiatrists at Alder Hey Hospital—apparently more than one was involved, and I assume my memory has conflated them—"were rather interested in the mother." The record (dated April 1952) goes on to observe that psychotherapy is "almost certainly indicated in this case as she appears to be suffering from ideas of persecution." As far as I know this diagnosis wasn't followed up. I was found to be imaginative but mentally fit, and my mother tried to solve the problem of the nightmares by sending me to a private school, Ryebank.

Another problem must have been that I was missing quite a lot of school. Asthma—psychologically based, I suspect—was the reason or at least the excuse. Almost the only memory of my time at Christ the King is of sitting with my classmates in the field outside a classroom in the sunlight while a schoolmistress read us a chapter from a book. I recall that whoever the young hero was, his adventures were intensely suspenseful, but I never learned what led up to this episode or happened after. I'm surprised I didn't ascertain the title of the book. Perhaps the teacher refused to tell me in case that would persuade me to attend more school.

Enrolling at Ryebank (where I gather the fee for each pupil was seven guineas per term) involved being interviewed and then, as I recall, having to wait in the grounds while the headmaster and my mother talked. She must have been very unhappy with Christ the King to remove me to a school that wasn't Catholic, even if special classes were provided for those pupils who were. While outside, I was accosted by boys from the senior half of the school, who poked some kind of fun at me—possibly at my size, since I was on the way to growing marvellously obese. I wince to remember retorting "I won't stand for it." How pompous of a seven-year-old was that? "Sit down for it, then," came the crushing riposte.

Thoughts of my size at that time remind me that on my birthdays my father would leave a book downstairs as a present, usually with a few pound notes concealed between the pages. Quite a few of the books were Frank Richards novels about the famously fat schoolboy Billy Bunter. Perhaps my father intended them as some kind of message to me, but I simply enjoyed them. More recently they've been accused of the kind of offence it has become fashionable to search for—fattism, I suppose the term might be—but if anyone back then had proposed suppressing them to protect the sensitivities of the overweight, I should have been wholly against it.

Either shortly after changing schools or in the summer holiday between them I began a novel, perhaps as a celebration. This was *Black Fingers from Space* by John R. Campbell (aged 7½), and illustrated by him too. The interested, not to say unwary, reader can find elsewhere in this volume all the chapters I wrote. It may have been this effort that prompted me to tell some adult at the bus stop by the school that I wrote books and planned to have them published in America. My comments were relayed to a member of staff, Miss Twomey, a fearsome Irishwoman, who demanded in front of my schoolmates if England wasn't good enough for me. Once she caned the whole class with a ruler for some offence that even then I failed to grasp. Perhaps I wasn't among the main culprits, since the anticipation proved to be worse than the sting when it finally reached me. Miss Twomey was also fond of telling unruly pupils how she had once spanked a rebellious girl on stage in front of the entire school. The reader must decide why this should have lodged in my memory.

In March 1954 I was examined by a physician at United Liverpool Hospitals, J. D. Hay. Hay "gained the impression that he [the young Campbell] was very much a mother's darling" and observed "twitching, indicating early habit spasm." I assume this was the eye-rolling noted earlier. Monstrous creations continued to emerge from my mind, not least the opening pages of an aborted novel, *Dogs in the Stratosphere*. Clifford Simak shouldn't be blamed, though his *City* was then a favourite novel of mine, which

I read more than once. Mine is lost, and the world may sigh with relief.

By now my grandmother was living intermittently in the Nook Rise house. She'd given up her flat in Southport to divide her time between her two daughters. When I was seven my father threatened to brain her with a heavy crucifix that hung above her bed, and apparently referred to her as Mrs Merrifield (who had been executed that year for poisoning the woman whose companion she was). I remember her only in glimpses: her singing "Just a Song at Twilight" to me in a high sweet voice, her groaning loudly on the toilet (a performance that emphasised the smallness of the house), her praying—"Through my fault, through my fault, through my most grievous fault" —and beating her breast so loudly I could hear it in my room. She found Charlie Chaplin vulgar, but I recall being horribly embarrassed at an early age when she and my mother were overwhelmed by sobs at a cinema showing of *Limelight*. She would ask me if I was learning gozintas yet at school ("Two gozinta four, four gozinta eight") and about something I took to be called globigerina oos. Not until secondary school did I grasp that it was ooze, a deposit found under the sea.

The school in question was St Edward's College, a Roman Catholic grammar school. I'd passed the eleven-plus examination, which suggests that on the whole Ryebank had been good for me. Then again, maybe I was too precocious for my own good. Shortly before starting at St Edward's I was on a bus that passed the gates of Sandfield Park, where the school is still based. As I recall I remarked to my mother "Note a bean my new school." I probably deserved to have the man seated in front of us turn around and say "I believe he means 'nota bene', madam, the Latin for 'note well'." I did, of course. My excuse for my behaviour was my youth; I'm not sure what his was.

On my first day at the grammar school we new boys were told what its various sections were called. One was Runnymede, but I heard "Running-Me." Mishearings seem to have beset me for some years. When my mother had our house redecorated downstairs, the decorator sent me to buy some paste. I knew its trade name couldn't really be Collapso, but I was too shy to ask him to repeat it. As in a game of Chinese whispers, I asked for this at the shop, and was miraculously rewarded with the item he needed—Lapcell. Perhaps my fascination with the pitfalls of conversation started there. It has certainly given me plenty of material.

Although my mother had balked at *Weird Tales*, for years she let me use her tickets to borrow adult books from Childwall Library, which in those days was no more than a narrow unit in a block of shops; it had shelves around the walls and space for just one row of central shelving back to back. Fiction was shelved in order of the author's name, not by genre, which made my search for the fantastic all the more of an adventure. At six I took out *Fifty Years of Ghost Stories*, which introduced me to the terrors of M. R. James; I also, despite my youth, much appreciated Edith Wharton's "Afterward". I borrowed all the science fiction I could identify as well, and at seven years old was powerfully disturbed by "The Colour out of Space" in Groff Conklin's *Strange Travels in Science Fiction*.

I believe that by the time I changed schools I was already writing my first completed book, *Ghostly Tales*. The stories in it were patched together like Frankenstein's monster from fragments of fiction I'd read. Now that I was eleven I was allowed to buy science fiction and fantasy magazines, not least *Weird Tales*. One of the earliest treasures of my collection was *Best Horror Stories*, edited by John Keir Cross. Besides specialists such as Poe, Bierce and M. R. James it included tales by Faulkner, Graham Greene and Herman Melville—his "Bartleby". The editor admitted that some readers might not consider this a horror story, but I thought my pocket money (which I'd saved up to buy the hardcover) well spent. I believe that more than any book this one persuaded me that horror fiction was a huge field, by no means wholly defined by narrow generic conventions, and part of literature. By contrast, when I read a paperback of a thirties *Not at Night* anthology—the series in which the editor declared she had set herself against literature—I found the gruesomeness of the material no substitute for good prose.

My writing had yet to catch up with my appreciation of the genre. Let me quote a single representative sentence from *Ghostly Tales*: "The door banged open, and the aforementioned skeleton rushed in." It must have been out of a mixture of desperation and maternal pride that my mother encouraged me to submit the completed book—the only copy, handwritten and illustrated in crayon—to publishers. She herself had published short stories in a Yorkshire journal before the Second World War, and during the war she wrote her first, largely autobiographical, novel. It was encouraged by my father, whom I gather she met through an advertisement she'd placed under a false name (possibly in a writers' journal) for pen friends. As their marriage deteriorated she set her hopes on writing novels, mainly thrillers, to make her enough money to bring me up on her own. My impression is that they were technically skilful but already dated. She used numerology to work out titles to bring her good luck, and posted the manuscripts in envelopes inscribed PLEASE DO NOT FOLD, NOR CRUSH. In my early teens she took to listening to "The Archers", a nightly radio soap opera, on the basis that the names and actions of the characters represented messages of hope for her. When her manuscripts were rejected she became convinced that the messages had been lies aimed at breaking her down. I think it was then I grew fully aware that all was not well with her, although there had been earlier signs; for instance, she'd insisted that the Moomin comic strip that appeared in a local paper must be the pseudonymous work of a freelance writer who lived in the next street, simply because nobody could have a name like Tove Jansson, and she regularly searched the strip for disguised references to herself.

This was by no means the whole of our relationship. She did her best to make up for my father's absence, though perhaps she never fully realised that his unseen presence was the problem. When I was younger we drew pictures together, played word games and board games and cards and ball games, the last of which must have been a trial for her, since she'd suffered a prolapsed womb at my birth. She encouraged me to write and to finish what I wrote. Her favourite film, to which I accompanied her dutifully on each reissue, was *Gone with the Wind*, though often when she revisited a favourite old film or book her disappointment would convince her that someone unspecified had changed the text (Edgar Wallace novels, which proved less surprising than when she had first read them, were among the commonest offenders). At home we listened to radio shows together—plays and serials and comedies, though she never liked Spike Milligan's "Goon Show" with its gleeful explosion of taboos—or simply sat by the fire and read (sometimes the same authors: Patricia Highsmith, Ray Bradbury, Cornelia Otis Skinner). I was always enthralled when she told me her memories: of Father Young, a Catholic priest who used to scuttle after her and her sister in Lon Chaney's latest role; of working at Rushworth's department store in Huddersfield where she eventually became a buyer and where her assistants used to confide all their problems to her; her years at the Ministry of War Transport, and the Christmas Day she had been working there alone while a man prowled the deserted street outside; her chaste love affairs that she always terminated; her pet dogs, one of which another dog-owner had kicked to death; the plots in great detail of films she'd admired, *The Barretts of Wimpole Street,* the Mamoulian *Doctor Jekyll and Mr Hyde,* the Claude Rains *Phantom of the Opera*... More than once she told me her most terrible memory, of the morning (five days before her birthday, I eventually realised) when she found her father burned to death, having had a stroke and fallen on the fire. Later I discovered she had passed on many of her memories in her several years of correspondence with my father. It was her way of sharing herself, which she did with a very few people—too few.

In January 1958 I was seen by yet another specialist, R. W. Brookfield of Rodney Street in Liverpool. I'd forgotten that back then the young chap "frequently suffers from urticaria." My genitalia were the main issue this time, however. The right testicle was "no bigger than a pea" while "the left scrotum seemed empty", and the penis was "small, buried". A course of Pregynl injections was prescribed. The doctor also noted my "rather intellectual manner" and recorded that I'd begun to talk at ten months and read books at the age of four. I assume this meant novels, not the tales of Rupert Bear.

Ghostly Tales, that first book of mine, bounced from publisher to publisher. Sometimes it ended up with children's book editors, one of whom told me it made her feel quite spooky sitting at her desk. (Childish the book may have been, but it wouldn't be for children even now.) By far the most positive response came from Tom Boardman Jr in August 1958. While Boardman was one of the few British houses to publish science fiction in hardcover, they didn't take ghost stories, but he concluded: "We should like to take this opportunity of encouraging you to continue with your writing because you have definite talent and very good imaginative qualities. It means a lot of hard work to become an author but with the promising start you have made there is every possibility that you will make the grade."

I was also being encouraged elsewhere. Brother Kelly, one of the Christian Brothers who ran St Edward's, was my first English teacher at the school. When he learned that I wrote stories he had me read them to the class. If he was offended by their grisliness, he kept it to himself; perhaps he found the tale that derived from Dennis Wheatley—I did say earlier that my writing had yet to catch up with my literary taste—commendably Christian. I'm very much afraid I grew resentful when he used my example to motivate my classmates. I considered myself to be the only real writer in the room, and had little patience with stories about, say, football. On one occasion I went to the ludicrous extreme of pretending to read stories from blank pages in a pig-headed attempt to hold the floor.

St Edward's gave me my first experience of editing. Brother Kelly suggested that I contribute a tale to the school magazine—that's to say, write a new one, since anything from *Ghostly Tales* would have been a bit too much. I duly wrote a relatively moderate tale, "Midnight Appointment", where two boys arrange to meet at a clock tower while a murderer is on the loose. Our hero Maurice Grant does indeed meet his friend Roger Hicks at midnight, but a newspaper report tells us Roger was murdered (gasp!) just before the hour. Imagine my bewilderment when I saw in the published version that he'd been killed just after! I actually wondered if I'd made that mistake myself, but when I raised the issue with Brother Kelly he told me that the editor (Brother Coffey, I believe) didn't like ghost stories. You can read the tale online on pp 201-2 here: http://magazines.ci-edwardians.co.uk/1957-58.pdf.

Brother Kelly was by no means the only good and enthusiastic teacher. Too much of the schooling, however, consisted of dictation—pages of text that the master read aloud with little or no commentary—or copying from the blackboard. I assume the intention wasn't to train us as secretaries. I recall that my boredom grew apparent when we had to write sentences that contained particular words; mine were defiantly gruesome and macabre, though perfectly grammatical.

I was briefly a cellist in the school orchestra. I'd obtained high marks in music lessons, but only by dint of learning the test piece by ear. I barely read music, and my orchestral playing was dismal. I'm reminded of this whenever I hear the suggestion that everyone is a poet or a writer. Of course everyone uses words, but that doesn't mean that most can do so to publishable standard, any more than my struggles with a Bach suite (had I tried) would have been worth inflicting on an audience. I wasn't able to avoid duty in the school choir, however, even after my voice began to change. At one school prizegiving at the Philharmonic Hall we performed the Polovtsian chorus from *Prince Igor*, but my contribution consisted simply of mouthing the words. At least my time with the choir gave me the background of "Never to be Heard".

I'd previously inflicted my musical struggles on the school in a different way. I was eleven or younger when I acquired a plastic ukulele, which my mother, ever indulgent if not worse, persuaded me I could play to accompany my singing, then heavily (and, I suspect, hideously) influenced by the skiffle singer Lonnie Donegan. When performers for the Christmas concert were invited I put myself forward, and as I've said elsewhere, put on an exhibition rendered all the more comic (to judge by the audience reaction) by my bids to hold up the instrument without having strapped it around my neck. I assume that it was next year I bought an acoustic guitar, and someone presumably suggested—however mischievously—that I form a band. Paul Ennis was the only schoolmate unlucky enough to be tempted. He was a far better guitarist than I, a contrast that became all the more evident when, after very few rehearsals, we appeared onstage to rapturous applause at the top of the Christmas bill as Campbell and Company. What key I tried to bring to *Frankie and Johnny* I have no idea, but I'm sure that unlike me, Paul was playing in the right one. That was the end of my St Edwards stage career.

I was excused Physical Education, largely because my mother feared that if other boys caught sight of my teeny penis in the changing room, any homosexuals present might find me attractive—a curious notion, but she succeeded in persuading the headmaster to have me dropped from the class. One gym master was fond of a game in which the boys ran about the gymnasium and attempted to smack each other's buttocks while avoiding the same fate. "Smacky bottom!" he used to cry, if I'm not mistaken—he certainly expressed his enthusiasm.

There was also the strap, which was applied to our hands for various offences and which was something of a hindrance to writing. I experienced it often enough that I became fearful of drawing attention to myself in class by offering to answer questions. This aspect of the school was epitomised by Robinson ("Gobbo", as he was generally known), a mathematics teacher who dedicated himself to terrifying pupils, not least with a kidney punch. What he thought this had to do with learning, if indeed he cared, I have no idea. In later years I was told that sixth-formers found him reasonable, but this suggests to me that he behaved better towards boys too old to be cowed, which simply makes him even more of a shit in my book. I was never in his class, thank God, but he summed up the dread that became central to my experience of school. Before long I was finding a range of excuses for my mother to keep me off—any hint of illness would usually do, even when I had to invent a symptom. Of course my education suffered even more, but one particular day of malingering began my career.

I was fourteen. At the weekend I regularly walked some miles to Bascombe's, a shop on Smithdown Road that was half devoted to books and magazines. Often I would find prizes in the window, and this time I was awestruck to see a copy of *Cry Horror*, an entire book by—I had to look twice to be certain—H. P. Lovecraft. I'd read and been enthralled by half a dozen of his stories—when I'd read "The Colour Out Of Space" I had found so horrifying I concealed it from my mother—but this was the first complete book of his I'd ever seen (indeed, it was the very first British paperback by him). I paid my half a crown and returned home in a daze with the book, and on Monday feigned sickness in order to read it from cover to cover. By the end I knew this was the kind of fiction I wanted to write.

And I did, altogether too slavishly. Though I'd never left England I set a bunch of tales in Massachusetts, rustic dialect and all. Alongside this I'd joined fandom. I'd recently discovered a science fiction and fantasy bookseller in Liverpool: Leslie Johnson, who, along with his family, had to suffer my phoning every night for weeks to learn if Arkham House books I'd ordered had arrived. He introduced me to the Liverpool science fiction group (LiG), and I set about becoming a drunken adolescent. I also became a member of the British Science Fiction Association, and Peter Mabey, the librarian, put me in touch with Pat Kearney, another horror fan. It was Pat who published one of my Lovecraftian tales in his fanzine *Goudy*, and he also suggested that I should send them to Arkham House, Lovecraft's publisher. That's how August Derleth came to read them, and he sent me a two-page single-spaced letter setting out in detail what was wrong with them. It was the most important editorial letter of my career, and once I'd recovered from the criticism I devoted myself to rewriting the stories and applying the techniques I'd learned to new work.

Meanwhile I was discovering the cinema—to begin with, horror. At fourteen I was able to pass for sixteen, the minimum age for admission to most horror films in Britain in the sixties; even Godzilla movies were burdened with the X certificate. Initially my mother took me into the cinemas, but soon I acquired sufficient confidence to bluff my own way in. I fear that school homework was too often crowded into second place by the feast of films that had become available to me. I knew many of them from stills and sometimes from whole articles in Forry Ackerman's *Famous Monsters of Filmland*, which I'd been collecting for years. Sometimes I was disconcerted when an image failed to appear in a film, often because the British censor had excised it. Even without stills, I could see that he'd made a mess of the genesis of the werewolf in *Curse of the Werewolf* (now available uncut on home video). I've been opposed to censorship ever since.

I don't think horror films influenced my writing significantly, but other films did. The very first subtitled film I encountered was playing second feature to *The Cyclops*, in which a chap enlarged by nuclear radiation pops up behind a mountain with his scalp hanging over his eye. While this made me jump, the supporting film, Luis Buñuel's *Los Olvidados*, stayed with me considerably longer. Filmed in 1950, it's as shocking as the director's work with Salvador Dali, but the surrealism is inseparable from Buñuel's unflinching view of life in the slums of Mexico City. It contains a nightmare that throws an extra light on the realism, while some of the realistic images are so grotesque as to border on the surreal. I think the film's interaction of social observation and the fantastic may have shown me how I could develop as a writer; certainly that's the route I took.

Filmgoing affected my writing in another way. Until my early teens I had very little sense of my birthplace. On the whole I kept to districts (Childwall, Old Swan, the Rocket, Wavertree, Taggart Avenue) within walking distance, all of them respectably suburban. I did take the bus or, until this mode of transport was done away with, the tram to the downtown shops, but much of the city centre was unknown territory, vast enough to make me lose all direction. Now I sought out every cinema that was listed in the *Liverpool Echo*, enough of them to fill an entire column of the front page with just the titles of their double bills. Many of them were in areas of the city that had been left in ruins since the Second World War. Simply making my way to them was an adventure of constant discovery, and before long their settings began to show up in my tales.

I was also reading far more outside my genre than within. Just as I'd discovered that mainstream films—Bergman's *Wild Strawberries*, Resnais' *Last Year in Marienbad*—could be more disquieting than most generic horror, so I began to value mainstream fiction that disturbed me: Beckett's later novels, for instance, and some by Thomas Hinde—*The Day the Call Came*, *The Investigator*. Alongside these I relished Graham Greene, Iris Murdoch, Malcolm Lowry, William Burroughs, Lawrence Durrell and many more. Nabokov—initially *Lolita*, after which I devoured all of his work I could find—was the greatest revelation. Even in an early tale like "The Stone on the Island" (1963) I'm beginning to share his delight in language and its myriad possibilities.

All this was backed by my family life. In my teens I sometimes came home at the same time as my father, who would hold the front door closed from inside to make sure we never met face to face. Very occasionally, when it was necessary for him to get in touch, he would leave me a note, for some reason in French. My grandmother was now living with us, and I shared my room and its single bed with my mother. It may be that the reason why she didn't share her mother's room was that she refused to believe there could be anything wrong with her sleeping with me: about then she started fulminating Freud and his dirty mind. At least I'd shed my obesity with adolescence or dieting, and so there was more space. Sometimes I would waken in the early hours, my mother snoring beside me, the glow of the dwindling night-light rendering the contents of the room—bed, dressing-table, my mother and myself—as unreal and ominous as their reflection in the wardrobe mirror.

My grandmother died of gangrene when I was fifteen. During her final illness I helped lift her onto the bedpan and had my first glimpse of a female pubis, which appalled me and made me think of a spider. After the funeral my mother told me that she had found one of her mother's toes in the bed. Nevertheless that was where she now slept, which meant I had my own room. I lay in the darkness praying that some undefined terror would stay away from me, since I no longer had the night-light my mother had always kept burning, whether in case she had to go to her mother in the night or lest my father came into the room. Some months later she saw her mother at the top of the stairs, wearing a nightgown that, she insisted, crumpled emptily to the stair and was still there when she went up. Now and then she would feel the ghost of her father tap her meaningfully on the shoulder.

The General Certificate of Education (Ordinary Level) was then the first major examination at secondary school. Most people who sat it did so at sixteen years old, but I and others in my class were thought to be worth putting in for it at fifteen. I performed dreadfully, passing only in English Language and (barely) in Religion, even failing English Literature. My skiving was certainly a reason, but I blame the style of teaching too. The following year we flops were taught by staff who, on the whole, were committed to helping us however they could, with very little beating. The best of them all was Ray Thomas, an English teacher who communicated his love of his subject with enormous skill and real feeling. I still recall his reading Matthew Arnold's *Sohrab and Rustum* to the class; he was clearly moved by the final pages, and I for one had to hold back tears. This was probably my favourite year at the school, marred mainly by an encounter with the loathsome Robinson, who found me away from my desk as he was passing the classroom during a study period and slapped my face. I'd been trying to retrieve a book a classmate had snatched while I was writing in it—the first draft of

The Inhabitant of the Lake. A version of this incident turns up in a summation of my experience of the school, the opening scene of "The Interloper".

Decades later I returned to the school, not least to reminisce with Ray Thomas. Who should be emerging from the staffroom as Ray ushered me in but Robinson himself? I've often regretted stepping aside without a word, but telling him that he was a shit to his face—or even just asking whether he remembered me and reminding him why he ought to—seemed unfair to Ray. At least, that's how I justify my inaction whenever I wish I'd confronted the fellow.

In a sense, alas or otherwise, my mainly enjoyable last year at school came too late. My GCE results were hugely improved—the splendid Brother Butler had even opened my eyes to the pleasures of mathematics, geometry in particular—and the headmaster wanted me to stay on to sit Advanced Level and qualify for a university. He did his best to persuade me, but I'd had enough of school, especially since I couldn't predict who might have taught me if I'd stayed. Besides, August Derleth was recommending me to find a day job that left me time to write, and so I did.

(At some point in my last few months at the school the entire upper fifth form was regaled with a lecture on the big wide world by a visiting monk. My only previous experience of sex education had been my mother's attempt, which got no further than the difference between boys and girls before I fled the room in embarrassed terror. I'm not sure how much of that was mine, but she left the rest of the job to some Catholic pamphlets that set out their version of the basics.)

I chose the Inland Revenue and commenced demonstrating my lack of social skills. (During the war my mother had worked for the civil service, but I suspect I chose this branch because others threatened to involve more contact with the public.) On my first interminable day in an enormous desk-filled room with a thin pervasive smell of cardboard and linoleum I spoke to almost nobody. That couldn't last, since I was a clerical assistant—a kind of office boy who checked other people's arithmetic and filed away their work or fetched files on their behalf—but for a while I was as fearful of drawing attention as I had been in my worst years at school. In time I discovered that some of my colleagues watched films and liked to talk about them, which helped. Talking, however, exposed my ineptitude with girls in ways that I suspect were apparent to everyone except me. While I wouldn't succeed for years in nerving myself to ask anyone for a date, I hung around more than one unfortunate young woman and did my hopeless best to chat her up. That she might have a boyfriend or, in one case, even be engaged seems not to have occurred to me until a colleague drew my attention to the ring on her finger.

Soon I was promoted to clerical officer, only to find that I was terrified of answering the phone. I believe one source of my fear was the notion that my old tendency to mishear words might prove to be lying in wait. I was now dealing with the tax affairs of hundreds of people, but if one of them phoned I did my utmost to be unobtrusive and to let someone else handle it. Of course this couldn't go on, and eventually the person in charge of the section insisted I take my own calls. Before long my panic subsided, and I developed an official manner.

Meanwhile I was still attending school. On starting work I'd found that anybody under eighteen was required to continue their education one day a week. My disgust was tempered when Mr Garley, the vice-principal of Childwall Hall County College, turned out to be a Lovecraft fan. I told him that I'd just published a Lovecraftian tale—"The Church in High Street", my first professional appearance—and in no time Miss Last, one of the English teachers, had me read it on tape and sit in her class to be questioned once she'd played the recording. I couldn't have predicted the result. The sound of myself on tape bore no resemblance to the voice I heard whenever I spoke, and if that was how I ordinarily sounded I found it well-nigh unbearable. It took me quite a while to slough off this extra layer of self-consciousness. Even now I'm sometimes thrown by realising how I actually sound, though nobody else seems to mind.

Soon after starting my first job I gave up religion. I'd grown suspicious of it in my last years at St Edward's: what sort of god would lend his name to the kind of sadism (not only physical) that was commonplace at the school? It's a naïve theological question, I know, but it did for me. As for Catholic repressiveness, I'd begun to lose patience with it pretty well as soon as I learned that it forbade my reading certain books. I read all of them I could obtain, along with books banned in Britain that August Derleth sent me—Henry Miller's *Tropics* and the like. Perhaps my faith finally crumbled when I had an idea in church for a story I was writing: to be precise, an image for "The Mine on Yuggoth", one of the tales I was revising at Derleth's behest. It occurred to me during Communion, and I waited for the thunderbolt or its modern equivalent until I realised none was due. When my mother began to miss church because she didn't like people in the congregation but insisted I continue attending, her example was all the excuse I needed. I went out every Sunday for the duration of a mass, but only to read a book. (In those days I frequently read while walking, a habit I imagine did my eyesight no good at all.)

Elsewhere I was making yet more wobbly attempts to get a girlfriend. When I took on the lunchtime task of phoning the local bakers to order food for colleagues and myself I fell in love with the delectable girl who answered the phone and whom I saw beyond the counter. For weeks if not months I struggled to nerve myself to ask her out when I'd finished phoning the lunch order, and every time the words refused to emerge. Eventually I must have given up.

I took Anita, a clerical assistant, out for a couple of weeks. One lunchtime I escorted her through a series of cellars in the business district, and this episode is depicted in "The Cellars", my very first Liverpool story. Later I based the protagonist of "Reply Guaranteed" on her, not as an act of revenge but simply because aspects of her personality had suggested the tale. There was also Anne, a girl I met on a coach back from London, where I'd taken to travelling to watch films that might not come to Liverpool. I must admit that although we talked throughout much of the journey, she had to suggest that I take her out while she was staying with her aunt for a week. She was with a girlfriend, and so I brought along a workmate, Jim Smith. I fear my inexperience was apparent to all. Our week and its aftermath are central to "Concussion", although I left out the other couple.

In 1964 Arkham House published my collection *The Inhabitant of the Lake*. Not long after I received copies I became unable to read fiction. I felt compelled to loiter so long on every phrase that by the time I reached the end of a sentence I'd lost any grasp of its sense.

I believe this began on the very bus I took to London (see the previous paragraph), and the book that defeated me was *Over the Edge*—specifically the Hodgson contribution, a dozen pages that took me hours to read or rather fail to read. The only explanation I can find is that proofreading my book had made me so aware of the discrete existence of words that I was hyperconscious of their presence in other people's prose. I was still able to read film criticism, however, and all the material that came my way in the tax office. One summer day, after months of struggling to regain my grasp of fiction, I sat in the front garden with an issue of *Weird Tales* and raced through the lead novelette, "The Hand of Saint Ury"—just another severed hand on the traditional rampage, but an invaluable text while it lasted that afternoon. I never suffered from the condition again, and have passed it on to Wilfred Lowell, a character in *The Overnight.*

In 1965 I met Kirby McCauley. I'd originally heard from him three years earlier, when he wrote to me care of Arkham House after "The Church in High Street" was published. We corresponded at great length about films and literature and music and much else (though Kirby's letters were much longer and richer than mine). He discussed my published work in detail, and was a hugely supportive, though not uncritical, reader. When he decided to tour England he suggested I should accompany him, and we continued our debates even more vigorously. He was a generous and cultured companion, and over the years he helped keep my brain awake.

I was twenty when my mother decided I was old enough to be left alone while she went into the Liverpool Homeopathic Hospital for the operation she should have had twenty years earlier, on her prolapsed womb. A neighbour of about her age, Miss Holme, took in my laundry, much to my embarrassment and resentment. Resentment and impatience and indifference were all I felt at the sight of my mother in a hospital bed. Her operation led to complications, but she believed she'd been misled about the operation and its aftermath, and refused to undergo a further operation to repair the damage. I don't know whether she originally made the homeopathic choice because she distrusted drugs and doctors. She left hospital as soon as she could and tried to sue the surgeon, but couldn't find a lawyer to take the case.

When I suggested that the lawyers weren't necessarily in league with the surgeon, she decided that some enemy of hers had got to me. I don't know if this was the first time I tried to persuade her that things weren't always as they seemed to her: Liverpool wasn't full of people conspiring against her, radio programmes weren't referring to her under an imperfectly disguised name. My friends were turning me against her, she retorted, or I was taking drugs (which I wasn't yet). She would accuse me of trying to drive her into a hospital or a home and make me swear never to have her put away. Increasingly, perhaps defensively, I accepted that this was simply the way she was and that I could do nothing.

I don't know how resigned to her behaviour her sister Kathleen became. It may have been around then that my mother developed a habit of arranging to stay with Kathleen and her husband Leslie, only to cancel at the last moment on some pretext, generally that she couldn't trust anyone to look after her cat Bonnie. If she ever asked to visit them only to be told that someone else was visiting, she became outraged that she wasn't given priority. I fear this fugue went on for years.

I was also twenty when I changed jobs. I'd progressed as far as I could in the civil service without sitting more examinations, a chore I'd determined to leave behind on quitting school. I applied for a post in the public libraries. I don't know if the book I was reading—E. M. Forster's *Howard's End*—looked like a calculated ploy, but I had no idea when I brought it to the interview that it was the city librarian's favourite novel. Whatever he made of that, I got the job.

In mid-1966 I started work at Wavertree Library in Picton Road. It was close enough to my house that I hurried home every lunchtime for a boiled egg to convince my mother that I was adequately nourished. (While I was at grammar school she'd provided me every weekday with cold sausage sandwiches wrapped in greaseproof paper, packages I'm afraid I soon took to dumping in the schoolyard bin.) I was taken under the wing of Derek Dorrity, the deputy librarian, who remarked on how fast I was learning the skills of the business: hardly a surprise, since I enjoyed librarianship, which in those days had a good deal to do with books. Derek was a diabetic and presumably unaware that the female staff derided him for having taken one of them on a date and tried to kiss her. An intelligent but lonely fellow, he soon invited me to spend a day with him at home, where he played me recordings of classical music before we walked up Bidston Hill. Some years later I heard that he'd hanged himself.

One Saturday in January 1967 a member of staff called in sick, and a substitute was sent from the Sefton Park branch—Rosemary Prince, a flautist. We chatted about culture, and when she learned I was a member of the Merseyside Film Institute Society she asked me to buy tickets for her and another girl. She expressed interest in other films I mentioned, but my timidity might have ensured that things progressed no further if she hadn't eventually asked whether I was inviting her to one of them (Hitchcock's *The Birds*). I stammered that I was, and three months later we were engaged.

Does that sound precipitate? I fear that both of us were desperate for a partner and unable to stand back far enough from the relationship to see that it was doomed. It was already plain that Rosemary didn't like horror in fiction or film. She began to try and coax me away from it, not least in my writing (I still recall her grimace as she read a passage I'd just penned of "Reply Guaranteed"). I retaliated by attacking classical music for valuing beauty above disquiet, which was both unreasonable and dishonest of me. I think the crux of the disagreement was whether lyricism and horror could co-exist within a work. They demonstrably can.

After six months Rosemary's parents terminated the relationship, apparently not the first time they had intervened in such a manner. Among the ways they found Rosemary superior to me was her being a professional musician. When I retorted that I was as professional a writer, great was their scorn. Admittedly I had just one book to my name, but a single book from Arkham House meant a good deal to the cognoscenti. Besides, having written "The Cellars" and "Cold Print" and "Reply Guaranteed", I had a clear sense of the new direction I was taking. I don't think it's unfair at this distance to reflect that Rosemary was professional compared to the orchestras with which I saw her performing, but—at least in those days—musicianship was by no means her profession. I was shown the back door and trudged into the night to buy a pack of cigarettes, which Rosemary had persuaded me to give up, or at least to pretend to. After a few miserable days I experienced a considerable sense of release and a rush of creativity that produced both "The Scar" and the final draft of "Concussion". Episodes from my time with Rosemary show up in "The End of a Summer's Day" and "The Puppets" and especially "Napier Court" (in which the unflattering self-portrait of the author is entirely accurate). No experience is wasted if it provides me with material.

Perhaps the most positive result of our broken engagement was that it cured me of desperation. (I hope it had that effect on Rosemary too.) If anything I became almost too relaxed about relationships. I'd been attending British science fiction conventions for some years, despite my mother's disapproval of such goings-on at Easter, and at the 1968 convention in Buxton I was introduced to Jenny Chandler, daughter of A. Bertram Chandler, the veteran science fiction writer. (Arthur C. Clarke and John Wyndham helped choose her name.) Too little came of our meeting, but next year in Oxford we were more than happy to encounter each other again. Brian Aldiss recommended a fine Indian restaurant for our first meal together—thanks, Brian! Before long we were visiting each other. Jenny lived outside Cheltenham in Gloucestershire, the very county in which I'd set *The Inhabitant of the Lake*. Visiting the area made me aware that my version of it had been almost as inaccurate as my attempts to depict Massachusetts; the Cotswold hills don't roll gently, believe me. Her mother made me welcome while her stepfather suffered my presence and Jenny's, whereas on Merseyside, since my mother wasn't offering a room, our splendid friends Norman and Ina Shorrock—the very folk who'd introduced us in Buxton—put Jenny and often me up.

1969 saw me into a second regular job: film reviewer for the recently established local BBC station, Radio Merseyside. Tony Wolfe, the producer of the arts programme, originally invited the secretary of a new underground film society to be interviewed, but the secretary wanted a member to support him, and in the end I did most of the talking. The other development that membership of the society brought me was a police raid at my home after I'd advertised the Marquis de Sade's *120 Days of Sodom* for sale in the newsletter. "Look what you've done now," my mother cried—unfairly, I thought—at my father as she pounded on his bedroom door. The four plainclothes policemen took away other items, not least Samuel

Beckett's *Imagination Dead Imagine*, apparently because it contained the word "arse". Ultimately all the books were returned except for de Sade's, the exact same unexpurgated translation of which can be found in any large British bookshop these days. In the Beckett a police person had underlined the naughty word in pencil.

I reviewed some of the underground films for Tony Wolfe, who then sent me off to cover mainstream cinema. I carried on doing so on Radio Merseyside for almost forty years, at which point a new managing editor saved the station the price of a pizza and terminated my engagement. Press shows are a welcome refuge from the stench of popcorn and the shrilling or, entirely as irritating, the illuminated text messages of mobile phones (but, to be measured about it, having to leave my desk in the morning to see any film that was put up for review wasn't always helpful to my tales). Just as I derived stories of mine from librarianship—"In the Shadows", "Root Cause"—so filmgoing gave me the background for tales such as "After the Queen" and "The Show Goes On" and the novel *Ancient Images*. For a few months I broadcast my reviews live on a teatime music and chat show that Tony produced, and his differences with the presenter suggested the basis of "Midnight Hobo".

In 1970 Jenny finished training as a teacher and moved to Liverpool, where she rented a bed-sitter. Her landlord proved to be an Irish Catholic who knew the headmaster of the Catholic school where she started teaching. He might almost have been inserted into the narrative as a symbol of the past I'd presumed to leave behind. One Sunday morning he came to the flat and interrogated us in separate rooms: were we sleeping together? You bet we were, but we weren't telling him. I found us a flat in Princes Avenue in Toxteth, and we moved in. Years later I would set tales in the area—"The Brood", "The Invocation", *The Doll Who Ate His Mother*. Arthur Dooley's spiky Christ still threatens to leap from the façade of the church on the next block.

On the first day of 1971 Jenny and I were married in Cheltenham. My mother wasn't there, since she didn't want to stay with anyone she didn't know. For our wedding night Jenny and I were booked into what proved to be Cheltenham's famous gay hotel. At the bar a chap expressed his condolences on my marriage and offered me a lovely vicar for the night. That summer we had a belated honeymoon outside Keswick in the Lake District. Some of our walks gave me the setting for "Accident Zone", while our later stays in the hotel and outings from it were the basis of a better tale, "Above the World".

I think it was actually on the first day of our honeymoon that my father fell (or, according to my mother, was pushed) downstairs at Holt's Fireplaces, the Liverpool firm where he now worked as a clerk, having retired from the police. My mother called me long distance to demand I go back to see him in hospital, but I told her she had to be kidding. I'd been considerably more affected by the news of August Derleth's death just a few weeks earlier. Although we never met, in his many letters August was the nearest thing to a father figure I'd had.

On our return to Liverpool a week later I let a couple of days pass before I made myself go to see my father, and then I couldn't find the hospital. My mother had told me it was behind a department store when in fact it was several streets away from the front of the building. I wandered about until visiting time was over. I wasn't trying very hard to find the hospital.

I did locate it the next day, and my father. He looked old and feeble and unfamiliar; he wore bandages on his skull and a tube up his penis. Only his blurred murmur, which he must have been unable to control, seemed familiar from all those overheard arguments. Jenny said he looked very much as I shall in old age, but I couldn't touch him or understand what he was saying; I simply felt repelled by my mother's belated concern for him. I left as soon as I could, and a few days later he died.

I attended his funeral in Toxteth Park Cemetery in the pouring rain. His sister Barbara peered into the open grave and cried "Where's mother?" Subsequently my mother claimed that policemen at the inquest had told her they weren't satisfied that my father had died of natural causes, but I heard no more of this.

The sense of relief I'd experienced on leaving home was short-lived, for my mother and Jenny disliked each other. The spectacle of their mutual politeness made me increasingly tense, not least because I felt as if I was somehow in the middle of all this. My mother's front room seemed unbearably small to me with both of them in it. She didn't want to visit us if she would have to take a taxi home, since she suspected all their drivers of wanting to rape her. Soon I found excuses to visit her by myself, but this only made her more suspicious of Jenny. She frequently accused me of discussing her with Jenny, though in fact over the years she'd managed to inhibit me against discussing her with anyone at all.

I wrote little new fiction in the first years of our marriage. Being married was the best kind of distraction. I also felt that having completed my second book, *Demons by Daylight*, I'd reached the end of some stage of my writing and wasn't sure how to go on. I delivered the book to Arkham House in the summer of 1968 and later substituted one story as well as removing the J for John from my byline when I decided to do away with the name. The collection would have been published sooner except for Derleth's death, and I may well have used the delay as another unstated excuse not to write much. Alongside all this I'd discovered cannabis, and soon fell into the habit of smoking a joint every day: Peter in *The Face That Must Die* is a self-portrait. Things had to change.

They did. Kirby McCauley moved from Minneapolis to New York and became a literary agent, having seen that many of his British correspondents—Robert Aickman and I among them—needed one. Jenny persuaded me that we ought to be buying a house instead of paying rent, and we managed to obtain a mortgage for a staggering sum—could it have been as much as four thousand pounds?—from the bank. Shortly after we took up residence in a terraced house in Tuebrook, *Demons by Daylight* was published, and a friend of Kirby's sent me a copy of his exegesis. He was T. E. D. Klein, one of the modern masters of the supernatural tale. His analysis included so much I'd hoped the stories would convey that it persuaded me I had the makings of a fulltime writer. Jenny felt that if I was going to take the risk this would be the time, before we had children, and so in mid-1973 I made the break.

I could have been put on display as an example of how not to write professionally. For a great deal too long I didn't start work until about nine in the morning, presumably in imitation of a day job, and on the same principle I took every weekend off. Before putting my pen to the exercise book each day I would read all of the story I'd written so far. I'd substantially reduced my cannabis intake, not least because in those days it was hard to come by, but I tended to make up for that on Sundays and spend Mondays with a hashish hangover. Nevertheless a bunch of tales resulted from all this, some of them set in actual locations close by—"The Man in the Underpass", for instance, and later "Mackintosh Willy".

Kirby sold quite a few of them in time but kept gently insisting that I should attempt a novel. In January 1975 I did, and completed it by the summer, even though I still hadn't discovered my ideal method; I would reread each chapter the day after it was finished and call this work. Now I'm at my desk by seven every morning if not earlier, having worked out at least the first line of the day's prose if it's a first draft. That's every day, including Christmas and my birthday. Any first draft goes with me on holiday or to conventions and continues to be written every morning there. In 1972, with a story called "Litter", I made the mistake of writing the first pages and then waiting until I felt inspired to go on. It's the only time I've suffered from writer's block, which lasted six months.

Much of our life in that first house of ours, at 54 Buckingham Road in Tuebrook, turned up in some form in my tales, but one incident was either too odd or too unlikely. Shortly after we moved there I was walking to the main road when I passed a neighbour's teenage or possibly not quite yet teenage daughter in the street. With no preamble that I noticed she took hold of my gonads and twisted them hard. I was so startled that I didn't react, and perhaps I thought in my befuddled way that because I wore my hair over my shoulders in those days she was ascertaining my gender. Decades later her younger brother contacted me as a potential witness on behalf of their father, whom she'd accused of sexually abusing her while she was a child. I mentioned this incident, but the defence lawyer may well have thought it was an ambiguous bit of evidence. I wasn't called to court, but in 2005 the father was found guilty and sentenced to eighteen years. While the *Liverpool Echo* didn't identify his several victims, it reported that he had sex with the youngest when she was eight years old.

The Doll Who Ate His Mother was published in October 1976 to largely indifferent reviews and worse sales. The solitary way I know to recover from that kind of blow is to write, and so I began another novel, *The Face That Must Die*. This was based to some extent on my mother's conviction that people around her were other people in disguise. It also drew on my own recent experiences with LSD. Those gave me material for quite a few tales—"Above the World", "The Pattern", and two stories based to some extent on trips I'd taken around the nearby Freshfield Nature Reserve, "The Faces at Pine Dunes" and especially "The Voice of the Beach"—but they'd led to a nightmarish extended flashback from which Jenny and several string quartets, Beethoven's Opus 135 in particular, had to some extent rescued me. Indeed, while writing a chapter of *The Face That Must Die* I saw my handwriting begin to writhe on the page. I don't recommend this as an aid to composition.

I thought and still think that the novel improved on my first. It traps the reader for chapter after chapter in the mind of the psychotic John Horridge and never attempts to sanitise the experience. For me the horror lies at least as much in his minute-to-minute consciousness as in the violence he commits (which, contrary to rumour, was never toned down in any edition of the book). I was thrown when more than one publisher of my first novel declared that Horridge was the problem with this one and either found him unconvincing or asked me to focus the book on more sympathetic characters. For the first time I baulked at editorial suggestions, and eventually the book was published as a British paperback original, although by then I'd lost so much faith in it that I agreed to cuts and made some myself. Robert Bloch championed even this version, and the first American edition and all subsequent reprints are restored to completeness.

The book wouldn't gain a reputation until the eighties, however. In 1977 its rejection forced me to concoct a commercial success. This was *The Parasite*, a novel about astral projection, stuffed with enough occult detail and film lore to have been split into two (possibly better) books. Its best sections are those in which I was sufficiently engaged with the material to forget about the market. We needed it to sell, because although Jenny had been supporting us by teaching, we were trying to have children. Publishers bought it, and it did well enough that from then onwards—with the partial exception of *The Claw* (1983), a pseudonymous commission that my British agent obtained while publishers caught up with my backlog—I was able to write whatever felt like the next development, inevitable in itself, and support my family as well.

In August 1978 our daughter Tammy was born. I almost missed the event, having nipped out for a bite to eat at a nearby Indian restaurant, where I had to leave my credit card while Jenny attempted to keep the baby in as I dashed back to the delivery room. The emergence of this small blood-streaked vociferous creature flummoxed me so much that when I was directed to dab her head I thought the nurse meant the baby's, not Jenny's. Many of the pratfalls executed by my characters are my own.

I have to confess that I'd planned two short stories so as not to be distracted from my writing by the new arrival. I'd reached the point of being afraid I might lose the impulse if I took any significant period off from my work. "This Time" went fluently enough, but when I began "Down There" it proved so reluctant to emerge that it might almost have been presuming to imitate birth. After several days I was ready to abandon it—something I've done with a handful of short stories in progress, though no novels—until an image of rain outside a window brought it to life. Perhaps I was secretly guilty about spending too little time with Tam.

She soon made her way into my fiction. *The Nameless* contains my first sketch of her and establishes the theme of parental paranoia. Despite being commissioned to order, *The Claw* soon makes personal subjects central—parents who turn monstrous and the vulnerability of children. The father who's transformed into a monster was already present in stories of mine, "The Chimney" in particular, but now he was me. Children at risk, and the unwillingness of witnesses to intervene, had shown up in my tales as early as "The Scar" (1967), decades before child abuse was to become a standard theme of horror fiction. I hope that writing about ghastly fathers prevented me from being quite as bad, but only our children can tell.

In a couple of years we decided where we lived wasn't ideal. I think the key detail may have been all the broken glass that bestrewed the route to the playground in the park. We moved across the river to Wallasey—beside the seaside resort that had inspired "The Companion" and that would be central to *The Count of Eleven*—before our son Mat was born in June 1981. Sadly, although this was right for us, it was too much for my mother. Though we'd moved less than six miles, it dislodged the last prop of her sanity.

I felt uneasy when she mentioned seeing faces in the foliage outside her house, although she assured me that she didn't find them frightening. Her state became more evident when we invited her for dinner on her birthday that October. I arranged to meet her at our local railway station, since I hadn't yet learned to drive. I waited several hours, phoning her house between trains, and eventually went home to a phone call accusing me of having played a trick on her. She'd been waiting for me at the station in Liverpool, where, she said, people had taken her for a prostitute.

One night soon after that she phoned me in terror, saying that the room was full of people watching her. For a moment I saw her cramped front room full of people whose faces I would have seen if the moment had lasted any longer. Most of the room was dark, but the figures were lit by a dying glare, exactly the light I remembered from nights in my adolescence when I'd wakened next to her in bed. The glare was enough to convince me that the faces of the figures would have had the clarity of a nightmare if I hadn't instantly shut my mind off from the perception. I couldn't bear to be that close.

Things quickly grew worse. Aeroplanes were being used to spy on her, though perhaps one of the pilots was on her side. Once, when she came for dinner, she took baby Mat for a pet animal. When we gave her a photograph of herself holding Tammy, she refused to believe she was the woman in the photograph, whose nose was too big. Her next-door neighbours had secretly bought her house from her landlord and were trying to take over one of the rooms for their daughter's use. Her neighbours on the far side were social workers who wanted her to look after a mad old woman during the day. She would phone me in a panic to say she was in the house that looked like hers but was miles away from hers. Sometimes she felt she was being drugged to cause her to hallucinate. When I tried to persuade her that none of this was happening she would accuse me of conspiring against her, trying to drive her mad.

Even I couldn't pretend nothing was wrong now, but more than thirty years of not discussing her at her insistence made me incapable of seeking medical advice on her behalf. I felt helpless and increasingly desperate whenever I thought of her. Usually on my visits I had to try and disentangle the truth from her account of something that had happened, or she claimed had happened, since my last visit; often we had violent arguments over nothing at all—sometimes we came to blows. More than once I grew so frustrated that I ran at a wall of the room head first. I wasn't always sane myself.

At about three o'clock one morning the police phoned me, having been called to my mother's house by neighbours because she was shouting from an upstairs window for help against the people who were attacking her. Not long after that, on the theory that living near me in a house she knew I owned would make her feel more secure, I managed to obtain a mortgage for one from the bank. Perhaps this seemed the perfect solution because I was at my wit's end, or because it was so close to the ambition she'd nursed throughout my childhood of owning her own home. I couldn't see (though Jenny tried to make me see) that it was too late for this, which might very well exacerbate the situation. Still, we found a house my mother was delighted with, a few minutes' walk away from ours.

The negotiations for buying it took months, as they will. Meanwhile she kept phoning to say that heads were looking at her out of vases or to plead with me to take her home from the house someone had left her in. She slept downstairs on the couch, because people came into her bedroom and pushed her out of bed. By now I left the phone off the hook when I went to bed, but more than once I woke in the dead of night convinced I'd heard its ringing.

Shortly after the contracts of sale had been signed, my mother decided she didn't want to move house after all: she felt at home where she was, she had friends among the neighbours. (Previously she had insisted that the neighbours were circulating a petition to have her put out of her house because she was only a tenant whereas they owned their homes, but a few were on her side and refusing to sign.) I managed intermittently to persuade her, sometimes by making wild promises, and spent the week before the move in packing her belongings, since she was either incapable or unwilling. Spending so much time in that house reminded me of my childhood. Remembering how she'd looked after me made me realise how unrecognisable she was now, and how little was left of our relationship. In the back garden I burst into tears.

At first she seemed happy in her new house and finding out

where the shops were, two minutes' walk away. She bought a television, which she'd wanted for many years. I imagined her settling in, making friends, taking strolls along the promenade down to which steps led at the bottom of her street. I was as trapped in a fantasy as she was.

It took me a while to notice she was no longer changing her clothes. People had stolen all the rest and replaced it with inferior stuff that she refused to wear, instead tying it in bundles that she hid around the house. I was visiting her every day, and now that I'd learned to drive I took her touring the nearby countryside. None of this helped; it simply let me believe now and then that it was a partial solution. Of course I knew it was nothing of the kind.

By now she often phoned me several times a day to go round and tell the people to leave her alone—the children, my sister, the man who looked like the devil. Often she told me I was there with her, or someone who was pretending to be me, who looked extremely ill and who had her worried sick. Occasionally I persuaded her that she'd just awakened from dreaming. Sometimes I rushed to her house to prove her wrong, but either she denied having called me or the people had just gone: this lady in the corner and the people in the curtains would confirm she was telling the truth, or were they afraid to speak? She knew they weren't really people in the curtains but photographs of people that someone kept putting in the room—hadn't I heard of talking pictures? That was as far as I could argue her back towards reality. What was I trying to do, drive her mad so that woman and I could have her house? Oh no, of course, it wasn't her house, though I'd said it would be. I'd shown her three houses and this was her least favourite, she hadn't really wanted it at all . . . She refused absolutely to believe that anything was wrong with her or that she needed help.

I did. For the first time in my life I considered seeking help on her behalf and was too desperate to behave as she had programmed me to. Even so, I spent months trying to persuade her to enrol with our family doctor, until one day I drove her there and dumped her in the waiting-room. She told the doctor I was her husband who had left her for another woman. The doctor[2] agreed with me that something had to be done.

[2] Dr Anne Biezanek, once famed for opening a Catholic contraception clinic and later noted for scoring cannabis to help her daughter's medical condition.

Nothing could be, since my mother refused help. The doctor referred me to the social services, who ran luncheon clubs and day care centres for the elderly. The case worker made two visits to my mother, at the second of which I was present and saw her fail to explain what services she was offering (presumably assuming, quite unjustifiably, that my mother would remember what she had been told the first time). She left after five minutes and put the case away among the dormant files. The few times I went to the social services after that she was usually on holiday, or not back from holiday when she was expected, or off sick. Once she told me that perhaps my mother's hallucinations were company for her. Her colleagues praised her professional competence.

So began the worst year of my life. I realised that my mother never went out of the house by herself, though she was convinced she did. Her calls became more frequent and more terrified, and all I could do was grow used to them, respond indifferently, tell her I'd be round later. I still visited her every day, though by now we loathed each other; either we had violent arguments in which she clung to the idea that nothing was wrong with her, or hardly spoke. Her grasp of language was failing, and often she would refer to something by a wholly unrelated word—she would call a car a house, for instance—or simply trail off, but although I almost always deduced what she meant I refused to admit that I did. I was becoming everything she feared and hated. Sometimes when I took her for a drive I was tempted to leave her miles from anywhere; sometimes I considered killing her, reaching across her on a deserted stretch of motorway and opening the passenger door. Perhaps she would leave the gas fire on unlit or finally wander down into the river.

The doctor could see how I was, and called in the community health officer to visit my mother. He was sympathetic, and more skilful than the social worker at the job she ought to have been doing, but all he could do was visit my mother regularly in the hope of establishing a rapport. Meanwhile my behaviour towards my wife and children grew steadily worse. When we took a fortnight's holiday in the summer of 1982, I made sure the social services knew I was away, but I was hoping that my mother would have to go out shopping by herself or starve to death. As I drove home after the holiday I listened to the local news in the hope of hearing a report that she'd died.

Her house smelled worse and was swarming with flies, but otherwise nothing had changed: the same arguments, the same helpless mutual loathing. She had clearly not been out of the house. She accused me of having stolen her key, and when I showed her she had several copies in her purse, insisted that they didn't fit the lock. She went to the front door to demonstrate, and I watched her trying to turn the lock with a box of matches.

Either I was able to see clearly at last that she needed constant supervision or two weeks' respite had left me even less able to cope. I spoke to the community health officer, who had concluded independently that part of his problem in establishing a rapport was that my mother felt (however bitterly) she could always rely on me. I told her I wouldn't be visiting her for three weeks; if she needed anything she would have to call on the services available, whose phone numbers I posted on the wall above the phone.

She called me a couple of days later to ask if we were still friends. Those were just about her last words to me. Nearly two weeks later I heard from the community health officer. He'd visited my mother's house two days running but had received no answer. I hurried round and let myself in.

The kitchen and most of the hall were flooded by a tap that had been left full on. My mother lay on the sofa, breathing but past waking. She was emaciated and looked decades older. The kitchen drawers were full of mouldering sliced bread, months old. The television was turned over on its screen; a mirror lay smashed in the hall. From the cuts on her hand it seemed she must have punched her reflection in the face.

I called the community health officer and drove to the social services. The case worker was off sick, and the officer I spoke to complained that it was nearly her lunch hour. She tried to make me feel guilty enough about my mother to go away, until I began to scream at her. I should not like to have to rely on most of the social workers I met, and perhaps after all it was to the good that my mother never had.

Our doctor and the community health officer had her admitted to hospital that afternoon. She'd regained consciousness, and was pitifully grateful both to see me and to go into hospital. I hoped this would be the first step towards her going into care, but every time I visited the hospital she seemed worse. Soon she didn't recognise me. Sometimes she lay with her eyes moving back and forth, very fast, like a metronome. I fed her water from a toddler's lidded cup, managing a cupful an hour if she didn't spit it out. Less than two weeks after she had been admitted, the ward sister called in the morning to say my mother had died during the night. I feel she died of my neglect and of my having destroyed her memories.

I was neglectful even after her death. I didn't view her body in the funeral home, not having realised that I could. I didn't place an obituary notice in any newspaper, which meant that none of her friends attended the funeral. She was cremated, and I took the ashes to the family grave in Huddersfield that weekend, only to find that there was nobody to tell me where the grave (which I'd seen once, twenty years previously) was. I set out to look for it, but found after an hour that I'd examined perhaps a tenth of the headstones. I gave up then, planning to come back on a weekday when someone would be in attendance, and wandered aimlessly through the graveyard until suddenly I halted, turned, and found myself looking straight at the family headstone. I had walked to it by the shortest possible route. I should like to think that my mother had managed at last to take me where she wanted to be.

During that last year I wrote much of *Incarnate*, by far my most elaborate and ambitious novel up to that date—perhaps even up to now. I used to think it was somewhere I could go and still be in control, but that wasn't quite the case. Since it was one of my books that came closest to writing itself, outstripping my initial ideas in order to create its own intricate structure, I think my need was to lose control, at least to the extent of entrusting myself to the energy of the narrative and the compulsion to write. The first draft was complete before I grasped that one of the several plots concerned a mother who grows alien and terrible. Perhaps I had to overlook this in order to write.

People may think she's still with me. My novel *Secret Story* is about a writer whose mother submits his work for publication without asking him. That's more coincidental than autobiographical, but my entire life is there to be drawn on, and even its earliest stages often give me insights. The foundation of my life now, however, is made up of Jenny and Tammy and Mat. They're all that's best about me, and without them I wouldn't be half the person I am, which means half the writer as well. You can find them in many of my tales; *Obsession*, *The Influence*, *Midnight Sun*, *The Count of Eleven* are just some. Jenny is my first reader and editor—the only other person who can read my handwriting—and my constant collaborator. The next piece she'll read is this.

I put together a version of this piece in 2004 at the request of *Contemporary Authors*. Since then the family has grown—Sam is Tammy's partner, and Cal and Isaac are their sons. I celebrate them all.

A Small Dose of Reality

LET ME RETURN TO WILLIAM SCHOELL, AT LEAST AS a way of introducing this piece. I mean his comment in *Fantasy Review* 73 that "literary" (Mr Schoell's quotation marks) horror novels are "a publicity department trick, aided and abetted by self-deluding horror novelists." In my case he's thinking of *Incarnate.* I hope it may be of interest to my readers to learn how that book came to be written. If Mr Schoell detects self-delusion in the process, by all means let him show where. I hope, though, that he won't fall back on the complaint that I'm taking him "much too literally"; I do expect people whose business is words to mean what they say.

Since every novel is a stage in the writing of later novels, I should begin by recalling how I came to write a novel in the first place. It was a bid to make my living as a writer, and also an attempt to convince myself that I could extend my audience. Ever since August Derleth published me in 1962, I'd regarded Arkham House exactly as Lovecraft regarded *Weird Tales,* as my only market, beyond which I dared not venture. My agent, Kirby McCauley, gradually demonstrated that I was wrong and at the same time encouraged me to attempt a novel.

This was *The Doll Who Ate His Mother,* which I worked on for most of a year before writing the first line of the manuscript at the beginning of 1975. I think it was the banality of that first line (which I still like) that got me going. So delighted was I to be writing a novel I knew I would finish (as distinct from several unfinished imitations in my early teens) that I overlooked the blatant contrivance on which the book is based, the circumstances of the car accident. Alas, the structure is too sound to let me take it out, though I did substitute a less bathetic fate for the title character in the 1985 version. For all its tentativeness and uncertainties of pace, the book does address issues I wanted to raise, particularly in terms of the unholy alliance of magic, Christianity and social conditions that help make the character what he is.

The book did, as my editor at Bobbs-Merrill put it, "dreadfully." In the intervening eighteen months I'd written three novels based on Universal horror movies (*Bride of Frankenstein, The Wolfman, Dracula's Daughter*) which enabled me to indulge the Gothic tendencies of my style almost to the point of purgation. (Later I was struck by aspects they had in common with my signed novels: protagonists searching for their homes, ambiguous familial relationships.) Given the news from Bobbs-Merrill, had I been reaching for bestsellerdom rather than writing what I felt driven to write, I should certainly not have written *The Face That Must Die* in the way I did. I welcomed returning to something more personal, especially since I'd completed several Robert E. Howard fragments after writing the Universal novels, and I thought it an improvement on *The Doll.* But apart from Piers Dudgeon at Star Books, who felt Star must wait and see how they fared with my first novel, none of my publishers would touch the book, which they felt was unpublishably grim. By the time Star brought out the first edition I'd come to share the general dissatisfaction with the book, and so protested only half-heartedly when Star's page proofs proved to have been edited without my knowledge. The response to the book persuaded me I'd been right about it in the first place, and I was glad to see a fully restored text into print from Scream/Press and Tor.

Meanwhile my wife was about to have our first child, and her teaching no longer supported us. For once I tried to write a guaranteed commercial success, *To Wake the Dead,* now available in a revised edition as *The Parasite.* I sought to include elements that

[1] *Claw* alias *Night of the Claw*, ultimately *The Claw*.

were regarded as commercial—sympathetic characters besieged by the supernatural, vivid unambiguous manifestations—but it turned out unexpectedly similar to my earlier novels: it too is a study of the derangement of a personality, specifically of the invasion of a female personality by a (dormant) male. My doubts about striving to be commercial at the risk of lowering one's standards are argued over by the central characters. But the book tries to pack in too much, and for every tightly written scene there's an underdeveloped and/or overwritten one, not least because I'd made the elementary mistake of having all the supernatural events befall only one character: as the menace of which she's aware escalates, there's nowhere to go but into her mounting terror, which is to say into overwriting, some of it unduly exploitative. That the central metaphor is rape seems relevant enough, but I agree with those critics who found the novel too dependent on the image of woman as victim. Still, I like the visionary (Lovecraftian?) scenes, and I try to recapture awesomeness in *The Hungry Moon.*

The Nameless was a conscious attempt to write a more succinct, more controlled novel. Stylistically and on the whole structurally, it's altogether more successful, but I was taken aback recently while reading the proofs of the revised version (revised mainly to take out a contrived scene) to realize for the first time that the book comes dangerously close to expressing attitudes I have little time for, the notion of evil as an external force—"nothing to do with us"—and the idea that independent women are suspect: not only does the protagonist blame her return to her career for the kidnapping of her daughter (a sense of guilt perhaps insufficiently contradicted by the book), but at the end she can't even rescue her daughter without the aid of her late husband, popping up ex machina to save the day.

Perhaps an unconscious sense of these flaws influenced the development of *Incarnate,* which I began to compose in 1979 but didn't start to write sequentially until the end of 1981, by which time it had ceased to be a novel about chronic insomnia. (In between I'd written a pseudonymous novel[1], the saga of whose composition I don't have room for here.) George Walsh, my editor at Macmillan, suggested changes in my synopsis: more unity of place (I'd had the characters converging from all over Britain throughout the book), more sense that one character was central.

His suggestions seemed to liberate me from depending on preconceived plotting, and for the first time I set out into the unknown to follow where a novel led.

Some changes were a matter of conscious choice. Chris Churchill, a young woman who helps two sisters run an old people's day centre until she's drawn into their obsession with an invalid who is taking over their home, became Geoffrey Churchill, both to give the book a marital relationship in which one partner's secret dream becomes incarnate and to dispense with Chris's fears of a recurrence of her experiences with drugs, which I thought insufficiently universal for the book (though I was sorry to lose a scene in which she copes for a while with the growing distortion of reality by telling herself that she's already experienced this kind of thing until she realises that her own physical metamorphosis isn't a hallucination—a moment that turns up in Geoffrey's last walk). In the original synopsis Molly Wolfe, the central character, was divorced, and Martin Wallace was ousted by her husband Jeffery. Learning belatedly that Jeffery has in fact been dead for years, Martin was to pursue them to an abandoned Scottish farm that has become a kind of commune for mystics. His rage enables him to break through the illusions and save Molly. In the novel, his rage simply flings him back into everyday reality, excluding him from the finale of the book: I'd had enough of scenes in which Our Hero charges to the rescue. Jeffery became Sage, the incarnation of the lure of occultism. More generally, I tried not to manufacture suspense, tried to avoid telling the audience when they were supposed to be frightened or disturbed. I wanted to let the material speak for itself where it could.

I thought the several plots would take their time about converging, and so I was surprised and delighted by how early in the book the order of events became inevitable; I enjoy form, but hadn't realised how much energy I could gain from it. I should be honest, though, and say that I wrote most of *Incarnate* during the last year of my mother's life, by which time she was utterly insane, besieged by terrible hallucinations. I became mentally unstable myself, except when writing *Incarnate*, which I take to have been somewhere I could go and be in control, and where letting go was beneficial.

I cut fifty thousand words or so from the first draft of *Incarnate* while typing, which is when most of my revision takes place. Macmillan felt it still needed to lose 150 pages or so, and sent back the typescript marked with suggested cuts. On the whole I think they improved the book, which was published in late 1983 to a generally favourable response. Reading proofs of later editions, I noticed eventually that besides an elaborately woven story, the book had a unifying theme: the abuse of authority, particularly over other people's perceptions.

Horror fiction at its worst (of which we've been seeing a good deal in recent years) is beneath contempt; horror fiction at its best is literature. Whether *Incarnate* is literature is not for me to say, but I should like it to be judged by the highest standards of the field, even if it's found wanting. I confess I don't know what Mr Schoell means by "the effort to be literary"; I rather made the effort in this and later books to clarify my style. Certainly comic strips have been based on the theme of dreaming—for instance, the superb work of Winsor McKay—but the fact that an idea has been used in comics hardly unfits it for use elsewhere: among those who have used the theme are Carroll, Somerset Maugham, Le Guin, Martinů, Peter Weir and Buñuel, and I mustn't forget Thomas Ligotti's superb "Dreams of a Mannikin".

One frequently quoted review of *Incarnate* said that the book "assails one's very grip on reality," making it sound like von Däniken or *The Amityville Horror*, but I hope that it rather encourages people to look again at what they may take for granted as reality, hardly an escapist purpose. For that reason I regret one cut that was made in the text, and I'd like to end by giving it here, though I should warn that it will convey little to those who haven't read the book. It comes at the beginning of chapter 43, before Molly glues the drawer together:

As Molly went into Mrs Shankar's grocery shop a woman said "If you ask me, they gave him drugs."

Her friend or her daughter, whose headscarf just reached around her piled hair and her chin, disagreed. "Why should they want to do that?"

"To make him say those things. Don't try and tell me he'd have said them otherwise. You can't believe a word someone says under drugs."

Mrs Shankar gave Molly a shrug as if the women were nothing to do with her, but Molly couldn't see why it should matter. "Just some glue," Molly said, and Mrs Shankar went into the back room, where she kept glue so as to be able to tell children she hadn't any. The older woman came to the counter at once and stood tapping her toe irritably as if she had been ready to be served when Molly had jumped the queue. "Are you asking me to believe that a policeman—a *policeman,* mind you—would confess all that in front of a camera?" she demanded, and Molly realised what the shrug had referred to.

"He might if he'd felt guilty."

"Never. Never in this world, Irene. You've been seeing too many films. If you ask me, the television people faked this film just like they did the other one."

It wasn't directed at Molly, whom she clearly didn't recognise: there was no reason why she should. Mrs Shankar appeared with the glue and another shrug. "I never was convinced they faked the other one," Irene said.

"Then you need your head examined."

"Says you. Who said it was fake? Only the police. They said the writing on the wall couldn't have been there, but they would, wouldn't they?"

Molly intervened before she knew she meant to. "Actually, it wasn't only the police."

Irene gave her a resentful glance. "So they scared someone into saying it. You would if the police got hold of you, wouldn't you?"

"No," Molly said.

Irene looked disbelieving beyond words as she turned her back on Molly. "And that policeman saying he was in church all the time. The cheek of him, saying he was in church."

Molly couldn't stop herself. "But he was."

Both women turned on her. "What do you know about it?"

"It isn't worth it, Molly," Mrs Shankar said as she handed over the tube of glue, and Molly had to agree, though the women were nodding as if they thought Mrs Shankar was talking about her prices. As Molly went out Irene said loudly "Some people will say anything to get attention."

The street was growing colder. It had been shady all day, since the January sun couldn't crane above the roofs. The conversation in the shop had made her nervous, with its fantasies of what had happened, for she wasn't sure what had happened at Rankin's herself. It must have been real—enough people had said so, including the police—but she was beginning to wonder if anything was . . .

Why I Write Horror Fiction

I

I WRITE HORROR STORIES, AND I MAKE IT PUBLIC that I do. Much of the time I could get away with saying that I write ghost stories, though the term "macabre fiction" might better cover what I produce. Either term might serve to dissociate my stuff from the mess which success has recently made of the field—from what seems like hundreds of books produced by far too many writers with no ambition beyond either imitating current best sellers or gaining fame by writing the most disgusting fiction of their generation. (God forbid we should see the field being influenced by *American Psycho* instead of just vice versa.) But whenever I'm tempted to save myself from any further guilt by association I can always reflect that Lovecraft suffered the company of a horde of uncollected hacks in *Weird Tales.* The worst thing that could happen to the field is to be deserted by the writers who care about it. Besides, I've no patience with people who make their reputation in a field and then pretend they never did.

There may be an element of bloody-mindedness in my public image, all the same (as no doubt in much else about me). Not so very long ago a lady who had for some years run the library of the British Science Fiction Association asked me at a party why I wrote that sort of thing, in a tone which suggested that she placed horror fiction on a level somewhat lower than child abuse. One might have assumed she would have remembered the decades during which science fiction was regarded with much the same sort of contempt, but perhaps it's unreasonable to expect a persecuted group not to take the chance to get its own back on someone else, or perhaps some science fiction fans are still so insecure about their reading that they need to find a scapegoat who will bear away their secret guilt. More recently a student (unpublished, I believe) at a creative writing course organised by Liverpool University expressed surprise that I had been invited as a guest lecturer. He had just been to the dentist, and I hope I conveyed the extent of my sympathy when I enquired if he was in pain.

Such encounters tend to make me protective of my field rather than of myself (of whom, in this context at any rate, I've learned to take care), and more personal attacks are merely amusing: a review of mine in *Shock Xpress* was objected to before publication by a vampire hunter, the author of the book reviewed, because he apparently felt I was "a pulp fiction writer... a hack... a bizarre and singularly inappropriate reviewer [whose] credentials limit him to reviewing fantasy/horror fiction." (Someone should inform the BBC that I've been reviewing films for them under false pretences for the past twenty-two years.) All this is fun, certainly, but it does occur to me that the vampire hunter is drawing on a widespread notion of what horror fiction is; and it occurs to me to wonder at what point "horror fiction" became an insult.

The question raises that of when the term came into use. I think we must hold Christine Campbell Thomson at least partly responsible both for the usage and, I fear, the bad reputation. In her foreword (written in February 1936) to the *Not at Night Omnibus* she wrote that "it has been interesting to see how the horror-story has developed during the last ten years.... From the first [as editor of the *Not at Night* series] I set myself against literature.... I think our courage in meeting a requirement [for "genuine, unadulterated horror"] has done much towards getting rid of the politely watered 'thriller'". The first volume and its successors were conceived as "the kind of book that a man would buy at a railway-bookstall, throwing down a single coin and running for his train".

One would like to know what Lovecraft, himself a contributor, made of such statements, and one may well guess. No wonder Montague Summers (in his introduction to *The Supernatural Omnibus*) and M. R. James took against the books. In *The Bookman* for Christmas 1929 James commented that the books were "merely nauseating, and it is very easy to be nauseating" (alas, even more demonstrably true these days). However, neither writer wanted to do away with horror in fiction: Summers objected rather to the lack of "spiritual horror, whether it be vampire horror . . . or Satanism", and in early 1931 James went so far as to say that "you must have horror" in the ghost story (although "not less necessary is reticence").

Like the field itself, the word experiences phases of relative respectability. The 1934 Hutchinson anthology *New Tales of Horror by Eminent Authors* (whose editor is identified by Bleiler as John Gawsworth) has on its cover a skeleton wearing a top hat and cloak and holding up its gory hands, but the blurb on the inside flap maintains (with some justice) that "the greater range of terror's facets are illuminated". Later in the thirties, as the British backlash against horror films began and heads (among other parts of the body, no doubt) were shaken over the sexy tortures on the covers of *Horror Stories* and its fellow pulps, Hutchinson might perhaps have felt the need to clean up their skeleton or even to tone down the title of the book.

In *The Bookman* James had blamed "the modern American taste" for the *Not at Night* series, and particularly in Britain xenophobia is a recurring element in the horror debate, a way of seeing horror fiction as alien, an invader to be repelled or done away with. By the mid-forties the stigma seems to have faded, however—at any rate, Maurice Richardson openly praised the contents of W. F. Harvey's *Midnight Tales* as horror fiction in his foreword—but soon enough horror was being deplored again, first its occurrence in comics (EC and their imitators) and, later in the fifties, films. For a change the British were offended by themselves, by Hammer Films and the ensuing minor boom: "When the horror is allowed to become realistic and nasty, the game ends" was one of the more restrained objections to [*Horror of*] *Dracula*. (Admittedly this was also the era where the film reviewer of the *Morning Star* was so offended by the violence of *The Seventh Seal* that she suggested a new certificate should be designed to exclude all ages of audience.) This time the cries of distaste seem to have been directed exclusively at films; at any rate, Herbert van Thal was able to launch the *Pan Books of Horror Stories* in 1959 without, so far as I'm aware, attracting unfavourable comment, even though the early volumes reprinted several *Not at Night* tales until van Thal began to build up a stable of writers who understandably preferred to remain pseudonymous. Even the xenophobic outcry of the media against the so-called video nasties failed to give the horror fiction of the day the same bad name, although the term "nasties" had originally been used by a British publisher as a marketing category. But horror fiction, like most things, tends to be identified as a whole with its most visible examples, and in the case of books these past few years, what has tended to be most visible is a glut of excess.

I've repeatedly said that horror fiction, like comedy, is often in the business of going too far and speaking the unspeakable. This is the simple truth, but my stating it shouldn't be taken as an endorsement of every excess, especially when some writers use it (I was going to say "quote it", but I'm sure that would be to overestimate my influence) to justify their intemperance. So let's be clear. There is nothing wrong with fiction which seeks solely to convey a sense of horror, any more than Laurel and Hardy deserve to be condemned for simply making people laugh (indeed, in my opinion they deserve to be immortalised). But horror fiction as a field isn't *only* about horror. The trouble is that too many of its present-day purveyors seem to think it is.

I began writing horror fiction in an attempt to imitate what I admired and, as I learned some basic craft, to pay back a little of the pleasure the field gave me. I've stayed in it because of its scope. So far it has enabled me to talk about any theme I want to examine, and I don't believe I've reached its boundaries by any means. In a sense I'm saying merely that all my fiction is horror fiction, with the exception of my stumblings in sf, and I can't expect everyone to agree, even with the assumptions I'm making. Better largeness both of definition and ambition than the reverse, though, say I.

Perhaps someone should be thanked for popularising the term "splatterpunk", which has been to some extent adopted by the media at large. I don't say this with a view to denigrating David Schow or anyone else whose use of graphic horror has some seriousness of purpose; I've remarked elsewhere that the introduction to *Book of the Dead* is a persuasive manifesto. Unfortunately or otherwise, however, splatterpunk looks set to be used by the media as the word for fiction which offers nothing but crude horror, and I'm afraid I think it is time there was such a word.

I don't know if I have inadvertently invented a contrasting term. On the acknowledgments page of *Midnight Sun* I paid tribute to those who had kept the tradition of visionary horror alive. "Visionary horror" is surely not a contradiction in terms; I'm reminded that in its day "The Willows"—certainly among the most visionary tales in the field—was praised as "pure horror". Now my bookseller friend David McClintock has taken up my usage, and it will be interesting to see if it gains wider acceptance. I certainly can't keep it for myself, since it hardly describes all of what I write.

Increasingly, when I read my stories to general audiences, people express pleasure that I write a kind of fiction they used to enjoy. It isn't that they want less horror, but rather more restraint, and I take the opportunity to encourage them to read T. E. D. Klein and Thomas Ligotti and K. W. Jeter and a gratifying number of others I can think of. There was a time when most anthologies of short stories would contain a significant proportion of macabre fiction, and I should like to see that situation revived in my lifetime. Horror fiction is a branch of literature, whether or not my own work is a twig of it.

Last year the debut issue of *Frighteners,* a new British horror fiction magazine (edited anonymously, and not by John Gilbert, he tells me), was withdrawn because of a story by Graham Masterton about a revolting person who does revolting things until he comes to a revolting end. I confess to missing the point of the story. The specific scene objected to describes at length how the revolting person buggers an injured calf while eating it alive. I take it this can be described as splatterpunk. As for me, I just write horror fiction. I write horror fiction.

II

THE H WORD: H FOR HONESTY

I write horror.

I've been saying so for decades, because it's the truth, simple or otherwise. Whenever anyone who creates horror fiction says they don't, it simply confirms me in my commitment to the field. No doubt they have their reasons, but I have mine, which is to support the kind of fiction I've loved pretty well ever since I can remember. I have to presume I'm not harming it by associating myself with it—I'm doing my best to be worthy of its great tradition in my limited way as a fiction writer. By espousing the adjective I'm also joining the tradition of writers who have given it a positive significance, and it occurs to me to wonder when this began.

It did with the Gothic novel, just about. 1797 saw the publication of *The Horrors of Oakendale Abbey*, but this is the only title of the period to include the word. We should also acknowledge *Horrid Mysteries* from five years earlier, both because the usage was immortalised by Jane Austen and since this was the second English translation of Karl Grosse's *Der Genie, oder Memoiren des Marquis von G. . .*; we might conclude that the adjective was introduced to make the book more saleable. After these two appearances anything like the word seems to have fled for a hundred years or so, but by the end of the nineteenth century the occasional short story had it in the title; Conan Doyle used it twice, for instance ("A Pastoral Horror" and "The Horror from the Heights"). It took longer to reappear on the covers of books. 1920 looks like the year of that rebirth—specifically, the first American edition of Maurice Level's *Tales of Mystery and Horror*—but this was the only sight of it for most of the decade. Even the *Not at Night* series didn't use the word directly at first, instead referring on the dust jackets to the weird and creepy (though reviews were quoted that included the supping image from *Macbeth*, that most respectable of references). The seventh volume (*At Dead of Night*, 1931) was the first to flourish the word on the front of the jacket (in the curiously worded slogan "A grim, creepy volume of horror and mystery of the supernatural"), and it dodged behind subsequent volumes again, the backs of which quoted the *Bookman* as enthusing about "a banquet of horrors". By then, however, Thomson's anthologies had been overtaken by several edited by Dorothy L. Sayers, which displayed the word in the title as early as 1929 (*Great Short Stories of Detection, Mystery and Horror, 1st Series*). Thomson drew largely on early issues of *Weird Tales*, which makes her series at least historically valuable, but famously or notoriously declared that she had "set her face against literature" in choosing stories to include. I believe Sayers had the opposite aim and perhaps even meant her books to function as a riposte to Thomson's (which had attracted the censure of commentators such as Montague Summers and M. R. James). Certainly Sayers reclaimed horror for literature, and revivals of this confrontation between definitions of the genre have been occurring ever since.

Gollancz published her anthologies and seem to have been fans of the adjective. In 1929 they promoted Visiak's novel *Medusa* as "a story of mystery & ecstasy and strange horror" and, perhaps more significantly, they brought out Dashiell Hammett's *Creeps by Night* (the first anthology to demonstrate that the best of the pulp horror writers could hold their own in literary company) under the title *Modern Tales of Horror*. In 1934 we find what I assume to be a more extreme attempt to stretch the definition of horror fiction and take it back from the Christine Campbell Thomson notion (which by that time may have been the popular concept of the genre, helped by the rumblings of press concern about horror films). This was *New Tales of Horror by Eminent Authors*, anonymously edited by John Gawsworth, which contains some tales that even I can't justify calling horror. At times the anthology seems to take its commitment to restraint and subtlety (both admirable qualities, especially in our field) a tad too far, or perhaps it's just that the editor was loath to turn down submissions by such eminences. The first tale by Machen, for instance, is very minor—more like a tale told over port in a men's club.

On the other hand, the reaction against explicitness can be very productive. Val Lewton conceived his fine films as a riposte to the Universal horrors, which he apparently saw as crude. Let me give one more example—the one that shaped my view of the field over fifty years ago. One of the earliest treasures of my collection was *Best Horror Stories*, edited by John Keir Cross—unless my ageing memory is playing tricks again, the first hardcover I ever bought. Besides specialists such as Poe, Bierce and M. R. James it included tales by Faulkner, Graham Greene and Herman Melville: his "Bartleby". The editor admitted that some readers might not consider this psychological study of a terminally apathetic character to be a horror story, but it seemed to me, like everything else in the book, to be entirely at home there. It, and the sense the anthology and this tale in particular lent me of the inspiring breadth of the field, has stayed with me ever since. I suspect the book was to some extent intended to make the genre once again respectable in the public eye after the controversy about horror comics (and just a year or so before the press pounced on Hammer Films and other new outrages the field had produced).

Best Horror Stories lets me make a few more points. The inclusion of authors such as Faulkner reminds me that very few authors of adult short stories haven't produced at least one example of our kind. Greene, for instance, wrote several. How many exceptions can you think of? In other words, horror came out of the mainstream and indeed was at home there; indeed, a good number of authors who didn't specialise in our genre are largely forgotten except for their work in it (W. W. Jacobs, Robert W. Chambers – add your own candidates). Now it may be objected that I've widened my definition of horror to make the point, but let me say this. As well as *Best Horror Stories* Faber had published *Best Ghost Stories* (Anne Ridler, 1945) and was soon to follow Cross with Edmund Crispin (*Best Tales of Terror*, 1962). The thing is this: tales from each volume would be just as much at home in either of the other two – "Who Knows?", "The Face", "Our Feathered Friends" and "Thus I Refute Beezly" from Ridler (indeed, "Friends" is actually reprinted in Cross); "The End of the Party" and "Oh, Whistle, and I'll Come to You, My Lad" from Cross; "Ringing the Changes" and "Three Miles Up" from Crispin. But perhaps the point was definitely made decades earlier. "Must there be horror? you ask. I think so." So wrote M. R. James in 1931, and he was talking about the ghost story. Of course many tales of horror don't involve the supernatural, but they surely convey terror, and I maintain that horror is the term that best contains all three fields.

Let me make a final declaration. If anything I've said so far makes it seem that I'm embracing horror from the mainstream in order to deny the work of specialists in our field, nothing could be less like me. They have handed down a great tradition. Elsewhere I tried to sum it up thus: Poe and Le Fanu refined the Gothic novel, rendering it terser and more psychologically focused. M. R. James stripped Le Fanu's methods to their absolute essence, developing his own genius for the spectrally suggestive phrase or sentence. Writers such as Walter de la Mare and Lovecraft learned from Poe. Lovecraft also subsumed the influence of writers such as Blackwood and Machen. Fritz Leiber united the traditions of M. R. James and Lovecraft. T. E. D. Klein does too, but Machen also comes to the fore in some of Ted's finest work. Stephen King rediscovers Poe for our time. Echoes of Robert Aickman can be found in M. John Harrison's profoundly personal fiction, and in Lisa Tuttle's and Terry Lamsley's – not to forget Reggie Oliver, surely our most elegant stylist and a great upholder of the best traditions of the field. Thomas Ligotti's tales can be Lovecraftian, but they are remarkably unlike anybody's work other than the author's, although Mark Samuels has an equally distinctive worldview that earns him the comparison. Ray Bradbury and Richard Matheson brought contemporary concerns to the field and revived close psychological realism, and their ground-breaking influence can be seen not just in Steve King but in the excellent Dennis Etchison. The overlap with crime fiction deserves an essay in itself; one excellent contemporary practitioner is Steve Mosby. I could name many more fine writers in our field, but add them yourselves to the canon and see where they fit in. Above all, be proud to write horror and say that you do. I am.

On Reading My Stories

THE LONELIEST THING A WRITER DOES IS WRITE—at least, if they are anything like me. Not only do I close myself up in my workroom and cut myself off from my family, whose intrusions I resent as much as any unwelcome phone call, but also there's no guarantee that when I emerge from the workroom the story I'm writing won't follow. I don't believe the imagination should be something you can shut in a room; the trouble is that the process of learning how to make it work for you may rob you of the ability to choose when it does. I always carry notebooks, and if scribbling random inspirations or descending into thought in company makes me appear rude, I'm afraid I would rather lose a friend than an idea. So when I say that social incompetence seems frequently to be a qualification for the job, I'm certainly including myself.

One piece of advice often distributed by writers, though not by this one, is that you should write as you speak. In fact few if any of them appear to take their own advice, to which in any case my retort would be that it surely requires you to be able to speak well in the first place. On the contrary, I would suggest that writing is often a way people who find it difficult to speak learn to communicate, and not infrequently a way of discussing subjects the writer is otherwise unable to address. (I remember the sense of liberation I had while writing the introduction to *The Face That Must Die.*) For evidence of difficulty we need look no further than the public performances some writers give, reading their work as if it had been written by someone else and dumped at that very moment in front of them.

I was one, but it took me years to notice. In my first year at grammar—which is to say, British secondary—school, Brother Kelly, an English teacher and one of the more human of the monks, had me read some of my *Ghostly Tales* to the class. I was happier with the general reaction to this than the response I provoked at a school concert the same year by performing skiffle songs while accompanying myself on a plastic ukelele which I'd neglected to strap around my neck and which I was in constant danger of dropping. The spectacle understandably became something of a school legend, though at least it taught me that the show must go on no matter what, and also that performance can be a way of hiding shyness rather than overcoming it. (Small wonder if for a while—less so in recent years—my writing tried to control the responses of the audience.)

I wasn't confronted with myself like that again until I went to college. This was a further education establishment which the law required me to attend one day a week for my first two years as a civil servant. An English teacher, one Miss Last (an unfortunate name to have on Merseyside, which is why James Last's album *Sounds Last* is a standing joke), learned I was a writer from Mr Garley, the vice-principal and a Lovecraft fan, and persuaded me to read "The Church in High Street" to one of her classes. No doubt at least partly to spare my blushes, she had me read it to a tape-recorder, and then I had to listen to myself read.

It wasn't just the sound of myself reading as though I hadn't heard the prose in my head while I was writing it, even if the quality of the prose suggests to me now that I hadn't: it was the sound of my voice. I can well imagine how Lovecraft's dismay at his own reflection may have prompted him to write "The Outsider". I don't think I read aloud again for almost ten years, except to my mother, at whom I sometimes used to drone my first drafts. Then came a couple of occasions on which I read to, or against, live music by a Merseyside jazz trio, Machineries of Mind. I read "The Shadows in the Barn" in a pub, and intoned an extract from the final version of "A Madness from the Vaults" on Radio Merseyside's arts programme.

Tony Wolfe, the producer, later made me one of the writers and performers of a comedy series on Radio Merseyside, *Are You Listening, Marconi?* (Other participants were John Owen, the "Frank Mace" of *Dark Mind, Dark Heart;* Arthur Powell, a distinguished poodle-trimmer; Phil Davis, an actor and pop promoter who was shortly to die of a brain tumour; and, for sex appeal, Sponge Polanski, a lady who didn't last beyond the opening episode.) I wrote a sketch each week, involving characters such as Brigadier Mangler-Mole and the composer Goldberg von Himmelhoch, but my report on the making of the latest Hamper Film Production, a vampire movie called *Christ Has Risen from the Grave,* was deemed too controversial to broadcast; I suppose it was a bit ahead of its time. The series was cancelled from on high after the tenth episode, in which I'd lampooned a journalist who was apparently the best the local daily paper could produce to review films—a pity, since the show had begun to acquire some polish. Still, insofar as it required me to adopt a variety of funny voices, it didn't prepare me for reading my own fiction aloud. Yet in 1975 I was persuaded to do so, first at Jack Sullivan's New York apartment and then at the World Fantasy Convention, and I realised that I ought to know where the emphases fell in my writing better than anyone else could. I've been a performer ever since, and not only when I have an audience.

This creates its own problems. One is that my autobiography has become something I perform, especially in interviews, having already written it. (It is also now available as a comic, which gives me the curious sense of seeing actors perform my relationship with my parents in settings I don't recognise.) Another is overconfidence. Anyone who heard my guest of honour speech at the 1986 World Fantasy Convention in Providence is likely to remember it as disgracefully shapeless and under-rehearsed. They may be glad to learn that I received what may be seen as my comeuppance the following year, at a literary society in Cambridge.

In February the secretary invited me to speak in November and asked for a title to announce. "The Truth About Horror", I said, which sounded vague enough to cover any talk I was likely to give.

Came November, and I drove to Cambridge to find my title posted around the campus. "I'll tell the truth if I can't think of anything better," I quipped, if that's the word, to the secretary, and immediately thought that would make a good opening line. He took me to University dinner, which proved to be on a Scottish theme: haggis of a hideousness I should like to think unparalleled in the species or anywhere else, served with some woeful vegetables and washed down with a tot of Scotch so fierce it might well have been intended to blot out any other tastes. The dessert was so traumatic I can't call it to mind. After that I was led to my audience in a long narrow room where, for some reason, their chairs faced one long wall, which meant the table holding my notes, such as they were, had to be placed beside me rather than in front of me. Still, I was a professional, and all the reassurance I needed was knowing my opening line. The secretary introduced me. "He's going to tell us the truth about horror if he can't think of anything better," he said.

Ah.

Well, I said. The truth about horror. What is the truth about horror? The truth about horror... (Pause for staring desperately at notes and praying that when I looked up the audience would have gone away.) The *truth*, now, the truth about *horror*... (By now the audience looked as paralysed as I and my brain felt, and all I could hope was that a fire alarm would go off.) As you saw from the posters, I'm here to tell you the, ah, truth about horror...

Perhaps my night at Kirklands in Birkenhead was even more nightmarish. This was a charity event organised by Billy McGinty, a local comedian, which indeed he was. All I knew in advance was that I'd be reading a short story to the audience in between other acts. It wasn't until I got there that I realised Kirklands was a night-club where I would be confronted by diners at tables, but after all, what's professionalism for? It transpired that I was to follow a performance by the Wallasey Girls Choir, who I'm sure were still girls in some sense or other of the word, of songs from *The Sound of Music.* I'd steeled myself for that by the time it happened, but I hadn't anticipated being introduced as the weird kid who sat behind you at school and made faces. Applause got me as far as the stool on which I was to perch, and then I saw what I'd walked into.

I used to assume that the scene in *Mickey One* where Warren

Beatty performs his act to a night-club in which he can see nothing except the glare of spotlights was exaggerated, but the only differences between that and my experience at Kirklands were even less encouraging. I could also hear the audience continuing to talk as I clutched at the microphone and set about doggedly reading "Call First", and if I looked up, a television monitor that seemed excessively large showed me myself trying to decide how to sit. It took me back to my performance with the ukelele. I'd chosen "Call First" because it takes under fifteen minutes to read aloud, but once I'd got through a page to no apparent diminution of the audience noise I reduced the story to five minutes' worth. Afterwards I learned that those sitting nearest the stool found the whole thing compelling. Nevertheless that has been my final appearance as a variety act to date, although I recently gave or tried to give a talk to a dormant audience at a paranormal gathering while a lady went around the tables selling raffle tickets and someone on the other side of the not especially large room told a client's fortune very much aloud.

A question interviewers often ask (about as frequently as "Do you ever write anything else?" and, sending me further into a stupor, "Why do people enjoy being scared?") is what I'd like to do if I didn't write my fiction. That's the same as asking who I'd like to be if I weren't myself, and the answer to both would be: a stand-up comedian. Not that I'm claiming any particular talent for it, though some of my performances have inadvertently come close. Indeed, when I first read "Down There" aloud, Kirby McCauley and Jack Sullivan led the audience in chortling, and it was also at Jack's and Robin's apartment that I was initially disconcerted to hear the listeners laughing at "The Chimney", though I was satisfied to find at as the tale progressed the laughter died away. Both experiences may have helped humour surface in my tales, so that when I read passages from "Needing Ghosts" in the same location I was happy to have at least one member of the audience in stitches.

. . . the truth about, you know, horror? When we say the truth, the *truth* about it, this thing, horror, what do we mean by horror? The truth is, well, then we have to say what do we mean by truth? The truth about *horror*, now, that's . . . And more words to even less effect, and many of them, or maybe fewer and more yawning silences. What happened, in case you're wondering, was that I told the truth—namely, that I was disintegrating in front of the audience, and that the reason must be that I'd set out not to tell the truth . . . which was, I suggested, that the source of my fiction was my childhood, which I proceeded to describe. I did say earlier that my autobiography has turned into a performance.

Still, as I promised, I got my comeuppance. The treasurer of the society was a spastic, and it took him ten minutes to write out the cheque for my fee. It wasn't until I examined it that I found it had been made out to Ramsay Macdonald. Would you have asked him to rewrite it? Neither did I, nor could I be so wicked as to entertain the suspicion that the society knew how to save itself money. Off I went instead, scribbling notes about my experience. That evening in Cambridge my autobiography led to other themes and saved my talk, but by God, that's closer than I care to come to disaster.

Nightmares

It seemed to be something like the end of the world. My wife and son and I (though not our daughter) had either taken refuge in or been confined to one of a circle of cages, unfurnished except for a metal seat which followed the line of the wall and on which there was just about room for the three of us to sleep. I'd befriended two initially savage Alsatian dogs which licked my hands as, in order to keep them out of our space, I led them along the corridor that made a circuit of the cages. Ours was the only cage which faced outwards from a cave in a hill or mountain. We were awaiting some kind of invasion whose nature for the moment was imprecise but which I sensed was filling Jenny with a terror she was managing totally to conceal. I told myself that if this was a dream and turned unpleasant I could wake up.

About then another family joined us, presumably from outside—a husband and wife, and two boys younger than Mat. While Jenny and the other woman talked I told the businessman that I wrote books of short stories. "Like *The Penguin Literary Short Novels*?" he suggested. It occurred to me that this family intended to share our cage, a prospect I found unwelcome, but now the children were moving closer to the adults, because the invasion was about to begin. Jenny told me that like myself, the businessman enjoyed using drugs, on which cue he told me that even a couple of drops of kangaroo urine on one's hand had a major psychedelic effect. I thought this comment ill-timed, because the spaceship which was now descending outside the cave (and of which I knew we were seeing only a minute portion) proved to be manned by Muslims. All the same, there was nothing to do but go down to the clothes and jewellery stalls they had erected at the foot of the mountain. When I chose a thin Indian jacket embroidered with gold to wear inside the ship the stallholder warned me that it might be cool in there, but I said it was hot. This disagreement made me feel nervous, and I awoke.

That didn't help much. The very pleasantness of what I took to be the aliens suggested to me how unpleasant the situation might turn if anyone opposed them. I thought of having a hand lopped off or of even having to watch this being done to someone else. Worse, I began to think that Jenny's calmness in the face of the invasion implied some complicity on her part. Eventually I groped my way out of this kind of night thinking, and remembered that when my bookseller friend David McClintock had sent me an article about nightmares I'd said I would write about mine. So here I am on the morning after that dream, beginning to do so.

Dave asked me whether I had nightmares which I was able to turn into fiction. Alas or otherwise, unlike Lovecraft and Wandrei and Edward Lucas White and others, no; though I enjoy dreams, and maybe that's just as good. I once dreamed of a figure repeatedly running towards me across a field at night, and it seems to me that even before I awoke I thought this would be the basis of a story, which indeed it was—"Run Through". As a child Jenny dreamed of a donkey which stood at the end of her bed and talked to her, and what made this considerably worse was that once when she awoke she could still hear its voice, a terror I liked so much that I used it in "The Trick". Our daughter Tammy (author of the shortest horror story ever told) was three when Lionel Jeffries' film of *The Railway Children*—specifically, the scene where the children are alerted to a minor landslide onto the railway by the sight of saplings on the move—made her wake up screaming about trees that moved. As for Mat, it takes the likes of Sam Raimi (his movies, I mean, not the man in person) to make him unwilling to sleep.

Writing *Needing Ghosts* was very much like dreaming at my desk, from the scene at the bus terminal onwards—specifically, from the moment Mottershead reads the destination boards—and of course one interpretation of the story is that . . . There was also the tale of someone who invoked a demonic force in order to shorten the First World War, only to have to choose between the destruction of a ship whose crew included his best friend or turning the force back on himself. He chose the latter course. I gather this was an obscure story by Arthur Machen, but the thing he'd called back sidled into view at the end of my bed—a luminous skeleton dropping its jaw in a silent laugh or shriek. I knew it was a story, and not even much of a spectre, yet both I and my son were trying to scream. I'm not sure if I awoke then; all I know is that I struggled to write the idea down, whether to record it as the work of the dream-Machen or to claim it for myself, but couldn't until I awoke the next day.

To return to my family, once I awoke to find a child standing beside the bed in the predawn glow. For a moment I thought it was Tammy or Mat, and then I gathered it was neither, and I very much didn't want to see its face. Instead I managed to waken, for exactly long enough to be aware that I was immediately falling asleep again, back into the same dream. This time I was terrified, and found myself struggling to use my voice to scream, but it was out of my reach. Somehow I succeeded in establishing contact with it and emitted the kind of cry which feels as though it is being produced at a great distance, and lurched awake.

I was lying next to Jenny in a night far darker than the one in the dream. These weren't circumstances in which I wanted to be alone with what had just happened to me, but I resisted the urge to waken Jenny so as to share it with her. After some indeterminate time I shook off enough of the lingering sense of the dream to be able to sleep until Mat roused me.

This time it was near enough to dawn that I could see he was wearing a Halloween mask, a skull. Well, if you're the son of a horror writer and a fan of horror movies, that isn't an especially odd way to wake your father up, but at that point it wasn't a sight I welcomed. I'd just had a bad nightmare, I told him, and I'd appreciate his taking off the mask. When he only stood there by the bed I reached out and took it off. Beneath it was another mask, or perhaps a face that looked like one, and I realised the figure standing over me wasn't Mat after all.

The following day I was walking to the nearby shops with him and his sister Tammy, and felt able to talk about this series of dreams. "Last night," I said as we went into a florist's, "I had the worst nightmare I've ever had in my life," and as I spoke I knew that mentioning it would cause it to begin again, and it did. And eventually, finally, and perhaps for the first time during the whole sequence, I managed to waken.

What is, at least for me, in some ways odder still is that someone else wrote all this down before I did. The evening after I'd dreamed it (no, I'm not about to reveal that I hadn't yet wakened) I was presenting prizes as one of the judges at the Liverpool Festival of Comedy and got into conversation with one of the many writers there, the mother of a prize-winner. Vinous garrulousness made me recount the dream, and some weeks later she sent me her version of it, which was eventually broadcast by our local BBC. Listening to her account seemed to steal my sense of how the dreams had felt to me, but now I think I've managed to regain it.

Precisely a week after the dream which I described at the beginning of this piece, I went to London to attend a preview, after which, having got involved in conviviality, I missed the last train home and stayed overnight in a hotel. There I had a series of bizarre dreams of which I recall little, other than a walk through an industrial ruin whose outlines and crepuscular gloom recalled Piranesi at his most oppressive (though in the dream I was unable to recall the artist's name). I awoke at twenty past six in the morning, for some reason thinking "Pizza Valdemar" and planning to write that down in case I could use it somewhere; but I was unable to move, even sufficiently to see whether my room had a bathroom attached, which I couldn't remember. As I struggled to move I heard someone breathing near me, and it occurred to me that this might be my own body, into which I had somehow to fit myself. This proved impossible. I tried to move, and tried to move, and tried to move, and after a considerable time I awoke in my bed at home, not having been to London after all.

One night I found myself in a Middle Eastern country ruled or at least held in thrall by an old railway engine on the front of whose boiler was a face of which I recall only the eyes—large and round and unblinking but, because they were composed of the same brass as the boiler, only gradually distinguishable. Another reason for the people to be nervous was that at this latitude gravity was apparently much greater, so that they lived in fear of being crushed by objects falling from everywhere else in the world. I made my way homewards by the immigrant route or at least a photograph of it—the Rieperbahn, a road lined with poplars. Was that a dream or a nightmare? Whichever, I enjoyed it, and such places are where I spend quite a lot of my time. Perhaps they will be what passes for eternity in my case, or maybe in the bookshops to which I often return in the middle of the night, unless I end up in one of the houses we move to in my sleep, buildings usually with a bewildering number of roofs and always with a view from the very top, often an attic with windows on every side. In the bookshops I always find books I want to read, but I never manage to do so or even to buy them, though recently I found a copy of an anthology containing Arthur Machen's "The Fulbright Scholar" in a bookshop in a village by a river. Perhaps eternity will give me that chance.

The writing of this piece seemed to make my dreams more memorably weird during the succeeding weeks. An instance placed me in an alley, one side of which was walled off by back yards, the other by a large unlit church. Though it was almost pitch black I could see that the church door was open and distinguish stone steps leading up into darkness beyond it, and I very much didn't want to climb them. Then a woman's voice asked if she could help me, and because her voice was coming not from the back yards but from the church, I hurriedly awoke. That may have been more or less a standard nightmare, for me at any rate, but later I was a koala bear which had somehow escaped from a Disney film about an organisation that wanted to destroy the world. What pursued me up a tree, however, was a baby, and when I managed to waken (yes, really, no question this time) I saw something behind my eyelids. I can best describe it as an aperture, about the size of the start of a migraine and—I thought and at first dreaded—related to that experience. It was brighter than the rest of my field of vision, and it showed me with absolute clarity the sight of a young girl dancing. The figure stayed in focus for about ten seconds, then vanished. Sometimes on waking in the night I see elaborate and vividly coloured patterns, and perhaps—like those, I believe—the apparition of the girl had to do with hallucinogenic experiments.

I don't think those can be held responsible for my two worst nightmares to date. Months after writing the above I had the first, made worse because all that I seemed to be able to recall on wakening was its emotional effect—an unutterable self-loathing. Then I apparently remembered having murdered Jenny and the children, yet underlying this was a suspicion that in fact I'd done something even more terrible, for which my mind had needed to substitute this memory. Jenny was breathing beside me, but the self-loathing and the weight of my impression of the dream didn't leave me for, I would guess, a quarter of an hour or more, not even after I'd stumbled to the bathroom for a glass of water. It took longer for me not to be afraid of going back to sleep. I suppose I was afraid of returning where I'd been, and I wonder if I still have reason to be. I've always told Jenny not to wake me if she thinks I'm having a bad dream, because I enjoy even those and because a dream, however bad, contains its own safety release. Until now I thought I could stand being proved wrong.

Of course dreams are symbolic narratives, and so shouldn't reading them in those terms render them bearable? But one night after Jenny and our daughter had had a blazing row I found myself back in the house where I lived with my parents, always a bad sign. Jenny and I had a large family of adolescents, all of whom had committed some crime so serious that Jenny told them to mutilate one another. I couldn't stand to watch, and went outside, only to find a small family picnicking on the grass. Their presence made me feel so guilty that I returned to the house, and met our daughter. She'd wrapped a bandage round one of her hands, all the fingers of which had been sliced off. I couldn't cope with her suffering. "Would you have wanted me to stop it?" I pleaded. "What do you think?" she said—and it's the look she gave me, rather than any interpretation of the dream, that stays with me even now.

Taking Drugs

I DON'T TAKE DRUGS IN ORDER TO WRITE. I BELIEVE in depending on as little as possible for that. As far back as *The Inhabitant of the Lake* I was identifying elements which seemed to crop up too often in my prose and trying to do without them in "The Will of Stanley Brooke" (no great shakes as a tale, but at least it tried). The same prompting was behind "The Stocking" and "Horror House of Blood", and it was why I erased all trace of the English cult from *The Claw/Night of the Claw*, a motif which I'd already used in all my previous novels apart from *The Face That Must Die.* (A journalist, Edna Stumpf, wanted me to take ten years off from writing in order "to flush the Lovecraft" out of my work; she has my permission to hold her breath.) The protagonist of *Ancient Images* suffers none of the malaise which afflicts most of my central characters, which admittedly meant that some readers thought her dull, and *Midnight Sun* attempts to relinquish even the threat of physical violence, on which I'd decided too many of my novels fell back. (I'm told that one American reviewer found that *Midnight Sun* failed to live up to the standards set by Shaun Hutson.) Amid all this creative puritanism a chap ought to allow himself some licence, and you won't be surprised to learn that the chief indulgences of someone who looked like the cover artist of *Tekeli-li* 3 appears to think I still look have been the milder drugs.

I don't mean cocaine, which I sampled in the early eighties before seeing it nearly destroy a friend of mine. What makes it so insidious is that by the time you've used it sufficiently to achieve the effects you're paying for, it's on your back. Amphetamine did absolutely nothing for me that I noticed the single time I sampled it; it didn't even suppress my appetite—just a few hours later I downed a hamburger, but perhaps that's typical of my gourmand self. Cannabis and LSD are other matters, though not necessarily less problematical. Overindulgence in cannabis can lead to habituation—psychological addiction—which brings its own species of hangover, a dulling of one's senses and responses the day after, no use to a writer or, I should think, to anybody else. I did find I was still able to write, but it demanded more effort than usual to produce comparable work. Since it apparently takes seven days for the metabolites of cannabis to work their way through one's system, perhaps once a week is the safe maximum. After all, the Sunday joint is an English tradition. Careless use of LSD—well, we'll return to that. As long as I'm in confessional mood, however, let me identify the pieces I wrote under chemical influence.

The first was a review of the Lovecraft issue of the underground comic *Skull*. I read it between tokes of a joint, and I don't believe I'd finished reading the first story when it occurred to me that there could hardly be a more appropriate state in which to write a review of an underground publication. So far as I can judge, its only effect was to encourage me to vary my sentence structures more, but it amused me enough to try it once again, for another project which seemed sufficiently unconventional: "Among the pictures are these", an account of some very odd sketches which I'd drawn at the age of fourteen and which I rediscovered over ten years later. In this case the grass was an aid to precision, as I think the few people who have seen the sketches will agree. Like the *Skull* review, this was meant to appear in *Etchings and Odysseys*, but when that little magazine perished, it ran in *Nyctalops* instead. What was my surprise when at a convention a reader brought me a copy of the piece to autograph, in an issue of *Etchings & Odysseys* published by R. Alain Everts ten years later! This business is full of surprises, like the publication of an early draft of my story "The Change" in *Shayol* and the appearance of a quote I provided for Jessica Salmonson's *Anthony*

Shriek on the cover of a Mark Morris novel, but I'm rambling off the point, man, and I've got to get my head together, right? Let me remember to mention that the only piece I ever wrote under the influence of LSD was the preface to a collection of early writings by HPL which originally appeared in the *Pawtuxet Valley Gleaner.* More exactly, I set about writing the preface to distract myself from waiting for the onset of the drug, and when I observed signs of that onset—sounds becoming isolated by an intensified silence, a restlessness of the words I'd written so far—I completed the next sentence and called it a day. Readers may care to discover if they can locate the aforementioned sentence and indeed the book, which was published by none other than that gangling teenager Marc Michaud.

By now some readers may have been reminded of Donald Wandrei's broad hint in his blurb for *Demons by Daylight* that some of the stories are about drugs ("let those who long for *The Enchanted Fruit* beware of the consequences of eating thereof") or Stephen King's comment in *Danse Macabre* that "in a Campbell novel or story, one seems to view the world through the thin and shifting perceptual haze of an LSD trip that is just ending—or just beginning". But Wandrei's comment, unlike Steve's, was made about tales I wrote before I'd had any experience of drugs other than tobacco or alcohol. However, the protagonist of "Potential", the grey-suited figure on the edge of a would-be psychedelic event, halfway between hopeful and nervous of being offered drugs, was of course me. I'd always valued unusual perceptions—childhood fevers had been fun—and shortly after completing the last tale in *Demons by Daylight* I was offered my first toke.

And was hooked. No, not really. Months, maybe a year, passed before I started smoking grass with anything like regularity. But there was a year in the early seventies when I would roll a joint of high-grade black Jamaican before listening to music, or watching a film, or going out for a walk. . . . At least this didn't rob me of ideas, but it may have sapped me of the energy to develop them. As to whether I would have had the ideas without the cannabis, who can say? Certainly the description of the park at night in *The Doll Who Ate His Mother* is derived pretty near entirely from walks I took under the influence (and perhaps my reluctance or inability to edit the chapter was too), and the final paragraph of "The Height of the

Scream" came to me in similar circumstances, as did the lines about the spider in human form in "The Guide", and several images which led me to write "In the Trees". I could go on. By now I was using drugs to compel myself to relax, particularly between novels, because the gap left by completing a novel makes me want to begin work immediately on something else. At one point I gave nutmeg a try—the contents of a supermarket jar stirred into a pint of milk. It took several hours to take effect, by which time I'd forgotten about it, but proved to be surprisingly impressive, especially when I listened to a Beethoven symphony (the seventh, I believe), which gave me a sense of enormously protracted time and colossally expanded space, into the depths of which the notes appeared to be progressing. I was also agreeably surprised to find that after a night's sleep the drug was still working the next day.

Unless you're Anthony Perkins (to quote what he allegedly told British customs officers), you don't take LSD to relax. I first took the plunge, having read as much about the substance and its effects as I could find, in late 1975: stared at the scrap of blotting paper, told myself I'd take it in a minute or two, swallowed it an hour or more later, went out with Jenny (who was probably more nervous about my imminent condition than I was) for a walk in the park, watched the early afternoon shadows of foliage appear to be about to undergo some transformation, was persuaded by Jenny to go home in case being in a public place caused problems, sat in the newly extended kitchen of our house and concluded that nothing more would happen, that my metabolism wasn't receptive to the drug. . . . Then the different colours of the new bare plaster intensified and began to flow like oil on water, forming Oriental patterns, and a sapling outside the window became transformed into the glass of the pane and reached for me.

If an acid trip consisted purely of such visions, I might still be inviting them. My experience, however, is that one has to put up with a good deal that is confusing to the point of irritation, and even banal. In that first instance it was panic which caused me to struggle to reduce the intensity of the visions, an act which led to hours of unsatisfactory forgettable stuff. That night I discovered something which is seldom advertised about LSD: even when the trip seems to be over it's virtually impossible to sleep. I snoozed for a couple of hours before dawn, and dreamed I was being initiated into an American Indian ritual. For the next two days my consciousness kept feeling poised to shift into an unfamiliar mode, not least while I was interviewing Roger Moore for the BBC about his new South African film; he appeared to be larger than I found entirely comfortable, and composed of bronze or plastic. (During that period I was also introduced to the anthologist Hugh Lamb, who assures me that my state didn't show, and to Piers Dudgeon, my first British editor.)

Nine months passed, and *The Doll Who Ate His Mother* was written, before I tried again. This time I went alone to a nature reserve near Liverpool, but the experience was just as frustrating. I remember looking at the profusion of flowers on the landward dunes and dismissing it as "psychedelic Disneyland". Feeling aimless, I returned to Liverpool and visited the Catholic cathedral, where I saw winged forms emerging from the wall of a chapel; then I walked through miles of streets where every face looked grey and pinched to meet Jenny from work.

I still felt awesome visions were possible if I could only achieve them. Perhaps if I had then discovered the gentler, more controllable, but otherwise similar experiences to be had from psilocybin—"worlds born of spores upon the twining psilocybe", as the poet has it—I would have come to a different end. During the next year or so I took four more trips. Once I saw my windblown shadow on a path and thought it was my late grandmother's (I was wearing a corduroy overcoat like hers), and there was quite a lot of such disconcerting unilluminating stuff. But I also watched the arch above the altar of a Norman church crack and disintegrate before gathering itself into muscular stone and rearing up again to support the roof. From a Lakeland fell I saw the fields and slopes gently rearrange themselves around me, and felt I was seeing the English landscape for the first time, as indeed I was; nor have I lost that sense of it. Later, on the peak, I watched distant mountains shudder and waken in the mist like gods. On the way down my vision became microscopic, and I saw deep into the heather. En route to the hotel I was able to see elaborate fossils in the pavement, and the pines above the hotel were transformed into a primeval forest, dark and mysterious.

The intensity of those hours should have been enough. A day or two later it was certainly sufficient to precipitate a migraine which shattered my vision and left me blind for perhaps half an hour. Nevertheless, back at home I continued to smoke most evenings, even when I noticed that the cable to a hi-fi speaker looked unpleasantly convoluted and scrawny. That ought to have warned me what I was risking, but it wasn't until one Friday night that I had to acknowledge something was very wrong. I was halfway through a joint when I felt too nervous to sit still. I went to the front door and tried gazing at the terrace opposite, but in the oily orange light the houses looked alien, not remotely reassuring. I went upstairs to splash cold water on my face, and saw myself in the bathroom mirror. My mouth was disappearing. The left side had already gone.

When his first marriage was ending, Evelyn Waugh wrote to Harold Acton: "I did not know it was possible to be so miserable & live." For "miserable" substitute "terrified" and you have my state then. I was afraid to admit it to Jenny, even when she remarked that the smell of me had changed; since a fly was buzzing about the house, I thought I was decaying. After perhaps an hour I owned up, having meanwhile tried to convince myself that she didn't know anything was wrong. The worst of it was that since I wasn't sure what had precipitated the flashback, I didn't know if it would ever end. I spent the next several hours struggling to see only the familiar, which made everything appear ominously, and in some cases hideously, changeable. Jenny helped me grow intermittently calm, as did several pints of Tetley's, by no means my favourite beer but the only alcohol in the house. Debussy's string quartet, and in particular Beethoven's Opus 135, were beneficial. Around four in the morning my fear of closing my eyes lessened enough to let me go to bed. I slept, but the following day I was still afraid—of looking in the mirror, or at paintings, or trees, or car headlights at night, and much else—and I grew more afraid as the weeks passed. I tried sleeping pills, Librium, an Ananda Marga meditation class; ultimately I consulted an acupuncturist and told him what I'd done to myself. Not very long after he started the treatment I was able to lie in bed without being assaulted by waves of light behind my eyelids, and so my recovery began, aided by a daily diet of Mozart's early symphonies conducted by Neville Marriner. Readers of *The Parasite* may recognise elements I borrowed for that book.

And that is ultimately the point. If no experience I undergo is too awful for me to write about it, then no experience need be wasted. My psychedelic dabbling left me with a store of material I haven't yet exhausted. Much of the Lakeland episode formed the basis of "Above the World", and "The Pattern" and "The Voice of the Beach" (among others) wouldn't have been written without psychedelic memories to draw on. Of course the stories were attempts to give form to them, though I even tried to convey the formlessness of most of my trips in a chapter of *The Face That Must Die* and later in *The One Safe Place.* My friend Poppy Z. Brite has written that some of these aspects of my tales helped turn her on to drugs when she was sixteen—I won't deny I feel responsible. And now? Well, I can remind myself of things I saw and experienced by leafing through a book of Dali's paintings, or through *Visions 1* (was there ever a *Visions 2?*), the 1977 Pomegranate Press book introduced by Walter Hopps—Bill Martin's *Garden of Life and Autumn,* and Gage Taylor's *The Creek,* immediately recall the kind of gestalt perception which made all the unsatisfactoriness worthwhile. So do fractals. But my days of dropping acid are over, man. I've too many ideas still to write, and who knows how much time?

FAME!

FAME!

"Hello, Mr Campbell. I'm Julie from the Ariel Trust and we're making a community radio programme about creative writing. We were wondering if you'd like to contribute."

"I imagine I might, yes."

"What kind of thing do you write?"

A relatively short silence. "Don't you know?"

"We got your name from Dave Ward who organises the writers' groups."

"I know Dave." Pause. "I write horror. I've been given the odd award."

"Have you written any short stories?"

"Oh yes, a few."

"Could you read one on our programme?"

"I should think so. I've written some that should be short enough."

"If you could send us a few to consider. . . "

"Perhaps you could buy the books in which they appear, or if that's a problem, borrow them from the public library?"

I list some likely tales, and feel suitably virtuous until the caller says "They're not too scary, are they?"

"I don't know how you would define that."

"Thing is, there might be children listening, and we don't want to scare them."

"Then I rather think you shouldn't have approached me."

A pause. "Maybe I'll read your stories and get back to you."

Fame!

I'm invited to address a group of pensioners formerly employed by a nuclear power facility. My wife and I share the obvious jokes about being able to see by the glow of the audience, so perhaps I deserve what I get. I'm met at the social club by the lady who invited me. "You'll be Mr. . . " she says. "Mr. . . " Once she offers me a drink I relent somewhat and am shown into a room off the main hall to await my introduction. While the chairman exhorts the owner of a hat left on a coach to claim it and talks about how many meringues were eaten on the coach trip, I regard the contents of the room: a broken mirror; several serving trolleys; a display of acrobatics by some tables and a good many chairs; a filing cabinet; some house-bricks; a fallen coat-hanger. . . I feel at home in their company. Eventually I hear my name and, having performed some impromptu slapstick with a microphone and chair, settle myself onstage. "The Guide" seems to hold the general attention, and the question session does too, though admittedly the chairman preceded his introduction by asking the audience not to talk throughout. At least he didn't introduce me, as he originally proposed, as Ramsay Macdonald. The old jokes may be best, but it's taxing to be one.

Fame!

I book my flight to the World Fantasy Convention in New Orleans at the local Thomas Cook's on my company Visa.

"Can I ask what kind of thing Waking Nightmares makes?"

"It's just me. I write horror."

A pause. "You're not Ramsey Campbell, are you?"

"Indeed."

"I read one of your books once."

"Which was that?"

"I can't remember." A longer pause which I'm not prepared to break, and then: "Something about a house with a wood behind it."

"That would be *Midnight Sun.*"

"Oh, right." A very long silence indeed . . .

Fame!

Peter Hough, a researcher into the inexplicable, and I are invited by librarians to sell and sign our books at the Cheshire Show. The venue proves to be the Cheshire Agricultural Show. As in a parody of a Soviet film, an audience applauds a procession of tractors which trundles round a muddy field. The two hapless authors are given a table in the open air, opposite the Mr Sweetie stand and beside a field in which a troupe of country dancers trip to the strains of "In an English Country Garden" as they struggle to hold arches of flowers over themselves against a rising gale. The public address system repeatedly asks the owner of Wiggles to come to the police office. An unsmiling youth approaches our table and asks if I can direct him to the zoo. I restrain myself. Mr Spot, a librarian dressed as a yellow dog, tells tales to children nearby. The gale increases, toppling the bottle of wine in front of me and inundating several novels in the source of their inspiration. Another humourless person asks me to direct him to the toilet. I can find no words sufficiently appropriate. At intervals herds of people plod past our table en route from one display of cattle to another. Peter Hough manages to engage some passers-by in talk of spontaneous human combustion, but none of them obliges with a demonstration. At the end of two hours I sell a copy of *The Nameless.*

Fame!

"Am I speaking to Mr Ramsey Campbell?"

"I believe that's what I said."

"Mr Ramsey Campbell the horror writer?"

"That one, yes."

"Do you investigate odd phenomena?"

"Ah. How odd do you have in mind?"

"Teenagers crushing pigeons to death in a ritualistic way. It's very sinister."

"I imagine it would be. I should say I'm a fiction writer, not an investigator."

"I've been to the police and they say they can't do anything."

"Oh dear. In that case I'm not sure what you think I . . . "

"Only they do it round here all the time, the teenagers. I only live a mile or two from where Jamie Bulger was murdered."

"I don't quite see what connection . . . "

"The boys who did it used to torture animals, didn't they? Do you want me to ring you again if I find out any more?"

"I think you'd be better off contacting the local press and radio. If you'll excuse me, I think that may be the door."

Fame!

I'm approached in my local pub, the one in which the Count of Eleven drank, by Steve King—someone of that name, at any rate. Will I read a story as an interlude in a blues concert he's organising? Will I never learn? I duly turn up at the concert to find listed in the programme "A Nasty Moment with Ramsey Campbell". The first set ends, and Steve King urges me on stage, and is suddenly nowhere to be seen. Nor is any of the audience, though this may the fault of all the lights trained, I would say, more on my eyes than on the stage. I speculate aloud as to whether the nasty moment will be for me or for my listeners, and wish I hadn't done so. I fall about amid a good deal more equipment than one might have supposed a small band to need, and manage to rest my book on a drum-kit. I explain that "The Companion" takes place less than a mile from where we are, and read most of it. The audience emits the occasional gulp, of drink rather than of fear. When I close the book someone either releases a bat into the darkness or applauds. As I stumble offstage half the audience asks whether I wrote the story myself. I assure her I did and show her the evidence, and she gives me a look which one might give a child claiming to be Batman.

Fame!

"Is that Ramsey Campbell?"

"None other."

"This is Gloucestershire Libraries and we'd love to have you come and do a talk."

"Then I imagine I should like to. When do you have in mind?"

"The second week in November?"

"Fine. I read and talk and answer questions as a rule."

"That sounds wonderful. We'll confirm in writing to you."

"What fee did you have in mind?"

Pause. "Oh, you want paying?"

"I would think so. Particularly for travelling across the country and spending two days away from my desk."

"I don't think we have any money to offer you."

"Another time, perhaps."

Fame!

I arrive at a comprehensive school to read and talk to a classful of twelve-year-old boys. I'm shown into the library and abandoned there with them. Boys cluster round my water-bottle for what I must assume is a ritual drink. Eventually a schoolmaster, a red-headed stool, trudges in and sits morosely at the back. His enthusiasm for his work is plain to see. Since he doesn't introduce himself, I tell him who I am, not that he seems to find it significant or interesting. Who's in charge, he wants to know. I suggest he's being paid to be, a comment that goes down less than well. I leave him to mope over his work, which seems mostly to involve shuffling a great many sheets of paper, and address the class. Who am I, a boy inquires. I explain and demonstrate by reading "The Interloper", which I introduce as being set in the kind of school I attended when I was their age. The red-headed stool attends more fiercely to his papers. Nobody seems interested in discussing "The Interloper". Questions multiply, however, until it's difficult to hear them. The stool lowers his head as I roar for order, with some success, and hear what I'm being asked. How many books have I had published? How much was I paid for them? What's my name?

Fame!

"Am I speaking to Ramsey Campbell?"

"This is he."

"Do you know Stephen Smith?"

"Oh yes."

"Stephen Smith the novelist?"

"Not the chap I know."

"He says he knows you. Meets you at a pub in Liverpool."

"I don't drink in Liverpool."

"I had a feeling there was something wrong. He says he has the same publishers as you. He used to be published by Little, Brown and now he's with Headline."

"Same as me, certainly. What kind of thing does he write?"

"Science fiction horror."

"Odd I haven't heard of him. Does he write as Stephen Smith?"

"He says so. He's got my daughter writing a script based on his novel."

"Published?"

"So he says."

"She'll have seen it, then."

"She hasn't. He says he only has one copy and he keeps that at home."

"I must admit that seems unlikely. Does he say what happened to the rest?"

"Might his agent have them? He says he used to have the same agent as you."

"If I were your daughter I'd insist on seeing the book. Give me your number and I'll check with the publishers for you."

Which I did, and my readers may not be surprised to learn that neither publisher had ever heard of Stephen Smith, author of—though the caller told me the title of the supposed book, it has slipped my memory. The daughter did ask to see it, but neither it nor its author was subsequently to be seen. Perhaps "Stephen Smith" is out there at this moment, claiming to know or even to be me. Perhaps he'll make a better job of it than I have.

Fame!

A School Visit

"AN AUTHOR CAME TO TALK TO US." SO SAYS THE cover of a giant pamphlet produced by eight-year-olds at a school where Jenny used to teach. There's the author in question on the cover, his tiny wide-set eyes peering out from under a jagged fringe. Beneath the upturned hook of his nose with its single nostril, a large if somewhat sinister grin displays piano teeth and a hint of a tongue the same purplish red as his tie. This monster waves a pencil in a minute hand at the end of a dwindling arm and emits a balloon that says "Hello year 3." It's me all right, and I can't resist reproducing the impressions I left on the class. Each account is titled "Yesterday our class had a visitor."

"We had a visitor his name is Mr Ramsey Campell he is an author an author writes books and sends them to the printer. He works 7.00 oclock in the morning to 5.00 oclock at night it takes him three hours to do a page. And two years to do a whole book and a front cover and a picture and his name on the front of it."

So writes Lindsey, and illustrates her thesis with the covers or title pages of two books: *Mr Ramsey Campell* [line] *The Doll Who Ate His Mother; Mr Ramsey Campell* [line] *The One Safe Place.*

"His name was Mr. Ramsey Campell. He is an author. An author writes books. Mr Campell writes Horror stories. I have read one of his books from the Wallesey library. He works from 7.00 A. M. to 5.00 PM. To get ideas for a book he carries a notebook as he travels. As soon as he gets an idea he writes it down, then he puts them together to make a book."

This unsigned tribute is accompanied by a picture of the author crouched behind a book at his desk. He's a cheery chap with glasses and a grin—both, like the rest of his face, bright yellow. Beside him and dwarfing him is a pink book: A HORROR STORY (crossed out—I assume a whisper may have been heard in an ear) THE DOLL WHO ATE HIS MOTHER by Mr. Ramsey Campell. The cover illustration shows a morose figure in a cage who is holding, if I'm not mistaken, a plaque bearing an identity number.

"Yesterday we had a visitor called Mr Campell he is an author he writes stories then he sends it to the printer he prints the words then it gets sent back to the author if there is anything wrong it gets sent back to the printers then he does it again then it is back to the author and if it is ok the it get taken to the publisher he puts the pages together and does a picture and it gets sent to the author and if he likes the picture he sends it back and sais ok."

Craig Windsor illustrates this with two decidedly irritated figures. Both have rounded turned-up feet. One stands by a purple table and waves its arms at what may be a door or safe, beside which the other lies and flourishes one arm while a red rectangle protrudes from its head.

"We had a visitor his name is Mr Ranisey Campell and he an author and he rats horror stories and it takes a years up rate one story and when he has finished he takes it to the printer and the printer does the standing out in blake print and when the printer has finishd whith it and he sendes it baek to the author and if he makes a mistak he marks it in red pen and sends it bak to the printer and givs it to the publisher and the publisher puts it in thu shops and sell it."

This optimistic view belongs to Sammy Parsons, who also draws Mr Campell as a winged blue object that appears to be the product of a Kafkaesque transformation and to be very pleased about it too.

"Mr Camell is An Author. He Deos Book horror Books. He Deos sceardey Books. He writes good. He gets 25000 pound. He Deos one Book a day. He Wake up at 70 o'clock and He gos to bed at 50 o'clock He hardle dosent gow to sleep He wake up and He Deos His Book He has Hie noet Book and He gets sum Words. in Hes noet Book. He Lice to gow to bed But He cont He hat to Deos His Book He Deos 200 pagegs. He gets He muny. For one Book For 25000 pound"

No wonder Lydia Jebb shows the visiting author with a broad grin and scrunched-up eyes. A bag stands by him and, more ominously, a table bearing a knife and possibly a gun. Above the table is a painting, I think, which may depict a multicoloured playing card, a five of some suit.

"he writes down Ideeis in a book the Ideeis or for a story fist he rits down he prins it den some peepl stick the pagis to geve Thay make a book if the author likes it it is the frunt kuver he taks it to a shop to sel it it taks two years to make one book if it is rong the book gos bak to the author so he can fix it it was the pisons folt he put the pages in the rong orde den Thay chek if Thay have put it in the rong orde"

This unsigned piece shows the spindly author at his desk with a rocket—a pen, I'm sure it must be—attached to one of his flourished hands.

"He was an author He was Mr Campell It is Miss Campell husband He write harror stories He sendse it to a publisher and He sens it back and said what is wong with it so Mr Campell dose it a gean and sens it back when the publisher said it is right and he sens it to a printer. When he has printed into a book and puts a caver on it and then it gose to the shop and people buy it"

Michelle Woods shows the author with a hunched right shoulder and a round head precisely like a smiling badge. A cover or a poster, "Mr Campells Horror Story", is a head taller than he.

"Mr. Campell is an Author. He carrieys a note book around with him were ever he gos. It takes him about three houers to do one page. If he gets ten things wrong he does a ree write wich takes him from some were around Twelv am to 5:00 pm. He does Horror stories. First is gos to the printer and then it gos to the publisher to make the words stand out. In other words Bold writeing. Then it gos to the Editor. the Editor makes sure that he doesnt make eney mistakes. He gets payed £25,000 pounds. He gets up at 7.00 oklock in the morning to start one Book it takes hin two years to make one Book"

The dwarfish purple-faced subject of this anonymous account sits next to a giant round table. On the table, we see from its labelling, is a Skript. On the other side of him is—what? A television receiving a broadcast of ten lumps of coal? A blackboard with a crimson border? An outsize electric fire?

"1 He was a author. a author is sume wan huw rets Books.

"2 He sed we hy has bun the braft he sends it to to printer and if the printer dus amstek he snds it dak and the author putet rayt and it gos dak to the printer hus it egen.

"3 afte the printer has finesht it gos to the publisher Juns the pajes and meks the frunt kufer of the book it neds a tatel and a piter.

"4 hy gets up at 7:00 klook and hy fineshes adawt 8:00 in the nayt.

"5 the Books hy rats of horor stoorays."

I'm not sure if Patrick Mooney means his picture to illustrate his final paragraph. Beneath a window through which the sun beams, the author bares his teeth and brandishes a pencil large enough to double as a murder weapon.

"Mr. Ramsey campell. Yester day we had a visitor and he is an author and he writes horror stories. And every time he has an Idea he puts it in his note books and leaves the other page for better ideas. He sends it off to the publisher and he publishes it and yesterday he asked us questions about being an author and he showed us the book and we showed him some of ours and then he went to year fours class and when he went to year fours he gave us his autograph."

Besides all that, Cairan Kavanagh illustrates the cover of *The One Safe Place*, complete with the way Headline positions my first and last names. Someone with an unimpressed expression looks out of a front door while a genial enough face bulges into the right side of the frame. It resembles a pudding with a raisin for a nose.

"He was an author, his name was Mr. Ramsey Campell. He told us what it was lake to be an author. He writes his ideas down in a littl red book. Then he make them into stories. He writer scary books. Then he takes his story to the printers. They print it out on a computer on paper They send it back to him and he checks it. when it is right it goes to the publisher and then to the shops"

Thus Rebecca Ravenscroft, but, alas, no illustration.

"Mr Campell is a author he came to see us yesterday and he told us all about Books. He write horror stories he had two Big piles of writeing. And he had don several Books of ideas he was a good man he starts when he was 11 I don't kone how mene books he has write."

Ricki shows the badge-faced author in a house with the sun outside. His face is purple, his left side green, his other red. A balloon clings to his left ear, announcing I WRITE BOOKS.

"Mr ramsey campell wroted horror stories how he had to write stories so fast he had to think some Idies Before he wrote the stories Mr ramsey campell came to see ws he is an authhe might do mistakes If he does do mistakes he will give It to the publisher he prints the story on a cumputer."

So writes Kerry Lane, and shows the elongated purple author either sitting on a chair beside a round green table with a case on it or performing some feat on a set of parallel bars.

"Yesterday we had a visitor called Mr. Ramsey Campell he showed us some things he did some Books he did spooky Book's he showed the printer it so she could print it out. my sister fort he was a post man because he had lowds of letter's he marked his writeing with Red pen. Mr. Ramsey Campell was an arther. We asx him question's. He told us about Himself."

Steven also illustrates the process, not to mention the author's final metamorphosis. "Me," a seated member of the audience, featureless apart from a round purple head and tubular yellow clothes, calls to him. "Yes you," he responds, hopping on one purple foot and waving his brown arms as he bulges his circular green eyes.

May I assume the children had a good time and much to dream about? That would be more than enough. My next visit will be to a prison. If I emerge to tell the tale, look for it here.

Writing and Depression

Among the more apparently depressed people I've met was the late Graham Chapman, who was brought by the film distributor to the Liverpool press show of *Monty Python and the Holy Grail.* Having members of the cast or production team at such events isn't always a good idea (though over the years we had the honour of meeting Lindsay Anderson at the Liverpool show of *Britannia Hospital*, where he lived up to his prickly reputation when I suggested that *Movie*, the critical journal that emerged from *Oxford Opinion*, was a successor to the short-lived but important magazine *Sequence**). At the end of the London press show of *History of the World Part IV,* for instance, it became apparent that Mel Brooks had been in the audience to listen to our protracted stony silence, and at lunch with Terry Gilliam after a showing of *Jabberwocky* (which had failed to live up to our expectations of another Monty Python spinoff) nobody so much as mentioned the film. On the other hand, the director of a then unknown film (the fine *Mad Max*) did his utmost to convince me at the Liverpool preview that it hadn't been trimmed by the British censor, though I was right to think it had. And I still recall a radio interview I had to conduct with a starlet who'd appeared in *Rosie Dixon, Night Nurse,* and who proved to be so shy of answering questions that the publicist who'd brought her

**Movie* has been revived online and can be found at www2.warwick.ac.uk/fac/arts/film/movie.

apologised to me afterwards, an encounter which turns up unexaggerated in my tale "Midnight Hobo". *Holy Grail,* however, was appreciated by the scattering of hacks at the Liverpool cinema, and we were happy to have lunch with Graham Chapman at a Greek restaurant afterwards. Maybe he shouldn't have tried to drink as much as us, but in due course it became apparent that he had, when he asked for a glass to smash in what package tours would have tourists believe is standard Greek behaviour, only to cut himself in the process. The next we knew he was insisting that he must be shown round Toxteth (later the site of the famous riots), where he was convinced he would find his real audience, and revealed his moroseness (his moorhens, my spellcheck suggests) when there was a general attempt to dissuade him. For a few minutes the black pit hidden by his comedy opened up for all to see, and then he was ushered protesting to his train.

I tell this tale not to blacken his memory but to suggest that, along with Spike Milligan and the suicidal Tony Hancock, he was more typical of comedians than is generally recognised. How many in their business are routinely asked by audiences whether they're depressed? Not many, I imagine, not that I'm suggesting more of them ought to be. But it's quite common for me to be asked whether I'm depressed by what I write.

The answer, of course, is that I would be depressed if I didn't write it. Let me hazard the theory that creativity is or can be a form of addiction, to the emotional highs and the imaginative pleasure it brings. The perhaps inevitable obverse or side effects are depressions of comparable intensity. Colin Wilson recounts that a writer friend of his, Negley Farson, was told by a doctor that curing his alcoholism would probably cure him of writing too, and if a determined optimist like Wilson can accept this view of the situation, I'm hardly likely to deny it, especially since my instincts don't. Depression is apparently the price I pay for having developed my gift to the point that it gives me my greatest pleasure. Sometimes that compensation can seem only just enough.

Maybe this account of how I am deep down will come as an unhappy surprise to some of my friends, or maybe that's to underrate their perceptiveness. It does occur to me that my public personality is a routine I perform to disguise myself—have performed for so long that it requires great effort to do anything else. Not that I'm claiming any uniqueness; indeed, I invite the reader to think of anyone for whom it isn't true. Creativity may exacerbate it, though. I'm put in mind of comedians again: Kenneth Williams, whose performances in the *Carry On* films were a toned-down version of the persona he displayed in impromptu comedy, itself a defence against the black boredom of being the character he otherwise would have been inside his head; Barry Humphries, a shy sensitive fellow best known as Dame Edna Everage, who is indeed the same person as the President of the Arthur Machen Society and the author (much to the disgust of Chris Morgan) of the introduction to Robert Aickman's *Night Visions.* Some writers are able to incorporate routines they perform for audiences into their prose—William Burroughs is a striking example—though perhaps this is only a more obvious version of the way writers' lives are a rehearsal for what they write. That said, all writing is ultimately about how it feels to the writer at that time to be alone, in a room or at least in their head.

Which means in my case that on occasion the fiction, even by my standards, gets pretty dark. 1976 in particular seems to have been, if we judge by the tales I wrote that year. "The Trick" is heartless; *The Face That Must Die* is meant to feel like all the months I spent in the company, or maybe the persona, of John Horridge; "The Brood" and "Loveman's Comeback" are further evidence of my mood, but "The Change" strikes me as grimmer still, since it deals with the possibility that the worst thing a writer does may be to write. On the whole I've ceased to believe that, despite the occasional stirring of guilt at the way I use those closest to me as material; at its best writing, along with reading to audiences, is as high as I get these days without chemical assistance. But I'm also convinced that it inevitably contains the seeds of its own destruction, as I do. That's why for most of my life as a full-time writer I've denied myself that most seductive excuse of writing only when I feel inspired. Slow I may be by some standards—I am right now, because for some reason this instalment of my column is proving unusually hard to produce—but by God I'm dogged (or, to quote my spellcheck, "God dogs me"). The temptation not to write is otherwise too powerful to resist, as I think poor Karl Wagner discovered at the height of his career.

Karl may be an extreme example, but only of traits I recognise in myself (though at least I've avoided the trap that was his downfall, of spending publishers' advances and then not completing the commission, so that he had to take on another commission only to leave that uncompleted too). By now some of my readers may suspect me of romanticising, however gloomily, especially if they've encountered me in the flesh (and what a lot of it, they could be forgiven for thinking). Can this column really be part of the truth about the avuncular hulk, the genial globe, whose name it bears? Rather too large a part, I'm afraid. It occurs to me that my public face sometimes hides too much, not least from my publishers, who may take me to be more resilient than I am.

That would help explain why one of my publishers once showed me another writer's sales figures—presumably to demonstrate how efficiently the firm could move books, but leaving me embittered by the revelation that the other writer's sales were ten times mine. Is his stuff ten times as good? I remind myself of the sales Robert W. Chambers (his popular stuff, not his horror tales) and Dennis Wheatley once enjoyed, not to mention Seabury Quinn's one-time popularity compared with Lovecraft's during the same period, and bide my time. (Wheatley's name means so little to my word processor that the spellcheck programme suggests I mean Dennis Wheaties. Mind you, the programme doesn't contain an entry for "spellcheck" either, and so I assume that on those occasions when the computer seems lethargic it's wrestling with this paradox of identity.)

The historical view is an intellectual trick I seem increasingly to need to play on myself, and it doesn't always work. The reader must decide how autobiographical *Needing Ghosts* may be, in particular the image of a writer wandering the streets of an unfamiliar town and not finding his books in the shops. Sometimes the experience is so dispiriting that it makes me consider not accepting invitations to read to audiences, but maybe the solution is for me to arrive with no time to spare to wander.

Perhaps some of these experiences have to do with my mid-life crisis—a phenomenon which, unlike the menopause and so much else, has still to be revealed as a male conspiracy—except that I'm not aware of being in the least bothered by my age, only by its symptoms, failing sight and the rest of the beginnings of decay. You would hardly believe how much fun forgetting which spectacles I'm wearing can be, but only the other day I was happy to be confronted by my age. Just as in my early teens I read Lovecraft's *Cry Horror*, the British edition of the Avon paperback *The Lurking Fear*, I understand that Poppy Z. Brite read *Demons by Daylight* when she was thirteen. If it had any influence on her writing then I'm proud to have been of some use. It helps me feel that I'm a part, however minor, of a continuing tradition. More importantly, it's heartening to discover such a talent so young. Poppy is already a better writer—more lyrical, more sharp-eyed, surer of her characters, at least as fond of language but more precise—than I am.

Which moves me and cheers me up, much like listening to the astonishingly young and talented violinist Sarah Chang—but can't distract me from my theme. If neither ageing nor my refusal to be conscious of it is the source of all this darkness, must we accept that it doesn't just come with the job but is necessary to it?

Alas, I think so, in my case at any rate. I recall that most of *Incarnate* was written during the last year my mother was alive, when she was hopelessly insane and I could often hardly sleep. My point isn't simply that I was still able to write under those conditions—it is that I wrote by far the most complex and elaborate novel I had so far written, and the least apparently effortful. Do I really have to feel that bad to write that fluently? Perhaps not, for I've learned more craft since then. Perhaps unsympathetic reviews are enough to lower my mood, and there's usually a set of sales figures to back them up, but I don't really need those either. I can always rely on feeling that my notion I'm improving as a writer is the opposite of the truth, as was the case with poor Frank Belknap Long in his last years—that any day now I'll be shown up as a fraud, if indeed people aren't too polite or too deferential to my undeserved reputation to pipe up. Of course if they did I probably wouldn't believe them. Maybe (to contrive some relevance for the opening paragraph) my habitual mood must inevitably worsen as the tone of my writing grows lighter and more comic.

Do I feel better for having written all this? Not especially, unless it reassures other writers to know they aren't alone. They are, of course—we all are—but we may not always want to feel unique. Knowing we aren't may help us to make better use of the ways in which we are. One thing I hope this column or the rest of my stuff never does is make it harder for good writers to write. If I thought that I would indeed give up.

Since writing this piece almost two decades ago I've concluded that depression is essential to the creative process, at least in my case. I commonly waken in the morning with the sense that I've too few ideas for whatever I'm about to write, only to be enlivened once I get some. It seems that I may need to feel inadequate in order to discover that I'm not so far as the day's work is concerned. I have the sense that the depression about my work actually generates its own cure in the form of inspiration, if I may use that term. In that case it's crucial to what I do, and I can only embrace it. Perhaps if I were too conscious of the process each time before it happens it might desert me. I'll live with it for the sake of the work.

Editing Horror Anthologies

EDITING A BOOK CAN BE AS HARD AS WRITING one, and with luck, as much intermittent fun. I had my first taste of the process of commissioning and judging other people's efforts at the start of my teens, when—on whose suggestion I can't now recall—I proposed to pulp myself and some of my schoolmates, or at least our stories, in what was to have been a magazine of fantasy and science fiction. Did I really propose to call it *Unknown?* Perhaps I felt that the title belonged to the Campbell clan. One of my collaborators dissuaded me, though not on the basis that the name had already been used, but the masthead is gone from my memory. I do remember that, apparently not having learned from the experience of submitting my handwritten *Ghostly Tales* to publishers, I wrote out the magazine by hand and illustrated it too, undoubtedly to its detriment. Not content with this level of control, I rewrote at least one of the contributions, a tale of a haunted graveyard which I thought trailed off at the end and to which I added a paragraph. The author, with who knows what self-control, professed himself amused by the line "A worm popped its head up and died of fright", but I can't imagine any tale to which that would be an improvement. My plan appears to have been to have the magazine photocopied and stapled for distribution within the school, but when I was told that I would need to write and draw the whole thing again onto Gestetner stencils, my interest dwindled. So there was only ever one copy of the magazine, and now not even that. It must pass into legend, the best place for it, I suspect.

More than a decade and a half passes. I have a British publisher at last—Star Books, which has bought *Demons by Daylight* after the book is turned down by Gollancz (on the grounds of excessive obscurity) and Neville Spearman. Hugh Lamb, already an anthologist, is the man responsible for commending me to his editor Piers Dudgeon. The three of us have lunch, and soon Piers (whose surname once prompted Manly Wellman to remark that if it had been his, nothing would have prevented him from calling his house High Dudgeon) suggests I edit an anthology of original tales of terror, presumably not having observed that I'm coming down from my first acid trip. Off I enthusiastically go, with not the least idea of how.

My saviour, here as so often elsewhere, was my old friend Kirby McCauley, who was responsible for more of my selections than the acknowledgements page makes clear. It was Kirby who sent me Aickman's "Wood", for example, and then got out of the way while Robert and I agreed terms. I rather think Kirby may also have brought Dave Drake to my attention; if so, I'm glad he did. (I hadn't realised until I leafed through the book for the purposes of this piece how much of an earthbound precursor of *Alien* Dave's tale is.) I must also thank Virginia Kidd, from whom I sought and obtained a Lafferty, for showing me Daphne Castell's poignant "Christina". If only I'd left the reader to discover unaided how poignant it was! But I felt compelled to praise each tale in the course of introducing it, as though its presence in the book wasn't sufficient evidence of my admiration. I did refrain from enthusing about my own story, and confined myself to a mysterious reference to another tale which I'd written for the book but which I'd been persuaded wasn't good enough to use. For the record, it was the first and less successful draft of "Through the Walls".

The book was called *Superhorror.* I'd emitted a variety of titles, and this was the one that stuck. Another had been *The Far Reaches of Fear,* not unlike the kind of title August Derleth favoured, and in Britain the book was transformed into this when it reached paperback, because Piers Dudgeon's successor wanted the cover to be uniform with those of my other Star books, on which long titles composed of a column of short words were embossed. I pointed out a further similarity in *Necrofile* 13.

I believe it was Thom Tessier, while he was my editor at Millington, who showed Nick Webb at Pan the book and suggested that together they should commission me to edit a *Dangerous Visions* of horror. Alas, Millington collapsed before *New Terrors* was ready, and so it never appeared in hardcover. It had proved more ambitious and taken longer to compile than I'd anticipated, not least because some of the authors I approached—J. G. Ballard, Brian W. Aldiss, Anthony Burgess—were busy elsewhere. Still, they left room for several writers to make their debuts in print, most of whom have gone on to greater things; I was especially pleased while reading *The 37th Mandala*, Marc Laidlaw's fine novel of visionary horror, to be reminded that I used his first professionally published tale. What Derleth did for me I try to do for others, and decades later, while co-editing *Gathering the Bones* with Dennis Etchison and Jack Dann, I was delighted to discover another major talent, Adam Nevill, the new British answer to Stephen King. (Even when I was alleged to occupy that position I never knew what the question was.) Sadly, Sonny Mehta of Pan asked me to drop some tales from *New Terrors*—Tom Monteleone's can be found in a volume of Dennis Etchison's *Masters of Darkness*—and still more fell to the hatchet of David Hartwell (what a title for a book in the tradition of Bob Bloch!) when the two volumes were done by Pocket in America. At least Pan eventually amalgamated their two as a fat omnibus.

New Tales of the Cthulhu Mythos was commissioned earlier but was published at about the same time as *New Terrors*, in Arkham House's steady way. Between my proposing the book and its being contracted for, Jim Turner had taken up residence, and had strong convictions about some of the authors who shouldn't be included, though to judge by his inclusion of "Sticks" in the revised *Tales of the Cthulhu Mythos*, in Karl's case he changed his mind. Shortly before his death August Derleth had mentioned to me that he was thinking of a sequel to his Mythos anthology, one reason why I intended mine as something of a tribute to him. Perhaps my memory of working with him was why I became more editorial.

Frank Belknap Long told me that he thought "Dark Awakening", his contribution, was "one of his strongest stories", but I felt it trailed off, and sent him a paragraph to suggest how it might end more ambiguously, which he apparently liked enough to have me add it as the final published paragraph. To A. A. Attanasio I proposed that "The Nightmarer" should be retitled "The Star Pools", an image I'd found especially evocative in the text, and that it shouldn't end quite so soon (originally, as I remember, at the words "plopped back into the water"). I encouraged Brian Lumley to drop a few more hints of something horribly wrong, and Martin S. Warnes (where is he now?) to develop his ear for Lovecraft, though what appearance such an appendage might have is best not dreamed of. Nor was Stephen King immune to my interference. Since saying "Coo" is not among the ways in which London policemen resemble doves, I quietly buried the utterance.

Editing a reprint anthology seemed a less exacting prospect, and soon a Glaswegian lady at Piccolo Books invited me to have a go. Though Piccolo was the junior imprint of Pan, she told me to deliver a book that would "turn the reader's troosers broon". This was *The Gruesome Book*—at least, it did its best to be one, and was published in Britain amid the controversy about children watching horror films on video. I also wanted *Stories That Scared Me* to live up to its name, but found myself wondering if I should have bothered, since Beth Meacham of Tor declared that the title would mean nothing to the public (hence its demotion to a subtitle). Still, it enabled me to revive several tales that had haunted my childhood and to find a home for some powerful new stuff.

Uncanny Banquet was the result of my ambition to bring to a wider audience the then fabulously rare 1914 novel *The Hole of the Pit*—a book which among the living only R. S. Hadji and Richard Dalby appeared to have read until I saw it listed in a dealer's catalogue and roused the genial bookmonger from his sleep at four in the morning to be certain of securing it. So far as I'm concerned, it justifies the anthology all by itself, but I trust there's at least as much to enjoy as Don Herron claimed in *Necrofile*. Nevertheless it isn't quite the anthology I envisaged, because editing a reprint book proved in this instance to be harder than expected. For instance, I should have liked to reprint a ghost story of about two thousand words by

Michael Arlen, but the agent for the estate wanted an advance against royalties of five hundred pounds. I trust I hear gasps from my audience. Can there really be reprint anthologies with the kind of budget such an expectation implies? If so, I live in hope of being asked to contribute. I had better luck in securing all the stories I wanted to include in *Meddling with Ghosts*, my anthology of tales leading to and from the work of M. R. James. Mind you, the British Library (who published it) conducted negotiations and made payments, and so I have no idea what may have been involved. They paid me generously enough.

There remain the collaborations. I was asked to come up with an idea for a Horror Writers of America anthology, and while waiting in an airport I did. Some members of the society were offended by it, though I thought it had made clear that a roving bunch of Aztecs—a race I take not to be around to feel insulted—were supposed to be the villains. Did Aztecs rove? I should have expected to have been put right by somebody if my transatlantic view was wrong. Only my title—*Under the Tarmac*—came in for improvement, since tarmac is apparently too British a term. As to *Deathport,* I can only quote my introduction: "I think the book fulfils its intentions—to display the range of talent, skill, imagination and style representing the Horror Writers of America. I thank every one of the contributors for helping me achieve that goal, and I thank Marty Greenberg for doing far more work than I did." Indeed, the book includes almost every story that I read for it.

Not so any of the volumes of *Best New Horror* on which I collaborated with Steve Jones. I'm proud of all of them, and Steve should be more so, but I think my withdrawal of editorial aid is far enough in the past by now for me to risk contradicting Steve's carefully worded press release. The pure truth is that I became dispirited by the amount of rubbish we had to read in order to reject it—material already published elsewhere which persuaded me that the mass of contemporary work in our field was becoming as contemptible as detractors of the genre suggest. Some of the last introductions to *Year's Best Horror* reveal that Karl Wagner was put in the same state of mind. I can only hope that Steve Jones continues to be more resilient than I proved to be, because he is certainly a fine editor. For the sharp-eyed, my departure is celebrated on the cover of *Best New Horror 6.* For the moment the image may suggest my interment as an anthologist, but whose hand is it we see clutching its way up from the earth?

A Transient Engagement

HOW ODD TO BE A BIOGRAPHEE! DAVID MATHEW, an interviewer and critic fast earning himself a good name, has made me the subject of a book in progress. I'm in progress myself, of course, and must hope I don't betray the image he pieces together. Already he and old friends pumped by him have reminded me of incidents I'd quite forgotten, but I'm too old to hide my face. Some significant folk have resisted being traced, and so I may have to tell such of their anecdotes as I can remember. One person, though, is more problematical in that regard, since I was briefly engaged to her. As long as she can hardly be excluded from the biography, I'll make the effort to be objective on her behalf as well as mine.

It was January 1967. I'd begun work in Liverpool libraries some months earlier—in Wavertree Public Library, to be precise. I'd been taken under the wing of Derek Dorrity, the deputy librarian, who remarked on how fast I was learning the skills of the business: hardly a surprise, since I enjoyed librarianship, which in those days had a good deal to do with books. (Derek was a diabetic and, unknown to himself so far as I'm aware, a subject of derision by the female staff for having once taken one of them on a date and tried to kiss her. Some years later I heard that he'd hanged himself.)

Often when a member of staff fell ill, a substitute would be sent from another branch. That Saturday the replacement was Rosemary Prince, a bespectacled (and, I think, possibly exophthalmic) girl about a year older than I was. In the lulls between readers we fell to discussing our interests, and my love of films inevitably expressed itself. When it emerged that I was a member of the Merseyside Film Institute Society (where, decades later, I was to give a rambling lecture on horror films, during which I allowed myself to be provoked by a drunken poseur into vilifying Beckett) Rosemary asked me to obtain tickets for a show for her and a friend. I forget which show, but I do remember mentioning that I meant to see Hitchcock's *The Birds* again and wondering aloud if she, that is, if she hadn't seen it and er, would, er. . . Was I asking her to go and see it with me? she inquired with perhaps as much compassion as eagerness. Well, I, that is, er, and so we did.

She jumped and cowered and clutched at me throughout the set pieces in a way that I'm sure would have gratified Hitchcock, and did me no harm either. (The poseur at my lecture declared the film banal in comparison with Beckett, hence my unhelpful defensive response.) I wonder now if Rosemary viewed the experience as a rite of passage never to be repeated, in which case little did she know, poor girl. I don't think I was taken home after that first date, but before long I was introduced to her house in Aigburth, an upmarket Liverpool suburb, and to her parents, an insurance salesman (Artie, as she called him) and an English teacher named Janet. Rosemary and I had cheese and biscuits in the front room, where I was delegated to warm a frigid lump of butter by the electric fire, and she played me records of classical music on the gramophone, not to mention performing for me on the flute. This was my first real contact with an enthusiast for the art—indeed, with a musician—and I owe some of my subsequent love of music to her. Whether any of my enthusiasms have remained with her I rather doubt, and surmise that she has avoided all my published stuff.

She certainly didn't like horror, and that was the inevitable beginning of the end of our relationship. Would it have lasted longer if I'd kept the genre to myself? I lost no chance to inflict classics of the genre on her—*Psycho*, which a friend of mine appalled her by describing as a comedy; Siegel's *Invasion of the Body Snatchers* (coupled with a dullie called *Castle of Evil* for which she was in one sense the perfect audience—every repetitive close-up of an android with an empty eye socket made her start afresh). I even tried to tempt her with Freddie Francis' *The Psychopath* on the basis that it used the adagio from Mozart's Clarinet Concerto to striking effect, but by then she'd had enough. I was simply trying to share my passion for cinema, but film after film proved to contain material that wasn't for her—the nude scene in *Blowup*, the violence in *The Pawnbroker*, the whole of *Les Carabiniers*, which I still regard as probably the single most direct fiction film about the stupidity of war. Of course sometimes we attended her choice of films, but things went wrong there too—I distressed her by suggesting that a ballet teacher in a now forgotten Disney second feature was a covert lesbian. Once I watched *Smiles of a Summer Night*, Bergman's delicate comedy which Robin Wood rightly described as Mozartian, on television at her house, but the first reel was scarcely done when her mother demanded whether the entire film consisted of people arguing. I mumbled politely but tersely, a response I fear I gave too often to her parents.

Music was another battleground, and in particular one of the very first performances of Britten's *War Requiem*. I was ignorant enough to suggest that the work owed something to that most derivative of composers, Carl Orff—specifically, to his *Carmina Burana*, one of the few pieces of, in the looser sense of the term, classical music I knew well in those days. (In fact both the Orff and the Britten owe something to Stravinsky's *Les Noces*.) My initial encounter with the *Requiem* impressed me less than it might have, though part of the problem may have been that it was conducted by Charles Groves, who I later realised was fond of giving the performers or more likely himself unscored breaks in even single-movement works (I once saw him cripple *Belshezzar's Feast* that way). My major objection, alas, was to Rosemary's claim that Britten's music rendered the textual themes beautiful. If that were the case I would still view it as a failing, but I think the truth is rather that the beauty of the music sometimes reflects the text, sometimes contrasts ironically with it (as in, say, *Don Giovanni*). Britten was to become a favourite English composer of mine, and the disclosure of his gayness added to my appreciation of his work, *Les Illuminations* in particular. (How Rosemary reacted to this revelation I have no idea—when I knew her she used to regard any kind of departure from straight sexuality askance, and as distantly as possible.)

Back then, however, Britten was only one casualty of a larger conflict. Rosemary seemed convinced that a choice had to be made between beauty and horror, and I'm offering no prizes to all my readers who guess which I felt I had to choose. It is, of course, a false choice, and some of my fiction—I'll venture to name "Above the World" and *Midnight Sun*—demonstrates that it needn't be made. Unfortunately my choice also entailed a reaction to beauty in music, which I decided was an escape from reality rather than a heightened aspect of it. (I at least hope Rosemary didn't end up with a sense that music and the cinema are mutually inimical; I gained some of my early affection for music from its use in films—Bach's second cello suite in *Through a Glass Darkly*, the adagio from Beethoven's Seventh throughout *Lola*, an arrangement for wind of Mozart's clarinet quintet, K. 581, in *Le Bonheur*). You might think that our distrust of the source of each other's creativity must have been fatal to our relationship, and so it was, but the situation was rather odder than that. I believe we had already reached this stage of hostility before we got engaged.

Was this a truly sadomasochistic relationship rather than the kind that's fun for the participants? Its basis may rather have been unacknowledged desperation. On my side there was hopeless inexperience; on Rosemary's, I learned after we'd parted, a previous engagement that her parents had terminated. Though I was twenty-one, I'd taken out just two other girls and snogged only one of them. In this area, knowing Rosemary was something of a retrograde step, since she permitted no more than the chastest of kisses until we were engaged and then, sad to say, endured my inexpert attentions more like a sufferer from lockjaw than with any apparent pleasure, a lack that soon communicated itself to me. Presumably I convinced myself that putting her through this had something to do with love. I think it, and our engagement, had far more to do with clinging forlornly to each other for fear of being cast back into our previous lonely state.

I bought a ring and went down on one knee and was guardedly congratulated by Rosemary's parents. I took her home to meet my mother and observed their mutual distrust. Troubled by my spectacularly teeny penis, I took it to the doctor for appraisal and was assured that it would do the job, though I should explain that it never had the chance with Rosemary. After we were engaged she behaved as if I'd made her a present of an erector set she enjoyed playing with while leaving it still wrapped, a tendency I found frustrating, especially on public transport.

Three increasingly argumentative months later we came to our end. Before I describe it, let me toss in a few more memories. Quite early on Rosemary took to bringing me books from the library where she worked. As I recall they were a decidedly eclectic lot, but I remember only one, a Brian Aldiss collection that included "The Girl and the Robot with Flowers". In this tale an immediately recognisable Brian discusses a downbeat science fiction story with his wife and wishes he could simply write about the summer afternoon they're experiencing instead. It was plain that Rosemary hoped I would be overtaken by the same change of heart. Perhaps she didn't notice that the author's wife can tell from his tone that he's less than wholly serious.

While I knew Rosemary I completed "Cold Print" and began "Reply Guaranteed". I wrote some of the latter in her house, and still recall her reading a passage I had just completed:

> A suspicion came to Viv. "You don't like your parents, do you?"
> "No, of course not."
> "Well, then?"

Perhaps Rosemary's expression should have made it evident to me that my irony doesn't always communicate itself to the reader as clearly as I assume. Her reaction may have been one reason for my writing "The Horror of Horror", an ill-conceived attack on horror films that appeared—dedicated to her—in the first issue of *Twylight*, and why I did something even more untypical of me: I brought to the attention of a senior librarian a medical textbook with photographs of birth deformities, a book I suggested ought to be locked in the restricted case. Censoriousness from Campbell! I hope the notion appals my readers as much as it dismays me. It shows how willing to please I was, even to the extent of changing my principles. It's a willingness I've overcome.

Other reminiscences I've dealt with elsewhere, in "The End of a

Summer's Day" (the basis of which was indeed such a guided tour, on which, as I remember, all the rest of the party were decades older than us). The fool I made of myself as a preamble to a performance of Debussy is described elsewhere in the present volume, in my introduction to *Dark Companions*. Let me bring all this to a close.

We'd been to see Antonioni's *Blowup*, not my first viewing of it. When we arrived at Rosemary's house her parents had clearly been preparing a showdown. Her mother did most of the talking. Artie confined himself to a promise that if I hurt his women he would split me from gob to navel. I was uneducated, said her mother; I'd no prospects and would get nowhere at the library; I would either fail to satisfy her daughter or grow impotent; my mother's mental condition would decline (true enough, as my readers know). In sum, I wasn't good enough for Rosemary, who was a professional musician. When I was moved to protest that I was as professional a writer, this was scoffed at. (Perhaps proving Janet wrong was one of my motives for completing *Demons by Daylight*, and I leave my readers to decide if I should be grateful to her.) I was shown the back door, my usual exit. Rosemary appeared at the bedroom window with a cry of "Whatever happens I still love you", to be replaced by her mother, who shouted "Go back to your kennel!" Readers may recognise echoes of this and more in a ghost story of mine.

I trudged off to the nearest cigarette machine, having pretended to give up smoking once Rosemary and I were engaged. For the next couple of nights I cried myself to sleep. This was the weekend, and on Monday evening I loitered for several hours in the library where she worked. These days I suppose I would be called a stalker. She was either not there or hiding—I never found out which.

I was moved from Wavertree to the central library in Liverpool, then to the music department. Staff were allowed unlimited borrowing of records, which was a great boost to my appreciation of music. One day Rosemary came in, returning a score, I think. At the sight of me she looked crestfallen. I was happy to talk, having more than survived—not a month after we'd split up I'd experienced a creative rush, and had written the final version of "Concussion" in just a few days—but she said as little as possible, nothing that I remember now. I would be saddened to think my presence in the library, presumably a favourite place of hers, kept her out of it, but I never saw her again. She had taught me more about music than I expect she would imagine, and our relationship had cured me of desperation. I was to wait a year before I set about wooing Jenny, my one true love.

[Since a version of the above will inevitably figure in David Mathew's book, it seemed only fair to let Rosemary see it. I'd heard she had moved to Yorkshire to work in the Bagshaw Museum in Batley, just a few miles from my mother's home town. A helpful curator agreed to forward the essay to her. I gather she was so wary of being located that rather than let him have her address, she collected the envelope personally. I hope reading my reminiscences did her no harm. Equally, I trust it isn't malicious of me to mention that when Sefton Park Library was reopened after refurbishment—the library where Rosemary worked, and the one her parents used—the city council invited me to make a speech and cut the tape. A plaque on the wall in the lobby commemorates the event, and later my name was displayed on the wall of authors outside the Liverpool Central branch. I got somewhere at the library after all.]

AFTERWORD TO *THE INHABITANT OF THE LAKE AND OTHER UNWELCOME TENENTS*

THE FIRST BOOK OF LOVECRAFT'S I READ MADE ME into a writer. I found it in the window of a Liverpool sweetshop called Bascombe's—Clive Barker and Pete Atkins were other customers, I learned much later, although we never met in the shop in Smithdown Road. I was fourteen years old, and went there every Saturday to search through the second-hand paperbacks at the rear of the shop once I'd made sure there was nothing in the window on the street. Sometimes, among the covers faded like unpreserved Technicolor in the window display, there would be a bright new book on which to spend my pocket money: an issue of *Supernatural Stories* written by R. L. Fanthorpe under innumerable pseudonyms (Pel Torro, Othello Baron, Peter O'Flinn, Oben Lerteth, Rene Rolant, Duetero Spartacus, Elton T. Neef were just some of them), a Gerald G. Swan *Weird and Occult Miscellany* whose back cover advertised studies of torture and flagellation and execution "for the mature student". But that Saturday, among the yellowing molls and dusty cowboys, I saw a skeletal fungoid creature, the title *Cry Horror*, and (believe me, I let out an audible gasp at the sight) the author's name I'd been yearning for years to see on a cover. For a panicky moment I thought I hadn't half a crown to buy the book and dreaded that it would be gone when I came back with the money. I read it in a single malingering day off school, and for a year or more

I thought H. P. Lovecraft was not merely the greatest horror writer of all time, but the greatest writer I had ever read.

Some (Stephen King and Charles L. Grant among them) have taken this kind of reaction to prove that Lovecraft is an adolescent phase one goes through—certainly a writer best read when one is that age. I can only say that I find his best work more rewarding now than I did then. Grant claims that "when you grow up you discover that what attracted you when you were fourteen was his rococo style and very little else", but I don't think it was so in my case; certainly I don't agree that "the style makes the stories". Indeed, I think that's precisely the trap into which too many imitators of Lovecraft fall.

I was one of them, of course, having already done my best to imitate Machen and John Dickson Carr. If I avoided the trap to some extent, I did so unconsciously—did so because I didn't merely admire Lovecraft; I was steeped in his work and his vision throughout the writing of my first published book. I began it as a way of trying to pay back the pleasure his work had given me, the sense of awesome expectation that even reading some of his titles—"The Colour out of Space", "The Whisperer in Darkness"—could conjure up. No other writer had given me that so far. I wrote my Lovecraftian tales for my own pleasure: the pleasure of convincing myself that they were almost as good as the originals. It was only on the suggestion of two fantasy fans, the Londoner Pat Kearney (subsequently to write some fine studies of erotic publishing) and the American Betty Kujawa, that I mentioned them to August Derleth at Arkham House. To be precise, on 16 August 1961 I wrote:

> Dear August Derleth:
>
> Being a great fan of HPL myself, I have recently been attempting a number of pastiches of the Lovecraft Mythos. There is obviously nobody better than yourself to criticize such work, and I therefore wonder if you could spare the time to discuss mss. of mine, if I sent them along to you. Several fans have praised my work (one of them is running a novelet* of mine in his fanzine) but I think you, as the greatest authority on HPL, should have the final word. Please let me know if you want them handwritten or typed (if at all!)

*I was then affecting American spellings, apparently.

Let me talk a little about the first drafts. "The Box in the Priory" (written in 1960) was the first of several attempts of mine to expand references I'd found in Mythos fiction (although back in 1957 I'd put a shoggoth pinched from Bob Bloch's "Notebook Found in a Deserted House"—which I'd encountered masquerading as "Them Ones", I suspect very much to the author's surprise, within the glossy covers of *Screen Chills and Macabre Stories*—into my tale "The Hollow in the Woods"). Here the inspiration is "serpent-bearded Byatis" from Bob's "The Shambler from the Stars" (itself a direct tribute to Lovecraft, who figures as a renamed character). My story exemplifies the stylistic overkill I mistook for writing like Lovecraft—see the narrator's entry into Arkham, for instance. It also demonstrates how right Derleth was to make me relocate the tales to England, given my curious notion of American history: how old is the castle supposed to be, and who would have built it? One aspect of the original I haven't replicated is the use of American spellings—"traveller", for example, and "gray". The ending owes much to the titan elbow disinterred by one of Lovecraft's narrators.

"The Tomb-Herd" (written probably in early 1961) opens by aping Lovecraft's early philosophy—indeed, the paragraph was the first piece of writing I based on an entry in his commonplace book (number 27, which compares life and death in order to conclude "Life is more horrible than death"). I could hardly claim a basis in experience; I'd seen little life and just one death (my grandmother's). The story regurgitates Lovecraftian tropes without his sense of structure or narrative logic, and is too headlong in presenting information (a tendency I still have to combat in some of my first drafts). The prose suffers much from this puppyish eagerness, and I even managed to cram in a reference to Zothique, although that won't exist for many centuries. I don't wonder that the neighbours are strangely reticent, although they manage to be loquacious too, but the greatest bit of deadpan comedy is that telegram. The tale expands a passage from the *Necronomicon* quoted in "Through the Gates of the Silver Key", proving that, in the Mythos as elsewhere in our field, less is more and should be left that way.

Far worse than any of the prose, however, is the way these tales (in their published versions as much as the first drafts) reinforce the claim falsely attributed to Lovecraft—"All my stories, unconnected as they may be, are based on the fundamental lore or legend that this world was inhabited at one time by another race who, in practising black magic, lost their foothold and were expelled, yet live on outside ever ready to take possession of this earth again." Even at that age I should have seen how much of his fiction can't be forced into that framework. There's no evidence that he ever said it, and it's dispiriting to find it attributed to him all over the Internet, not to mention in at least one recently published book. It has been established that Derleth was quoting not Lovecraft but Harold Farnese, who occasionally corresponded with Lovecraft and, after his death, misremembered passages from Lovecraft's letters (as well as apparently believing that Frank Belknap Long's name was Bellknap Jones). The quote misses the essential cosmicism of Lovecraft's vision and so, I'm afraid, did I.

"The Face in the Desert" was the only tale Derleth rejected outright, understandably enough. Arabia (or "Araby", as I insisted on calling it in emulation of "The Nameless City", which my story struggles to resemble) was no less exotic to me than Massachusetts. Of course Lovecraft hadn't been to Arabia either, but he had more imaginative experience to draw upon. Like others of my early characters, the narrator reads as if he's parodying the stubbornness of some of Lovecraft's, who venture into the menacing unknown despite the omens that warn them. I must have been trying to outdo Lovecraft by declaring that the author of the *Necronomicon* wasn't entirely human. A similar ambition led me (in "The Tomb-Herd") to miss the point about Azathoth and suggest that this symbolic deity once had "mind and will".

"The Horror from the Bridge" all too obviously attempts to imitate "The Dunwich Horror", not just in the relative sobriety of my prose but in the structure, although the story borrows from other Lovecraft sources too. Wentworth's soliloquy takes its cue from Dr Armitage's in the Lovecraft tale, and his formula is all too reminiscent of the one Armitage flings at Wilbur Whateley's brother. The monsters are my bid to equal Lovecraft's monstrous inventiveness in that story, but apparently I had to scrounge an element from Smith's "The Dweller in the Gulf". While the final shift into first-person narrative is borrowed from "The Shadow over Innsmouth", it appears to express the writer's dream of having a Lovecraftian experience. The tale was based on note 217 from the Commonplace Book: "Ancient (Roman? prehistoric?) stone bridge washed away by a (sudden and curious?) storm. Something liberated which had been sealed up in the masonry of years ago. Things happen."

In "The Tower from Yuggoth" I was striving to tone the prose down further, taking "The Thing on the Doorstep" as a model. The letters between occultists plainly derive from those in *The Case of Charles Dexter Ward*. Of all the first versions this was the most substantially rewritten, because Derleth was unhappy about the fanzine publication of the original draft. I even changed the title to "The Mine on Yuggoth".

"The Insects from Shaggai", written in late 1961, was drawn from my favourite Commonplace Book note, which I painstakingly ruined. It was number 221: "Insects or other entities from space attack and penetrate a man's head and cause him to remember alien and exotic things—possible displacement of personality." I encountered it in *The Shuttered Room and Other Pieces*, where Derleth appended Lovecraft's account of the dream where it originated, but even then I overlooked the point that Lovecraft had simply meant insects, not giant ones. The guilt of my mistake haunted me for decades, until I did my best to rectify it by reviving the original idea in *The Darkest Part of the Woods*. Clark Ashton Smith shows up as an influence again, with the blossom from Xiclotl and perhaps the hashish dream as well (I wouldn't have one of those for quite a few years, although the visions that the insect bestows on the narrator were written when I was off school with a fever). The insects' chronicle was my variation on the history of the Old Ones in "At the Mountains of Madness". My old schoolmate Kevin Bulger (one of the original dedicatees of the book) pointed out that "The Place of the Cone" sounded like an ice cream parlour.

And so at last we come to the book as published, starting with the foreword by the youthful author. This was originally written in March-April 1963 as "Cthulhu in Britain" after Derleth invited me to contribute a piece to his Lovecraft compendium *The Dark Brotherhood*. He decided it was too specific to the present book and kept it to be used as the introduction, as which he edited it somewhat. He had me approaching the task of rewriting the tales "with youthful enthusiasm", but I thought it sounded arch or worse to appear to be referring to myself as youthful, and so my enthusiasm became cautious instead. Decades later Lin Carter told me that Derleth had described me as a lovely young boy, although we never met. As T. E. D. Klein said in his essay on my tales, the foreword errs in telling too much too soon.

"The Room in the Castle" (the rewritten "Box in the Priory") was completed in November 1961. This wasn't my first try at redrafting a tale; before setting about the Mythos I'd had two stabs at a detective story very much in the manner of John Dickson Carr, *Murder by Moonlight*, which I abandoned after about fifty pages and recommenced from scratch a year or so later (though that version remained uncompleted too). I imagine my impressions of the reading room of the British Museum were derived from the scene in Tourneur's great film *Night of the Demon*. Alas, my research wasn't always even that thorough; I managed to have a writer refer to a kaleidoscope in a prose style much earlier than the word was coined, and "flying mouse" as a phrase for a bat doesn't seem too likely either. The drumbeats in the forest seem to have lingered from the Massachusetts version of the tale. I was plainly much more taken with italics in dialogue and elsewhere in those days than now. I've corrected some typos that somehow survived in the Arkham House edition: for instance, "the meaning of that peculiar group" was misprinted as "the meeting of that peculiar group".

At this stage I seem to have wanted to salvage as much of the first drafts as possible. On 22 January 1962 Derleth sent a note:

Dear JRC,

If I am to see a story for possible inclusion in my new anthology of hitherto unpublished horror tales—DARK MIND, DARK HEART—I must see it posthaste.

I zipped "The Tomb-Herd" off to him at the end of the month, and on 7 February he responded

Dear JRC,

All thanks for yours of the first. I have now read THE TOMB-HERD, and while I am not altogether satisfied with it, I believe I can use the story in DARK MIND, DARK HEART, subject to certain conditions, as set forth below:

1) that the title be altered to THE CHURCH IN HIGH STREET;

2) that I be given a free editorial hand to alter and delete as I see fit. For instance, the initial paragraph should go. Following the quotation from Alhazred, the story should begin with: "If I had not been the victim of circumstances, I know that I would never have gone to ancient Temphill."—"rotting, ancient" is a bit too much at this juncture. I want, in short, to make the story a little more direct, in some places less clear, in some places more, and I want to guard against overwriting, of which there is a bit in this MS . . .

Since it never formed part of the Arkham edition of *The Inhabitant of the Lake* and is so extensively edited that it could be regarded as a collaboration with Derleth, I've included it among the appendices.

The next two tales here were revised early in 1962, mainly by changing names and locations and adding dialogue. "The Horror from the Bridge" does acquire some additional scenes. I suspect that the operation Phipps refers to performing on his mother derives from the Hammer film *The Man Who Could Cheat Death*. The tale reinforces Derleth's version of the Mythos, in which star-signs have the same sort of conventional power as crosses exert on Hammer's vampires. God knows what accent the woman's soliloquy after the flood is meant to be in—she appears to have strayed out of Dickens' London, as does the man from the builder's yard. It's evident that I've been nowhere near Gloucestershire. "But you don't know what the devil I'm running on about," Chesterton remarks. Indeed, although I think his ramblings have their roots in some of Lovecraft's more desperate rewrites of his clients' work. As for the final confrontation, I suspect it was suggested by Frank Long's *Horror from the Hills*.

The first draft of "The Insects from Shaggai" was written after I sent Derleth the original batch of tales, and so he never saw it until I revised it along his lines in April or May 1962. Although the rustic lingo in this one owes less to London than the patois in "The Horror from the Bridge", it's pretty haphazard—at one point it appears to veer into Lancashire. This was the first of my tales ("The Moon-Lens" was another) where the protagonist loses interest in the proceedings and nods off, or rather the author's imagination does. Elsewhere I imagined too much and continued missing the point about Azathoth, even consigning the god to Derleth's roster of creatures exiled by forces of good. In a letter to me Errol Undercliffe was scathing about the last paragraph.

In April 1962 Derleth sent me a copy of "The Church in High Street". I'd written the first couple of paragraphs of "The Inhabitant of the Lake", but reading his revision of "The Tomb-Herd" appears to have triggered inspiration. I abandoned the story in progress—not an error I would ever make now—and began one that excited me more, "The Render of the Veils". I remember sitting in the sun in the back garden at 40 Nook Rise and writing with a new fluency—it felt as though the spring day were expressing itself or at least helping me do so. Certainly the style becomes lighter and brighter. In retrospect I wonder if my dissatisfaction with some of the changes Derleth had made in "The Tomb-Herd" prompted me to develop his editorial advice along lines of my own. Still, I wasn't equipped to do justice to the theme, another one from the Commonplace Book (number 204: "Disturbing conviction that all life is only a deceptive dream with some dismal or sinister horror lurking behind"). The name Gillson may sound like an Innsmouth joke but was in fact the surname of a schoolmate.

"The Inhabitant of the Lake" began life as "The Thing in the Lake", since I hadn't heard of the Eleanor Ingram novel. It was completed in July 1962, apparently while I was on holiday with my mother in Colwyn Bay. On reflection the idea that a family would abandon a house and leave all the furniture struck me as worse than far-fetched, but then some folk believe the Amityville Horror nonsense. The Brichester estate agent has a decidedly unorthodox approach to selling properties, and even if he knows something we don't, his methods are a little too conveniently shaped to the purposes of my tale. In this story I appear to have been trying to eschew my earlier overwriting, but the finale is too understated, I think.

"The Plain of Sound" dates from July 1962. I've no idea why I set it four years earlier than it was written. The sounds that figure in the story may have been suggested by my earliest encounters with electronic and concrete music. It's the first story here in which the aliens are (at least apparently) benign, which—together with the final fragmented vision of horror—makes its roots in *At the Mountains of Madness* obvious. The Mao rite may suggest a political reference, but like the mention of Alala, it echoes Arthur Machen. Despite his reservations about the occasional vulgarism in my text Derleth let "balls" stay here.

I believe "The Return of the Witch" was written in late 1962. It's based on entry number 99 in the Commonplace Book ("Salem story—the cottage of an aged witch—wherein after her death are found sundry terrible things"). The development was mine, but not only mine. In 1969 I was delighted to find in *Tales of the Cthulhu Mythos* a Henry Kuttner reprint I'd never read, and then unnerved to discover that "The Salem Horror" had the same plot as "The Return of the Witch", scene for scene. I fear that my protagonist's reactions to his situation would have struck Lovecraft as lightweight, and he'd have been right. Here and elsewhere I seem to be making references to later Mythos tales of mine—I suppose I already had them in mind—and it looks as if I meant to claim Lovecraft's evil clergyman for Severnford.

"The Tower from Yuggoth" was reworked twice, the more radical version probably dating to September 1962 (though I planned back in November 1961 to develop the tale beyond the ending of the first draft). The published tale, reprinted here, reads more like a sequel than a rewrite. Are Edward's reading habits a sly reference or an unintentional one? By the age of eight I was reading Lovecraft ("The Colour out of Space") and many other classics of the field myself. At a guess, the scatological detail about the fungi has wandered in from William Burroughs, probably *The Ticket that Exploded*. Derleth replaced my forthright single syllable with offal. Elsewhere, "soron" was certainly an echo of Tolkein. Here and in the other later tales in this book I seem to have pared the narrative down a little too much, missing opportunities for dread suspense.

"The Will of Stanley Brooke" may have been my last tale of 1962. It was the first example of a discipline I've often imposed on myself—doing without some element that seems essential to my tales in order to learn what may happen. In this case, at this stage of my career, it was the dependence on evocative adjectives and atmosphere. Alas, I was insufficiently equipped with other skills, and the characters too often resemble the cast of a bad country-house mystery, naïvely depicted to boot. The theme derives from Lovecraft's "The Festival", although at the time I didn't realise it did.

My old letters imply that "The Moon-Lens" was written in January 1963. It was suggested by number 189 of the Commonplace Book entries ("Ancient necropolis—bronze door in hillside which opens as the moonlight strikes it—focussed by ancient lens in pylon opposite?") I hadn't then read Merritt's "Moon Pool", and presumably Derleth didn't think the similarity worth remarking. The attempt at a suspense scene in the hotel owes a good deal to "The Shadow over Innsmouth", but this is another of my tales where the protagonist can find nothing better to do than nod off. Originally he screamed "What's all this shit you're talking?" at the manager, but Derleth did away with the vulgarism, even though he'd left it in a Burns poem in *Dark of the Moon*. He was right, I think, given the context of my tale—I remember feeling uncomfortable decades later when such words showed up in the equally stylised context of a Hitchcock comedy thriller, *Family Plot*—but simply deleting the word left a line of dialogue even more awkward than many others in this book. I should have made a substitution in the proofs, but in those days publishers warned us sternly about the cost of such changes. I've added it here, though, and made one very slight revision to clarify what the celebrant in the square may be wearing around his neck (Derleth had inserted "a man", which altered my point). I've also changed a frankly silly gynaecological reference—why Derleth didn't alter it we'll never know, unless he thought I meant to convey Shub-Niggurath's alienness.

I delivered the complete final version of the book (together with "The Stone on the Island", written immediately afterwards for Derleth's anthology *Over the Edge*) on 11 March 1963. In June, having had a couple of unsuccessful shots at Olympia Press's magazine, I offered Derleth my next horror stories, "The Childish Fear" and "The Offering to the Dead" to add bulk to the book, but they weren't needed or even appropriate, and Derleth bounced them. At least they were a little more closely based on actual observation, whereas the *Inhabitant* stories were founded very largely on fiction I'd read. It was time for me to deal with my personal fears and experience, and very soon I began.

There's still the question of the book's title. In August I suggested *The Inhabitant of the Lake*. Derleth thought we might add *and Other Unwelcome Tenants*, and I liked that too. Alas, when he sent Frank Utpatel instructions for the cover art, he misremembered the addition as *and Less Welcome Tenants* (perhaps with his own forthcoming *Colonel Markesan and Less Pleasant Persons* in mind). The title had to be changed to match the cover, though I felt few tenants could be less welcome than Glaaki. Now, for the first time ever, the book bears the chosen title. Welcome!

FOREWORD TO *DEMONS BY DAYLIGHT*

THIS WAS MY SECOND PUBLISHED BOOK, AND MY first real one. Its predecessor, *The Inhabitant of the Lake* (now available from PS Publishing in its first complete edition) was my attempt to sound as much like H. P. Lovecraft as I could. There's nothing wrong with learning your craft by imitation: Beethoven began by sounding like Haydn, Wagner's symphony could be a lost Beethoven, Richard Strauss's first opera sounds like Wagner, early Bartók sounds like Richard Strauss. Oddly, however, writers often seem suspicious of this way of acquiring the necessary skill. While there's plenty to be said against making a career of it—the kind of composition which is to good writing what starlings are to birdsong—I suspect that the aversion to learning by this method has more to do with a fear of never finding your own voice. My experience is that gaining some skill first gives you time to discover your themes, and they are what shapes your voice. If you can't progress beyond emulation, then I fear that means you haven't anything new to say.

I thought I had when I wrote the stories in this book. Having imitated Lovecraft, I rejected him with all the obstreperousness of a fanzine contributor determined to make a name for himself at the expense of his betters. These days I regard Lovecraft as crucial to the field, but however unreasonable my reaction against his writing was, it was necessary to let me move on. (It's worth noting that Lovecraft's own work was to some extent a product of his mingled admiration for, and dissatisfaction with, his predecessors Machen and Blackwood.) I wanted to write a kind of horror fiction which, it seemed to me, wasn't being written—a kind which addressed real life and yet retained the appeal to my imagination which had brought me into the field. I should correct that statement: it seemed to me that this kind of fiction hadn't been written by anyone except Fritz Leiber. I was conveniently forgetting writers as diverse as Richard Matheson and Robert Aickman, but then, that awareness might have lost me the necessary focus. So I used *Night's Black Agents* by Leiber (who I still think is the most important living* writer in the field) as a basis for development, and set about writing this book.

It took me five years, from 1963 to 1968. Most of the period up to early 1966 I spent in writing first drafts and growing increasingly dissatisfied with them. The one exception to this was "The Cellars", which I meant to include in *Demons by Daylight* but which August Derleth bought for another Arkham House book. That story derived much of its strength from its autobiographical elements (an intentionally unflattering self-portrait) and its detailed observation of a real geographical setting, but I stumbled through several first drafts of other tales before I regained my hold on these qualities, in the first and only version of "The Stocking". This time, perhaps because I'd reduced my technique to its basics, I maintained my grip, and the next two years saw me writing the final drafts of most of the tales in this book—in the cases of several, the only drafts. At times I believe I fell victim to the myth that effortless fluency, rather than regarding the first draft as a laying out of the material for further shaping, is ideal: "The End of a Summer's Day" and the final version of "The Interloper" were each written in a single day, and I fear it shows in both cases. I feel too distant from them to attempt any retouching, and so they must stand, or sag, as they are.

Any sureness which the tales display didn't last much longer than the act of writing. As I recall, the first person to see typescripts of them was the Belgian fantasy writer Eddy Bertin, who discussed them in the course of a series of essays on Lovecraftian writers for

*Alas, no longer!

David Sutton's British fanzine *Shadow*. Although he wasn't hostile to all of them, I understood his underlying view to be that admirers of my Lovecraftian work would be disappointed or bemused. I hardly needed to be told that; I was afraid that August Derleth, who had published my first book because it was Lovecraftian, wouldn't like this one for all sorts of reasons, not least its (in those days, in this field) relative sexual frankness. Accurately or otherwise, I tended to feel that nobody else was writing horror fiction quite like this, and perhaps that meant everyone else was right and I was wrong. I should have gained more encouragement from selling several of my tales of this period to Derleth, as well as one ("The Scar") to Robert A. W. Lowndes for *Startling Mystery Stories.* On the other hand, when I submitted "The Enchanted Fruit" to the late Graham Hall, one of the editors of *New Worlds* during Moorcock's tenure, he told me in advance that he wouldn't like it, and proved not to do so, opining that whatever talent it displayed was too diffuse and misapplied (like, he suggested, Eliot writing about Macavity the cat). Admittedly it is probably the weakest story in the book.

Oddly enough, one further blow to my self-esteem made me determined to succeed. At the beginning of 1967 I became involved with a fellow worker (also a musician) in the Liverpool libraries. It was a decidedly ill-matched pairing—relationships in which those involved agree about virtually nothing seldom last, Hollywood romantic comedies to the contrary—and our brief engagement (during which I was persuaded to hyphenate myself temporarily as Ramsey-Campbell) was terminated by the girl's parents. When the mother claimed that one proof of my inferiority was that her daughter was a professional musician I retorted that I was a professional writer, only to be jeered at. Well, perhaps one Arkham House book wasn't much to show the general, but I knew I had already progressed beyond it, and I think at that moment I vowed to show the world I had. I hope Rosemary (now married, I understand) has done as well in her chosen career. Shortly afterwards I began to write the final draft of "Concussion" to explore my growing confidence as a writer and to announce the end of my sexual adolescence.

I completed the last tale to be written—the third draft of "Made in Goatswood"—in mid-1968, and then typed the whole book.

Perhaps I shouldn't have driven myself to finish the task late at night, something I've almost never done since, but when the typescript was done I was seized by a black depression, an experience which was then unfamiliar to me. I was certain Derleth wouldn't like the book; I didn't think it would be worth spending postage on submitting it to him. But I did, and shortly afterwards he sent me a contract, though without comment. In the Arkham catalogue he wrote that it was "adequate proof of [my] creative growth".

Lack of self-confidence never really leaves a writer; at least, it hasn't yet departed from me. I was still unsure enough about the contents of the book to be persuaded by the poet Alan David Price that "Reply Guaranteed" was a boring failure, and I removed it after Derleth had announced the contents, substituting "The Lost", one of my one-day efforts. In 1971 Derleth died, and the book was delayed for two years. Probably for that reason, something of the sort also befell my career. But *Demons* was published in 1973, and the essay of appreciation T. E. D. Klein then wrote was enough to give my dissatisfaction with librarianship a goal. I'd been trying earlier that year to change jobs—I'd been interviewed by editors of local newspapers and had even tried to get back into the civil service—but now, with my wife Jenny's support, I took the plunge into fulltime authorship, planning to write a science fiction novel (*Cold City*) of which I never wrote a word apart from a disarray of notes. So it may be said that this book changed my life; certainly Ted's essay did.

How does the collection look to me in retrospect? More representative of its period than I intended it to, and not only because I loaded it with an excess of contemporary references as well as in-jokes. Donald Wandrei suggested obliquely in the blurb of the first edition that one underlying theme of the book was drug use. He was right, but I hadn't been aware of it; the adventure of meeting my own subconscious was still to come. However inextricable this book may be from the era during which it was written, I hope it is rooted in something more lasting—in the tradition of the literature of terror and the supernatural. It was a turning point for me, at any rate, and a record of five years during which I was becoming myself.

INTRODUCTION TO *THE HEIGHT OF THE SCREAM*

WHY DO I WRITE HORROR FICTION?

Because there's nothing I enjoy more than writing.

But why *horror* fiction?

Because it's what I do best. And it seems to me one ought to spend as much time as possible doing what one does best.

By God, I needed that. Now here's some (I hope not too random) observations on this book, my writing, and allied matters.

Why the predominance of sexual themes?

Because some of the best horror stories have been based on such themes. Don't get me wrong. I'm not suggesting that "Oh, Whistle, and I'll Come to You, My Lad" is a disguised treatment of sexual problems (though I've seen that case argued skilfully). But think of most of Machen, or "How Love Came to Professor Guildea", or "Carmilla", or *Dracula,* for that matter. Such themes were largely abandoned or disguised or used as the basis of uncomplicated erotic fantasy in the *Weird Tales* era, yet I'm sure there was more to be done with them. (More recently and more disturbingly, particularly in Britain, horror anthologists have increasingly been sneaking in what I can only describe as pornography without sex: sexless sadism for readers who can't even admit the real appeal of the stories. I reckon it's time to put the sex back in horror; it's healthier.) What I've tried to do is to bring these themes closer to the surface, in order to take a closer look at them.

Why? Probably the best reason is that a while ago I began to come upon them unawares, lurking beneath the surfaces of my stories: for example, "The Inhabitant of the Lake". You think I'm exaggerating, or "reading in"? I would have thought so too, until I reread the story and fell over the buried sexual theme. Consider: the story deals with a creature covered with spines that come erect to enable it to inject fluid into the bodies of its victims. It is finally put out of action by one of the characters, who lops off one of its spines (on which, in a disturbingly unmotivated act, he has impaled himself); the story juxtaposes this image with the castration of a zombie. Now if I read all that in someone else's story I would feel pretty safe in discussing the sexual symbolism. Yet believe it or not, when I wrote "Inhabitant" I wasn't aware of what I'd written. So I thought it was about time I was.

Hence the theme of the fear of (and suppressed desire for) homosexual rape which becomes progressively more explicit in "Cold Print", "The Second Staircase", and "The Telephones". I don't mean that I set out to write a mini-trilogy; only that as the theme kept recurring, I felt more equipped to approach it directly. In fact I had the first telephone conversation of "The Telephones" in reality, at the Pier Head in Liverpool at midnight, during a bus strike. I've no reason to think that the man at the other end was a menace in any way. Nonetheless, I found the situation so disturbing I could only make a hasty date which I didn't for a moment intend to keep, and flee; which tells you a lot about me.

My life often gets tangled up in my stories—at least, written into them. It first did so in "The Stone on the Island", where I tried to sneak the Lovecraft mythos into the office where I was then working. The attempt wasn't too successful, but it pleased August Derleth sufficiently to show me what I ought to be doing. After all, however much one admires and wants to emulate Lovecraft, it's a dangerous trap to seek to use his method. His minimal characterisation and plot work because they are right for him; I had to find by trial and (much) error what was right for me.

I wrote the first, scrapped, drafts of most of the stories in *Demons by Daylight;* they took me years, and read so. Then I wrote "The Cellars", and I had it at last: my method. Most of the first long episode is autobiographical, characters and all. I have it now, I thought, and proceeded to write an appallingly inept first draft of "Concussion", which consisted largely of verbatim reporting of the relationship on which the story was based: there's egotism for you. (It took the second draft to show me that besides making for a better story, the imaginative elaboration of characters and incidents also gives a truer sense of what "actually" happened.)

It wasn't until I wrote "The Stocking", deliberately paring it down to the muscle, that I began to learn the crucial skill of selection. But I think my intuition grasped the secret then, at last; I wrote the final drafts of all the *Demons* stories (with the exception of the later "Lost") in about eighteen months. Lovecraft had rooted his horrors in recognisable settings; I wanted to root mine in recognisable human behaviour, an altogether more universal thing. And I'm still trying, I dare to say with fewer errors: Kirby McCauley heads off most of those.

But don't I ever hear a tiny voice, questioning the worth of distorting my experience to provide these nightmares? "Isn't there enough horror in the world already?" Yes, of course I hear it. And I'll tell you who put it there: the public, the sons of bitches.

I hardly need to say that I don't mean you who bought this book. I mean the people who, when I tell them what my job is, say "Good heavens" smirking, or "Oh, really?", or "Can you make a living writing that sort of thing?", or, in one fascinating example of human behaviour, pretend not to have heard and proceed to recount the plot of an archetypally banal spy story for quarter of an hour (in an attempt to convert me to higher things, perhaps). These are the people who brought me to the pass of saying I write "Oh, science fiction, ghost stories, that sort of thing" or replying "I suppose you'd describe them as, er, tales of unease" or muttering "Er um er ah horror stories, actually." I know exactly how Errol Undercliffe felt. Well, the hell with that, and the hell with them. I write horror stories, and I reckon I've written some pretty good ones.

Nevertheless, I'm occasionally dispirited to realise that of the serious popular forms, horror fiction is about the last that still embarrasses its readers. You can safely admit to reading sf these days, in fact it can be culturally smart to do so, but horror gets disowned the way sf used to when Mr Average and Mr Chi-Chi thought it was all about little green men. You don't agree? Remember all those people who asked you if you'd read (or seen) *The Exorcist:* did you take the chance to recommend to them the horror fiction that you thought was superior? I wish I had.

Still, this preaching isn't really part of my job. "Isn't there enough horror in the world?" There's far too much of some kinds of horror. But there's always room for more of Mahler's kind, or Berio's, or Richard Strauss's, or Ingmar Bergman's, or Hitchcock's, or Magritte's, or Albright's; and there are hundreds of names I could add, including all those good people still writing worthwhile horror fiction (as distinct from adolescent morbidity and sadism). I hope there's room for my kind too. And you know, I seem to be meeting more people who don't sneer at my job—people who actually admit to reading horror themselves. Maybe one of these days well be fashionable. Don't let me hear anyone saying it'll be less fun!

Well, this has been a right old ramble; you can see what it's like inside my head. I've some comic relief for you in a couple of paragraphs; but first, in case anyone's interested, here are a few stories and thoughts behind the contents of this book. I suspect that the form of "Missing" derives from "August Heat", one of the perfect horror stories, while the idea for "Jack's Little Friend" came from a good friend of mine, Tony Edwards. In "Beside the Seaside" (and in "The Companion", published elsewhere) I had nearby New Brighton in mind, even though it's Merseyside pretending to be seaside (with its eyes shut, surely). "The Cellars" existed, and may still do so, but are inaccessible now—for Rumford Place, under which they lay, has been walled off. I smoked so many cigarettes while writing "Smoke Kiss" that I gave them up forthwith, and for good. "The Words That Count" was suggested by a Nabokov tale which, like much of his work, I greatly enjoyed: "The Vayne Sisters". I once experienced the treatment meted out to Tim in the first scene of "The Telephones": in the Crown pub on the Charing Cross Road, of all places, in London. Oh, one clarification for "The

Words That Count": The National Viewers' and Listeners' Association is an extremist organisation which, as such things will, presumes to represent the silent majority (in demanding stricter censorship).

Now then. I remember when I was a Lovecraft completist I used to read the poor man's juvenilia with respectful solemnity. Who knows, maybe that would have appealed to his sense of humour; but I feel I was doing him an unpardonable injustice. I'll tell you one thing: nobody is going to do that to me. A while ago, sorting through old notebooks, I turned up one of my early masterpieces. I'm about to share it with you, exactly as written, capricious spellings included, on the understanding that you won't be solemn about it—except perhaps while noting the Pinteresque minutiae of bus-routes, the intrusions of surrealism, the Godardian jump-cuts, the Hollywood bombardments, the vaudeville routines, and the echoes (psychical, presumably) of Mrs Radcliffe.

For the benefit of future bibliographers I ought to reproduce part of my first published work, which appeared in the *Liverpool Echo*'s Children's Corner, no doubt with its face to the wall, in 1951. I recall that it began

Wag is my dog.
He's out in the fog.
When he comes in,
He'll lick my chin.

An unashamedly primitive piece. There was more, but it seems to have been too traumatic for my memory. I give it here as the first appearance of a personal theme which, as you will see, recurs below—and which is treated more fully in the later *Dogs in the Stratosphere,* whose 20,000 words you should be heartily glad I've spared you. But as for the following, I can't bear to live alone with it any longer.

The Contents of the Red Exercise Book

(It is a thin red exercise book, its pages covered by a painstakingly neat pencilled handwriting. Many disturbingly primitive drawings, ambiguous and almost indescribable, are omitted here.)

BLACK FINGERS FROM SPACE

by John R. Campbell (aged 7½)

(No. 1. Science Thriller Library)

Chap. 1. The Dead Scientist.

JOHN sat up. Was that the 'phone? It might well be. This was the fifth case.

John picked up the 'phone. "Click!" it said.

"Oh," said John. "Are you cut off?"

"No," said the 'phone. "I've got a case. A black hand is seen at night, crushing houses. It's a whopper, too!"

"Come round and tell me about it," said John.

"Right," said the 'phone. "Ta-ta!"

John hardly heard him. He was thinking about the case. Space? That meant rockets. Earth? A sudden thought struck him. Would the man get there? Lost? No. Murder.

He thought of the last case. The man had been shot through the brain. This man might be next.

* * *

Bong! Bong! Bong! Bong! Bong!

"Funny!" said John. "He should be here now!"

He decided to go and look for him. So loading his rifle, he went down the road.

The first bus was a 78a. The next was 22, and the next was his, a 78.

* * *

"We get off here!"

John got off the bus. He knew the road. Fitzwilliam Avenue—that was it.

He walked along the road. 15, 17, 19, 21, 23, 25, 27, 29, 31...

Ah! Here it was. No. 37.

"Now!" said John. "Now for the shock! OPEN UP!"

"Wait!" said a voice. Then to someone inside: "Now I'll shoot!"

"No!" said a voice. "Don't! Don't! I—I'll join——"

"Well——" said the other. "We-ell. I'll——"

"OPEN UP, I SAID!" said John.

"Oh, he's still there!" said the murderer. "Oh, I'll shoot!"

CRACK! CRASH! TINKLE!

"I'll get in," panted John.

CRASH!

"I've done it——too late!" The scientist was sprawled on the floor. There was no doubt. He was dead.

Chap. 2. The Disappearing Corpse.

AS John had been too late, he thought he might as well sleep in the scientist's house. Little did he know——!

* * *

Later he was awakened by a faint scrabbling noise. He got up and went downstairs. Nothing there!

Scrape! Scrape! There it was again. What was it? Suddenly he stopped. Something had moved! The Black Hand!

The Hand was creeping towards the corpse.

"Stop!" said John.

The Hand took no notice. Instead, it picked up the body and went off with it.

"An' yer got im'?" snarled a voice.

"Yeah," said the monster.

"Is 'e dead?"

"Yes."

"How's the 'tec?"

"Alive an' awake."

"Didn't yer shoot 'im? Why?"

"As you know, I can't handle a rifle," said the monster.

"Yes," said the murderer slowly. "Ah, well! I'll have to do it meself!"

"Now what can I do?" thought John. "I think I'll go home."

So he got the bus home. He was thinking hard. Where was the man? Who or what was the Black Hand?

"He (the murderer) must be on another planet now," said John. "Phew. Who CAN he be?"

"I think I'll go to Pluto," thought John. So he went to the ramps.

"A passage to Pluto. How much?" he said at the pay-box.

"£1.16.5," said Jones, the tax man.

"Projectile CD5," said John.

"Good," said Jones. Then to himself: "Wonder what 'e's goin' for?"

"Step in," said Jones, pointing to the lift.

John got in. He was thinking hard. Where had he heard Jones's voice before?

He was still thinking as the lift neared the top. Too late he saw he had a companion. It was a man, who, rifle to shoulder, was aiming at the light.

CRASH! The lift was plunged into darkness. Hands groped at John and the last he remembered for a long time was something crashing down on his head.

*   *   *

When John woke up he was lying in a metal compartment, bound and gagged. The "dead" scientist was lying by him——and that was all!

Chap. 3. Message in blood.

FOR a long time John lay like that. Then he began to examine the place. Then he spotted a notice on the floor. It was like this:

AT 7 O'CLOCK TONIGHT. BRING A GUN. T.

It was done in blood. He looked at it, and then a movement behind made him start.

It was the scientist! He tried to get up, reared up, and fell forward.

"Collapsed! Isn't that a pity?" sneered the man by John. (He had a gun in his hand.)

"He did not collapse! Can't you see the fresh bullet hole through his arm?" John snapped.

"You know too much," snarled the man.

"Where are we now?" asked John.

"In an area covering Russia," said the man. "Where would you rather go. In the sea, or in Russia?"

"I—I—I—" said John. "In Pluto!"

"Right," said the man. "Get in this jet!"

Click! KARR-K!

WHEEE!

Suddenly he was confronted by a strange monster. It was a robot.

"What is it?" thought John.

"KAA-RK! Stop!" said the robot.

"Fire!"

BOOOO-OOM! WHEE! CRUMP! CRUMP!

A groan came from below. Looking down, John saw Wag, his bloodhound, with a bullet wound in his leg, with the patrol.

Silently John set down and let Wag in.

"How did you do it, Wag?" John said.

"I've got no swag!!" answered Wag.

"I SAID, 'HOW DID YOU DO IT?'" yelled John.

"Mm——I do rue it," said Wag.

"HOW DID YOU DO IT?" screeched John.

"I met the murderer," said Wag.

"Oh," said John.

"Well," he said, "up we go!"

WHAM! WHIZZ! BOOOOM!

They crashed. But when they got out——

"Hey! This isn't Earth!"

"No!"

It certainly wasn't Earth! From sun, houses, men on Earth, this was dark, soundless, wierd—

Soundless, did I say? Yes. Well, John could not get to sleep that night. He lay awake, wondering what fate might meet him the next day. Then—he saw *it*.

It was something glinting on the floor. He picked it up and whistled. It was a dagger, stained with fresh blood.

Chap. 4. Broad "Daylight" Murder.

The next morning he found he had a four-legged murder alarm. It was Wag.

"Come quick! We've been robbed! Roger's been murdered!"

"Wha-at?"

"Yes! He—he—he——."

"Come on, quick! We—"

John's speech was interupted by a scream. Then Richard, with Wag's friend, Rover, yelled: "A black hand took Roger's body!"

"The Black Hand!" gasped John. It certainly was gone! The place was wrecked. . . .

"EEEEEE!"

"What was that?"

Well, readers, read the next chapter!

* * *

On Earth, Mrs. Brown heard a scream. She went downstairs.

"Joe! Where are you?"

Complete silence was the only answer. She ran into the dining-room. Nothing was there. Into the attic. . . .

"EEE!"

Joe was lying on his back. A chest, which had long remained locked, was opened revealing——well—a white object.

Mrs. Jones could not see it clearly, for it was mostly covered in black cloth. She gave it a pull. It came away to show—a skeleton!

Chap. 5. Cavern of Death.

True pop art. I'm sorry to have to leave you on the cliff-edge, but I never did have the staying power to finish writing a novel. That won't be true of the one I'm writing now, however. With that you're on your own. I hope you enjoy the book. It gets better now.

II

That's how I introduced the Arkham House edition of the book. I can't help reflecting that the prose of *Black Fingers from Space* is scarcely more perfunctory than the style of some books I've seen professionally published. In 2004 the book was reprinted by Babbage Press, and I provided this afterword:

Still Shrill After All These Years

My third published book! How long ago it seems. It appeared in 1976, which means the photograph of the author and his wife gazing from the back cover must have been taken the previous year. Whatever happened to that shirt of many colours? It might not fit me now. The moustache has vanished with it, along with a good deal more than half of the hair that trailed over my collarbones. People must have thought the man in the photograph was a pervert, or on drugs, or trying to prefigure Kim Newman. As for my wife, she grows more beautiful than ever.

But you're waiting patiently to be told about the contents of the book. I'll reminisce about the tales in the order of their writing. "The Cellars" (1965) is the earliest, and sent me off in more than one direction: maybe it shows. It was the first story I set in Liverpool, and it uses actual locations, the cellars included. It was also the first tale in which, having acquired a delight in language from reading *Lolita*, I tamed that tendency sufficiently to use it in the service of the story rather than burying the story under it—a temptation I still have to watch. One aspect of "The Cellars" that may have given me control was its commitment to autobiographical realism. Only the name of the girl in the tale was changed, and I did indeed escort her through those cellars one lunchtime. As for the creepy male lead with his undeclared sexual agenda, that was the author, Turkish cigarettes, grey civil service suit and tie and all.

This ill-assorted couple turns up again under different aliases in "Reply Guaranteed" (1967). Kirby McCauley, not then my agent but already my first critic, who read my work in typescript, was offended by the opening line. It makes me squirm too, but the real girl said exactly that, and I thought it was a vivid image of her character. I might not pen it now, nor indeed the tale, which is very much of its time in terrorising its female protagonist with a sexual threat, but I've no compunction about reprinting it. It isn't meant to disturb a female readership more than it disturbed me, which is considerably. It dates from a time when I was determined that my tales should be as frightening as I could make them, and there's nothing dishonourable about that.

Both these tales were written while I had my second published collection, *Demons by Daylight*, in view, but were omitted—"The Cellars" ended up in another Arkham House volume, and a friend persuaded me "Reply Guaranteed" was boring. I'm about to write the introduction to his first published book. "The Scar" (1967) was a candidate for *Demons* too, but since August Derleth had turned it down for an anthology of his, I assumed (wrongly, I later learned from him) that he wouldn't want to publish it in a book of mine either. In the midst of being interviewed by Caitlín Kiernan (whose fine supernatural novel *Silk* I enthusiastically recommend) on stage at the 1999 World Horror Convention, I realised "The Scar" is where my recurring theme of the vulnerability of children first appears. I'm also struck by how, aged twenty-one, I managed to sketch a convincing nuclear family of a kind I'd never had myself. My commitment to observation (would that more writers of the fantastic devoted some of their energies to it!) was paying off.

There's some in "Cyril" (1968) too. Both characters are based on people I knew, and I was intrigued to imagine what might have happened if they had ever been thrown together by circumstances. Inevitably the tale altered them to its own ends. The late Jim Turner, my editor on the book, felt there was insufficient reason for the doll to behave as it does. I suppose I thought that animated dolls were such a staple of the genre that they no longer needed too much explanation, and that few forces are as powerful as sexual frustration—powerful enough to have magical qualities, in fiction at any rate.

By contrast with all the foregoing, "Ash" (1969) was just my attempt to work out a ghostly idea, and ought to have been better. The clotted first paragraph will warn you what to expect, I'm afraid. I would tell the tale much more simply now. It contains a couple of images I like. Like "Cyril", it was surrounded by other experiments in fiction that I made, not included here. Once I'd completed *Demons by Daylight* I felt I'd finished something but wasn't sure what to try next, though I won't presume to offer that as an excuse.

"The Telephones" (1969) grew from an incident where, Jenny and I having travelled to London one hot summer day, I was refused a pint of Double Diamond by a barman in the Crown public house on Charing Cross Road because of the length of my hair. It can often be the unpleasant moments of life that germinate a tale. What else underlies this one I leave my readers to decide, and that's pretty much all I can find to say about "Beside the Seaside", which I wrote in the winter of the same year: I don't remember anything about the act of writing it or where the idea came from, except perhaps from my morose enjoyment of seaside resorts out of season. I'm now of an age when my early, and sometimes not so early, work is distant enough for rereading it to be like reading someone else's stuff. Just as unnerving, if more rewarding, was my encounter with the English writer Russell Flinn's short tale "Subway Story", which reads like a tale I'd forgotten writing, though a better one than most of those I did. He cites me as an influence. His story is included in *Best New Horror 3*, which Steve Jones and I edited in 1992.

Back to 1970 and "Second Chance", a pretty self-indulgent piece. Jenny was my wife to be, Anita her flatmate at a teacher training college in Hereford. Anyone who knows the field will recognise that the central notion is far too reminiscent of one used by Walter de la Mare. I'm also indirectly reminded by the tale that I once went to Hereford to visit Jenny for a weekend, only to assume that the train had stopped short of the station when in fact it was merely my carriage that had. By the time I realised my mistake and raced to a door that let me onto the platform, Jenny had despaired of my arrival. Four hours later, when the next train was due, we caught up with each other at the station, but I still miss those hours of our life.

All I remember about "The Dark Show" (1971, the year we were married) is that it was written for or at least submitted to an anthology by Peter Haining of, I think, fantastic tales related to pop music. The Hippodrome cinema existed, and was worth using more appropriately and accurately, which was its fate in a later tale, "The Show Goes On". It has only now struck me that the latter sounds like a sequel. Such are the tricks writers can play on themselves without realising.

I do remember writing "Litter" (1972), and it's worth sharing the experience, particularly with any of my readers who have ambitions to write. It involved my worst—indeed, so far my only—case of writer's block. I wrote a page and a half of it, and failed to continue it as soon as I next had a chance. The lost day became two, then a week, and so time piled up, until six months later I managed to trick myself into recommencing with the line "That's how he enters the story, or this is." Of course I should have begun the final draft at that point and incorporated the preceding material into the body of the tale, but I'm rather glad I let it stand as a horrid example to myself and others of what happens if you wait for inspiration to strike. Inspiration is something you work for, seven days a week until the story is completed.

For all its flaws, "Litter" found a home in the anthology *Vampires, Werewolves and Other Monsters* ("Roger Elwood's family of fictional horrors", says the cover—"monsters obsessed by evil, unnatural cravings!"). How my tale fits into that isn't clear, as can be seen from the contents page. "Litter" is preceded by a tale tagged with the line "What do you eat after you've finished your brother's eyeball?" (to which the reader is presumably not expected to respond "A light dessert") and followed by one summarised as "When boys refused him, he cut them apart and laughed!" The worst Elwood can visit on my story, however, is "Trapped by malevolent bottles, napkins and straws!" What a man.

"The Whining" (1973) was written for Michel Parry, then a prolific anthologist. We had corresponded about horror films and fiction while we were still at school. For his first book, *Beware of the Cat*, he'd persuaded me to write a feline spectral tale, and now wanted something appropriate for a companion anthology, *The Hounds of Hell*. The cat story was an excessively calculated attempt to work up a catty atmosphere, and was justly criticised by Fritz Leiber, but "The Whining" has its roots in my dislike of some canine traits. Karl Edward Wagner, I remember, didn't like it much for that.

1973 was the year I went fulltime as a writer, and pretty prolific, not to say determinedly experimental. The title story of this book was one result of the latter. The notion of the occult power of apathy, however, was far better handled by M. John Harrison in "Running Down", to be found in his splendid collection *The Ice Monkey*. All that needs to be said about my tale is that I originally thought it complete when I'd penned the penultimate paragraph.

S. T. Joshi feels my liking for "The Words That Count" is explicable only by my being a lapsed Catholic. I thought of it as being liberating rather than daring, but perhaps his view still applies. I've never been sure if readers realise that the protagonist is writing more than she knows, as the narrators of "August Heat" and "The Vayne Sisters" did. Or is this so obvious that people can't believe I imagine it will come as a surprise? It may be worth noting that a French version of the tale by a careful translator completely missed the point about the structure. Perhaps, like Stravinsky's orchestration of Rachmaninov's Paganini Variations for cimbalom and string orchestra, the story is best treated as an experiment worth trying once to see what happens.

"Missing" lifts a title I didn't know Walter de la Mare had used, later to be borrowed by my friend Poppy Z. Brite. No doubt Jacques Barzun would accuse us all of unimaginativeness—he deplores such unemphatic titles in his introduction to *The Penguin Encyclopaedia of Horror and the Supernatural*—but for me the very neutrality of a title in this field can convey ominousness. In this case it is meant to suggest what has happened after the last scene.

"Smoke Kiss" may have been one of the very few instances where a tale of mine has proved therapeutic for the writer. (I've met people, generally at writers' groups, who would like to think that has been the purpose of all my stuff, but what an introverted purpose it would be!) Certainly I kicked nicotine not long after finishing the story. The open ending was intended as a warning, but Stuart Schiff, who bought "Smoke Kiss" for *Whispers*, asked me to deliver a more final paragraph. Those interested in reading it must seek out that appearance.

Michel Parry commissioned "Jack's Little Friend" for, I think, the first but not the last anthology of tales about the notorious Jack. It was yet another attempt to find out what would happen if I did without something I relied on as a writer—in this case, a defined protagonist. The second-person narration simply causes problems,

I fear, though later I was to find a more effective use for it in tales such as "Heading Home".

And last, as I struggled to discover my identity as a fulltime writer, "Horror House of Blood". Jim Turner was especially taken with its technique, but then he saw only the final draft. Kirby McCauley saw the first version, and must have thought I'd taken his advice to experiment too much to heart, because he showed the tale to another client of his, David Drake. David exhorted me to write a stronger finish, and no wonder. At that time the story ended with Frank's line "It's yours and you're stuck with it." Presumably I'd decided to see what happened if I denied the audience the pleasure of any resolution, even more than the film director Richard Brooks did by having one of the participants in an imminent gunfight freeze to death at the end of *The Last Hunt*.

What more can I say? Some of the tales seem alien to me, the work of someone I no longer am. Some I wouldn't mind having just written. All, like anything I write, are bits of myself I left or tried to leave behind. I'm happy to see them still trailing in my wake. The most experimental are probably the ones I feel most distant from, but that's by no means to say I intend to stop experimenting when it's appropriate. Part of the fun of writing is to surprise yourself—to strive not to repeat yourself. I doubt I'll return to the extremes you'll find herein. I'm too old to think it clever—though I hope never so old I don't notice—to end a story or even a paragraph before it's

AFTERWORD TO *THE DOLL WHO ATE HIS MOTHER*

THIS WAS MY FIRST COMPLETED NOVEL, AND IF I were writing a preface rather than an afterword I would ask the reader to be kind to the book. Admittedly my earlier attempts are even more in need of special pleading. We'll pass hastily over *Black Fingers from Space,* the opening and only chapters of which I wrote when I was seven and a half,, and there isn't much more to be said about *The Pit,* a ramble after Machen I composed (hardly the word) without the advantage of a plot in my twelfth year. It was intended as the first volume of a trilogy—which in itself would no doubt be sufficient to guarantee it a publisher's contract these days—but it foundered after sixty pages or so, with nothing else to show for itself except the name of the trilogy, *The Trail of the Narg,* and the title I'd conceived for the third volume, *The Broken Moon.* The first chapter was enough to cause my English teacher to regard me askance and intone a warning about morbidity, and two years later some, to put it mildly, mild sinfulness in *Murder by Moonlight* raised the eyebrows—only those, I hope—of a Christian Brother at the same grammar school, St Edward's. This was the second, less uncompleted, draft of a detective novel which I'd written in emulation of John Dickson Carr and which included characters with names like Hartley Darwin and clues such as a life-size cardboard policeman found at the scene of a murder. Who done it, and how, I forgot long ago. The manuscripts of both drafts are in the Local History library in Liverpool for the interested to mull over. After that I wrote nothing but short stories, most of which saw publication, for fourteen years. Since the advent of the pulp magazines this has tended to be the way writers of the fantastic and macabre have learned their craft before embarking on a novel. (These days more writers get their start in semi-professional magazines, some of which are unfortun-ately pretty bad or worse and self-congratulatory in proportion to their lack of worth, and which seem unlikely to provide much valid editorial advice.) Learning to walk before attempting the marathon of a novel has considerable advantages, but in my case it began to assume the characteristics of a more elaborate form of writer's block, in this sense: every day one fails to continue writing a story adds to the difficulty of doing so—at least that was my experience—and as my career progressed, every short story began to feel like a hindrance to my composing anything more ambitious. I did write a few tales which were stronger on plot and less reliant on atmosphere—"The Tugging", "Dolls"—than my average, but "Medusa", one of my lurches into science fiction which got out of hand and became a novella, rather soured me on writing at greater length. However, my old friend and American agent Kirby McCauley persisted in gently suggesting that I should have a go, and about halfway through 1974 I had an idea for this book.

I thought I had an idea for a new monster. As Steve King points out in his essay on the book in *Danse Macabre*, that wasn't so, but it was enough to make me enthusiastic about developing the notion at length. (Steve also suggests that the book's "slumbering, semi-sentient monster" may be Liverpool itself—specifically Liverpool 8, better known these days as Toxteth—which seems uncannily prescient of both of us.) Developing it sufficiently for me to feel confident enough to begin the first draft entailed filling many pages of a notebook with bits of scenes and characters, then working out the entire plot in advance, then breaking it down into chapters in an exercise book and using that to index the notes so that I knew which chapter each related to. Since *Incarnate* I've relaxed sufficiently with the form of the novel that I don't feel the need to bind myself to a preconceived plot, and I think that even in the case of *The Doll* I eventually became aware that poring over the plot was a substitute for writing the book. Even that awareness didn't spur me to begin, but in earliest 1975 I awoke one morning and thought of the opening line, and once I'd sat down at my desk to write it I found myself continuing to write.

The first draft took only five months, and I believe it shows, as does my inexperience. For instance, the description of the park at night in the chapter taking place on 4 September celebrates the greater scope which I felt I now had, but is largely irrelevant. Whenever I finished a chapter I read it through the next day and called that the day's work; I'm surprised I didn't find myself blocked. (In 1973, in my early months of writing fulltime, I would read through however much I'd written of the first draft of the current story each morning before starting work, and took Saturdays and Sundays off. What a one I was for learning from my own mistakes!) Having rewritten the handwritten draft onto the typewriter, I sent the typescript off to Kirby and, I rather think, the uppermost of two carbon copies to the British publisher of *Demons by Daylight*, Piers Dudgeon at the now defunct Star Books. God, was I professional. Piers sold the hardcover rights to Thom Tessier at Millington, and meanwhile Barbara Norville at Bobbs-Merrill bought the American hardcover rights, and I was convinced that my career as a novelist was assured.

I thought so until the Bobbs-Merrill edition appeared, in late 1976. I was in New York for the second World Fantasy Convention, in time to look for copies in the shops, though not to find them. (I still think that if I don't find my books in a bookshop the shop isn't buying them, whereas if I find them that means they can't be selling, though at least finding them gives me a chance for surreptitious improvement of the display.) I needed the encouragement of finding the book on sale in New York. Kirby had been disconcertingly reticent about reviews of it, eventually admitting that there had been one bad review and one mixed. He duly produced the *Publishers Weekly* notice—". . . contrived plot . . . wooden characters . . . purple prose . . . "—and, having to some extent recovered from this, I asked to see the mixed review, only to learn that was it. As for sales, I had to spend a night of jetlag and insomnia and noisy central heating before I ascertained over pre-lunch cocktails with Barbara Norville that they were, as she put it, dreadful. I have never been so grateful to fans, at the convention I duly attended, for making me feel other than worthless.

Nor were the poor thing's tribulations over. A later review by one Bernice Williams Foley in the *Columbus Dispatch* spent three sentences giving away the plot twists (such, admittedly, as they were) before disposing of the novel with the line "Thank goodness, this distasteful manhunt is fiction." Star Books did rather better with it in Britain, however, and Millington even received a request from a bibliographer for a copy so that she could list it in *Books about Dolls and Doll-Making.* Still later the literary editor of *The Times* included it in a list of the silliest titles of 1987, along with (among others) *Get More from Your Deep Fat Fryer, Seaweed: A User's Guide, Taxidermy: The Revival of a Natural Art,* and *The Mental State of Stuart Women*—none of them titles in whose company I would be unhappy to find myself. My title has indeed alienated some people, but I'm as unrepentant about it now as I was before starting the novel, when it seemed the only title for the book.

Despite its flaws and falterings, and despite/because of the title, the book has seldom been out of print, and the prices asked by dealers for a copy of the first edition have become increasingly unnerving—$400 was the most recent I've seen. I confess to a certain indulgent fondness for it, not least since I rewrote the scene of the death of Chris, originally a bathetic episode in which he hopped on a bicycle and immediately fell under a lorry, no doubt one reason why my friend S. T. Joshi, the American critic, declared the novel "very poor". Since Steve's *Danse Macabre* continues to encourage people to seek it out, I don't mind seeing it revived. After all, it did persuade me I could write novels, and I think I'm beginning to learn how to do so.

AFTERWORD TO *THE PARASITE*

ALL PROSE IS TO SOME EXTENT ABOUT HOW THE writer was when it was written, and perhaps that's my excuse for this book. It was a frankly commercial concoction, or at least it tried to be. After the early editions of my first novel sank almost without trace, and my second was declared unpublishable by practically everyone who had published the first, I felt the need to court success. I'd been writing fulltime for nearly four years, but my wife Jenny was the breadwinner, and now she wanted us to have a child. My American agent Kirby McCauley suggested that I might consider writing about characters with whom readers would identify more readily, and sent me some examples of the kind of horror novel that was then popular: *The Exorcist, Audrey Rose,* and a book—called *Suffer the Children,* I think, and if it wasn't it should have been—by John Saul. From these I gathered that the public liked to read about middle-class characters being besieged by some menace for which they were in no way responsible, pretty well exactly the opposite of the kind of fiction I'd been writing since I began to sound like myself. On the other hand, the notion of writing an extravaganza of supernatural terror had appealed to me ever since I'd regretted staying up late by myself to finish reading Richard Matheson's *Hell House,* and it occurred to me that this might be the opportunity to try my hand at one. An early working title, before I conceived the parasitic theme, was—prepare to wince—*The Haunting of Rosabill.*

I suspect it has been apparent to all but the kindest reader that I tried to stuff too much into *The Parasite:* a German interlude for the tourist-minded, lots of cinema lore (much of it of the kind subsequently employed by Theodore Roszak in a better novel, *Flicker*) because I loved the movies, some occult history and related bullshit to attract the Dennis Wheatley brigade, American characters for the Americans. . . . (In the American edition of *The Count of Eleven* I was persuaded to turn a minor character into an American to placate the Yank book trade; readers of the unAmerican version may amuse themselves by guessing which character it was.) I was self-aware enough to have Rose and Bill discuss exactly the kind of commercialism I was espousing, but that hardly compensates for my inability to bring this Frankensteinian patchwork to life as a whole. The early scenes with Rose's parents, for instance, seem to lie there on the page, and some of the episodes involving her premonitions are dispiritingly bathetic. Alas or otherwise, it's too distant now for me to attempt any doctoring.

By the time it saw print I felt I'd edited it quite enough. The version I initially sent to my agents sprawled about for at least another forty thousand words, and my publishers understandably felt that it needed further work. Thom Tessier of Millington and Tim Shackleton of Fontana took me off to lunch, where I disarmed them before they could propose cuts by listing forty thousand words' worth of my own. If I say my cuts included several complete chapters you may gather how sloppily constructed the book was. Soon the book found an American publisher—Macmillan—and a reader there suggested more work. I recall that she objected to the description of skyscrapers as resembling computer cards on the basis that "New Yorkers like to read nice things about New York". My reaction to this was the same as Bill's to being overheard on the phone at the National Film Theatre, and I had as little time for the suggestion that the passages from *Astral Rape* should be severely cut. George Walsh, my editor at Macmillan, advised me to trust my own instincts, and that was how the book had different endings on either side of the Atlantic, but more of that later.

Came publication, and I felt, as one frequently does in those circumstances, that it was my best work to date, and so I was taken aback by some of the reactions it provoked. The first I encountered was during my debut on television, in the now defunct *Book Programme*, hosted by Robert Robinson. The other guests were the psychiatrist Anthony Clare and David Punter, author of *The Literature of Terror* (rather good, but rather less so as it homes in on what was then the present day). Now, as a fan of Robert Robinson's radio show "Stop the Week", I should have been used to the playfully contentious introductions with which he sparked discussion, but I fear I was thrown when he started mourning a golden age of horror fiction which he implied had been betrayed by the current practitioners, whose publishers apparently (though perhaps he was making this up, because I've never encountered it elsewhere) described us as writing "squirm fiction". "Do you write squirm fiction, Ramsey?" Well, er, no, I hope not, stammer, blush, and that's all I remember of my television debut, except that the producer was aggressively disapproving when I mentioned that my wife was recording it for me to watch. Perhaps deep down I realised that Robert Robinson had a point about my book.

Mary Gentle had some in an essay for the British Science Fiction Association's journal *Vector*. Though she begins (perhaps mischievously) "Horror fiction, as a genre, is the hardest to justify as being worthwhile literature", her comments on the book are worth considering. "There are two types of horror fiction written today, the supernatural (which has its roots in fantasy) and the pathological", and she takes *The Parasite* as a paradigm of the latter. "The question of pathology arises when we consider: is the writer using the subconscious or is the subconscious using the writer?" There's no doubt which she thinks is the case with *The Parasite*, but ironically, the problem with the book (even though it may well have reflected my doubts about the imminence of my wife's and my first child) is precisely the reverse. My experience is that I write my best work when the subconscious (which some writer friends of mine would call "the muse") takes over, whereas much of *The Parasite* is the product of a conscious attempt to be as scary and shuddery as possible—so much so that in rereading some passages I wonder how I could ever have presumed to criticise Shaun Hutson for being gratuitously horrific. This intention on my part creates the further problem that since the book insists on showing its horrors entirely from the viewpoint of the victim rather than of anyone less aware of what's happening to her, the tone becomes steadily screechier—very much as in Tobe Hooper's film *The Texas Chainsaw Massacre*, another case of an attempt to push scariness as far as it will go, and beyond.

Well, there it is—*The Parasite.* By now it should be apparent that I like it the least of my novels, and there may be some cynics out there who are wondering why I'm reissuing the bugger at all. Amid the prose which makes me squirm—ah, so *that's* what "squirm fiction" means—there are passages, and occasionally whole scenes, which convey to me at least a hint of the visionary quality which I'd hoped the book might contain, and others where the characters seem to be roused to something like life. Apart from that I can only plead that it's a book I wrote before I knew better, and it would be dishonest of me to pretend I never did. At least it rather surfeited me with trying to be scary and nothing else at novel length.

Mary Gentle argued that the ending was a cop-out. The ending she meant—the one which precedes this afterword—was my final choice. I'd thought the last chapter was weak, and so when the American reader suggested an alternative, I wrote it, too late for it to appear in the British edition published as *To Wake the Dead.* (Mary's suggestion was that I should have let Rose give birth, but—like my original ending—that might have led me towards the kind of book I think it would most bore me to write, a sequel.) While it may have been an improvement, the novel needed many more. Too late now, alas—too many new tales to tell.

AFTERWORD TO *THE NAMELESS*

MOST OF MY NOVELS HAVE TAKEN LONGER TO conceive than to write, and that seems to be all to the good. I suspect that if a book doesn't feel ready to write I'm probably not yet technically equipped to do so. Thus it was four years after I began to develop the basis of *Incarnate* (originally along quite different lines and with a different central theme) that I set about writing the book, and at least five years after I conceived the notion of a haunted film starring Karloff and Lugosi that I began to write *Ancient Images.* Occasionally I've been required to start work on a novel with much less preparation, as I describe in the afterword to *Claw,* and sometimes a theme suggests itself to me so forcefully that the book insists on jumping the queue of novels waiting to be written. So it was with *Obsession,* thanks to Sylvester Stallone, and so it also was with *The Nameless,* which dislodged *Incarnate* (to its considerable benefit) from my writing schedule. After the over-written and too consciously horrific *Parasite* I needed to write something simpler and more restrained in order to improve my craftsmanship.

Not that I was conscious of this at the time: I only knew that *The Nameless* was urging me to write it. Our daughter was less than a year old, but she had planted the seed of the book just by existing (hence the dedication). This genesis could have been a problem, insofar as consciously autobiographical fiction can be fuller of pitfalls than any other kind. One reason why so many second novels are a letdown is that, if autobiographical, its predecessor has used up too much of the author's experience. If I didn't fall into that trap, it was because I had already made the reportorial mistake in short stories (as the late Robert Aickman told me he did in "Just a Song at Twilight"), and indeed kept on doing so even once I should have been aware what was wrong: "The Other House", for instance, was autobiography without perspective and with the merest seasoning of the fantastic, though years earlier I'd discovered (in "Concussion") that to harp on what "really" happened was the least convincing way of writing fiction based on real events or people, that this kind of fiction may require more selection of detail and more imagination than any other. Sometimes a strong theme can bring these qualities with it, and I should say (though a few readers have disagreed) that they are more present here than in *The Parasite.*

Over the years the flaws in the novel—some of them, anyway—have become clearer to me. The opening is something of a mess, which is a pity. I liked the form described by the first six chapters (the flashback which leads up to its starting point, from which the book moves forwards) enough that I used it again in *Obsession,* where its first pages bewildered Tom Monteleone, author of a comic Vietnamese ghost story called, I think, "New Ears". When Kirby McCauley, my American agent, read the typescript of *The Nameless,* however, he suggested that the book was missing a prologue introducing Kaspar Ganz. That made sense to me, especially when I found myself beginning to think in the voice of Santini, the warder. I suppose I should have been self-critical enough to recast the six chapters which followed, and I hope the book survives all this narrative wriggling.

Other flaws are more pervasive. Is there a suggestion that Barbara lost her child by going back to work? It was certainly not my intention, but of course that doesn't mean it isn't there. I find the ghostly husband one ghost too many, and I'm not entirely happy with the Wheatleyish notion of supernatural evil at large. Though perhaps it works as a symbol of the growing tendency to regard one's own moral decisions as someone else's responsibility, I think the view of random violence I presented in "The Depths" may be more useful.

Chapter 22 of *The Nameless* has a different ending in all English-language editions published before 1985. This first version bothered me as being unnecessarily contrived (if hardly as bathetic as the scene in early editions of *The Doll Who Ate His Mother* where the monster hops on a push-bike and immediately gets knocked over by a truck), and when I thought of a development which I found more convincing, I substituted it. Originally Barbara had noticed an old lady reading *Fate* and *Prediction* in the hotel lounge, and after the line "She could watch the faces and pretend she was looking out for Ted" the scene continued as follows:

She hadn't reached the foyer when she turned back. It was a desperately slim chance, but how could she ignore it? She went to the corner of the lounge, where the glow of the table lamp sat on the old lady's lap. "Excuse me," Barbara said, "is that your magazine?"

"No, certainly not."

"Do you happen to know whose it is?"

"I really couldn't tell you." She threw it on the table as if it were an indecent publication she had picked up by mistake. "I assume it belongs to the hotel."

At the counter in the foyer a businessman was questioning every item on his bill, a pear-shaped man with a tankard in one hand was patiently insisting that the key he was holding belonged to this hotel. By the time she was able to speak to one of the girls Barbara felt that the question wasn't worth asking, but she made herself sound forceful. "I wanted to ask about those occult magazines in the lounge."

The girl glanced away quickly as a phone rang. "The manager's spoken to the one who leaves them."

"I wasn't complaining," Barbara said, sensing her defensiveness. "I only wanted some advice."

"Oh, is that it? Then you'll want Fiona. She'll be here in a while." Perhaps she felt her faint amusement might offend Barbara, for she said "I thought you might be like the vicar who stayed here. He said it was wicked to leave such things for folk to read."

Barbara sat near the counter and waited. She was wasting precious time, she had to follow every lead: her thoughts turned back and forth, monotonous as the revolving doors. Old people paced by, fragile as sleepwalkers, and eventually there was Ted. No, she wasn't waiting to complain, she had to speak to the staff who just might be able to help her in her search. When he'd gone upstairs she wished she hadn't treated him as though he was uninvolved, even if that was what he was. No doubt he would worry even more about her now.

Light fluttered like a trapped moth in the revolving doors, faint luminous unconvincing crowds went by beyond the glass, and at last a fat sulky girl in a bulging black uniform joined the girls behind the counter. When the others pointed Barbara out to her, she turned her back on the foyer and busied herself at the pigeonholes. Barbara had to wait at the counter and call "Excuse me" twice before the girl reluctantly approached. "I understand those magazines in the lounge are yours," Barbara said.

"What if they are?"

"Only that I wondered if you knew of any—" Barbara noticed that the other girls were glancing over at them and whispering, and she could see Fiona had noticed them too. "Shall we talk somewhere else?" Barbara suggested.

"I'm all right where I am."

Barbara lowered her voice. "I only wanted to ask if you know of any occult groups here in town."

"What do you want to know that for?"

"Because I believe in such things." She was speaking lower still, in case Fiona's colleagues heard her talking nonsense. "I'm searching for truth."

"I wouldn't know about all that." Fiona peered suspiciously at her. "I don't buy those books. My mother gets them and gives me them when she's done with them."

Barbara was afraid she would burst out laughing at herself, at her waste of an afternoon. She heard Angela saying "I need you" and was no longer in danger of laughing. "I'm sorry to have bothered you," she said.

Perhaps she looked as disappointed as she felt, for Fiona took pity on her. "Well, maybe there's one lot I know of. My mother was telling me about them. They meet down on Broomielaw, under the bridges. I think she said Thursday nights."

That was tonight. Barbara's voice rose inadvertently: it was a lead, there might be people in the group who could help her, who might know of other, more secretive groups. "What do you know about them? What do they call themselves?"

"That's all I know. My mother couldn't find out anything." She turned back to the pigeonholes. "I don't know what they're called."

That didn't matter, it was still a lead. It took Barbara to the occult fringe: what better place to seek information? She was nearly at the stairs when she heard Fiona's colleagues whispering. At once she was hurrying upstairs to tell Ted she must go to the meeting, for one of the girls had said "Maybe they haven't got a name."

I've made one further change which may mean more to some readers than others. The acknowledgements in previous editions included one to Bob Shaw, a Glaswegian science fiction fan rather than my late friend the science fiction writer, with whom the fan apparently enjoyed being confused (one way to make a name for oneself, I suppose). When I was about to visit Glasgow to research settings I contacted the fan for suggestions, and after the novel was published he told me he had sent me on a wild-goose chase. In fact I had followed my own instincts once I was in his city. Inertia has meant that my thanks to him have persisted in reprints of *The Nameless*, but I'm happy to expunge him now. (The word "expunge", I note, derives from the Latin for "prick".)

While *The Nameless*, unlike *The Parasite*, wasn't thought up as a commercial success, I thought it had some breadth of appeal. I was therefore not entirely happy with the British blurb ("As the evil longing surges up inside them, and the knives lie ready... no one can hear the screams"), especially when a few months later I encountered a blurb on another book (by Leigh Nichols, which is to say Dean Koontz) from the same publisher which could pretty well have described the kidnapping-by-cult plot of my novel. I'm quite certain that the similarity was a coincidence, but the Nichols blurb did emphasise what I felt was the drawback of the description of my own book—its one-note quality. (In fairness I should say that it was by no means the worst of its kind that I've suffered.) The notion that seems to be common to many book designers and blurb writers—that all horror novels are about violence, or at best terror, *and nothing else*—is one I've devoted much of my career to trying to combat, with some gradual success. After all, colleagues more talented and subtler than myself have been burdened with worse blurbs.

To sum up this book as I see it I'm tempted to misquote Lovecraft's famous dictum and suggest that if the oldest emotion of mankind is fear, the strongest fear is parental. Certainly being a parent, particularly of a first child, gives one a crash course in neurosis. Whereas Jim Herbert has vowed not to victimise children in his fiction, and regrets having written the scene with the baby in *The Rats,* Steve King and I seem driven to keep imagining the worst. In this context it occurs to me that *Claw* is a kind of companion piece to *The Shining* insofar as while in that novel the reader may be reassured that isolation is one cause of the madness, in my book the possessed parents are surrounded by friends and acquaintances, who either see nothing out of the ordinary or find reasons not to intervene. What a neurotic view of the world, but is it a true one? I also reflect that my daughter will be thirteen years old when the present edition of *The Nameless* sees print. I suspect I may have nightmares.

INTRODUCTION TO *DARK COMPANIONS*

I

TO THE INTERVIEWERS' FAVOURITE QUESTION—why do you write horror stories?—there are many answers, all of them true. Here are some. My most vivid memories of my early childhood are of being frightened: by Hans Andersen and the girl cutting off her feet to rid herself of the dancing red shoes; by the deformed creatures that swarm out of the mine in *The Princess and the Goblin;* by (most unlikely of all) an edition of *The Rupert Annual,* a British children's book, in which a Christmas tree stalks home to its forest one night, creaking away in the dark and leaving a trail of earth through the house. The cinema got to me too: I spent most of Disney's *Snow White* in a state bordering on panic, and then there was the scene (meant as a joke) in Danny Kaye's *Knock on Wood* where a corpse is hung up like a hat and coat on the back of a door. I began to read adult horror fiction when I was six years old, but I'd already known for years that fiction could be terrifying.

So when I began to write stories, they had to be tales of would-be terror. At the age of eleven I had finished a short book of ghost and horror stories, patched together like Frankenstein's monster from fragments of tales I had read. Most writers start by imitating their favourites. Mine, three years later, was H. P. Lovecraft, now that I'd found a complete book of his stories. Lovecraft's style seemed easy to imitate, and so did his monsters. I wrote half a dozen stories in the manner of Lovecraft, with titles such as "The Tower from Yuggoth", and sent them to August Derleth of Arkham House, Lovecraft's American publisher. Derleth liked them enough to tell me how to improve them—by describing fewer things as eldritch and unspeakable and cosmically alien, for a start, and by rereading the ghost stories of M. R. James to learn suggestiveness—and eventually he published a book of them. You can tell I was seventeen when I finished the book—one character thinks nothing of buying a house sight unseen—but all the same, it began my career.

Literary imitation is rather like ventriloquism—trying to say things in someone else's voice—and just about as limited a skill. My next book was a reaction against this, and sometimes so personal as to be wilfully incomprehensible. By now I'd left school and was working in the tax office, where I wrote stories at my desk in the lunch hour, surrounded by bureaucratic activity and ringing phones. No wonder my surroundings began to appear in my stories, and so did my growing obsession with movies and the dying cinemas where I caught up with films of the previous thirty years. Since my first book was an imitation of Lovecraft's horrors, it had been a way of sidestepping my own fears—I sometimes think that is why so many amateur writers imitate Lovecraft today—but now I was beginning to write about them, perhaps because I was gaining enough confidence as a writer to be more honest about myself.

While the supernatural elements in these new tales weren't autobiographical, the feelings were—particularly the descriptions of how it felt to be afraid. During my schooldays I'd often been terrified of going to the Catholic grammar school, where they were fond of using corporal punishment, but now that I was growing up I found that there were many other things to fear: women, and answering the office phone, and talking about myself, and going to parties where I knew almost nobody. . . Well, I needn't go on; most of it is in my stories somewhere. All the same, I'm convinced that good horror stories nourish the imagination, and so I hope these stories do.

I had four years of the tax office, and another seven of public libraries. It wasn't until my second collection was published that I decided to try to write full-time. I was growing bored with irrelevancies: at least everything you do as a writer is relevant to the job—no cramming yourself for examinations (a pet hate of mine) with facts you will never use again, no dressing up and looking servile at interviews. The first couple of years were hard; if my wife hadn't then been working, they would have been impossible. At least writing for a living persuaded me to make myself clearer, and so, I suppose, did reading my stories to audiences—for me, the most enjoyable part of my work. I use many of the stories in this book.

With the exception of "Napier Court", all the way from 1967, the stories here were written since that freelance plunge in July 1973. They can more or less speak for themselves, I hope. The very short stories ("Heading Home", "Out of Copyright", "Calling Card", "Conversion", and "Call First") are the best of a group of tales I wrote as a kind of tribute to the old EC horror comics such as *Tales from the Crypt* and *Vault of Horror*, which in fact I never read until my twenties. Horror and humour have much in common, and it was often difficult to see where the horror comics ended and EC's other comic, *Mad*, began; perhaps these tales of mine are black jokes. "Out of Copyright" is one of my attempts to be clearer, since another acrostic tale of mine ("The Words That Count", where the entire story was an acrostic) left many readers bewildered. "Calling Card" was written (as "First Foot") in response to a commission from the Liverpool *Daily Post* to write a ghost story for Christmas and the New Year, which the newspaper then refused to publish. "Drawing In" probably belongs with these stories, since I was trying to discover if there was still any terror to be had from the best-known (and most domesticated) horror character of all. Many of the stories grew out of their settings; the setting of "Mackintosh Willy" is real, and so is the graffito that gave me the idea for the story; the location of "Above the World" is real, down to the hotel, a favourite of mine; the cinema in "The Show Goes On" was real until they knocked it down—and so on, for almost all the settings. Of course, they may not look quite like that to anyone else but me.

Three of the stories have been given awards. "Mackintosh Willy" tied with Elizabeth Lynn's "Woman Who Loved the Moon" for the

World Fantasy Award in 1980; "The Chimney" took the same award in 1978, again for best short story of the previous year. "In the Bag" was given the British Fantasy Award for best short story in 1978. (The story was published in November 1977. Up to that time the award had been based on the previous calendar year, but after that, for one year only, it was based on the period from July to June. Harlan Ellison®'s "Jeffty Is Five" became eligible for a second time, and this time it won, all of which has caused some confusion in reference books.) All three stories are about childhood in some way; make of that what you will—perhaps that I often return to the theme that deep down, we are all still as vulnerable as we were in childhood; sometimes it takes very little to break through our defences. It's a disturbing thought, but then I believe that horror fiction cannot be too frightening or too disturbing. Too much of it seeks to reassure, often by reinforcing prejudices.

And that's as good a way to end as any. Now you're alone with the stories and yourself.

II

That was how I introduced the first edition back in 1982. For the recent Samhain reprint I had this to say:

This was my fourth collection to see print, and the first not to appear through the eldritch portals of Arkham House. After imitating Lovecraft in *The Inhabitant of the Lake* I'd spent five years developing my own approach, which was loosed upon the world at book length in *Demons by Daylight. The Height of the Scream* was more experimental, too often wilfully so, and less sure of itself. I'd say *Dark Companions* leaves those problems behind. Only the title was a compromise: I'd meant to call it *Just Behind You* until I learned that my old friend Manly Wade Wellman had that in mind for a book of his own. In fact he never used the title, and so I did just a couple of years back.

Let me reminisce as best I can about these tales, written by the long-haired genial freak who appears in a zippered suede shirt on the back flap of the first edition. I'll go at them in the order they appear herein. "Mackintosh Willy" was written in 1977—to be precise, the first draft was begun on 22 August and completed six days later. In those days I kept a diary in a ledger and recorded the progress of my first drafts, though not of the rewriting. As for the story behind the story, there isn't much to tell. For several years Jenny and I did indeed live across West Derby Road from Newsham Park, where I often took a hashish-eater's stroll. One day I misread the graffiti in a shelter as the narrator does, and noticed footprints set in new concrete around the nearby pond. This was all my imagination needed. Alas, when I took J. K. Potter on a tour of my locations years later, the shelter had been demolished. The tale brought me a World Fantasy Award in the short story category, which I shared with Elizabeth Lynn, and we hugged onstage in Baltimore.

"Napier Court" was the last tale I wrote in 1967, in the midst of the *Demons by Daylight* bunch. Like several of those stories, it was a radical rewrite of a first draft. The 1965 version had a male protagonist laid up in bed, but Alma Napier is based on my solitary ex-fiancée, from whom I'd parted several months before writing this version. Along with "Concussion" it's among my most nakedly autobiographical tales. Before August Derleth bough it I sent a copy to Kirby McCauley, then a friend and later also my agent. Kirby showed the typescript to J. Vernon Shea, who commented that if I was like Peter in the tale I couldn't be much of a catch. Indeed, and I knew it, which was why I tried to depict myself as honestly as possible: perhaps it was a means of outgrowing that personality as well. Basing the tale on my experience was also certainly a way of bringing it to life.

I've a confession to make about "Down There". It was begun on 9 September 1978, less than three weeks after our daughter's birth. Indeed, four days after she was born I set about writing another tale, "This Time", completed a week later. I may have been afraid that the change in my life might hinder my writing, but was this really an excuse to devote so much time to proving the reverse? The first draft of "Down There" took seven days and is described in the diary as "laboured"—serve me right, you may think. As I often do, I reassured myself that it could be rewritten, and so it was. It certainly needed it, which I can demonstrate with the opening of the first draft:

"Hurry along there," Steve called as the girls trooped down the office. "Last one tonight. Mind the doors."

The girls smiled at Elaine as they passed her desk, but their smiles meant different things: just like you to make things more difficult for the rest of us, looks like you've been kept in after school, suppose you've nothing better to do, fancy having to put up with him by yourself. She didn't give a damn what they thought of her, which was part of what irked them, and she was quite content to be alone with Steve—if only he wouldn't make a joke of everything.

Even the lifts, one of which had sunk to the sub-basement every time it was called today. Presumably the sub-basement was no longer so disgusting, but Elaine was glad she hadn't had to go down there, even momentarily. Glancing back through the window that sealed her off from the lobby, she saw that the lift was out of order now. Its twin was stuffing people into itself, closing its doors whether or not they were ready, leaving the girls behind. They loitered near the other lift as though by pretending not to notice it they might persuade it to relent. When one of them caught her eye, Elaine looked away. She wasn't about to let them think she was envying them.

There was nothing to envy, especially when they would have to face the November night, the downpour. Around the office building the warehouses looked like melting chocolate; the river and the canals were opaque with tangled ripples that almost extinguished the reflections of streetlamps. Cottages and terraces, some of them derelict, crowded up the steep hills towards the disused mines. Through the skeins of water on the glass their infrequent lights looked shaky as the flames of candles.

"Goodnight comrade," Steve said like the title of a song as Mr Williams went by, and Elaine had to stifle a grin. Mr Williams had tried to dissuade Elaine from working tonight, from being exploited as he'd called it, long after the rest of them had desisted. It was all very well for him: his father wasn't an invalid, he earned enough to keep his parents without working overtime. He had only annoyed her by harping on the things that were wrong with the place: she had to work overtime—how could it help to remember what might go wrong?

Still, he'd given up finally [unlike this turgid prose, its greying author grumbles], and she was alone on the sixth floor with Steve—alone in the otherwise untenanted building except for the caretaker, wherever he was. Ranks of cabinets like bookcases divided the long room down the middle; they were stuffed with blue Inland Revenue files. Beneath a fluttering fluorescent tube protruding files drowsed, jerked awake [much like the author as he transcribes this]. Smells of dust and old paper drifted about the room, which was growing oppressively hot. Through the steamy window above an unquenchable radiator, Elaine could just make out the frame where the top section of the fire escape should be.

"There goes our Red," Steve remarked. "Into somebody's bed rather than under it, from what I hear." She smiled a little timidly across the stretch of desks at him and lit a cigarette for confidence. Being alone with Steve and his risqué joke made her feel queasy and nervous, an odd sensation like the start of an adventure, but at least the length of the office separated them. She began to compare a tax return with last year's.

"You can understand these union men, especially round here," Steve said. Perhaps he'd taken her shyness for disagreement. "The trouble is, it's never the employers they hurt most, always the public" [or the long-suffering reader who has to trudge through this mire of dialogue].

He reminded her of her father: fair, but not too fair. Was Mr Williams a genuine Red? [Was their author a genuine bore?] Certainly he'd opposed the move to the building long after the rest of the union had accepted it, very temporarily. Of course his father had lost his job when the mines were shut down, but need that mean employers were always wrong?

Steve was gazing at her, blank-faced again. "Are you feeling exploited again?"

Mr Williams had called her the employers' weapon against solidarity. "No, certainly not." She wished Steve would let her be quiet for a while; she would chat when she felt more at ease. "I'm feeling hot," she said.

"Yes, it is a bit much." He stood up, mopping his forehead theatrically. "I'll go and sort out Mr Tuttle," he said. "Maybe he can do something about this bloody awful first draft we're stuck in . . ."

Well, you get the idea, probably more than you want. For the record, the story came to me when the light failed in the lift at Radio Merseyside, where I then worked as a film reviewer.

"Heading Home" was written on 14 January 1974 and, I suspect, little altered in the rewrite. It was the fourth of six such tales I wrote that month, having heard from Kirby McCauley that Marvel Comics planned to resurrect horror comics, short filler stories and all. They needed tales about 1800 words long on traditional themes, and the idea seems to have fired up my imagination. Marvel would abort the proposition, but my offerings all found good homes. Later "Heading Home" was reprinted in *Read*, a classroom magazine aimed at grades 6 to 10. Among the suggestions for classroom work was this one, apparently provided by a Junior High School Middle School Assembly: "Presumably, the narrator will have his head back on, but it will be held in place only by the regrown nerves and the thread. That's pretty wobbly. Continue the story, telling what happens next." And they call us horror writers warped!

"The Proxy" started life as "The Bed beyond the Window" on 28 April 1977 but adopted the present title on the first of May, and was finished one day later. I hope it doesn't show senility is creeping up on me because I've absolutely no idea where the idea for the story came from. David Lloyd adapted it with style for the *A1* comic.

I spent a couple of days researching the locations of "The Depths" (though the diary suggests it was "an excuse for a day off, really.") Certainly I met our old friends Stan and Marge Nuttall, veterans of the Liverpool Science Fiction Group, for a drink in the Crown. Marge is heard to sing on the first page that she's glad she's Bugs Bunny, which she had already done in *The Face That Must Die*. This wasn't a lapse of memory on my part; I'd simply despaired of seeing that book published, given the responses of various editors to its oppressive grimness. I plunged into "The Depths" on 28 July 1978 and surfaced from the first draft on the sixth of August. Again, I can't trace the idea to its source, which may be somewhere in my many notebooks and a quest for someone else to make. I once claimed that the tale was written out of dissatisfaction with my handling of a similar theme in *The Nameless*, but "The Depths" precedes that novel by a year—so much for the chronology in my cranium. I don't think horror fiction has to be a holiday from morality, as Angela Carter once declared it was, and perhaps that's why I keep writing about scapegoats and the rejection of responsibility.

In early July 1977 we had a contingent from Carolina to stay in our little house in Tuebrook—the Wellmans and the Wagners (Karl and Barbara), I believe, and David Drake. I had "Out of Copyright" in mind and asked Dave for a likely Latin phrase, which I used in the tale. When he got back to Chapel Hill he airmailed me his revised thoughts, but too late—I'd written "Out of Copyright" in three days, starting on 10 July. His off-the-cuff response still seems fine to me, but don't blame Dave for my use of it.

"The Invocation" owes its inspiration to *The Godfather*. Perhaps it was party because I knew of Coppola's roots in horror (specifically the film he made for Roger Corman, *Dementia 13*, which was hacked to bits by the British censor at the time) that I thought the Hollywood mogul would find worse than a horse's head when he peeled back the sheets. What I anticipated happens to Ted in my tale. I saw the film at its first Liverpool showing in August 1972, but didn't start the story until 5 September 1975, completing it on the 12th. When the story was reprinted in *Dark Voices 2*, a copy-editor presumably assuming ignorance on my part changed Mrs Dame's citation of *Finian's Wake* to *Finnegan's Wake*. Sometimes I'm tempted to provide footnotes to make absolutely certain I can't be misunderstood, like so*.

"The Little Voice" was apparently to be called "The Playmate" when I made notes for it in early April 1976. I set about writing it on the 30th and finished it on 9 May. Where did it come from? I have no idea—perhaps just a train of thought that made me scribble notes. By now I carried notebooks with me everywhere I went, though previously I'd made life harder for myself by writing notes in the diary ledger. Charlie Grant bought "The Little Voice" for his *Shadows* anthology series but suggested I should prune it a

* (joke)

little. I believe I rid it of about two thousand words, and that's the published version.

"Drawing In" was written over the last three days of May 1977. At a guess the idea came out of cracks in the walls of our Tuebrook house, waving its spindly legs as it emerged. I don't mean I actually saw this happen, despite having taken several acid trips in the preceding couple of years. Strangely enough, I'd dreamed in August 1973 of dropping acid, a year before I ever did. That diary entry records a "genuine sense of growing intensity and muted panic" and notes "powerful images which I constructed in the dream and which remained: a silent avalanche of clouds; walking between amber buildings like banks of sand at sunset". Incidentally, elsewhere I've said that "Through the Walls" was written as a kind of preamble to venturing on my first trip, but in fact it was written just a few days after that experience.

A trip I took in the Cotswolds in May 1975 gave me the seeds of "The Pattern", and so did my impression some days later of the Freshfield coast near Liverpool, which may have echoed the trip. The diary entry describes "green symmetry everywhere, the more complex the more minutely you look: glimpses of larger mandalas" and "a sense that there may be an enormous pattern (only one? or many?)" The next day (the last of May) saw the start of the tale, completed on 6 June. Halfway through I changed the title from "The Screamer". In retrospect I think that the lyricism of the story had to give way to or at least include horror because otherwise its pattern would have struck me as incomplete. In any case lyricism needn't be inimical to horror: see the work of Poppy Z. Brite or Caitlín Kiernan, for instance, or Robert Dunbar.

"The Show Goes On" started out as "The Usher" on 24 May 1978. By the 27th it had the title it bears now, and the next day it was done. The cinema was based on the Hippodrome in Liverpool, converted from a variety theatre (the Royal Hippodrome) in 1929. A maze of dressing-rooms survived behind the cinema screen, and one night I got lost among them while searching for an exit. Eventually I came to a pair of double doors, and as I made to push them apart I seemed to glimpse a large dim room beyond, full of figures that rose or tottered to their feet to await me. Perhaps they were homeless, but the light reminded me of waking from a nightmare in an ill-lit childhood bedroom, and I made haste to find another way out. Need anyone ask why I write as I do?

"The Puppets" returns to the failed relationship that's at the heart of "Napier Court". One crucial disagreement with Rosemary (the real girl) was over horror fiction, which she didn't care for, not least mine. Dentistry represents or at least is substituted for it in this tale, and the village pageant is an objective correlative for a spectacle Rosemary coaxed out of me, perhaps because she thought it was remote from horror. At a performance in Hoylake of Debussy's *Prélude de l'Après-Midi d'un Faune* she was one of the orchestral flautists (not the soloist) and persuaded me to read Mallarmé's poem as a preamble, in French and then in English, to the hapless audience. When at last I'd struggled through the original in an accent worthy of Inspector Clouseau I looked up to see the mayor of Hoylake on the front row, clutching his head in his hands. Afterwards, having fortified himself with at least one glass of wine, he described my performance as a tour de force. His accent was better than mine had been. Still, I don't waste material if I can avoid doing so, and a decade later the memory was nothing but fun. According to my diary the writing of the tale (then known as "Curtain Call") was pretty hesitant, stretching from 29 June 1978 to 8 July. On one day, admittedly with a hangover, I wrote just a single paragraph.

I started "Calling Card" on 24 November 1978 and completed it two days later. At that stage it was called "First Foot", a reference to a common New Year's Eve tradition in Britain. It was written in response to a request from the local newspaper for a two-thousand-word ghost story set on Merseyside during the festive season. Alas, the commissioning editor found it too gruesome—presumably he didn't know the kind of thing I wrote. Lin Carter was made of sterner stuff and bought it for *Weird Tales*, but told me on the train from New York to a World Fantasy Convention in Providence that the title wouldn't mean much to his audience. A few minutes later I gave him the title it bears now. Alas, the anthology series died before he could use it, but by a splendid irony a new editor at the local paper asked me for a Christmas tale five years after the original request, and this time the paper published the tale with no changes (except for entitling it "The Calling Card").

Even more than "The Pattern", "Above the World" owes much to LSD, especially once the tale climbs to the heights—specifically, the last acid trip I ever took (in July 1976, up Bleaberry Fell near Keswick) before a nightmare flashback some months later put me off the drug. The following June I researched Knox's ascent to the Bishop of Barf, and the story was written in three days, starting on 18 July. Alas, the Swan Hotel has been turned into apartments. A nearby hotel that closed recently was called Barf House. I wonder if some folk may have found the name ominous, and perhaps a question on the hotel's web site—"Why Barf?"—didn't help.

"Baby" began on 29 November 1974 and drew to a close on 4 December, which is pretty well all I know. The entry for the 25th notes "some rather nightmarish pram images" but doesn't specify them—I'm guessing that an everyday sight set them off in my head, as frequently happens. I suspect it may have been the swollen faceless plastic head.

I recall even less about the genesis of "In the Bag". The ledger shows only that the first draft was begun on 20 November 1974 and completed two days later. No doubt the sense of random unreasonable severity came from my schooldays, though the headmaster isn't based on anyone specific. "Conversion" was written on 18 January 1974, but the other EC tale—"Call First"—took all of two days, starting on the 8th. In both cases, as with "Heading Home", I wrote copious notes at speed and incorporated nearly all of them.

I find this as hard to believe as anybody would, but when I wrote "The Chimney" I didn't know it was autobiographical. It was conceived on Christmas Day 1972, after Jenny and I had watched that splendid tale of television terror *The Stone Tape*. "Child afraid of Santa Claus—Perhaps from a very early age has associated horror with the large fireplace in his bedroom? His parents tell him of Santa Claus—But when they tell him the truth about SC, the horror comes flooding back—And something's always moving in there towards Christmas—He sees it emerge each year: but this year he sees it in more detail . . ." I got as far as the charred apparition but not, at this stage, its real identity (which, as David Drake pointed out, it has in common with L. P. Hartley's "Someone in the Lift", a tale I'd read back in the early fifties). Often my ideas lie low for years, and I didn't start "The Chimney" until 20 June

1975, finishing it on the 27th. Only when I read the tale aloud at Jack Sullivan's apartment on the Upper West Side years later did I remember how terrified I'd been on most Christmas Days of my childhood—not by Santa Claus but by having to go upstairs and knock on a bedroom door to invite my unseen father down for dinner. That he stayed unseen, then and for nearly all my childhood and early adulthood, only added to my dread.

And so to "The Companion", which took years to get itself together. On 30 June 1969 I had an idea about the derelict fairground in New Brighton. At this stage the protagonist is "a young girl, frightened of people generally". The place seems to be partly operative, with "white faces like papier-mâché at some pay windows". Two years later I had thoughts about a ghost train in a fairground, but they weren't incorporated—maybe, having rediscovered them in the process of writing this afterword, I may develop them. Then on 13 September 1973 there's a page of notes for "The Companion", including a version of the final line and thoughts for an unused encounter with a fortune-teller. The 14th sees most of the ideas for Stone's last ride, and the next few days gather more material, but I have to conclude I was writing the story by then. Certainly once Stone heads for the abandoned fairground I finished the tale in a single session.

If I had the time I'd rewrite much of my old stuff, and "The Companion" is a case where I like some of it (the second half) enough to wish the rest were better. Well, my time is limited, and I'd rather work on something new—perhaps I'll write that ghost train tale from forty years ago. In any case, some people have liked the story—Steve King declared it a favourite, and more recently Jeremy Dyson did. Jeremy and I gave a public reading in Liverpool last month, and "The Companion" seemed to go down pretty well with the audience. Maybe there's life in these old tales yet, and even in this old writer. I'm happy to see *Dark Companions* rise from its grave.

AFTERWORD TO *THE CLAW*

THIS BOOK WAS ORIGINALLY PUBLISHED UNDER A pseudonym, and I'm frequently asked why. Not to fool anyone, let me say at once. In 1981 I had sold both *The Nameless* and *Dark Companions* to my American publisher, and it seemed reasonable to give him time to bring these out before I wrote another book for him. I discussed this with my British agent, Carol Smith, rather expecting her to have me commissioned to contribute to the Nightshade series of Gothic romances she was then editing for Fontana, my British publisher at the time (a series which included fine work by Rosalind Ashe and in particular by Thom Tessier—his remarkably dark *Shockwaves,* a precursor of his even bleaker later books). Instead Carol negotiated with a different publisher what sounded like a better deal, under which my pseudonymous novel would be promoted as the first work of a new British horror star. More of that later, believe me, if you're wondering why you never heard of him.

My original choice of pseudonym was Jack Ramsay, until I discovered that someone of that name had written a book called *The Rage.* (Indeed, in some editions of *How to Write Tales of Horror, Fantasy and Science Fiction* the editor, J. N. Williamson, describes me as "the author of such unforgettable novels as *The Rage,*" in which case I must have forgotten writing it.) I settled on Jay Ramsay instead, which appealed to me as making the authorship obvious to anyone who knew my work; my first book and some other early stories had been published under the byline of J. Ramsey Campbell, though Gollancz preferred to reduce me (on the jacket of *Travellers by Night*) to J. R. Campbell. Years after this novel had been published I learned there was already a Jay Ramsay too, the poet responsible for such books as *Psychic Poetry* and *Raw Spiritual* (the latter illustrated with photographs by Carol Bruce, who sees them as "a reflection of her own inner process, through which her relationship with the Earth is manifested"). I became aware of the other Ramsay when someone brought me his books to sign, but of course I declined, though I wouldn't have minded taking the credit for some of the imagery—"Face", for instance, is a poem about a human face found, possibly alive, on a pole near the sea. Whether the real Jay has ever been asked to sign anything of mine I have no idea.

However, I'm getting ahead of myself. Carol Smith and the commissioning editor suggested that the book should be about a child in peril—a theme less common then than since—and Carol thought cannibalism ought to be involved. With these germs in my brain I went away to Mundesley in Norfolk for two weeks' holiday with my wife and our three-year-old daughter. I spent the mornings in trying to plot the book and was even more difficult to live with than usual. Mundesley, I need hardly say, is the English setting in all but name. Home again with the central idea of the Leopard Men, I began to research Nigerian settings, helped by friends at Millington, my first British hardcover publishers (in particular Phil Edwards and Thom Tessier). I disliked writing about places I had never visited—it was a mistake that had dogged me since my first book—but I couldn't afford the trip to Africa. After a couple of months or so I felt comfortable enough with the plot to let Carol know I was ready to start work, and I was invited down to London to meet my editor.

One of the joys of publishing is lunch. Many are the happy hours I've spent in restaurants with editors. Perhaps I should have felt uneasy about my perceived status on discovering that this editor was offering not lunch but a coffee in her office, but I was too thrown by being asked to tell her the story of the book from beginning to end. Writers are vulnerable creatures, prone to allow demands to be made on them which they're entitled to resist much earlier in their careers than most of them believe, and so—despite having been published for almost twenty years—I gave in to this ill-conceived request. I should have known better, but so should my editor. Nothing is more likely to rob a book of energy than telling the story before it's written, and I advise any of my readers who are writers to refuse any such proposal point-blank.

The editor enthused about the story, and asked me to write her a detailed synopsis, which I did. These days my publishers encourage me to depart from any prior synopsis (which in any case will be sketchy and terse) if the book wants to, but in 1981, having signed a contract, I felt bound to stay as close as possible to what I had said I would write. The process took about nine months, as I recall. I delivered the typescript to Carol, who liked the book, and then there was a prolonged silence until I gathered the courage to phone the editor. Was she happy with the novel? I asked. Well, no, actually, which was why she hadn't been in touch. She found too much of it menacing: both of Anna's parents rather than just one, the overall atmosphere, even the sea and the beach.

This relentlessness was hardly untypical of my work up to that point, and one might have expected her to know that in advance. When I protested that I'd written almost exactly the story I'd told her and synopsised, she informed me that she needed to see the novel written before she could identify what was wrong with it. Oh. I agreed to rewrite the book as substantially as I felt it needed, not least because I'd noticed some glaring flaws which escaped her until I pointed them out. Worst of all (if you can imagine this, having read the final version), I'd managed to write the entire first draft without a single scene from Anna's viewpoint. I also junked an entire sub-plot involving British black magicians who want the claw for their own use and who, having failed to kill Isaac and Alan in Nigeria, befriend Liz in Alan's absence. While this was to some extent intended to counteract any racism implicit in the story, it was clear to me in retrospect that I'd fallen back on a theme I had already dealt with in *The Parasite* and *The Nameless.* It also distracted attention from the central theme which the book had begun to develop, that everyday domestic savagery can be blacker and more dangerous than any magic. I must say that the scenes involving the

British cultists look to me now like a conscious bid on my part for bestsellerdom. Here's an encounter with them, which immediately follows chapter 32. I've resisted all impulses (pretty strong, I can tell you) to touch up the style of the original typescript.

> They looked out of place, the two men in raincoats. Under the downpour and the giant trees their umbrellas looked pathetic. They might have been two businessmen who had taken the wrong road. The smaller man wore steel-rimmed spectacles which he had to keep wiping, the other had a greying beard which hid his mouth completely. Even when Alan saw that the bespectacled man was toying with a heavy knife, something like a machete, it seemed more incongruous than sinister. He might have been expecting to hack his way through the jungle like a Rider Haggard character.
>
> They might be police, whatever they looked like. As Alan and Isaac approached, Isaac drawing himself up almost imperceptibly, the two men turned toward them. "What is your business in this territory?" the bearded man said.
>
> "We're on a field trip from the University of Lagos," Isaac said.
>
> The bearded man ignored him; he might not have spoken. "You," he said to Alan.
>
> Alan thought it best to hold to his original story. "I'm from the Foundation for African Studies in London. As my colleague says—"
>
> "I don't see any colleague." The bespectacled man's accent was impossible to place, like his companion's. "Just a nigger," he said.
>
> Alan managed to keep his voice steady. "As my colleague says, we're researching the forest tribes."
>
> "Forest tribes?" The bearded man seemed amused. "You speak all their languages?"
>
> "My colleague is the interpreter."
>
> "That makes sense," the bespectacled man said, grinning fiercely and wiping his spectacles on his collar. "Hire a bush man to talk to niggers."
>
> There were few worse insults you could offer a Yoruba than

to call him a bush man, but Isaac neither moved nor spoke. The bearded man seemed impatient with his companion. "Which tribes have you visited?" he said.

Alan's limbs felt cramped, desperate to move. He was sweating profusely, as far as he could distinguish that from the rain. "Just the one you saw us coming from, so far."

"And what did you learn from them?"

What could Alan say? He'd brought this on himself, he'd talked himself into a corner. The bearded man was shaking his head sadly. "You have no camera and no recorder, yet you say you were here to study the tribes. You can't really expect us to believe that, can you?"

Alan lost his temper. "Who wants to know?"

The bespectacled man tossed the knife into the jeep and in the same movement reached into his coat. He looked delighted. The next moment, the barrel of a gun was pointing at Alan's chest. "This does," the bespectacled man said.

Alan's buttocks clenched. For a moment he was afraid that he wouldn't be able to control his bowels. Then his whole body grew prickly with rage, not least because he didn't dare to speak. If he had kept his temper, perhaps it wouldn't have come to this.

The bearded man looked faintly distressed by the show of force. All the same, he unbuttoned his own raincoat so that the gun tucked into his belt was visible. "I think we had better separate them," he said to his companion, and to Isaac: "Come with me."

When Isaac hesitated, the bearded man pulled out his gun and prodded him across the road, into the forest. Lightning flashed, trees reared up around them, gleaming like metal. Alan was cursing himself silently: if he hadn't talked back, Isaac might not have been led away. What might be done to Isaac now?

Alan turned to the bespectacled man, despite the threat of the gun. The round black mouth looked enormous and deadly. "Who are you?" he demanded. "You're not the police."

"You'll find out." The man raised the gun toward Alan's face, a warning while he cleaned his spectacles.

There was nothing Alan could do except hope that whatever was going to happen would not be as bad as he feared. He'd never fought a grown man, let alone a gunman; what use were a few childhood victories in the schoolyard? He turned to watch Isaac and his captor. At least that meant he didn't see the gun that was pointed at him.

Lightning shook the forest, lit up rain as it dripped from the foliage; the forest screamed. Isaac was in the forest now, but he seemed to be walking too slowly for his captor, who prodded him forward with the gun. "Go on," the bearded man said; Alan could just hear him. "You brought this on yourself. You should have taken notice of what we did in Port Harcourt. That's what happens to blacks who see and talk too much."

That seemed to freeze everything, more violently than the lightning. For an endless moment Alan couldn't even hear the rain. Isaac had halted, shoulders hunching up around his neck. Alan's captor stepped forward, jamming his spectacles back onto his face, poking the gun into Alan's right side, below his ribs. "Now you know," he muttered.

The next moment, Isaac twisted round and knocked the gun out of the bearded man's hand. At once he was running, slithering on the drenched undergrowth, dodging between the trees. The bespectacled man pushed Alan away—Alan was dismayed to learn how strong he was—and aimed his gun at Isaac. Just as he pulled the trigger Alan rushed him, clutching at his right arm, for the gun.

The shot went wild. The two of them fell struggling at the edge of the rough road, the bespectacled man underneath. Alan felt the impact through the other man's body. The gun was jarred out of the man's hand, skittered a few feet across the stony surface. His spectacles flew off and smashed.

Alan held him down as he stood up himself, then he let go in order to lunge for the gun. That was his mistake. Though the other was blinking rapidly, from rain or shock or blindness, he was by no means disabled. As Alan pushed himself away from him, the man kicked out at his groin.

The kick fell short, but only just. Alan staggered back against the jeep. His thigh felt as if it had been torn open. For the moment he could only cling to the jeep and wonder if he was going to vomit for the second time that day.

The man clambered to his feet, glaring at Alan to make sure he was incapable of intervening. So he could still see that far. His eyes were bright, fanatical, more dangerous than the tribesmen and their chief had seemed. He was something to do with the influence that had driven Alan out of his home, away from his family: so much was clear from the bearded man's words. He was a visible enemy, something solid at last to attack. As he turned from Alan and made for the gun in the road, Alan heaved himself desperately along the side of the jeep, though his leg was blazing with pain. The man was stooping for the gun when Alan flung the heavy knife.

His aim was poor. He'd meant to strike the man's body, even his head—anything that would put him out of the running. Instead, the blade chopped into the man's wrist just as he reached the gun, and sliced the flesh from the back of his hand. Blood poured down his wrist, over the exposed tendons of the hand.

The man was screaming, digging the fingers of his other hand into his injured wrist. When he bent toward the road, Alan thought he was collapsing. It took him a moment to realise that the man was still determined to pick up the gun. Alan hobbled toward him, as fast as he could—not fast enough. The man's injured hand closed on the gun. Alan could see the raw tendons working.

Surely he could wrest the gun from that hand. In any case, surely it wouldn't be capable of aiming the gun at him. But the man was holding the gun with both hands and lifting it toward him. Alan flung himself aside, toward the knife. In one movement he had grabbed it, lurched upright and brought the blade down with all his force.

Even now he missed his aim. His bruised thigh made him stumble. He felt the knife chop home, like a cleaver into meat, before he saw what it had done. It had hacked off the right side of the man's face; the cheek, the ear and part of the scalp. His skinned hand was reaching up toward his face, afraid to touch, to find out what had been done to him. Alan could only stare appalled at his handiwork, his stomach churning.

The man was losing his balance, tilting onto his uninjured side, but it took him a long time to fall. He lay on the stony road, the ruin of his face turned up to Alan. Through the gaping hole in his cheek, Alan could see his tongue squirming. His eye stared up accusingly, stared and blinked. At last it stopped blinking, even though rain was splashing on his eye-ball.

As soon as the eye died, Alan ceased feeling appalled. The man was just a piece of meat now. He was surprised, and dizzily exhilarated, how little he was shocked by his own actions. . . .

The bearded man escapes, returning in chapter 39, where he kills Isaac. Alan kills him, and then the Leopard Man seizes Alan.

As he staggered against the trees, borne backward by the leap of the figure that was clinging to him, the nails clawed at his neck, reaching for his jugular. The dried-up wizened face was panting into his. Its skin looked like a mummy's, leathery and ancient; its breath stank of stale blood. Though the head was so small, the mouth with its pointed brownish teeth looked far too large for the head.

He managed to force his clasped hands up between its wrists, dislodging its claws from his throat, and at the same time drove his knee into its groin. It convulsed and fell to its knees. He stepped back out of reach at once. He was dismayed by its strength; it didn't behave like an old man at all—was that the effect of its food? Perhaps it had attacked him because it knew what he meant to do. He made himself step forward, drawing back one foot. He had no other weapon, and he had to finish it off.

He hadn't reached it when it came scrabbling at him on all fours, limbs stretched out like a spider's. He should have known it was swift by the way it had crept up on him. Before he could kick out or retreat, it seized him, grabbing his ankles and swarming up him, wrapping its limbs around his legs. He felt its bones scraping over his.

He couldn't move his legs. As he struggled, desperate to free himself from the thing that was grinning mirthlessly up at him, enormous mouth and shrunken eyes, he lost his balance. He clutched at the nearest tree, but couldn't reach. He fell backward, arms flailing, and the ground thumped all the air out of him. The spidery man was on top of him. Before he could draw breath it was crouching on his chest, fleshless knees digging into his ribs, claws reaching for his throat.

He managed to seize its scrawny wrists, but he couldn't force it backward, nor could he raise himself. However ancient it looked, it was as strong as he was. Its long stained nails were clawing the air inches from his throat, his wrists were trembling with the effort of holding it off—and then it ducked its head toward him, toward his right eye. Its great mouth opened, its teeth closed in him. It raised its head again, tearing away part of his face.

For a moment he thought it had taken his eye. It had ripped away some of his cheek, just below the socket. His cheek felt as though a red-hot coal was burning deeper, deeper, into his flesh. He blacked out momentarily, unable to believe what had been done to him. In that instant he lost his hold on its wrists. The long nails went straight for his throat.

He'd dug his chin into his chest before he was aware that he had done so. At least his reflexes were with him. The nails were scratching at the flesh that bulged out from under his chin; the skinned flesh began to blaze. His own blood was spilling down his cheek, into his mouth. That maddened him, made him equal to his attacker. He darted his hands at its eyes, to gouge them out.

The lids closed tight at once. He could feel the eyes moving behind them, out of reach. He clawed at the lids to try to prise them open, he dug his thumbs into their corners, but it was no use. The long nails were ripping away flesh from beneath his chin, demoralising him. He grabbed the hands, in a last desperate bid to snap the fingers, but they wouldn't bend back, they wouldn't leave his flesh for a moment. When something gave, at first he didn't know what it was. He'd torn out one of his attacker's fingernails.

The fleshless creature made no sound. The loss of a nail seemed not to have troubled it at all. Perhaps that was the

> worst—the silent single-minded concentration of its attack, more bestial than any animal's. The nails were still clawing at Alan, clawing until he had to raise his head and let it reach his throat. Its mouth lowered toward his face again, to tear.
>
> His head snapped forward instinctively. Civilisation had taught him some responses. He butted the dried-up head under the chin, just as it came down at him. He felt something break inside the face, and his attacker turned away, shaking its head like an injured animal, dark blood dribbling from its mouth—its own blood and Alan's. For a moment it was taken off guard, and Alan was able to heave it away from him and stagger to his feet.
>
> It came for him at once, heedless of its injured finger, determined to savage him with whatever was left of its teeth and jaws. Even when he kicked it in the face, it kept coming. The third kick flung it onto its back, and then he brought down his heel with all his force on its chest, on its heart. He felt ribs splinter. He kept grinding his heel deeper, as he might have on an insect, until the limbs stopped twitching, the eyes dimmed like ash.

The problem with all this is less its unsatisfactoriness as action than the level of violence, which seemed to leave me no choice other than to continue its escalation. (I wrote myself into a similar trap by using a single viewpoint in *The Parasite.*) So Liz's friend Barbara, to whom Liz has sent a letter in this version, turns up only to be murdered, and then Isobel is, by the cultists who have befriended Liz at the hotel. In a disastrously literal re-enactment of the Leopard Man ritual, both Liz and Alan join in chasing Anna along the beach until her parents have a last-minute change of heart and the book falls back on splatter:

> Both Liz and Anna screamed as the claw bit deep into flesh and tore onward. Then Anna was free, and wavering desperately between the men and her mother. Mark stood behind her, his arms waving limply and aimlessly, his mouth wide with shock—too wide. The claw had torn away most of his lower lip, which hung over his chin like an extra tongue. . . .

> Alan tore open Norman's hand with the claw. Liz saw the metal points catch among the tendons, wrenching them half out of the wound before the claw jerked free. . . .
>
> She saw Norman groping his way out of the murk. What was wrong with his eyes? They looked even more like the eyes of a mask. Suddenly, appallingly, Liz realised they were flat, deflated—punctured. . . .
>
> As Norman stumbled into the midst of the carnage, David dragged him off his feet and tore at his raw throat with his teeth, ripping loose a chunk of flesh. Blood sprayed over Frank, and the scrawny figure leapt on him, biting and scratching. . . .

And so, it seems almost interminably, on. I suppose I was trying to compensate for having lost my grasp of the characters, because the scene stumbles to its end with the following speech from Alan: "Anna, I don't know if you'll understand this. I expect you must feel you can't trust me or your mother any more. But do you understand that we were made to do these things? It was like being hypnotised—you know what that is. We wouldn't have done these things if we could have stopped ourselves. You might say we weren't ourselves at all. Do you believe me?" to which Anna responds (admittedly indistinctly) "Yes." Presumably I was hoping that my readers would be as credulous.

Expunging the cult from the book and including Anna's viewpoint seemed to me to solve the problems, and the only deletion I regret is an Ibo novel which Alan skims in the second chapter: "Her youthful fidelity was exhausted and they delved into a romantic blast. . . . His sexual instinct was in its worst intensive urgent. . . ." (Genuine quotations, though I can't now recall where I found them.) I submitted the new version of the book, which was on its way into production when Tom McCormack of St Martin's Press expressed interest in publishing it in America. He had some reservations, however, particularly about the final chapter, and over Scotches in his office in the Flatiron Building I came to agree with him. I rewrote the ending and some other scenes a second time, and this is the version you are holding.

Given Tom's considerable enthusiasm for the book, I had every right to expect that the British edition would be published with the kind of fanfare that had been promised (though not written into the contract) at the outset. Not so. It was published as a paperback original with a dingy cover and no publicity at all, in a series which included such lasting work as *Omen 4* by Gordon McGill, *The Medusa Horror* by Drew Lamark and *Possessed* by Alan Radnor, and sank without trace (along with a library edition, which is the true first hardcover). In America it did much better, both in hardcover and paperback. While the British edition carried a short biography I'd faked for my pseudonym, the American revealed on the back flap that the author was pseudonymous. *Kirkus Reviews*, who had thought little of my novels up to then, were rather taken with it, but *Publishers Weekly*, one of my staunchest supporters in the trade, reviewed it as a mediocre first novel. It was published as *Claw* in Britain, in America as *Night of the Claw* (a transformation reminiscent of the change which often overtakes horror films as they cross the ocean). My original title, *The Claw*, had just been used by Norah Lofts.

Despite the Hollywoodish processes the book underwent on the way to publication, or quite possibly because of them, I think now (not having opened it for years) that it represented a step forwards for me as a novelist. I'm happy to give it my name and see it reappear. It deserves a second chance.

AFTERWORD TO *INCARNATE*

INCARNATE WAS THE NOVEL WHERE I THREW AWAY my sketch map and set off into the unknown. I had already published eight novels—four signed, one under as undeceptive a pseudonym as I could invent, three under a house name—all of which had been written from preconceived plots. Indeed, I didn't feel safe in beginning a novel until I knew or thought I knew what every chapter would contain. My first two novels hardly deviated from the chapter breakdowns I'd prepared in advance, except in the final chapters (the preconceived endings acting as a kind of safety net, allowing me to reassure myself that I had a way of finishing the book if I couldn't think of anything better), and the same is true of the early drafts of those which followed, though I later cut approximately forty thousand words from the first revision of *The Parasite* and substituted about twelve new chapters at the same stage of reworking the pseudonymous book. By then I must have known that preconceiving the plot wasn't the ideal way for me to approach the writing of a novel, but perhaps it was a habit which I needed help in breaking. Hurrah for George Walsh.

He was then my editor at Macmillan in New York, and saw five of my books into print, starting with *The Parasite.* By the time of which I'm speaking he had started to commission my books in advance. This entailed my sending him a synopsis of what I had in mind. For various reasons, *Incarnate* had been blundering around inside my head for some years—indeed, it had begun as a treatment of quite a different theme, until the plot was so thoroughly hijacked by the notion of the experiment in dreaming and its aftermath that the original theme was left behind, perhaps still to be turned into a novel of mine—and so the synopsis was almost as detailed as a chapter breakdown. George, let me say, was very much a gentleman, and he presented his criticisms of the synopsis to me as no more than suggestions I might like to consider. He felt that instead of having several plots which only very gradually intersected I might want to make one character somehow more central, and he thought that to have the characters converge on a particular location would give more unity of place. Minor changes, I thought, and ones I would have no difficulty in accommodating—but I had scarcely begun to write the novel when they took over. The ideas they brought to life were so much livelier than those I'd written down for George that I don't think I consulted the synopsis again for the year and a half I spent on the book. Appropriately enough, none of my other novels has felt so like a dream I was having at my desk, though most of two decades later *Needing Ghosts* did.

Now, that was happening alongside events I discuss in *Near Madness** ("So began the worst year of my life . . . "). I used to believe that *Incarnate* was somewhere I could go during that period and still be in control, but it seems more likely that the book was somewhere I could lose control, at least in some senses, as part of the process of letting the book and its structure be themselves. I wouldn't want this to read like yet another admission of guilt on my part; I don't believe any writer should feel guilty about the compulsion to write or to look upon their life as the raw material of their art. In some cases, indeed, that compulsion may be a way of retaining sanity, and I rather think this was true in my case.

One consequence of allowing the book to explore itself was that it was much longer than the published version. Even the edited typescript I delivered to Macmillan was over 750 pages long. Macmillan, however, were extremely enthusiastic—so enthusiastic that they wanted to be into print with the book in time to display copies at the American Booksellers Association (much like the

* Expanded in the present volume as "How I Got Here".

Frankfurt Book Fair) that year. They edited the typescript for the printer and sent it for my approval, as any good publisher will. It arrived on a Friday, and I had until Monday to read it. I think that's the only period in which I've lost my voice from snarling and screaming even though I was by myself in the room.

Don't assume that I'm about to take revenge on George Walsh or on his consistently helpful assistant, Ilka Shore Cooper, with whom I had a prolonged transatlantic conversation that Monday afternoon. When I needed a break from reading the typescript over the weekend I found myself leafing through Tom Dardis' *Some Time in the Sun*, an account of the experiences of novelists in Hollywood, and chancing upon F. Scott Fitzgerald's plaintive protest to Joseph Mankiewicz: "I'm a good writer, honest.... Can't producers ever be wrong?" To judge by some of the material Mankiewicz cut from Fitzgerald's script for *Three Comrades*, any writer can sometimes use an objective opinion of their work, but I still wished that if (as was certainly the case) *Incarnate* needed further cutting, I had been given time to carry out the rewriting myself.

The book has seen several editions since then, all of them based on the Macmillan version, which was the product of my discussion with Ilka of the changes I agreed with and those I wouldn't countenance. By now I regard it as the authorised version, more or less. Two cuts have always bothered me. The first passage occurs at the beginning of chapter 43—the scene in Mrs Shankar's shop—and I've never quite understood why anyone should want to cut it, given the themes of the book. The other, however, is almost a complete chapter, and while I think it gives one kind of strength to the book, its absence is responsible for another kind, insofar as Martin remains an ambiguous figure until much later in the book. It should follow chapter 15. Dream it for yourself, or seek its rare appearance.

AFTERWORD TO *OBSESSION*

THIS BOOK SHOULD BE CALLED *FOR THE REST OF Their Lives*. Many of my titles have been altered between my conceiving their subject and delivering it to the publisher: *To Wake The Dead* became *The Parasite* in order not to be confused on Macmillan's list with a novel by John Dickson Carr; *The Nameless* in embryo presented itself to me as both *The Loud Houses* and *Home To Mother*; *Incarnate* might have been known as *The Incarnations* if Hugh Lamb hadn't suggested to me that it sounded like a florist's; *Scared Stiff* might have been *Horror Erotica* (arguably appropriate, since some readers of various sexes have found it more erotic than horrific) and *Cold Print* was almost *The Voice Of The Beach*, until my Californian publisher pointed out that few Californians would derive much of a shiver from the image of a beach. I admit that I wish Melissa Singer at Tor had persuaded me to change the name of *Secret Stories* (not a collection, despite how it sounds) to *Secret Story* soon enough that I could have renamed the PS edition too. *The Communications* became *The Grin of the Dark*. *Think Yourself Lucky* began life as *Bad Thoughts*, which is subsumed into the book itself, and *The Kind Folk* was *The Black Pilgrimage* until the book moved so far from the original conception that I plan to use both the name and the idea in a future novel. In general, the title I've settled on has appeared on the book; I didn't, for instance, have much time for the notion that *Ancient Images* would be improved by naming it *Ancient Evil*. But in the case of the present book, and in the face of the transatlantic unanimity of my publishers, I gave in.

The purpose, I believe, was to make the book more marketable, never a bad idea in theory. Although the title *Obsession* made me think of Brian de Palma's rather fine fantasy of incest, and might also have recalled from my years of librarianship various gatherers of dust on the shelves, I found the dictionary definitions—"persistent attack, especially of an evil spirit" and "morbid persistence of an idea in the mind against one's will"—variously appropriate enough to be appealing. But of course the title was also more comfortably generic than mine, and unfortunately some publishers (not, let me say, all those who published the book) react to anything unconventional by making it appear to be the opposite, thus often putting off those readers who might enjoy it and alienating those whom it reaches. Other writers have suffered from this more than I have: I'm put in mind of the late Brian McNaughton, a talented and inventive writer whose work I originally avoided because of the packaging (*The House Across The Way*, for instance, was published as *Satan's Surrogate*, volume four, in a non-existent series). But once a blurb claimed that *Obsession* offered ". . . such horror, such terror . . . death, violence and bloody vengeance . . . " I should have recognised that it was wooing the wrong audience.

Soon I did, when a review in the Herts Advertiser by one "A.A." (presumably the initials of the reviewer rather than of any organisation to which this person had recourse) complained about a similarly packaged edition of *The Nameless* that "those who revel in bloodthirsty gore will certainly be disappointed". ("Bloodthirsty gore"? Well, blood will have blood.) Now, a hostile review from someone who regards that as a criticism is a compliment, but I confess to waiting with even more nervousness than usual for the response to *Obsession*. Interestingly, some of the most favourable comments referred in passing to the way my books were perceived and marketed: ". . . if Campbell were not already pigeonholed as a writer of horror . . . " ". . . if anyone ever bothered to look beyond the genre labels . . . "

"Pigeonholed as a writer of horror"? Well, I suppose so; it's hardly surprising after more than fifty years of writing it, and I dislike the idea of courting success at the expense of one's peers. At least there is no literary equivalent for being doomed to play out one's career in the company of Abbott and Costello. I'll admit, however, that I'm unhappy with the kind of guilt by association one sometimes has to suffer. It may be peculiar to this field; at least, I'm not aware that (for example) Dashiell Hammett was ever blamed for the excesses of Robert Leslie Bellem, S. J. Perelman's favourite hard-boiled writer ("You crazy dimwit!" I yeeped. "Do you realise you've dumped me in the grease up to my dimple?") or that even in the fifties Brian W. Aldiss was held responsible, heaven forbid, for the prose of his fellow Digit science fiction writer Nal Rafcam, an understandably pseudonymous figure whose writing reads more like an alien trying to communicate with Earthlings than anything else I have read ("Apropos to the feast of delicately prepared foods a state of complete submission overpowered them. They were so to speak under the influence of external vibrations, thought compulsions of some guiding dominant locomotion close by them . . . "). But the hackwork and exploitative rubbish the field of horror fiction includes, of which there is far too much at present, tends to be more visible and more likely to be seen as dominating, if not indeed entirely constituting, the field.

Ah well. I can only do my best (though when I say so Clive Barker twits me for sounding like his old schoolteacher) and wait for the verdict. Let me end by identifying a couple of common fallacies: that the best work in a field must be done by writers who don't specialise in that field, and that the ghost story (whether or not it overlaps the horror story) is dead and can only be revived from without. Not so in either case, as I trust I may sometime demonstrate. Meanwhile, I shall continue to write horror fiction and say that I do. I just hope that damn title didn't fail to attract too many readers who might have liked the book.

That's what I wrote in 1989 (though I've slightly updated it) for a reissue of the novel. Proofreading this new edition for Samhain has been an eerie experience. The first section of the book was historical when it was written, and now the entire novel feels that way—the work of someone I hardly recognise, and the product of processes I don't recall. It's me all right, however. Twenty-five years later, while writing my most recent novel, I gave to the manager of

Waves Radio a slogan I'd forgotten Robin Laurel's mother had used here.

Should I have preserved the text as it was originally published? I've left the title alone despite severe temptation, simply because I wouldn't want anyone to be tricked into buying a book they already own under its previous name. In any case, perhaps it's more appropriate than I thought at the time: the narrative itself becomes obsessive—it's one of my earliest comedies of paranoia. However, I'd forgotten that the book had been invaded by a swarm of italics wished upon it by a copy-editor in the eighties, and I've rid it of them, along with an infestation of unnecessary commas and unwanted paragraph breaks. I've also changed a very few words to get rid of inadvertent rhymes and repetitions and some untypically staccato prose—no more than that—and fixed printer's errors that have gone unnoticed ever since the first edition. (The worst, I think, is "Going quietly mad, she thought of saying, 'Why do you ask?' ", which now correctly reads "Going quietly mad, she thought of saying. 'Why do you ask?' " What a difference a single punctuation mark can make!) The computer also gave us a few giggles while scanning the text: we had Steve puffing out a key rather than pulling it out, and in this very introduction the Herts Advertiser became the Hens Advertiser.

I'm happy to find that the book has a life of its own. I'm surprised how vividly the chapters set in 1958 evoke my own impressions of the time, where the post-war greyness had begun to dissipate, though it seems to linger in most contemporary photographs, in which every man wore a suit and tie. The characters feel like their own people now, though they must have been part of me once. Some commentators have found them too English: well, that's their nationality, and mine too, and I make no apology for it. One reviewer complained that the Waters children were whiny, but as far as I can see they just behave like ordinary youngsters. Perhaps the reviewer didn't like children; I like these myself, not least because they ring true to my experience even where they aren't drawn directly from it (they mostly are). If my characters don't convince me I can hardly expect the reader to accept them, but I don't believe it's also the writer's job to make characters sympathetic just so the reader can identify with them. The point, surely, is to tell the truth. On the other hand, do I feel involved with my characters? Indeed I do, even with a quarter of a century between us. If they and the tale didn't engage my imagination I couldn't have written them—the defensive distancing of post-modernism doesn't inspire me much. I write as I do because that's how it feels to me, and if I didn't feel it I don't believe I could write it at all.

AFTERWORD TO *THE HUNGRY MOON*

HOW IDEAS CHANGE! THIS BOOK BEGAN LIFE AS A riff on Jim Herbert's *The Dark*. I thought more was left to be done with the notion of a supernatural darkness, not least because of the discipline imposed on the writer by having to do without the visual. I'd already tried that twice, in a macabre tale ("Hearing is Believing") and, immediately after writing that, in a fantasy ("The Mouths of Light"). Believe it or not, I hadn't realised I was restricting myself the same way in both tales until I came to write them, so unconscious, in whatever sense you care to take that word, was my creativity. At least they persuaded me in due course that the dark was worth another crack, even if it had been dealt with magnificently by William Hope Hodgson in *The Night Land*.

Somewhere in a pocket-sized red notebook, a bunch of which accompanies me everywhere, are my earliest thoughts about *The Hungry Moon*—mutterings about a darkness sent back from an apocalyptic future where everyone is blind. That notebook eludes me just now, but I do have those in which I continued to work up the novel. By this point I'd decided that the dark should have a purpose, that of making the characters grateful for any light at all. Gullibility had become my theme, and quite right too, given the spread of it. I see that the book might have been called *The Man with the Moon's Face*, or *Dreadful Night*, or *The Hungry Dark*, or *Blind Dark*, and it was only after one hundred and fourteen pages of notes, an unusually large number of them unused, that I lit upon the present title. Mind you, the book itself almost didn't see the light of publication.

We'll come to that, and blame the British Fantasy Convention. Meanwhile, I recall that once the embryonic novel emerged from that most frustrating of states where the writer doesn't know the names of the characters, or what they do in life, or where they live, or just about anything else concerning whatever is trying to get itself written, it was some fun to research. Not only fun, either: I found it slightly unnerving to learn how much corroborative detail I was able to snaffle from actual legends and folk traditions to back up a myth I had myself invented. Of course there are clowns around who would argue that proves my subconscious was privy to occult truths I wouldn't admit consciously—they say the same of Lovecraft, who was a most rational fantasist—but that idea deserves the other kind of privy. What unnerved me was rather the ease with which one can rustle up evidence to support any kind of nonsense.

I'd had a somewhat similar experience when researching *The Parasite*, but I'd thought it would be clear to the reader that I was playing with the material. When I referred to a painting by Hitler's favourite artist, showing Wotan with a forelock and a small moustache and painted the year of Hitler's birth, I assumed it wasn't necessary to point out to the reader that the most likely explanation was that Hitler modelled his adult appearance on the painting. In the context of my view of the book it was disconcerting to receive a letter from an American reader thanking me for turning her on to the occult. Robert Aickman used to say that humour and the occult were very close, but I don't know if he would have related this incident to that view.

This may sound as though I'm readying myself to make claims for the knockabout qualities of *The Hungry Moon*, and indeed I am. Having mocked evangelism as I more than ever think it deserved—very little of that aspect of the book was imaginary, and I've encountered far worse since—I wasn't about to risk sowing the seed of a druidic revival. That could be my excuse for the amount of naked absurdity the book tries to contain, as identified by Rob Latham in an unimpressed account of the book in *Fantasy Review*, but I cannot tell a lie. Having reread the novel in order to write this afterword—these days half the time I can't remember stuff I wrote, poor old sod—I think Rob had a point, though I'd put it differently. It seems to me that *The Hungry Moon* was trying to be too many books.

Everything one writes is a stage of the journey to whatever one writes later. I see where I was beginning to think along the lines of *The Influence*, and the feeble grabs I made at the kind of visionary horror *Midnight Sun* attempts. Perhaps the father who becomes monstrous prefigures events in *Nazareth Hill*. Eustace Gift is clearly a relative of my homicidal friend Jack Orchard, and wouldn't it be fair to say that *The Hungry Moon* struggles to incorporate the kind of increasingly macabre pratfalls which form the heart of *The Count of Eleven*? I was much more unsettled to find that Eustace Gift might also have acknowledged kinship to the superannuated comic Joey Hanover, with his catch-phrase "That's my name and that's my nature", in Peter Ackroyd's 1989 novel *First Light*. Joey's wife Floey has precisely the same habit of mangling everyday phrases I gave to Edna Dainty in *Midnight Sun*, though I hadn't then read Ackroyd's remarkable novel, in which "Stone Age gloom" rises from a pit and affects archaeologists. Perhaps, like the three little would-be Buddhas in Bertolucci's film, Ackroyd and I are aspects of a single reincarnated personality, and there flaps a pig past my window.

I mustn't forget to mention that Ian Watson rang me in a panic around publication time. He'd discovered that this book had an uncanny amount in common with his forthcoming horror novel *The Power*. We decided, and were right, that the similarities didn't matter: we were different writers who'd written different treatments of a theme. Ian's book was apparently regarded as too leftist to be published in America, and mine did far less well there than my previous novels had, even though I'd stuck some Yanks in it to give it transatlantic appeal—less blatantly, I hope, than Jerry Warren, who not only dubs Mexican horror films into American but shoehorns American actors into them.

Other unexpected things have happened to this book. I own up to not making life easy for my translators with my delight in the ambiguities of English. (I imagine Shaun Hutson's translators raise a cheer and a yippie whenever he lets fall a new book.) I hope nobody will mind if I suggest that the translations of "Harry Moony", a song which I hope to record one day, add some fun to my foreign editions. The J'Ai Lu paperback, with its beautifully sinister cover, encourages the reader to chant

> Descends, Harry Moony, jamais plus ne nous nuis,
> Plein de fleurs, pour te plaire, on depose a ton huis.

Not only does it rhyme throughout, but I've successfully sung it to its old tune. Knaur, my German publishers, invite us to make the rafters of the bierkeller ring with

> Hi nab, Harry Moony, und lass endlich aus,
> Wir legen dir Blumen vor dein einsames Haus.

Splendid stuff. It too rhymes throughout, and I've roared it to considerable effect in lonely places with just a few walkers in ear-shot. Should I ever tire of it, there are other versions, for instance that in *Luna Sangrienta*, which I trust no bemused Spaniard will mistake for a prose version of the legendary Jesus Franco's movie *Bloody Moon*:

> Baja, Harry el Lunático, no nos acoses mas,
> fibres tenemos para darte, en tu puerta las vamos a dejar.

Ah. Well, perhaps that might call for some prefatory use of Rioja. It does all rhyme, though. How about the Italian?

> Stai giü Harry Moony, piü non ci tormentare,
> Abbiamo dei fiori, per farti contento,
> Alla tua porta Ii veniamo a lasciare.

I envision that and all its verses set by Verdi, or better still Rossini in his comic mode, or maybe chanted by Goblin on the soundtrack of a Dario Argento film of the book. (Hell, I'd like to see an Argento version of just about anything of mine.) But in terms of the translations which have so far appeared, I think the palm for euphony goes to the Swedish, the jacket of which describes me as "en skräckforfattares skräckfrfattare" and quotes the Washington Post as saying "Campbell skriver mera skrämmande skräck":

> Ner nit, Harry Mane, lämna oss i ro.
> Vi kommer med blommor att smycka ditt bo.

And what of the edition you hold in your hands? Despite severe temptation, I've left it almost entirely alone. It would have made no sense to change the elements which date it: for instance, the missile base, which may well be out of date only until we find another bugbear to justify defending ourselves that way—any time now, I fear, even if that makes me sound like Jerry Pournelle. Other aspects have, alas, not dated at all. Just the other day my daughter was handed in the street a copy of the *Jesus Revolution Streetpaper*, published by the Jesus Army, in which you can find out where to buy a music tape called "Bleeding with Jesus" and every single piece of news tells us how some alleged unfortunate found Jesus. Jesus. Sometimes I think I don't invent fiction but simply anticipate.

I have, however, tweaked the text where I found it tweaked. I'd forgotten—perhaps preferred to forget—that I'd caved in to the interference of some copy-editor. The kind of detail I mean may seem petty, but in that case it should reflect the taste of the person whose name is on the title page, not of somebody anonymous whose commitment to finding something wrong would not disgrace an Eastern European clerk. I confess to being even more depressed than is my frequent state by the sight of a typescript where my punctuation and usage have been messed with, and it may be that depression which has sometimes deterred me from taking an eraser to the hundreds of alterations. I foam on this and related subjects at greater length in an instalment of my regular column in the American critical journal *Necrofile*.

Let me summarize. If you read in a book of mine (to contrive an inelegant sentence in order to demonstrate)

I said, "I've no patience with the kind of unnecessary, piddling, trivial changes that find their way on to my pages" then I didn't write it. What I would have written is

I said "I've no patience with the kind of unnecessary piddling trivial changes that find their way onto my pages".

I can only hope that is how this book now reads. I take responsibility for everything except printers' errors, even the oddly perfunctory climaxes which end some of the chapters, not to mention my inability to contrive a way to get all the survivors to the missile base for the finale; the best I could do was convince myself that the return of the sunlight resembled a nuclear explosion. Rereading the whole thing wasn't quite as dispiriting an experience as I feared, though I've yet to proofread the wretch. Perhaps I have a special affection for it since I had to rescue the only copy of the first draft from a Birmingham hotel safe after a panicky return from home, the award which the British Fantasy Convention gave me for Incarnate having driven all thought of it out of my head. May whatever imaginative appeal it has outlive its timeliness.

All that is the afterword I wrote for the 1995 reissue of the book, and here's the novel again at even more of a distance. The Scragg school revives memories of the first schools I attended, Christ the King and Ryebank. There's little exaggeration involved, believe me (though both schools employed good teachers too). Perhaps even more disconcertingly, the Scraggs' rules in chapter twelve were in force at a local school when I wrote the novel. Quite a few of the characters and incidents are put together from experience; for example, Brian Bevan's provision of porn and his offer of a vibrator was the aftermath of a dinner Jenny and I once had at the home of two science fiction fans. (We found an excuse—quite a desperate one—to leave.) In a different autobiographical sense, perhaps the book is an early stage of my journey into agnosticism—I'd used my adolescence with the Christian Brothers as an automatic excuse for atheism long enough.

Am I making the book sound more coherent than it is? If you've read it you decide. It was my shot at an extravagant supernatural novel splashed on a large canvas, the kind of book that was quite common back then (though I may have been unconsciously influenced by a classic predecessor, *The House on the Borderland*, especially in Diana's vision of the birth of things). Perhaps several of us needed to have a go at the form, to see what it achieved or to find its limits. In my case I think the experience led to greater control in at least some of my later books, but there are a few scenes in here I quite like. Some readers have too.

AFTERWORD TO *SCARED STIFF*

NOBODY REBELS LIKE A GOOD CATHOLIC BOY, and I spent quite a stretch of my childhood in fighting the repressiveness of my upbringing. I needed to. At an early age I was infected by my mother's blushes at anything that might conceal a double meaning, and anything more explicit than that made me horribly uncomfortable: I squirmed when Bluebottle and Eccles in the Goon Show looked up someone's trousers to see who he was, and felt physically ill when Victor Borge introduced the messy soprano who came in a single pile. I couldn't go through life like that, though I'm sure too many people do, and by the time I reached adolescence at a grammar school run by Christian Brothers I was beginning to grow mutinous. I'd no time for the spinsterish way one master wrinkled his nose at sex in pop songs and denied us a hearing of the Porter scene in a recording of *Macbeth*. No doubt I resented his disapproval partly because pop songs and dirty jokes, some of which would have taken a David Cronenberg to visualise, were all the sexual experience I had. Sex education was thoroughly absent, except for a talk on the ways of the world, delivered on one of my last days at school by a visiting monk who referred to girls' "headlamps" and boys' "spouts". Still, perhaps the beatings that were frequent at the school were popular with some; in that year's issue of the magazine a school governor reminisces at unhealthy length about them. Myself, I agree with Gore Vidal (and all of its practitioners whom I know) in approving of corporal punishment only between consenting adults, a theme I'll return to later.

But my strongest resentment against the church and my upbringing at that time was over the forbidding of books. I had the impression—how accurate I can't say—that as a Catholic I was prevented from reading all sorts of things on pain of some unspecified and therefore daunting penalty. Having persuaded my mother over the years to let me borrow adult ghost books from the library, and eventually, when I was ten, to allow me to buy science fiction magazines and even *Weird Tales*, I now felt ready to confront censoriousness—or at least, I thought I did. This was the year *Lady Chatterley's Lover* was first published in Britain, and while I don't think any of my schoolmates were brave enough to bring a copy to school, quite a few claimed to have read it; undoubtedly some of them had. The best I could do, however, was to skulk near bookstalls where it was displayed and clutch the three and sixpence in my pocket in a vain attempt to goad myself into picking up the book. It wasn't until I left school that I determined to make up for lost time by reading whatever I liked.

So I bought Nabokov's *Lolita*, having seen it recommended by Graham Greene, and found it liberating in several ways, not least as a writer. In order to write anything lively enough for publication I'd needed to unlearn some of the restrictions I'd been taught at school—you couldn't contract "I had" to "I'd", for instance—but the effect of reading Nabokov was an instant lightening of my style and a greatly enhanced enjoyment of language (a pleasure which, I fear, at least one teacher of English literature had had no apparent time for). Meanwhile my first published stories, imitations of Lovecraft, had begun to appear. Pat Kearney, a friend who published the very first in his fanzine *Goudy*, told me about the Olympia Press, *Lolita*'s original publisher. A house devoted to publishing books banned in Britain sounded fine to me, particularly since I was incensed to discover that so many books were banned, and so with the advance paid on publication of my first book, I took my mother and myself to Paris, where I met Miss Olivia Pringle in the Olympia office. I returned with William Burroughs' *Soft Machine* and *The Ticket That Exploded* and a copy for Pat Kearney of a book of bawdy ballads pseudonymously edited by Christopher Logue. How I intended to bluff my way through Customs I have no idea, but a rough and protracted Channel crossing came to what I was able to regard retrospectively as my aid. Faced with the sight of me, wavering and pale-faced and bespattered with remains of that morning's croissants, the Customs officer waved me through. In the introduction to his bibliography of the Olympia Press, Pat Kearney celebrates this incident with a description that makes me think of Anthony Cronin's last grisly sight of Brendan Behan.

Another source of banned books was August Derleth, my friend and mentor and (in the days when Arkham House was pretty well his one-man operation) first professional publisher, who sent me Henry Miller's *Tropics* and Lawrence Durrell's *Black Book*. This led me to assume he wouldn't mind if I introduced a different kind of shock into my Lovecraft imitations, but he took the shit out of a line of dialogue. I still think it's what the character would have said, but I see that that may not be relevant to such a stylised form as Lovecraft pastiche. I therefore tried writing for the Olympia Press, who were then publishing a magazine. "A Third-Floor Withdrawal" was an attempt to deal with my adolescent sexual turmoil, and the editor of *Olympia* gave me the impression that it might have been published except for its brevity (it was about a thousand words in length). I tried again with "The Folding Socket", a plotless fantasy influenced by William Burroughs, which I wrote at my Civil Service desk in the lunch hours. This, I imagine, was too gross for the magazine, which was aimed at the British and American bookstalls. Both stories are lost, and certainly the latter need not be mourned.

Years later—1969, I think—I had a different sort of experience involving Olympia Press. In the first newsletter of a short-lived Liverpool underground film society, I advertised for sale the Olympia edition of de Sade's *120 Days of Sodom*, whose three volumes I'd found somewhat tedious. Of course the nondescript fellow who called at the house to examine the book proved to a plainclothes policeman, who had no doubt been planted in the film society so as to keep an eye on things, though I didn't realise this until he returned with three of his colleagues and a warrant to search the house. They were unfailingly courteous, and seemed to be impressed by both my naïveté and my having been published.

Weeks later I was invited to the police station to be given a cup of tea and the news that the Director of Public Prosecutions had decided not to prosecute, and almost everything they had seized was returned to me, including Kenneth Patchen's *Memoirs of a Shy Pornographer* and Samuel Beckett's *Imagination Dead Imagine*, in which page 12 had been marked in pencil, apparently because it begins with "the arse" ("the arse against the wall at A, the knees against the wall at B and C, the feet against the wall between C and A, that is to say inscribed in the semicircle ACB . . . "). I don't think Beckett had previously been regarded as a pornographic writer. I had to sign away my rights only to the de Sade, a book which caused the policeman to wrinkle his nose in exactly the way pop songs had affected my old schoolmaster*.

By then I had completed *Demons by Daylight*, my second book, though it wasn't published until 1973. It may not seem especially radical now, but it certainly was then, not least in dealing with characters whose guilts and fears and sexuality and, especially, emotional clumsiness were based on my experience. Indeed, if I hadn't felt driven by the need to bring horror fiction up to date, in line with the contemporary fiction I was reading, I might not have had the courage to continue; I felt that these stories were unlikely to receive August Derleth's approval—so much so that when I'd finished typing the book I fell into a horrible depression, because I both regarded Arkham House as my only market (as Lovecraft regarded *Weird Tales* as his) and was convinced that Arkham wouldn't touch it. But Derleth bought it, though he never gave me his opinion of it, and I was set on my course.

It is sometimes suggested (by Paul Schrader, for instance, in an attempt to justify his vulgar remake of *Cat People*) that all horror fiction is about sex. This is nonsense, and unhelpfully reductionist even when applied to tales with sexual themes: it's too easy to slide from "that's what the story is about" to "that's all the story is about". But it's true that many horror stories have a sexual subtext, and I think many of us in the field tended to assume that if the underlying sexual theme was made explicit, it would rob the fiction of its power.

* How times change! These days not only the novel but Pasolini's bleak and distressing film of it are openly on sale in Britain.

It was the anthologist Michel Parry, an old friend, who gave me the chance to test this theory, though I don't think he quite realised what he was helping to create. After editing three volumes of black magic stories for Mayflower, he complained to me that nobody was submitting tales on a sexual theme. Aroused by the suggestion, I wrote "Dolls", which enabled me both to explore what happened to the supernatural story when the underlying sexual theme (not always present, of course) became overt and to write a long short story that was stronger on narrative than atmosphere, a useful preparation for writing my first novel. Michel hadn't expected anything quite so sexually explicit, and I was amused when his publishers, Mayflower, felt compelled to show "Dolls" to their lawyers for advice. The lawyers advised them to publish, and over the next few years Michel commissioned several more such tales, all of which are included here.

My original title for this book was *Horror Erotica*. The one it bears was the inspiration of Jeff Conner at Scream/Press. At least we didn't call it *Wanking Nightmares*. My correspondent Keith B. Johnston of Goshen came up with *Eldritchly Erect*, and Poppy Z. Brite suggested I should write a second such collection set in Liverpool and called *Mersey Beat-Off*, though admittedly that was after I proposed she call a book *The Phantom of the Okra*.

I don't know if much need be said about most of the following stories. "The Other Woman" has offended some readers, and I probably wouldn't write it that way now if at all, but I think it's a story about fantasies of rape rather than merely being such a fantasy itself. "The Seductress" was filmed for the cable television show *The Hunger*, quite faithfully, I thought. "Merry May" (which was written to tumefy the first edition of this book) became transformed into "Merry Way" on the cover of the American Warner paperback, which also toned the original subtitle ("Tales of Sex and Death") down to "Seven Tales of Seduction and Terror". "The Body in the Window" was written for the *Hot Blood* paperback anthology series, while "Kill Me Hideously" suggested itself as soon as I agreed at a British science fiction convention to offer as an auction item the chance for the highest bidder to appear in my next novel. That was *The Last Voice They Hear*, but the charming bidder had nothing in common with the unlucky Lisette in the present book.

"The Other Woman" and "Loveman's Comeback" were written for the short-lived *Devil's Kisses* series of anthologies of erotic horror Michel edited as Linda Lovecraft, who was in fact the owner of a chain of sex shops and who is one more reason why asking for Lovecraft in a British bookshop may earn you a dubious look. Perhaps the anthologies were ahead of their time, because the second in the series was pulped shortly after publication, apparently in response to objections from Scotland Yard. Rumour had it that the problem was a tale reprinted from *National Lampoon*, involving a seven-year-old girl and a horse. Michel held on to "Stages" for a possible anthology about drugs, but after the above incident the story went into limbo. I confess to being more amused than irritated by the banning of *More Devil's Kisses*, much as I felt upon learning that my first novel had been seen (in a television documentary) on top of a pile of books for burning by Christian fundamentalists—something of a compliment as far as I'm concerned. On reflection, though, I think I wasn't entitled to feel quite so superior about censorship. Though my sexual tales had been, on the whole, progressively darker and more unpleasant, I'd suppressed the third of them, "In the Picture". It was the initial draft of the story published here as "The Limits of Fantasy".

At the time (May 1975) I believed I had decided not to revise and submit the story because it wasn't up to publishable standard, and that was certainly the case. However, the reasons were more personal than I admitted to myself. All fiction is to some extent the product of censorship, whether by the culture within which it is produced or by the writer's own selection of material, both of which processes tend to be to some extent unconscious. Perhaps the most insidious form of censorship, insofar as it may be the most seductive for the writer, is by his own dishonesty. For me the most immediate proof is that it wasn't until Barry Hoffman asked me if I had any suppressed fiction he could publish in *Gauntlet* that I realised, on rereading "In the Picture", that my dishonesty was its central flaw.

One mode of fiction I dislike—one especially common in my field—is the kind where the act of writing about a character seems designed to announce that the character has nothing to do with the author. On the most basic level, it's nonsense, since by writing about a character the writer must draw that personality to some extent from within himself. More to the present point, it smells of protesting too much, and while that may be clear to the reader, for the writer it's a kind of censorship of self. I hope that "In the Picture" is the only tale in which I succumb to that temptation.

"In the Picture" follows the broad outline of "The Limits of Fantasy", though much more humourlessly, up to the scene with Enid Stone, and then Sid Pym begins to indulge in fantasies of rape and degradation which I believe are foreign to his sexual makeup and which are contrived simply to demonstrate what a swine he is—in other words, that he is quite unlike myself. Nothing could be further from the truth. In response to Barry Hoffman I treated "In the Picture" as the first version of the story and rewrote it exactly as I would any other first draft, and I had the most fun writing Pym's boarding-school fantasy, which is at least as much my fantasy as his. For me his presentation of it is both comic and erotic.

It seems to me that even the most liberal of us employ two definitions of pornography: the kind that turns ourselves on, which we're more prone to regard as erotic, and the kind which appeals to people with sexual tastes unlike our own and which we're more likely to condemn as pornographic. In my case the absurdity is that the group of scenarios which I sum up as the boarding-school fantasy (which is obviously as much fetishistic as sadistic) is the only species of pornography I find appealing, and it was therefore especially dishonest of me to include no more than a hint of it when I collected my sexual tales in *Scared Stiff*. I suppose, then and in my original suppression of "In the Picture", I was afraid of losing friends, but that really isn't something writers should take into account when writing. I suspect I was assuming that my readers and people in general are squarer when it comes to erotic fantasy than is in fact the case. Since the publication of *Scared Stiff* I've heard from readers of various sexes that they found parts of the book erotic, and a female reader gave me a copy of *Caught Looking*, a polemic published by the Feminist Anti-Censorship Taskforce, in which one of the illustrations (all chosen by the FACT designers on the basis that they themselves found the images erotically appealing) is a still from *Moral Welfare*, a British spanking video. (The Spankarama Cinema in Soho, rather unfairly chastised in the winter

1982/83 *Sight and Sound* and touched on by association in *Incarnate*, is long gone; perhaps I should have had a publicity photograph taken under the sign while it was there.) Incidentally, perhaps one minor reason for my reticence was the notion that this sexual taste is peculiarly British, but a few minutes on the Internet will give the lie to that. I keep feeling there's a novel in the theme, to be called *Adult Fun*, but who would publish it? Meanwhile "The Limits of Fantasy" adds variety to this collection, which has sometimes struck me as too mechanically including the standard variations in tale after tale.

So I trust this hasn't been too embarrassing. I haven't found it so, but then I may sometimes lack tact in these areas: I once greeted a friend in a sex shop, who immediately fled. Still, I'm committed to telling as much of the truth as I can, as every writer should be. If we can't tell the truth about ourselves, how can we presume to do so about anyone or anything? Secretiveness is a weakness, whereas honesty is strength.

If I'm told my field is incapable of something, I'll give it a try—hence these and others of my tales. No doubt the irritation of censorship also has something to do with it: here it seems to have behaved like Spanish fly. On that basis I should like to thank censors, especially the self-appointed, for helping me write. I love them all. After all, as they must recognise, we hate most in others what we can't admit about ourselves.

INTRODUCTION TO *DARK FEASTS*

SOME HORROR STORIES ARE NOT GHOST STORIES, and some ghost stories are not horror stories, but these terms have often been used interchangeably since long before I was born. I'm in favour of this. Many horror stories communicate awe as well as (sometimes instead of) shock, and it is surely inadequate to lump these stories together with fiction that seeks only to disgust, in a category regarded as the deplorable relative of the ghost story. Approximately half of the thirty stories collected herein to represent the first twenty-five years of my career are ghost stories, and I hope that at least some of the others offer a little of the quality that has always appealed to me in the best horror fiction, a sense of something larger than is shown.

"The Room in the Castle" (written in 1961) was my first professionally published story, my first attempt to sound like Lovecraft. Once I'd finished trying to do that for most of a book, *The Inhabitant of the Lake,* I set out to sound like myself. Imitating Lovecraft had let me avoid talking about my own fears, but now I ventured to do so, still hanging onto Lovecraftian conventions in "Cold Print" (1966/67) before venturing further into the unknown with "The Scar" (1967). My memories of my schooldays do turn into a rather more Lovecraftian nightmare in "The Interloper" (1968), although by this stage of my writing, everyday life tends to be the Siamese twin of horror. In "The Guy" (1968) I sought to use the M. R. Jamesian ghost story in the service of social realism, so long as it was still supernaturally frightening: if I'm led to believe that my field can't achieve something, I'll give it a try. As for "The End of a Summer's Day" (1968), I'm happy to say it remains an enigma to me, and so I've let the originally published version stand verbatim, despite the clumsiness of some of the writing.

The next two are taken from my third book, *The Height of the Scream.* Rather than include the title story, I recommend you to read M. John Harrison's remarkable "Running Down", which deals with the same theme far more powerfully. "The Whining" (1973) is here at the suggestion of my publishers. "The Words That Count" (1973) was suggested indirectly by Nabokov's ghost story "The Vayne Sisters". I hope it is able to undermine the moral glibness I find in too much horror fiction.

In July 1973 a growing recklessness, fed by T. E.D. Klein's critique of my second book, caused me to take up writing fulltime. "The Man in the Underpass" (1973) was almost the first tale I wrote then, feeling that it might help my style remain supple. I wrote "Horror House of Blood" (1973) on similar principles, this time attempting to avoid any reliance on atmosphere. I hoped that by now my readers would know me well enough to recognize that the title was deliberately excessive. "The Companion" (1973), like "The End of a Summer's Day", was a story it seemed less important to understand than to write. One strength of horror fiction can be that it lets the subconscious speak for itself.

Alas, none of this new batch saw print for years, and so I tried to focus on existing markets. I heard of a market for tales in the manner of the fifties horror comics, the best of which owed more to writers such as Poe and Bradbury than their detractors recognize (*Haunt of Fear, Tales from the Crypt* and their kin, now available in impeccable bound sets from Russ Cochran of West Plains, Missouri). By the time this market proved to be a mirage I'd written several brief tales, among the best received of which was "Call First" (1974). I was glad to rediscover terseness, which I sometimes need to do.

"In the Bag" (1974) is a ghost story I submitted to the *Times* ghost story competition, though it wasn't written with that in mind. I rather hoped it might appear in the anthology derived from the competition, but the judges (Kingsley Amis, Patricia Highsmith and Christopher Lee) must have decided otherwise. However, it did gain me my first British Fantasy Award. As David Drake has pointed out, the punning title is inappropriately jokey—a lingering effect of writing the horror-comic tales, perhaps—but I try not to cheat my readers by changing titles once a story has been published.

"The Chimney" (1975) is disguised autobiography—disguised from me at the time of writing, that is. You can learn more about me than you may want to know in the autobiographical introduction* to the complete *Face That Must Die.* I can't recall where "The Brood" (1976) came from, except from one of the grimmer periods of my life. By 1977 my mood seems to have improved enough for me to write "The Voice of the Beach", an attempt to return to Lovecraft's first principles (which is to say, those of Blackwood and Machen) in order to convey a little of the awesomeness I still find in his best work. Perhaps that attitude of mind led me to produce a group of ghost stories later that year, "Out of Copyright", "Above the World" and "Mackintosh Willy", and another group in early 1978, including "The Ferries" (which, like many of my tales, is derived from a landscape). I don't know what you'd call "Midnight Hobo" (1978), but it comes of working in local radio.

Angela Carter has suggested that the horror story is a holiday from morality. It often is, especially when it uses the idea of supernatural evil as an alibi for horrors we are quite capable of perpetrating ourselves, but it needn't be, as I hope "The Depths" (1978) and others of my tales confirm.

"The Fit" (1979) was written for my anthology *New Terrors,* and I think it may be one, as seems to be the case with "Hearing Is Believing" (1979). In 1980 I wrote, among others, two stories I would call pure horror, "The Hands" and "Again". My lapsed Catholicism may account for the first, while the second is told as it told itself to me. One British magazine found "Again" too disturbing to publish, while a British Sunday newspaper magazine dismissed it as "not horrid enough". Who would have expected Catherine Morland to take up editing?

*expanded in the present volume as "How I Got Here"

Two novels occupied my time for the next three years, and while picnicking in Delamere Forest to celebrate having finished *Incarnate* I thought of the basis for "Just Waiting" (1983). My touch here and in "Seeing the World" (1983) is lighter than it used to be, or so I like to think. "Apples" (1984) was my contribution to a Halloween anthology; "Boiled Alive" (1986)—another intemperate title that I trusted would be recognized as such—was written in response to an invitation from David Pringle of *Interzone*. It looks to me as if I'm becoming less interested in telling the reader how to react, more inclined to let the story be itself, though I hope my work will always be disturbing.

Introductions to collections such as this one often end with jokes, but I hope the jokes are already in the stories and inextricable from the terror; certainly some of these tales have produced a gratifying amount of laughter when I've read them to audiences. However, it was less with laughter than with a sneer that a hypnotist who claimed to reawaken people's memories of their past lives once advised me to study his career for when I "started writing seriously", rather as if those responsible for *The Amityville Horror* had accused, say, Shirley Jackson of having her tongue in her cheek when she wrote *The Haunting of Hill House.* I see no reason why dealing with the fantastic requires one to write bullshit, and I submit this collection as evidence.

I had to be alone with myself and these stories, and now I invite you to be. Turn the page, and I'll let you down gently into the dark of my mind. But I don't promise not to let go.

Of all the introductions and afterwords collected here, I fear this needs a postscript more than most. I was about to leave on an American tour to promote the Tor edition of *The Hungry Moon* when the proofs of *Dark Feasts* arrived and went with me. They proved to be the worst set of proofs I've ever had to deal with—riddled with errors of every kind. I spent most afternoons of those three weeks in correcting them. Imagine my reaction when I learned that any number of uncorrected proofs had been bound and not merely sent out as review copies but apparently delivered to shops. This state of the book can be identified by a computer command (End of File) left at the end of "The Ferries" on page 233. Was I happier with the corrected edition that the publisher issued? To the extent that I prefer a headache to a hangover, perhaps. Somebody gave no kind of shit, since half the errors I'd taken such pains to correct remained in this version, and it is still the most misprinted book of mine ever to appear. *Alone with the Horrors* expands the collection and supersedes it except for the most dedicated collector.

AFTERWORD TO *THE INFLUENCE*

"IT SADDENS ME THAT THIS SORT OF MORBID potboiler is being published under the 'Fantasy and SF' label. It appeals to gullible readers whose minds are back in the pre-scientific Dark Ages. How much better it would be if Campbell were to employ his talents in bringing them up to date by writing about the real contemporary Merseyside in the honourable tradition of proletarian mainstream writers."

Thus ended a review of *The Influence* in *Vector*, the journal of the British Science Fiction Association, by one Jim England. Is this the kind of thing people had in mind when they used to propose closing their eyes and gritting their teeth while thinking of England? I did ask several other writers what they could tell me about him, but heard nothing I'd wish to repeat. In any case, he's hardly unique among science fiction fans in viewing supernatural horror fiction as—well, as the kind of contemptible stuff which science fiction used to be accused of being. Perhaps it comforts them to find a victim of their own. Don't we all like to feel there's someone even worse than ourselves?

Though for some reason the thought of Jim England does bring with it an image of a boiling pot, this book wasn't conceived or written as a pot-boiler. (*The Parasite* was, as I describe later in this afterword, but even then I wasn't quite able to pursue a purely commercial plan, not that I'm claiming any virtue on my own behalf.) Like so much of my stuff, *The Influence* was an expression of some of my fears and doubts about my life and my heredity. It was also an attempt at a book-length ghost story, and I suspect that somewhere in my mind was the idea I had while watching *The Exorcist* on its original release—that if I had been telling that story I would have told it from the young girl's viewpoint. What strikes me most in retrospect about *The Influence* is how much it resembles the kind of fiction my daughter read when she was in her early teens: the novels of Lois Duncan, for example. Very little alteration, maybe none, might be necessary to render it marketable as a book for teenagers these days.

My agents seemed to like it, my editors too. You might think this, and possibly even my reputation, would have allowed it into print more or less as written; naïvely, I did. The Americans indulged me; not so the British. If curses worked—if we really lived in the world Jim England seems to think I have to believe in to imagine it—several vacancies would have occurred in British publishing as I read through the copy-edited manuscript. Indeed, at times I felt I was dealing with vacancies of a different kind.

The copy-editor's attitude can be summed up by her comment on an image in the book: "I see what's meant but cut it because it seemed too sophisticated an image for the readership." Since I wouldn't dream of regarding my readers as inferior to me, I take that personally. What an unsophisticated gullible lot we are, unable to read anything that makes demands on us or to distinguish when a text is fiction! But on the evidence, the copy-editor had only been doing what she'd been encouraged to do. Her letter to my editor (to be found, along with a sampling of her version of my pages, in my archive at Liverpool University) refers to chapters she rewrote at the editor's suggestion to shorten them. In other words, the editor didn't think it appropriate to ask me to consider revising my own work, instead preferring to confront me with something which I hadn't written but to which I was supposed to lend my name. Of course I was shown the revisions for approval, but what a way to make a writer feel unsure of his worth, as though he isn't constantly doing that to himself! The talented Joe Donnelly tells me he had similar problems with the same publisher, and worse things have happened to better writers than either of us—read David Lodge's introduction to the reissue of his novel *Out of the Shelter.* (Indeed, read all of David Lodge. If you're like me, you'll be glad you did.)

The experience sketched above might have suggested to me how much the publisher valued the book, but perhaps someone felt I was still too high by several pegs. On publication day I went to London to celebrate publication day with my editor, as was my habit then. While awaiting her in Reception I found the catalogue which listed my new novel. Or did it? Not in the index of new titles, where one might find *Aroids: Plants of the Arum Family, The Nanny Guide: The Complete Low-Down on Nannies, Au Pairs and Mother's Helps, The Healing Power of Crystals,* and much that is less memorable (along with, to be fair, the likes of James Ellroy and Harry Kemelman). Just as my editor emerged from the restricted area of the building, I found myself, under "Library Fiction". There was my name and the title of my eighth novel, with no description of either, and shortly I had my hands around a copy of the book itself.

A library edition is essentially the paperback with slightly stiffer covers and pages apparently designed for instant yellowing. In *Danse Macabre* Stephen King commented about the way my first novel was published and promoted that it "makes a writer wonder if publishers don't practice their own sort of voodoo, singling certain books out to be ritually slaughtered in the marketplace." At least one of us has forged ahead since those days. My editor took me out for lunch and ordered champagne, a gesture I couldn't help finding ironic, and explained to me that her enthusiasm for the book had failed to reach the people at the top. Alas, her explanation and the champagne combined to afflict me with a depression bad even by my standards, and I still recall walking by the Thames in a state of mind which frightened me and from which I was ultimately rescued by the companionship of my good friend Steve Jones.

I said at the outset that *The Influence* promised to write itself. Now that I ponder it, most of the buggers play that trick on me, until I start trying to organize my ideas. I see that the characters don't even have names until page 7 of my notes (which I indexed into an exercise book where the headings were the characters and in some cases the settings) and Rowan was called Emma until page 25. Here's a note for a scene in which Rowan's appearance as an old lady in the school play upsets Hermione. Here's the idea, which I didn't shake off until page 10, that Hermione has a child too, who becomes Queenie's first prey until Hermione kills both the child and herself. On page 19 I was still planning to begin the book with Queenie's funeral; after making notes for various false starts, I came up on page 58 with the published opening. I see that the pair of binoculars was originally a Victorian stereoscope, that Queenie had the power to make old dolls move, that she had a pet dog that slept on her bed and survived longer than dogs should and wouldn't look away when people met its eyes—by implication, a familiar. The stripping away of much of this reflects the way Queenie became progressively humanised, I think, and more generally the process of letting a novel be itself.

It's worth saying here (not least to remind myself of this before I start my next novel) that the process often involves feeling that I've no idea where it's going. Increasingly I find that writing the first draft, especially the early chapters of it, is a way of setting out the material so that I can shape it later, which does mean that I have a good time cutting as much as I can once I reach the keyboard (the first draft being handwritten). Some of the cuts I remember are minor: for instance, on her journey home Rowan was originally disconcerted by faces in the clouds, until I found that Peter Ackroyd had used such an image more deftly in his (highly recommended) ghost novel *Hawksmoor.* One longer passage I deleted as too strange for the context is perhaps also strange enough to include here. It leads into the latter section of chapter fourteen, where Rowan is awakened by the sound of a drill at the school:

> Rowan lay in her refuge as the curtains blackened at her window and the night seeped out of the walls, and listened in case her parents were saying what they couldn't say in front of her. Putting it that way made her feel anxious, but not enough to stay awake until she heard. Sleep let her anxiety overwhelm her as she trudged down a long dark stony tunnel cold as a hole in a black iceberg and found her father in the depths at the end, caged like a beast for beating up Jo and his accountant and stealing from the houses where he worked. He was naked and filthy and crouching over a dish of dog food, teeth bared

in case anyone tried to take it from him. "It's the money troubles," said Rowan's mother, who was covered with bruises, and tried to drag her away from the cage. When Rowan reached for her father's hand through the bars, which felt crumbly as chocolate sticks and began to melt at her touch, her father shrank back, snarling "Don't sully yourself." It was no use, her mother had dragged her home in a moment to where they lived now, a single windowless room that might be underground, piled high with all their furniture. An ache was swelling Rowan's belly, and she limped to her bed that was the only clear place in the room. As she lay down, the precarious ceiling-high piles of furniture swayed toward her. "It's only natural," her mother said, running about to steady the furniture, but it couldn't be, not all this blood that was soaking the bed as Rowan's legs opened like a sluice. Somewhere in the distance she could hear a drill grinding through stone, and she realized it was her father, breaking out to come home. The idea of his seeing her like this appalled her so much that she gasped herself awake.

Her stomach was aching, and she could hear the drill. . . .

The source of *The Influence* was simple and powerful: at times my daughter Tammy looked or sounded like my mother, whom she barely remembers. Who else but Tammy could have played the role of Rowan when, in 1987, I took my friend and illustrator J. K. Potter on a tour of the locations I used? And that's my wife Jenny you see in the role of her mother (which of course she is). During his stay J. K. also took the opportunity to photograph our son Mat, who appears with his sister in the October 1987 issue of *American Politics*, both of them sporting armbands to illustrate "The New Scarlet Letter", namely AIDS. As for his work on *The Influence*, his ability to depict nightmares in photographic detail is as powerful as ever: see the inhuman guard on the train—a creature as grotesque as I imagined it to be and yet unmistakably a product of Potter's subconscious—or the street of soft houses, which Tammy is attempting not to notice as she flees along it, or the Liverpool warehouses whose stones appear to be lit from within by the moon. There's an especially subtle menace about some of the images:

Tam's double coming for her by the lighthouse or watching her sidelong under the streetlamp. (I recall keeping traffic out of the way on the street outside our house while J. K. took the time he needed for the shot; the sharp-eyed may spot the artist waiting in the picture, rather like Dalí gesturing Africa to hold still.) Best of all—and I like to think that it may have been some quality in the book that helped awaken this new sensitivity on J. K.'s part—are the images of pathos: Jenny cradling Tam's body (a picture in which one of Jeff's achievements was to give them both a straight face) and above all Tammy's ghost alone in the night outside our house.

These pictures have a special meaning for me: they're the most lyrical portraits imaginable of Tammy at the age of nine, whether writing in a diary (my own) or taking refuge behind a cross in our local graveyard in Rake Lane (where the *Weird Tales* writer G. G. Pendarves is buried). Like my book, they're transformed by J. K. Potter's inimitable imaginative technique. It makes me proud to think I may have written the source of them, and I'm proudest of all of Tam. They were created for a limited Scream/Press edition of the novel, but the publisher imploded before publication. I'm delighted that Jerad Walters and his excellent Millipede Press have given them their due.

Introduction to *Alone with the Horrors*

THIRTY YEARS IN PRINT, AND THESE THIRTY-NINE tales to show for them—at least, these are the ones my editor Jim Turner and I think are representative. I hope most of them can speak for themselves, and I intend to let them do so without too much delay, but I feel bound to mention that the opening story ["The Room in the Castle"] was the first of my tales (in the order of writing) which ever saw professional publication, hence its presence here. Otherwise I can only crave indulgence on behalf of my fifteen-year-old self and for the way I had a clergyman refer to the kaleidoscope a century before it was invented and thought nothing of having my narrator drive on country roads at night without headlights. Lovecraft, of whose work the story is of course a poor imitation, would undoubtedly have pointed out such flaws.

"The Room in the Castle" was the lead story in *The Inhabitant of the Lake*, my first published book. In 1964 I was several kinds of lucky to find a publisher, and one kind depended on my having written a Lovecraftian book for Arkham House, the only publisher likely even to have considered it and one of the very few then to be publishing horror. In those days one had time to read everything that was appearing in the field, even the bad stuff, of which there seems to have been proportionately less than now, but I'll rant about this state of things later. Suffice it moment to say that much of even the best new work—Matheson, Aickman, Leiber, Kirk, as vastly different examples—was being published with less of a fanfare than it deserved. Some of these writers still are.

I mentioned imitation. I've made this point elsewhere, and I do my best not to repeat myself, but this bears repeating: there is nothing wrong with learning your craft by imitation while you discover what you want to write about. In other fields imitation isn't, so far as I know, even an issue. It's common for painters to learn by creating studies of their predecessors' work. Beethoven's first symphony sounds like Haydn, Wagner's symphony sounds like Beethoven, Richard Strauss's first opera sounds remarkably Wagnerian, and there's an early symphonic poem by Bartók that sounds very much like Richard Strauss, but who could mistake the mature work of these composers for the music of anyone else? In my smaller way, once I'd filled a book with my attempts to be Lovecraft I was determined to sound like myself, and *Alone with the Horrors* may stand as a record of the first thirty years of that process. The reader must decide when I started to succeed.

The Chicago and San Francisco tales of Fritz Leiber were now my models in various ways. I wanted to achieve that sense of supernatural terror which derives from the everyday urban landscape rather than invading it, and I greatly admired—still do—how Fritz wrote thoroughly contemporary weird tales which were nevertheless rooted in the best traditions of the field, and which drew some of their strength from uniting British and American influences (something Lovecraft had achieved before him*). So several of my stories here—"The Man in the Underpass", "The Companion", "Mackintosh Willy", "The Show Goes On", "The Ferries"—try to invoke ghosts suggested to me by actual settings in and around Liverpool. Others, beginning with "The End of a Summer's Day", explore the sexual implications of horror fiction and what happens to the fiction when the sexuality—or, in the case of "The Fit", what one might call Freudian knowingness—becomes explicit. "The Interloper" was a strange kind of revenge on the sort of schooling I'd had to suffer at the hands of Christian Brothers and their lay staff (not all of either,

* It occurs to me that Steve King unites the American traditions of Poe and Mark Twain and makes of the combination something productively personal.

I should add); the incident involving the maths teacher and the poetry notebook actually happened, and the teacher was fully as much of a shit as I portray, though the book in question was actually the first draft of *The Inhabitant of the Lake*. "The Other Side" was my attempt to equal the surrealism of J. K. Potter's picture on which it was based, and "The Voice of the Beach" tries to scale Lovecraft's peak of cosmic terror. I think that is enough about the stories.

In these thirty years I've seen horror fiction become enormously more popular and luxuriant. I use the last word, as tends to be my way with words, for its ambiguity. There's certainly something to be said in favour of the growth of a field which has produced so many good new writers and so much good writing. One of its appeals to me ever since I became aware of the tales of M. R. James is the way the best work achieves its effects through the use of style, the selection of language. On the other hand, lately the field seems to have been sprouting writers whose fiction I can best describe as Janet and John primers of mutilation, where the length of the sentences, paragraphs, and chapters betrays the maximum attention span of either the audience or the writer or more probably both. There are also quite a bunch of writers with more pretensions whose basic drive appears to be to outdo one another in disgustingness. "It is very easy to be nauseating," M. R. James wrote more than sixty years ago, and the evidence is all around us. However, I hope that in time the genre will return to the mainstream, where it came from and where it belongs.

What to do? Nothing, really, except keep writing and wait for the verdict of history. The field is big enough for everyone, after all. I came into it because I wanted to repay some of the pleasure it had given me—particularly the work of those writers who, as David Aylward put it, "used to strive for awe"—and I stay in it because it allows me to talk about whatever themes I want to address and because I have by no means found its limits. Perhaps in the next thirty years, but I rather hope not. I like to think my best story is the one I haven't written yet, and that's why I continue to write.

Introduction to *Far Away and Never*

THESE TALES DATE FROM MY BRIEF STINT AS A writer of pure fantasy. All are set in a mythical world. Of course, the version of New England I perpetrated in my first Lovecraftian stumblings was pretty mythical, not to mention the juvenile sketch of Arabia ("Araby") that I persuaded myself was good enough for "The Face in the Desert". But the present tales, with one exception, are of the planet Tond, and that's where the problems begin.

I made Tond up as the theme of a paragraph from *The Revelations of Glaaki* (which my spellcheck would like me to call *The Revelations of Glasgow*) for quoting in "The Inhabitant of the Lake". Neither the idea nor the paragraph was too inspired, but Pat Kearney, my first fan publisher, liked them enough to suggest I write a history of Tond for *Goudy*, his fanzine. I produced a sample of twaddle off the top of my head, where I generally keep a store, but then lost interest, luckily. Instead, having fallen in love with the imagination of Clark Ashton Smith and with "The Abominations of Yondo" in particular, I determined to use Tond as the setting for a complete tale.

This was the first draft of "A Madness from the Vaults", and it was published by Graham Hall, then a fanzine editor and later a less receptive editor of *New Worlds.* Having peopled Tond with creatures other than human in the "Inhabitant" paragraph, I apparently felt bound to stick with them, and with two suns as well. These elements persisted into the second draft, though not much else did. When I used Tond again less than two years later, however—in "The Stages of the God"—the protagonists had become men.

The excuse for this transformation, I fear, is sloth. I couldn't imagine my way inside my characters unless I regarded them as human. The tale was printed in *Whispers* as by Montgomery Comfort, a little joke using two names borrowed from dullards of the British cinema. Since then it has appeared under my byline, most recently in the British fantasy magazine *Beyond,* where it proved most unpopular with the readership.

The following year I was asked to write a sword and sorcery tale. Tond seemed the only place to set it, but by now I couldn't be bothered with an extra sun or even a green one, and Tond remained terraformed to this extent for the rest of its stories. Am I entitled to account for the inconsistencies by claiming that they relate to different periods of its history? I can imagine what my old and, alas, now late drinking pal Bob Shaw would say to that idea. I did announce at the outset that these tales were pure fantasy, but I'm not sure that would placate a science fiction writer.

"The Song at the Hub of the Garden" was the result of the commission. It saw print in *Savage Heroes,* edited by "Eric Pendragon", who cast off his armour for the American edition five years later and stood revealed as Michel Parry. (An outbreak of a different typeface halfway through the American introduction is caused by the burgeoning in the genre of Karl Edward Wagner's career—sadly, to about its full growth even then, in 1980.) Meanwhile I'd invented a hero for myself, or at least as much of one as I could believe in.

He was Ryre, and more than twenty years later it seems to me that he came complete with his first adventure as I watched *Bloody Fists,* a martial arts film that had been refused a certificate by the British censor but had been granted exhibition by the local council in Wrexham. I take "The Sustenance of Hoak" to owe its existence less to the film than to my loss of interest in the events on the screen.

Memory suggests I decided at once that the central issue of the story was too fantastic to be developed in a realistic setting, and so the place for it was Tond. I sent the completed tale to Kirby McCauley, hoping he would have more idea where to place it than I had, and surprisingly soon it was bought by andrew j. offutt, that typographically modest fellow, on the understanding that its pace should be increased a little. I edited four thousand words out of the story, and that improved version appears here.

Getting on for two years later, andy offutt asked me to bring Ryre back. I hadn't planned a sequel—I never do—but I was happy to find out where he went next. His brief saga allowed me to work out ideas too weird to be incorporated in the kind of thing I usually write. At least, that was my view, but Hugh Lamb expressed the opinion that the events of "The Changer of Names" could perfectly well have occurred in Liverpool. I hadn't realised that the image of my home town I'd presented to the world was quite so odd.

Ryre underwent two more adventures before Zebra Books had had enough of *Swords Against Darkness.* Deprived of a market, he entered that limbo to which the passing of the pulps consigned so many of his predecessors, though in the case of Solomon Kane it was the suicide of his author that did. In 1975 Glenn Lord chose me to complete three tales of Howard's British adventurer. The completions are all in the new Baen Books edition, together with a revised introduction. Otherwise all that occurs to me to mention here is that "Hawk of Basti" became a kind of sketch for *The Hungry Moon.*

Howard's ghost wasn't done with me, however. As the first Conan movie hove into view, Milton Subotsky of Amicus Films approached me to prepare Solomon Kane for filming. I wrote a treatment based on the African tales, but he didn't see a film in it. Shortly afterward, rumour has it, the financing for a Thongor film he'd started was lost, leaving him with the bill for some Eastern European special effects, and his enthusiasm for sword and sorcery ventures waned. I later heard that he revived the Solomon Kane project with a view to having it scripted by the team responsible for *The Monster Club,* but he died before this could be perpetrated. I hope my last involvement with Howard was more genuine than I can believe that would have been. It was a chapter of a tale based on a Howard fragment called, presumably by him, “Genseric’s Son”.

So here are all my fantasies that are other than sexual. Some writers seem to use pure fantasy as something to hide behind—at least, they try. It can’t be done, of course. I hope I haven’t tried, whatever shortcomings the tales may have.

All the Ghosts That Made Me

Once upon a time I presumed to break with the tradition of the horror story. I was in my latish teens, and had just finished writing my first published book, imitating Lovecraft as best I knew how. Completing the book (*The Inhabitant of the Lake*) seemed to break Lovecraft's hold over me, and I grew impatient with his work. Whereas I'd been enthralled by his ability to suggest terrors far larger than he showed, I now felt that he explained too much—indeed, I found his mythos as confining as he had found Algernon Blackwood's use in fiction of the "trade jargon of occultism" to be. Before long I wasn't impatient only with Lovecraft but with just about everything that had been written in the field. I felt it was time to bring it up to date and acquaint it with a few of the developments that had been taking place in the wider field of twentieth-century literature. Long before I'd finished rewriting *Demons by Daylight*, my second book, to my satisfaction, I felt as if I were writing horror fiction as nobody else ever had, an experience as often nerve-racking as it was exhilarating.

I was wrong, of course. The urban supernatural stories of Fritz Leiber, then (with Robert Aickman) the greatest living writer in the field, had given me a direction. Long before the invasion of everyday settings by the supernatural had become a cliché of the genre, Fritz was writing stories in which the supernatural arose from the everyday setting. What Chicago and, later, San Francisco were for him, Liverpool already was for me, and I needed only to use his example to help me draw on my experience of my home town and be true to myself.

Paradoxically, I was also being true to the tradition I had set out to progress beyond. In retrospect I don't find this surprising. Striving to be untypical often proves to be a way of rediscovering the essence of the field or of one's work. Some of Lovecraft's finest stories seem to grow from his dissatisfaction with the way their themes were handled by other writers, and some of my early tries at sounding like myself appear to have had a similar basis, though I wasn't conscious of it at the time. A tradition often gains strength from attempts to work against it, and vice versa. This strikes me as all to the good, and so I'm saddened that so many contemporary horror writers seem bent on succeeding at the expense of the field as a whole.

I don't only mean those writers who achieve commercial success and then deny that they ever wrote horror fiction at all, though that is certainly a betrayal of the tradition that created them and perhaps one cause of a tendency I deplore—the growth of a generation of horror writers who are either contemptuous or ignorant (and perhaps one leads to the other) of the old masters. Of course, this isn't new. Most pulp writers, including most of the forgotten contributors to *Weird Tales*, appear to have had no impulse other than copying what was currently marketable: no wonder Lovecraft was unhappy with the company his stories kept. Far worse than ignorance, though, is pride in ignorance, and a generation raised on that is a dismaying spectacle.

Some of us have tried to counteract this. On realizing how many of the submissions to *Twilight Zone Magazine* came from writers who had never heard of anyone earlier than Stephen King, T. E. D. Klein commissioned a series of essays on the masters and reprinted examples of their work. David Hartwell's huge anthology *The Dark Descent*, displaying the breadth of the horror field, is both excellent and timely. Alas, there are writers and editors who would have their audience believe that today is all. In a book addressed to budding writers (in which my own contribution was infected by a fever of italics, much to my surprise when I saw them in print), J. N. Williamson wrote:

"I doubt with all my heart and knowledge that Verne, Stoker, Lovecraft, Wells, [Mary] Shelley or Stevenson—or Edgar Allan Poe—starting in writing today would write even one novel or story exactly as he wrote it for his contemporary audience . . . If reincarnation theories are correct and Eddie Poe is hard at work today. . . he himself would never see a connection between 'The Tell-Tale Heart' or 'The Fall of the House of Usher' and the yarn he just sold to *Night Cry* or *The Horror Show.* Suggesting anything to the contrary would, I believe, be actively bad advice."

For myself, I believe that if one is regarded by neophytes as an authority on their field, part of one's duty is to demonstrate how the old masters achieved what they achieved rather than to dismiss it as irrelevant. It seems to me that there is nothing whatsoever wrong with modelling one's work on something that has stood the test of time in order to develop one's craft while one discovers one's themes, as I did with Lovecraft. On the other hand, if an artistic personality is so weak that it can't progress beyond such imitation, then is it worth expressing at all?

My disagreement with Williamson's stance was one reason I welcomed the invitation to write "The Guide" for *Post Mortem,* Paul F. Olson's and David B. Silva's anthology of supernatural tales in the best tradition. (The scope of the book proved to be considerable, and at the end Dean R. Koontz chased away the wraiths with an essay damning television fantasy as "brought alive with electricity conducted through rough bolts in its neck, a shambling Frankenstein of wonder" and citing *A Christmas Carol* as perhaps the greatest ghost story of all time on the basis that it "takes the hope that is a buried element of all ghost stories and raises it to the surface of the tale".) In his essay on *Demons by Daylight,* T. E. D. Klein pointed out that I revived Jamesian techniques in a contemporary context (another skill I must thank Fritz Leiber for). I wanted my story for the Olson and Silva book to go further, to be both a tribute to M. R. James and a demonstration of how his techniques could—can—still be used.

Writing tales within the limits specified by an editor can be a valuable discipline, and productive of ideas one might otherwise not have. The core of the Jamesian paragraph Kew finds added to James's guidebook ("Imagine . . . a spider in human form . . . ") I extemporised for my nine-year-old daughter as we were walking through Delamere Forest one day (oddly enough, a setting where I also announced the plot of "Just Waiting" as it occurred to me). I'd already decided that the book within the story would be by James himself, and once I had the annotation, the story developed itself.

I had fun with it, not least because I felt it was worthwhile. I hope that if it invokes James, it will not invoke his displeasure. I must have forgotten to replace my copy of *Suffolk and Norfolk* properly after consulting it last, and that is why it is standing out from its companions on the shelf. Now I think I've said everything I have to say, and I shall remove my spectacles to rest my eyes after spending the day at the word processor. Surely my spectacles aren't very like those James used to wear. Surely I won't see anything beyond the lenses as I place them on my desk—accusing eyes, or whatever occupies their sockets now.

AFTERWORD

WHAT AN AMOUNT I HAD TO SAY FOR MYSELF! NOT all of it is here. Most of the columns that give their name to this collection are, and I'll end by explaining the title. A few of them are too trivial to reprint. Other stuff has been excluded to spare the reader boredom or myself embarrassment. Thus my brash attack on Lovecraft isn't present, nor my diatribe against *King Kong*, which moved Ray Harryhausen to retort in the letter column of *L'Incroyable Cinema*. I later repudiated both of these excesses of mine and published my second thoughts. Neither of the essays I wrote for *Twylight* magazine is here; not "The Horror of Horror", dedicated to my old ex-fiancée Rosemary (which I assume is why I made it so censorious) nor my survey of British horror film directors. Like the list of squibs I wrote about actors in *Supernatural* magazine, the latter took Andrew Sarris's *The American Cinema* as a model, though both read more like parodies of it. Various reviews aren't in here either. The disappointed may search the dealers' catalogues for issues of *Alien* and *L'Incroyable Cinema*, *The British Fantasy Society Bulletin*, *Shadow* and *All Hallows* and *Castle of Frankenstein* and no doubt other journals I can't bring to mind just now. The dedicated collector may seek *The Questing Penis*, the column I kept up in a men's magazine (though when the magazine grew more respectable my title was transformed into *The Honourable Member*.)

Most of the contents of the book don't need propping up with afterthoughts, I hope, but here are a few late ruminations. A version of the Leslie Fiedler essay to which I responded appeared in *The Penguin Encyclopedia of Horror and the Supernatural.* Mrs Whitehouse is dead. William Schoell is still with us—the chap who convicted me and others of the effort to be literary; he recently published a book on Lovecraft. I have a 1988 novel of his, *The Pact*, which contains lines such as "The face that was now nibbling on her own belonged to the largest spider she had ever seen and *it wasn't harmless* [italics certainly not mine] . . . Then out of one uncovered eye she saw past the spider's legs to see that a few dozen more of its fellows had come to join it in its feast." The reader must decide what effort was involved in this. More recently a review complained that a sentence from *Nazareth Hill*— "He took out the little he had and emptied the great deal for which it was the solitary egress" —had too much style about it. Maybe I should write more like "He took out his small dick and had a big piss."

Anyone who finds my piece on the Highgate Vampire saga flippant may read a more sober account in *Raising the Devil* by Bill Ellis, an Evangalical Lutheran and associate professor at Penn State Hazleton. I wonder if he was approached to contribute to a biography of Sean (now Seán) Manchester? Years after my essay about him was published I heard from one Katrina Garforth-Bles, writing from the address of Gothic Press, Manchester's publisher. "I am presently collecting commentary about Seán Manchester from people who both know him and not, who might have something interesting to say." I thought I had already done so. I fear that I neglected to respond, and also failed to order a cassette of the chap performing his own music on a tenor saxophone and reading from his sequel to *Dracula*. Images of the Highgate Vampire after staking can be found on the Internet.

And the title of my column and this book? In the January 1991 issue of *Fantasy and Science Fiction*, Harlan Ellison® wrote an essay heralding the end of the horror boom and castigating those who insisted on applying the word "horror" to their fiction. "What possibilities that existed were explored . . . prior to 1974 . . . Then along came Stephen King . . . *Sui generis* . . . he was the new Poe, the latest Lovecraft, the direct lineal descendent of Polidori . . . There never was a blossoming for 'horror'. There was only Stephen King, and everyone else."

I hope some of the pieces I've collected herein will suggest that this is simply Harlan being Harlan. In any case, the passage that stayed more strongly with me—so much so that I took my title from it—reads:

"... all those who existed merely because Stephen King dominated the landscape will find themselves homeless. Dean Koontz will remain, and Joe Lansdale; Rick McCammon and John Saul; Lisa Tuttle and Dan Simmons (if he chooses to write in that vein); Bloch, as always, and Ramsey Campbell, probably."

No probably about it, mate.

Ramsey Campbell
Wallasey, Merseyside
3 August 2015